Apocalypse Later
Books by Hal C. F. Astell

Apocalypse Later
Filmography Series

Charlie Chaplin Centennial

Keystone

Apocalypse Later Press
Phoenix, AZ

Apocalypse Later Filmography Series
Charlie Chaplin Centennial: Keystone

ISBN-10: 0-9894613-3-5
ISBN-13: 978-0-9894613-3-7
Apocalypse Later Press catalogue number: ALP003

Reviews by Hal C. F. Astell

These reviews originally appeared, albeit in evolutionary form, at Apocalypse Later. Each review was originally posted in 2014 on the centennial of its original release in 1914.
http://www.apocalypselaterfilm.com

Front cover art by Adele Hentz of Mad Hatter Designs
http://madhattersdesign.tumblr.com

Published through CreateSpace
https://www.createspace.com

Typeset in Gentium
http://scripts.sil.org/FontDownloadsGentium

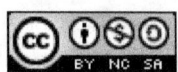

Dedication

This book is dedicated to two people without whom this project would never have been started and this book would not exist.

One is Charlie Chaplin, for making the world laugh during some of its darkest days. We will not allow you to be forgotten.

The other is Jim Politano, a good friend and a good filmmaker, wherever he chooses to shoot his movies.

Acknowledgements

No book is ever created by one person, regardless of whose name is on the cover. Many other people deserve credit, along with my undying gratitude and appreciation for their part in bringing this one to print. Thank you, one and all!

Most obviously, thanks to Dee Astell, my long suffering better half. She watched everything reviewed here with me, sometimes more than once. I read all my reviews aloud to her, which helps me proof my own writing and her to highlight odd other errors in my assumptions. This wasn't as painful a project for her as some that I drag her through but it had strict deadlines and she worked them with me without complaint.

Thanks to Jim Politano, for the conversation that sparked the original idea for the project, and answering further questions about that crazy experience later. For more on that, see my introduction.

Thanks to Flicker Alley, who released *Chaplin at Keystone*, without which this project would have been thoroughly different. Most of these films are available elsewhere but in awful copies that negate any possibility of reaching the sort of insight I believe I was able to find. Your support during this project was also much appreciated.

Thanks to the many friends, acquaintances and strangers who commented on these reviews after I posted them, including by the power of synchronicity, one man who I quote a number of times in this book, John Bengtson.

And thanks to Mack Sennett and Mabel Normand, for watching a vaudeville performance and believing that the actor who stumbled around the stage in a believable state of fake inebriation could be worth inviting to join you at Keystone Studios. Without that single invitation, the twin histories of comedy and film would have been very different indeed.

Contents

Introduction

A few years ago, a film friend of mine experienced something that he found rather shocking and he shared it with me. I not only found it rather shocking too, but felt like I should do something about it and the end result evolved into this project which ran at my review site, Apocalypse Later, throughout the year of 2014.

It's all about Charlie Chaplin, the greatest name in film comedy, and just how recognisable he is and was.

Only a couple of years into his career, which began at Keystone Studios one hundred years ago in 1914, he had become not only the most recognisable actor in the world but also, arguably, the most recognisable image, period. Wherever on the globe you might have happened to be back then, the locals would know the silhouette of his most famous character, the Little Tramp, whom he portrayed in the majority of his films.

Today, a century later, the modern equivalent might be the golden arches of McDonalds, Mickey Mouse's ears or the Statue of Liberty, but surely the Little Tramp hasn't been forgotten? Well, apparently he has, as my friend discovered.

That friend is Jim Politano, a local filmmaker who won an I.F.P. Phoenix Audience Favourite award for his short film, *Love Sucks*, and who cast my better half in his thematic follow up, *The Sisters of St. Mary's*. The occasion was Ed Everroad's "Intro to Cinema" class that he was taking at Scottsdale Community College (S.C.C.). The spark was a textbook, *Flashback: A Brief History of Film*, by Louis Giannetti and Scott Eyman.

I have a copy of this book too, but mine is the third edition with Forrest Gump on the cover. The edition Jim was handed was a custom 2006 edition for S.C.C. with a front cover featuring Charlie Chaplin, dressed in his famous Little Tramp attire, standing next to an old furnace. It's taken from a scene in his 1925 classic, *The Gold Rush*, which the cinematic establishment at the American Film Institute voted as the 74th greatest American feature of all time in their original *100 Years... 100 Movies* list and the early film aficionados at SilentEra.com voted the 6th greatest silent movie ever made.

The class Jim was in numbered about thirty, most of them young adults of the sort of age you might expect to be in a college class but with a handful of mature students like him too. A dozen or so of these folk were working through the film program at S.C.C. While such students would surely expect to learn something about the history of film in an "Intro to Cinema" class, you might also expect them to have brought at least a little background with them.

Yet the student in front of Jim turned round and asked him, "Who is this dude on the cover?" Apparently, a few of these folk had at least heard of Chaplin but nobody except Jim knew who he was.

To Jim, and to me, that is a scary thought. The Little Tramp has deteriorated from being the most recognisable image in the world to being an unrecognisable "dude on the cover" of a textbook. The man who did more than anyone to move screen comedy forward from its juvenile slapstick days to something approaching high art has been forgotten even by students in a college cinema class. I can hear the collective sigh of classic film fans everywhere at this news. To use a more recent quote that the people in this class might have recognised, it's "as if millions of voices cried out in terror and were suddenly silenced."

Jim's experience resonated with me for a few years until I realised at the tail end of 2013 that the coming February would mark the centennial of Chaplin's debut on film in the Keystone farce comedy, *Making a Living*. The time seemed ripe for me to revisit the 36 films he made in 1914 and review them from the perspective of how they evolved over that year because of the new approaches that Chaplin was bringing to the screen.

Another trigger was the new availability of these films in remastered editions in the Flicker Alley DVD box set, *Chaplin at Keystone*. This contains all 33 of the extant shorts that Chaplin made at Keystone Studios in 1914 (*Her Friend the Bandit* is still believed to be a lost film), along with the first American comedy feature, *Tillie's Punctured Romance*. What's more, it also featured half of the recently rediscovered short, *A Thief Catcher*, featuring Chaplin as a Keystone Kop. Flicker Alley later released the entire short in *The Mack Sennett Collection, Vol 1*.

I'd seen the majority of these films before, but only in the public domain prints that are readily available for pennies, viewable for free online at the Internet Archive or even uploaded to YouTube.

These are frankly awful: they're washed out to the degree that it's usually tough to ascertain any detail whatsoever and they're often incomplete because of skipped frames and missing reels. Intertitles are mostly absent or later additions to re-released versions. I wasn't particularly impressed when I worked through them most of a decade ago.

It's no understatement to suggest that watching them afresh from the *Chaplin at Keystone* box is a revelatory experience. They're certainly not the classics that Chaplin would go on to make in later years, but they're so much better than I could ever have believed possible from those cheap prints. Now I can see faces and subtleties that bring whole new life and meaning to the films and even the original intertitles have been restored, where possible.

Don't just take my word for it. SilentEra.com has compared the different releases of some of these films and found most seriously wanting. Unless someone discovers *Her Friend the Bandit* or waves some sort of magic new digital wand, *Chaplin at Keystone* is likely to remain the only recommended release of these films.

I should emphasise here that, while I have become associated "professionally" with Jim Politano, as he kindly allowed my left arm to appear as an extra in his short film, *Flight Fright* (I'm more visible in the most recent trailer), I have no such association with Flicker Alley. I'm simply a satisfied customer who believes that they did Chaplin's legacy a great service with this box set. Hopefully I can add a little more with this set of reviews.

I worked through these films slowly, as if I was watching them in 1914 not 2014, and I posted each review a hundred years to the day from its original release. I also included in that schedule the half of *A Thief Catcher* that was available at that point but revisited it afresh after its full release. I also attempted to cover *Her Friend the Bandit*, even though it remains a lost film, reviewing from the information at hand.

Hal C. F. Astell
Apocalypse Later
December 2014

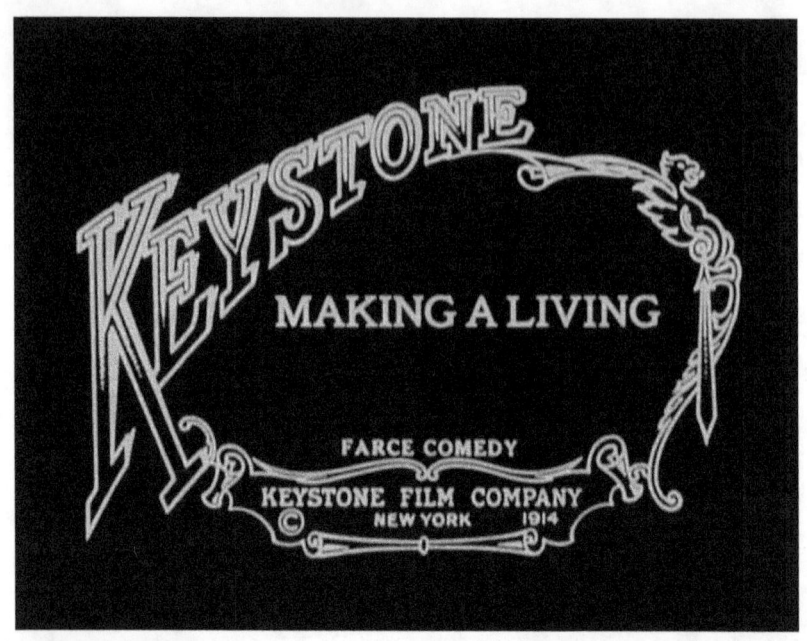

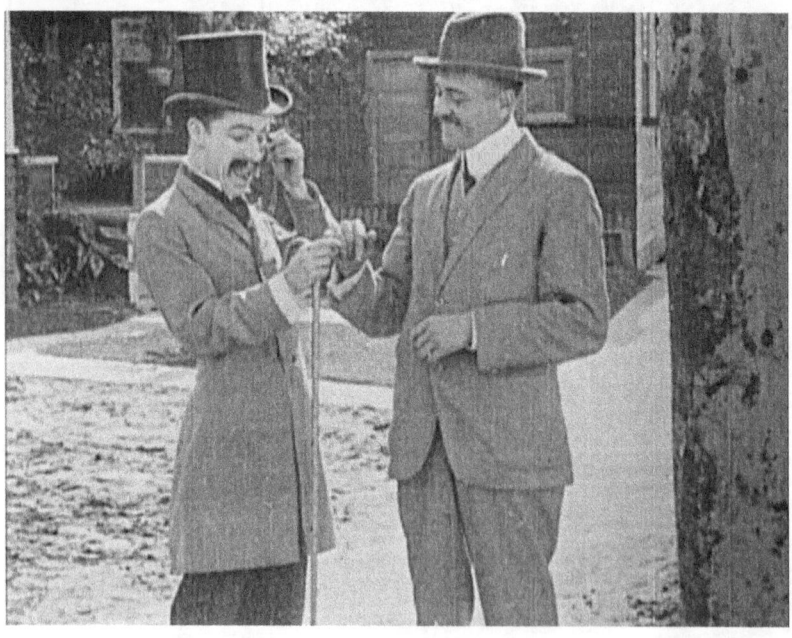

Making a Living
2nd February, 2014

Director: Henry Lehrman
Writer: Unknown (possibly Reed Heustis and/or Henry Lehrman)
Stars: Charles Chaplin, Chester Conklin, Alice Davenport, Virginia Kitley and Henry Lehrman

Monday, 2nd February, 1914 turned out to be one of the most important dates in the history of cinema, though nobody knew it at the time and very few even glimpsed the possibility. However, the release on that day of *Making a Living*, a one reel comedy short film from Keystone Studios, marked the screen debut of a former stage actor, Charles Chaplin, whose most frequent screen character, the Little Tramp, would quickly become the most recognisable image in the entire world, the equivalent perhaps of Mickey Mouse's ears today.

The tramp wouldn't show up until Chaplin's second picture, *Kid Auto Races at Venice, Cal.*, although that arrived in theatres a mere five days after his debut. To suggest that he was a busy man at Keystone understates the case; he made no less than 36 pictures in 1914, as many as he made for a variety of other companies over the following seven years. This wasn't anything he was used to; as a vaudevillian for the Fred Karno troupe, he spent months rehearsing new routines. Keystone didn't even work with scripts, at least not in the sense that we know them today (and more on this later); they took ideas, improvised them into chases and were done.

The man behind Keystone Studios was Mack Sennett, known in his day as "the king of comedy" because he was synonymous with the genre, at least as far as Americans were concerned. Before him, the art of comedy was a European, often a French, creature: the Lumiére Brothers had invented it as far back as 1895 and the first international comedy star was Pathé's Max Linder, whose screen debut was in 1905; amazingly, he had made 170 films before Chaplin had made one. Even in the United States, Keystone weren't the originals; when Sennett left Biograph, where he had learned his craft under the greatest American director of the day, D. W. Griffith, to become the production chief at Keystone in 1912, there was an established comedy star already. That was John Bunny, a rotund but engaging actor who worked for Vitagraph, but his star had waned even before his death in 1915. Under Sennett, however, Keystone were prolific and reliable. They became comedy, pure and simple, but at a time when comedy meant slapstick.

If you've ever heard of an early American film comedian, then chances are that he or she worked at Keystone. Major stars at the time included Mabel Normand, Louise Fazenda and Harry Langdon, all Keystone regulars. Some were known only by their nicknames, such as Roscoe Arbuckle, Mack Swain and Chester Conklin, who were respectively "Fatty", "Ambrose" and "Walrus". Some Keystone players went on to greatness elsewhere, such as Gloria Swanson, Harold Lloyd and future Academy Award winner Marie Dressler, the star of the first feature length comedy, *Tillie's Punctured Romance*, which was made at Keystone in mid-1914 and released just in time for Christmas. Other less remembered names, such as those of Slim Summerville, Al St. John and Edgar Kennedy, are still recognisable today as members of the Keystone Kops, perhaps the one name that conjures up slapstick best. Needless to say, they worked at Keystone Studios too. However, it was Ford Sterling, their lead star in 1913, who inadvertently paved the way for Chaplin, by planning to leave to form his own company.

Needing a new face, Sennett and Normand remembered an actor who had impressed them on stage as an "Inebriated Swell". He was part of Fred Karno's London Comedians, so they fired off a telegram asking simply for a man called "Chaffin... or something like that" to contact Kessell and Baumann at the Longacre Building in New York.

This reached Chaplin, who realised that the Longacre Building housed lawyers, so believed his great-aunt had died and left him an inheritance. He was disappointed to find that he was only being asked to join a motion picture company, though he did sign a year's contract for two reasons: one, his salary would immediately double to $150 a week, to increase again after three months, and two, he recognised the power of film to reach a large audience.

He intended to use this year at Keystone to build publicity. "A year at that racket and I could return to vaudeville an international star," he wrote in his autobiography. By the end of 1914, however, he had become even more of an international star than he could have dreamed and the stage became firmly anchored in his past.

Such ambition wasn't in anyone else's mind during the filming of *Making a Living* and it didn't arrive once it had been completed. In fact, most of those involved in making it thought it would be a flop. Henry Lehrman in particular, who served both as the film's director and Chaplin's on screen foil, was furious with his co-star and cut most of his best material out of the finished product. Chaplin had choice words to say about that later. "It broke my heart," he wrote, "for the cutter had butchered it beyond recognition." Neither Mack Sennett nor anyone else at Keystone were impressed either.

In reality, it isn't that bad, merely showing us yet again what any other Keystone movie showed us. Only one contemporary review is known today, but the anonymous writer for the *Moving Picture World* proved rather prophetic. He singled out Chaplin for praise, though as no actor was given credit in a Keystone film at this point, he had no idea of his name. He called him a "comedian of the first water, who acts like one of Nature's own naturals."

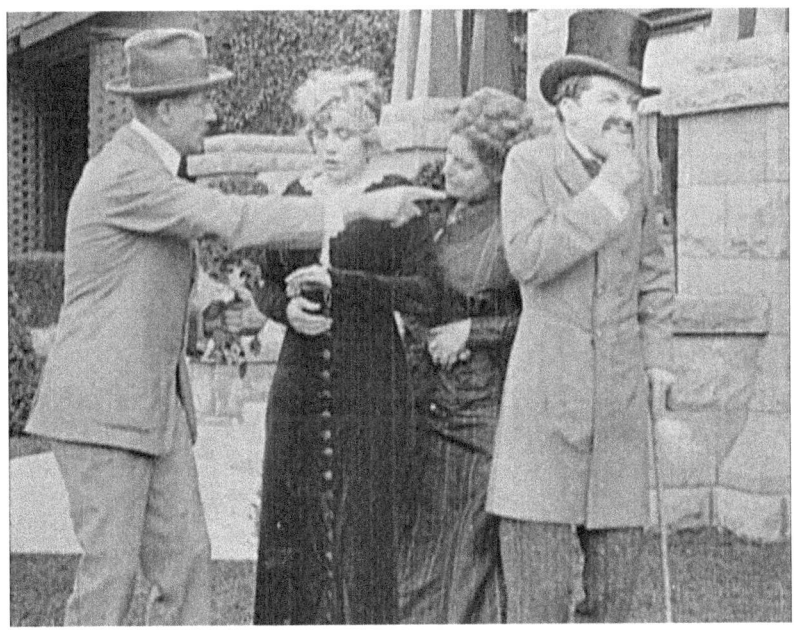

He's recognisable to us, of course, with the benefit of a hundred years of hindsight, but still only just. With the Little Tramp not yet created, Chaplin drew on an old vaudevillian costume for his role as a "sharper", a sort of middle ground between beggar and conman. He wears a top hat, monocle and tight frock coat and he carries a cane; all of which were designed to make him look like an English gentleman who had fallen on hard times.

Unfortunately, he also has a thick and drooping moustache, of the sort we can't fail to see today as anything but silent movie cliché. Surely American audiences of the time wouldn't have seen the English gentleman but the serial villain with a set of inevitably dastardly schemes. Given that Chaplin does play an opportunistic villain here, that wouldn't have felt out of place, but he's still the most watchable character.

While that *Moving Picture World* journalist saw something that most wouldn't have seen, Chaplin clearly steals the film out from under Lehrman without appearing to try and even though his best material was apparently cut.

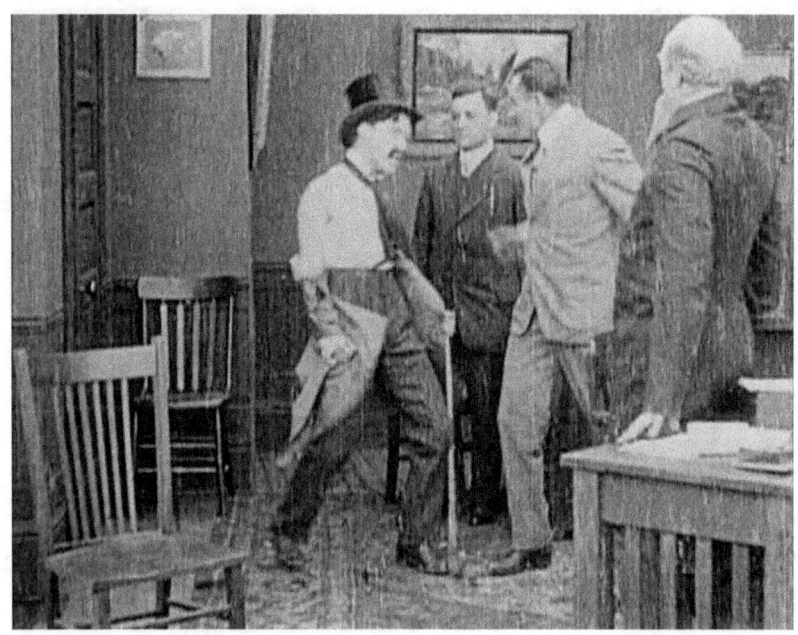

His best scene is his first one, which runs surprisingly long for a Keystone short. Jeffrey Vance, the author of *Chaplin: Genius of the Cinema*, highlights that Chaplin's opening scene in *Mabel's Strange Predicament*, the second film he would shoot at Keystone but the third to be released, was allowed to run uncut for a full 75 feet, or about a minute. However, he neglects to mention that the same thing happened in this picture, as Chaplin is introduced not only to this particular story but also to the world at large.

The sharper, apparently named Edgar English in the idea, stops a random stranger in the street in an attempt to persuade him out of some money. For a full minute, we watch him ply his trade while Lehrman, playing the stranger, seems flummoxed by the whole affair. Clearly, we're supposed to be watching the sharper play his mark, but we also find that we're watching a novice actor play his more experienced director and there's no doubt as to who will win in each instance. Edgar English breaks the ice, engages in chatter and raises an unsavoury topic; he even refuses the proffered gift before quickly grabbing it. It's good stuff.

Unfortunately it goes downhill from there. After taking money from Lehrman's character, he finds that he bumps into him again and again. Chatting up a young lady, clearly under the suggestion that he's a notably rich and important man, he finds that Lehrman is wooing her too. Deciding to seek work, he tries out for a job as a journalist, only to find that Lehrman already works there. And, for no better reason than it's the way Keystone pictures always worked, this is all riffed on until it becomes a chase.

As impressive as Chaplin was in the first, notably static, scene, he's unable to match that as things get progressively frenetic. He does, at least, dominate every scene that he's in, not only because he's the only character with three dimensions. Everyone else in the film might as well have been a cardboard cutout and, when he isn't on screen, we do start to wonder why we're watching. Even the Keystone Kops, who show up towards the end, don't seem to have as much to do as usual and scenes arrive and depart with abandon.

Making a Living was completed and shipped from California to New York on 14th January, but it didn't arrive on screens until 2nd February. That's a gap of less than three weeks, but by the time the first audiences saw this first picture, Chaplin had completed and shipped another three.

As I mentioned earlier, Keystone Studios weren't interested in hanging about. When Chaplin joined their roster, they were in a routine of churning out a dozen one reel comedies every month, plus a couple of two reelers.

His second film, *Kid Auto Races at Venice, Cal.* followed his first by a mere five days, with his third, *Mabel's Strange Predicament*, so hot on its heels that it reached theatres only two days after that, meaning that regular audiences saw his first three films in a mere week.

It's worth mentioning here that, technically, the latter film was started first, so it features the first true appearance of the Little Tramp, while the former is merely where audiences saw him first. However, because of how that was shot, guerrilla style at a public event, it could be argued that the people in the background are the first Chaplin audience, captured on film for us to examine a century later. However the public saw these films a century ago, though, it's fair to say that, to us, they mark the birth of modern American film comedy.

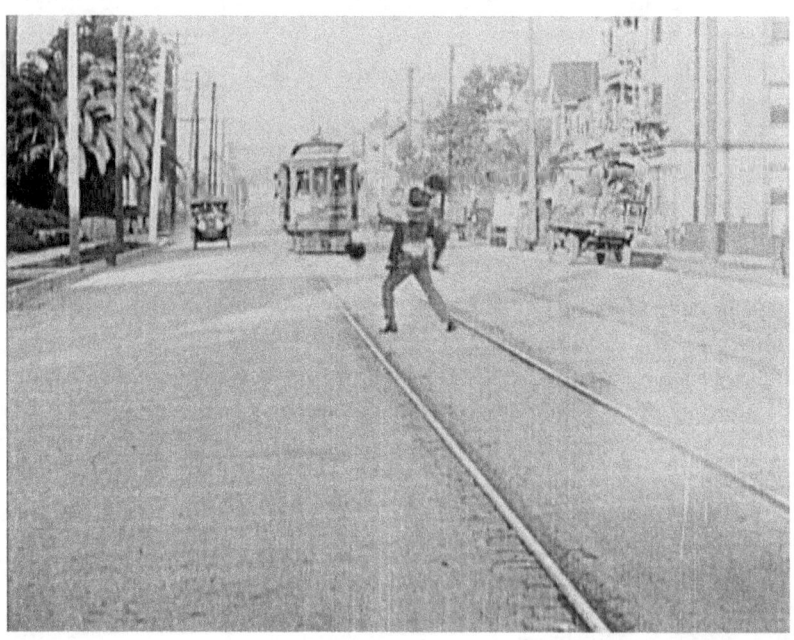

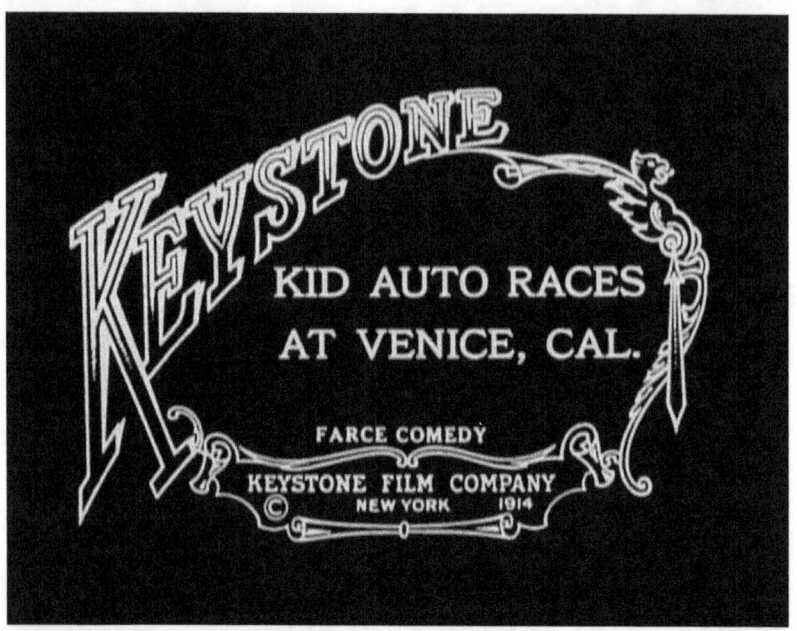

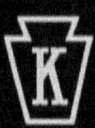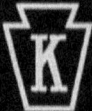

Kid Auto Races at Venice, Cal.
7th February, 1914

Director: Henry Lehrman
Writer: Henry Lehrman
Stars: Charles Chaplin, Henry Lehrman and Frank D. Williams

Almost a decade ago, when I watched most of the films Charlie Chaplin made at Keystone Studios in 1914 in cheap public domain copies, this seemed the weakest of them all.

On the face of it, there's nothing here: just a tramp loitering in front of a camera to annoy the people behind it as they shoot the auto races of the title. There's no story, little more than an initial idea that doesn't progress any further as the film runs on. We might be forgiven, as many of the unwitting extras were, for assuming that the tramp is the only character, though of course the film director and cameraman that he annoys are characters too. There's neither a leading lady nor any other supporting roles, at least not scripted ones played by actors. What's more, there aren't even any of the components that we might safely expect to see in a Keystone picture: no Keystone Kops, no pies in the face, not even a single chase. The most recognisable moment is that old slapstick standard, the kick in the ass; Chaplin finds himself on the receiving end of one and naturally hits the dirt.

Without context, the movie feels more valuable for the auto races going on in the background that had obviously started before this guerrilla shoot began and continued after it ended. We see children racing in what seems to be some sort of soapbox derby event with little apparent structure, though perhaps that's mostly due to the editing which didn't care about the races in the slightest.

It was really the Junior Vanderbilt Cup, a children's version of the first major auto racing event in the U.S. which had been founded in 1904 in New York. It stayed there until 1911, when it started moving around the country. In 1914 it found its way to the west coast for the first time, to be held in Santa Monica, CA, the only city to ever sponsor an equivalent race for children, which took place a mere couple of miles down the coast on the boardwalk at Venice Beach.

Given that this six minute film may have only taken forty five to shoot, it's somewhat surprising that director Henry Lehrman managed to stage three completely different set-ups: one on a straight, another on a bend and the third just below a ramp being used to launch the engineless vehicles.

Of course, adding a little context provides a rather different understanding. A century on, nobody has even heard of the Junior Vanderbilt Cup, which appears to have been held just this once, and, if any have heard of it without the Junior prefix, it's probably because it was rebooted in C.A.R.T. racing in the late nineties for a decade or so, that being a rather appropriate acronym that stands for Championship Auto Racing Teams.

That context, of course, entirely revolves around the film being shot there at the time. If you went back in time to Sunday, 11th January, 1914, and suggested to anyone in the masses crowding the boardwalk at Venice Beach that the strange man annoying a camera crew would become one of the funniest actors to ever be seen in the movies, lauded for inventing modern American film comedy, they'd probably laugh in your face. Clearly the throngs are here to watch

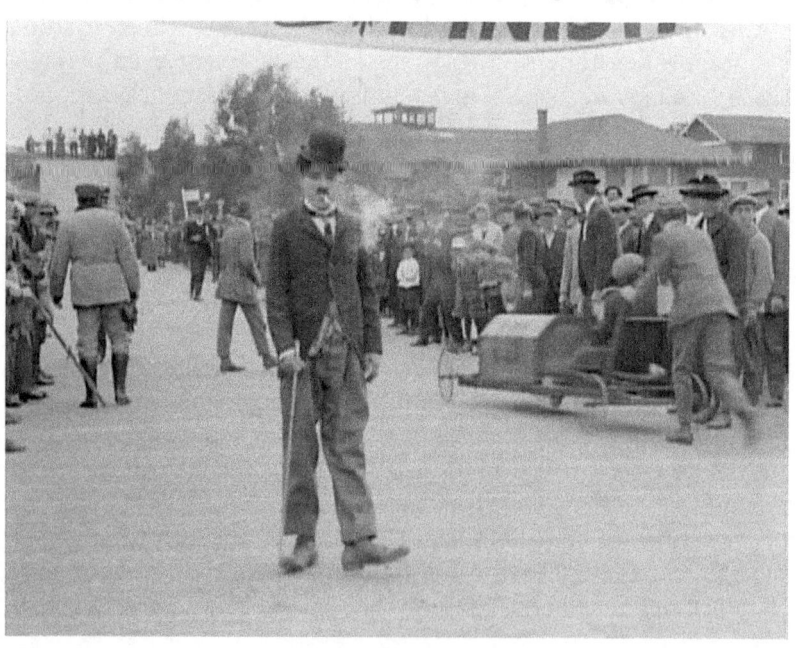

the races, not a movie being made, and they initially appear to be as annoyed by the Little Tramp's antics as are those whose camera he keeps obscuring. In fact, if we look at this from the perspective of a "reality", a sort of early documentary that merely captured a slice of life as the camera ran, he's just as annoying to us too. Yet this was, in so many ways, the beginning.

Technically, Chaplin made his screen debut five days earlier with *Making a Living* but, in that picture, he played a more traditional villain in a more traditional story; here he plays the Little Tramp, the character that would make him world famous. He played other characters in other films, but in almost every one he made up until *The Great Dictator* in 1940, he's either the Little Tramp or some sort of close approximation to him.

Hilariously, the most famous character in the world of silent film was apparently an afterthought. Mack Sennett, the man who ran Keystone Studios, wanted Chaplin to put on some sort of comic turn in a Mabel Normand picture called *Mabel's Strange Predicament*; perhaps he could walk into a hotel lobby and create some laughs. His list of instructions to Chaplin were absurdly minimal: "Put on a comedy makeup. Anything will do." Chaplin apparently thought up his costume on the way to Wardrobe. "I wanted everything to be a contradiction," he wrote in his autobiography, "the pants baggy, the coat tight, the hat small and the shoes large."

Because Sennett had apparently been surprised at Chaplin's youth when he first arrived at the studio, the actor felt he should add another little detail, which would soon become one of his most memorable attributes and which may well remain his most defining feature today. "I added a small moustache," he wrote, "which, I reasoned, would add age without hiding my expression. I had no idea of the character. But the moment I was dressed, the clothes and the make-up made me feel the person he was. I began to know him, and by the time I walked on to the stage he was fully born."

Certainly this most famous character of screen comedy was an inspired creation, but it wasn't entirely original. It was influenced by many generations of comedians who played tramps or clowns on the music hall stage. When he first stood in front of the camera, in *Mabel's Strange Predicament*, he's a variation on characters Chaplin had portrayed on stage himself for Fred Karno's London Comedians.

Yet this film creation was somehow something more.

Clowns come and go. Tramps come and go. The genius of what Chaplin created on the fly is the sort of genius that isn't often seen, those contradictions he aimed at becoming definitive ones that others would reinvent over decades, yet nobody has quite matched this character in a century.

From the waist up, he struggles not to burst. His coat is clearly quite a few sizes too small for him but he buttons it up anyway. His hat perches precariously on top of his head as if he's hoping it'll stretch to fit; of course he loses it often in his films. Even his famous toothbrush moustache appears too small for his face, just another contradiction to film audiences in 1914, even if it's always going to be a reminder of Adolf Hitler to us. It's worth noting that Hitler was only 24 when this picture was released and it would be five more years before he would join what would become the Nazi party, so Hitler appropriated Chaplin's moustache rather than the other way around. That realisation, of course, makes *The Great Dictator* even more delightful.

Mabel's Strange Predicament was a regular one reel comedy, like *Making a Living*. One reel in 1914 was a thousand feet of film, which would contain between ten and twelve minutes of footage. Unlike those movies, *Kid Auto Races at Venice, Cal.* was a split reel film, a shorter picture that shared a reel with another film, in this instance an educational short called *Olives and Their Oil.*

Partly because of its shorter length and mostly because it was such a quick shoot even by the standards of Keystone Studios, it was completed and shipped before *Mabel's Strange Predicament*, which means that the public saw it first and it would go down in history as the first appearance of the Little Tramp. These two films served as a one two punch for audiences over a single weekend, as *Kid Auto Races at Venice, Cal.* arrived on Friday, 7th February, while the more substantial *Mabel's Strange Predicament* quickly followed up a mere two days later on Monday, the 9th, still only a week after *Making a Living*. Charlie Chaplin had emphatically arrived.

Contemporary reviews were positive. The anonymous *Bioscope* reviewer talked of "sensational happenings" but his equivalent at *The Cinema* was effusive with his praise. "*Kid Auto Races* struck us as about the funniest film we have ever seen," the review said, adding that "Chaplin is a born screen comedian; he does things we have not seen done on the screen before." I don't know when this was written, but it must be more recent than the other as the actor is called out by name, impossible to do when Keystone didn't credit them; in the *Bioscope* review, he was simply referred to as "the funny man".

It's difficult to understand this praise today, though it is a little easier if we watch the newly restored version released by Flicker Alley. Restored at the British Film Institute's National Archive in London from two nitrate prints, it shows us far more than we could see in the print that has circulated for years. Most importantly, we can see facial expressions, which we soon realise are massively important, both on the Little Tramp himself and on the audience watching him from the Venice Beach boardwalk.

It could fairly be argued that the first time audiences saw Chaplin as the Little Tramp was not when *Kid Auto Races in Venice, Cal.* hit theatre screens but as the picture was being shot, as this timely restoration allows us to realise that initially they had precisely no idea who he was or what he was doing. Some folk do keep an eye on

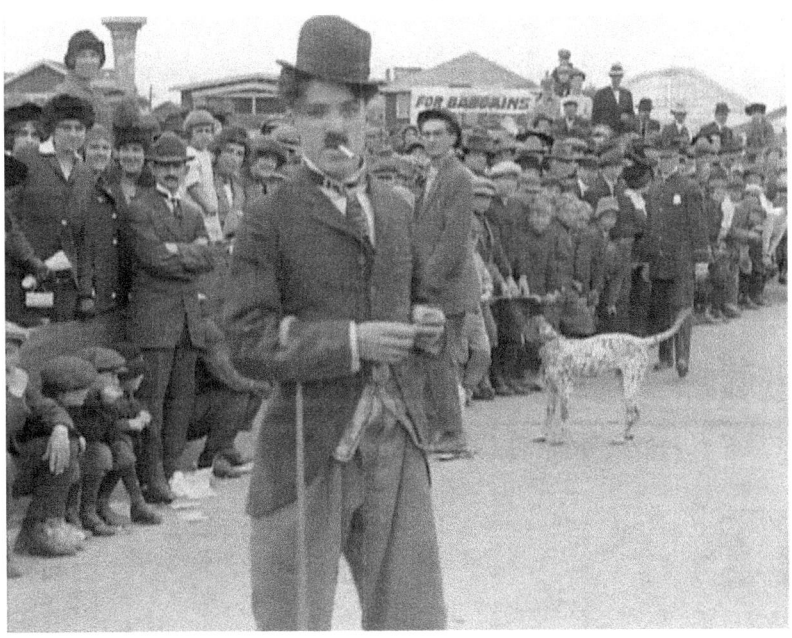

"the funny man" but more watch the races which, of course, they'd come to see. As they realise that those races were not the only entertainment unfolding on the boardwalk, more begin to watch Chaplin until, to a surprising proportion of the crowd, he becomes their focus and the cars become just an afterthought.

Their faces clearly change too. Initially, they're bemused, as they attempt to figure out what's going on. The camera shooting the camera shooting Chaplin explains that they're on the set of a movie, playing out guerrilla style against a real event. The shoot was not a long one but by the end of it, the crowds are laughing; the Little Tramp has won them over with antics that are all the more funny now we can read his face.

Make no mistake, this is still weak stuff but it is, at least, a lot better when we can see faces and join in the contagion. Instead of being distracted into trying to figure out what sort of cars the kids are driving or why the cops vainly attempt to keep the crowd from spreading onto the track while ignoring the many dogs who wander around as if they own the place, as we do in the regular print that's been issued on cheap videos and DVDs for decades, we see exactly

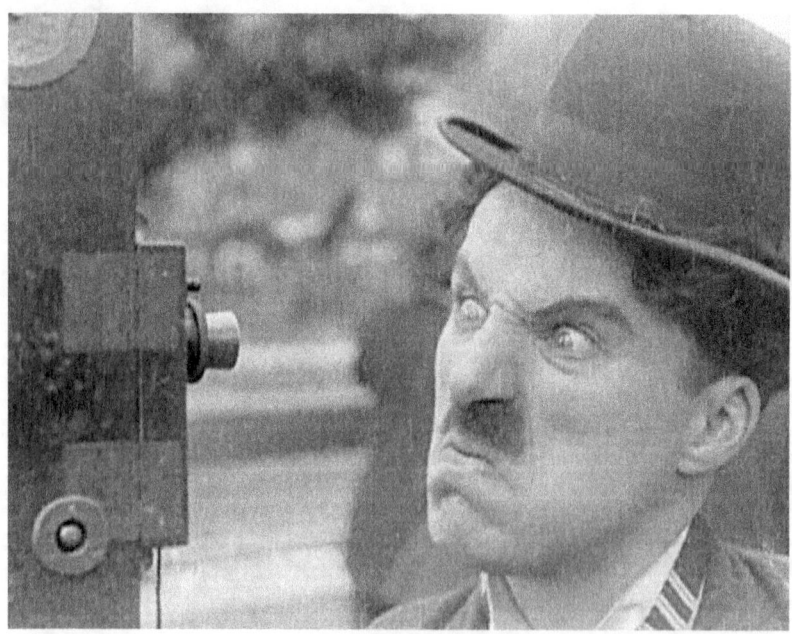

what we are supposed to: Charlie Chaplin as the Little Tramp.

As in *Making a Living*, he's dominant, but director Henry Lehrman edited out his best footage from that film "because, as he put it, he thought I knew too much." Here, he couldn't edit Chaplin because Chaplin was all there was. Certainly, now that we're able to see, we don't pay any attention to Lehrman, who directs himself as the director whom the tramp annoys, and we don't care about Frank D. Williams, either, as his cameraman. We're watching Chaplin finding his lovable rogue character. It really is still early days but the seeds are clearly there and they didn't take long to sprout.

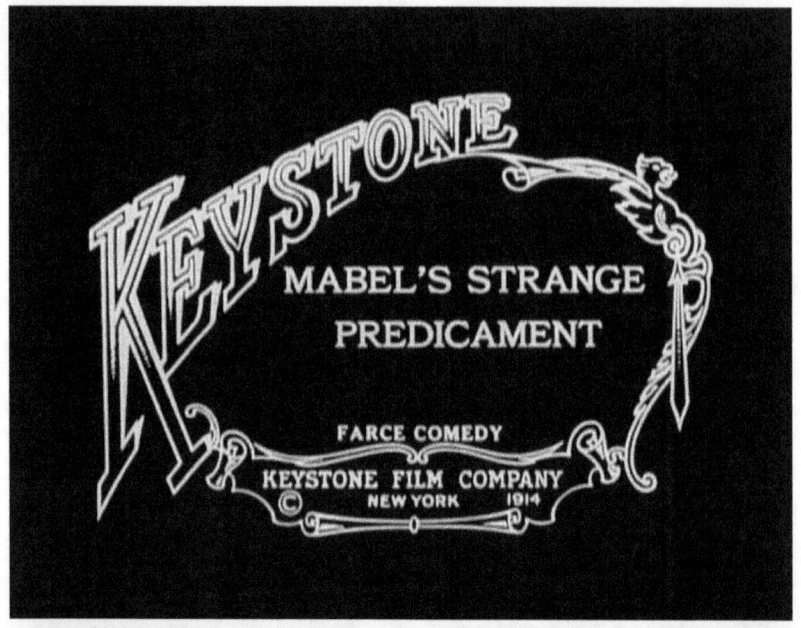

Mabel's Strange Predicament
9th February, 1914

Director: Henry Lehrman
Writer: Reed Heustis or Henry Lehrman
Stars: Mabel Normand, Charles Chaplin, Chester Conklin, Alice Davenport and Harry McCoy

I first saw *Mabel's Strange Predicament* in a horrible, washed out French print in a cheap public domain DVD box set under the title of *Charlot à l'Hôtel*, or *Charlie in the Hotel*.

This change of title is important because, even though it was surely done to reflect the bigger star at the time of reissue, it does underline a very obvious truth: that this is undeniably a Charlie Chaplin picture. Nobody watching today would remotely believe that anyone else was the lead actor, because he's clearly the focus of attention.

He's rarely off screen, for a start, and he owns the opening scene, which runs long for a film from 1914, let alone one from Keystone Studios. Mack Sennett, founder of Keystone, originally intended to have Chaplin stage some routines in the hotel lobby, presumably to warm up the picture and to give his new actor some screen time. However, Chaplin made it obvious, even during the shoot, that his new character clearly deserved more attention, which he promptly got and Sennett bulked up his role to appear throughout the story.

It's important to remember that at this point in time, Chaplin had only hinted at what he could bring to the screen. This film hit theatres on Monday, 9th February, 1914 and he wasn't yet the world famous star he would soon become. He'd debuted on screen only a week earlier, in a role that didn't fit him, then showed up again five days later as the Little Tramp. Theatre audiences were beginning to notice this funny actor who did things a little differently from the norm, and this was an emphatic follow up to the oddity that was *Kid Auto Races at Venice, Cal.*

In reality, he shot this film before that one, but it took longer to reach theatres because it was a far more sophisticated production. That's not to suggest that anything Keystone produced at this point was particularly sophisticated, but everything feels sophisticated when compared to a 45 minute shoot at a public event where the height of comedy is having the Little Tramp walk in front of the camera for five minutes. It was groundbreaking and historic, but it was hardly high art.

At this point, as the original title suggests, the star was Mabel Normand, perhaps the biggest name on the roster at Keystone. Not incidentally, she was also four years into a tumultuous relationship with Sennett, whom she had met at Biograph a few years earlier when they were both working for D. W. Griffith, Normand in front of the camera and Sennett behind it. He brought her with him to California in 1912 to found Keystone and he quickly made her a star.

By the time she found herself in the strange predicament of the title, she had become the establishment, with nearly 150 pictures behind her, many as her regular character, simply named Mabel. Not content with starring in so many pictures, she had also become a pioneering female writer and director who would have her own studio by the end of the decade. Her star fell eventually, aided by two major scandals: the unsolved murder of film director William

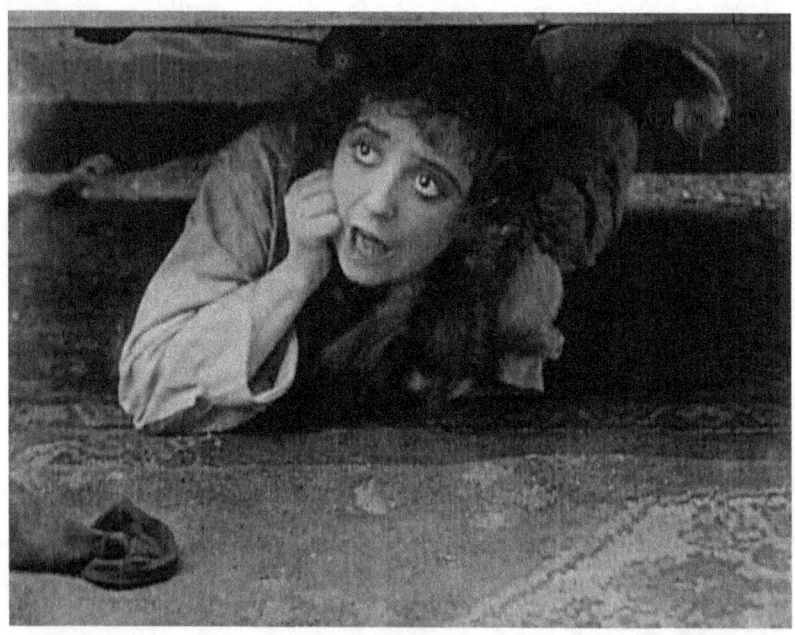

Desmond Taylor and the shooting of millionaire Courtland Dines. It has been argued that the former was a hit to stop him assisting the authorities to bring down her cocaine dealers, while the latter was performed by her chauffeur, Joe Kelly. She died from tuberculosis in 1930.

Watching *Mabel's Strange Predicament* a century on, especially in the restored version that Flicker Alley put out on DVD in 2010, we can't help but wonder what she thought she was doing here. She appears just like a silent movie stereotype, flailing her arms around in panic and chewing up every piece of scenery she can find. She isn't alone, of course, as most of the rest of the cast do the same, including Keystone regulars Chester Conklin and Alice Davenport as a husband and wife who find themselves inadvertently caught up in the assorted mishaps which set up the strange predicament of the title.

However, all these routine slapstick shenanigans merely make it palpably obvious that Charlie Chaplin doesn't chew up any scenery at all. Instead, he's a surprisingly realistic drunkard, a "drunken masher", who sups too much in the first scene and spends the rest of the film notably under the influence. It's a believable, grounded performance that makes good use not only of his hat and cane but of many other props carefully littered around the hotel.

Officially, of course, it's all about Mabel and another nice mess that she gets into (a phrase we associate today with American film comedy, courtesy of Laurel & Hardy, who didn't use it for another sixteen years, but which originated perhaps with W. S Gilbert, who used it in two operettas, *The Mikado* and *The Grand Duke*, back in the late nineteenth century, so audiences would have recognised it in 1914). It's hardly a complex idea on which to build a picture; she just checks into a hotel, changes into her 1914 pyjamas and plays with her dog: bouncing a ball, falling over a lot and generally driving the couple across the hall nuts.

The fun begins when she bounces that ball into the hallway; she goes to retrieve it and the dog shuts the door behind her, locking her out of her own room. Conventional wisdom would suggest that this is probably as far as the script got, because that's how they worked at Keystone and the rest was gags built upon gags. That's not strictly true but it's very believable nonetheless.

The next scene, in which a drunken Charlie stumbles upon her in the hallway and decides to woo her, results in her hiding under the bed. In the room across the hall. The one that houses the couple who are already complaining about her. It's hardly sophisticated, even by Keystone standards, but it moves along capably enough, with a set of decent opportunities for Davenport to rage, Conklin to gesture and Harry McCoy to get crazily jealous as her lover.

None of them impress. It's great to see them properly in a well restored print but they do nothing here that hadn't been done a hundred or a thousand times already, such as in most of the dozen one reel comedies that Keystone churned out every month, often featuring these very same actors.

What makes this particular picture special is Charlie Chaplin, not because he does anything we wouldn't see him do again later on in better pictures with better scripts and better performances, but because he hadn't done it before this moment. This is the film that first showed us just what Chaplin could do.

He didn't do much in *Making a Living*, because he was clearly stuck playing a clichéd villain in a movie that refused to slow down and director Henry Lehrman cut out most of his best bits anyway. I enjoyed *Kid Auto Races at Venice, Cal.* a lot more in the Flicker Alley restoration, but it's still far more important as our first experience of the Little Tramp than it could ever be seen as enjoyable.

It's a shame that that film reached theatres first, because this would have been the better debut. While *Kid Auto Races at Venice, Cal.* features more of one of his most appealing traits, namely his eagerness to stick his nose up at authority, this has more of the rest.

He's notably drunk for most of the film, for a start, making him an outsider wherever he goes, even if the hotel staff treat him with deference because he's aware how to tip. In playing this drunkard, he gets the opportunity to exercise his craft and demonstrate what he could do, but he also gets to do it at length within the confines of a story based picture.

The superlatives that some contemporary critics used to describe him in his first two films would have been far more appropriately used here. He got better, make no mistake, but he effortlessly and emphatically outclassed every one of his co-stars in this picture. He dominates, pure and simple, with every movement an opportunity for another little nuance, whether it's to bash himself on the head with his twirling cane, fall off a chair or just hang up his tight coat on a hook that isn't there. He's the centre of his own universe, one that only we can appreciate.

With three films reaching theatres in eight days, Chaplin was well on the way. This picture in particular showcased his talents, highlighted how he could steal every scene, apparently effortlessly, from his far more experienced and far more established fellow cast members, and clearly emphasised that the future was his to grasp.

Yet he was still new at Keystone Studios and he was still adapting his stage expertise to screen. *Mabel's Strange Predicament* shows us that he had an instinctive feel for the camera, but he would hone his skills over many further pictures until he had mastered not only the role of actor but most of the other roles needed to make a film work too. David Robinson, author of a number of books on Chaplin, explained that "no other filmmaker ever so completely dominated every aspect of the work, did every job," famously adding that, "If he could have done so, Chaplin would have played every role and (as his son Sydney humorously but perceptively observed) sewn

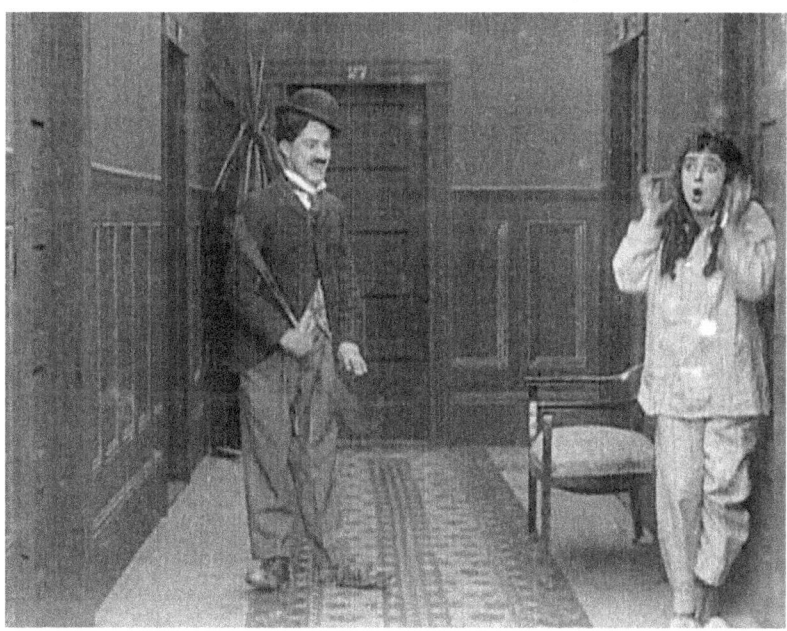

every costume." From here, we can start watching him grow.

And I found myself really looking forward to doing that over the course of 2014. I'd seen most of Chaplin's Keystone pictures before, but only in the generally poor prints that have circulated for years. I quickly found the Flicker Alley restorations eye-opening because I saw things in each of these films that I've never seen before, even if I watched an older copy immediately before its new restoration. Each one of Chaplin's first three pictures played better to me than the previous time and I laughed more and more often.

However, like Chaplin's career, I was still only at the beginning. I knew his films got better as the year progressed and as he gradually took over as actor, writer and director and I wondered here if this was why Mabel Normand is so frequently cited as his mentor. It certainly wasn't because of her acting, as he effortlessly eclipsed her in their first screen pairing. There were twelve more to come in 1914, culminating in the first feature length screen comedy ever made, *Tillie's Punctured Romance*.

As I wrote after revisiting this one in 2014: "It's going to be an interesting year."

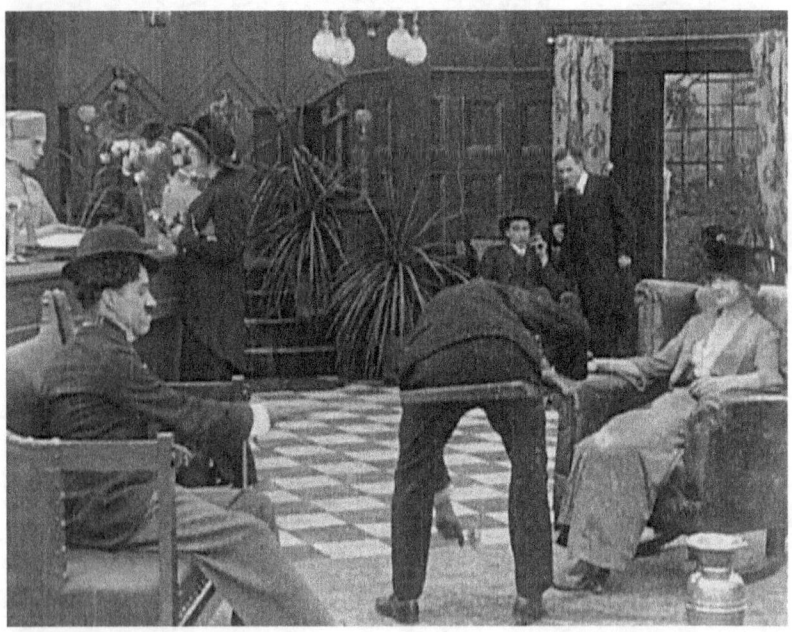

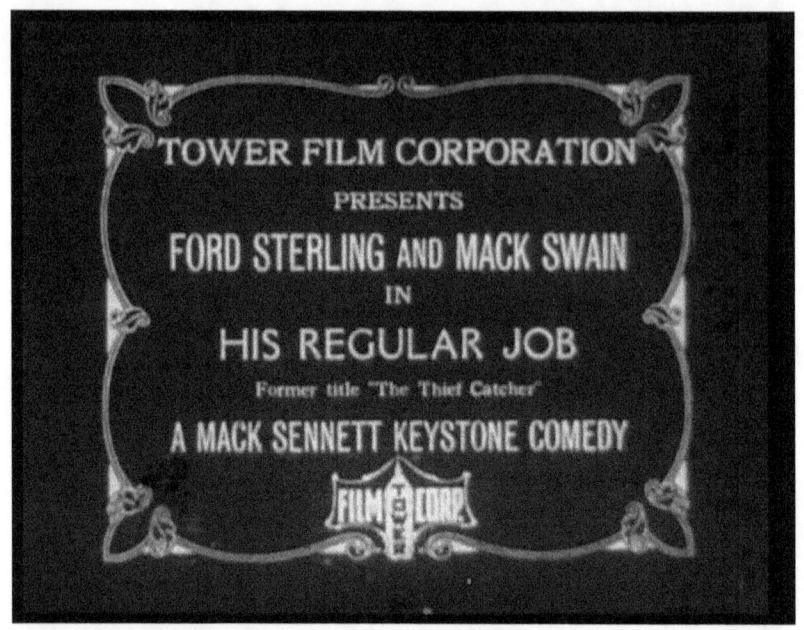

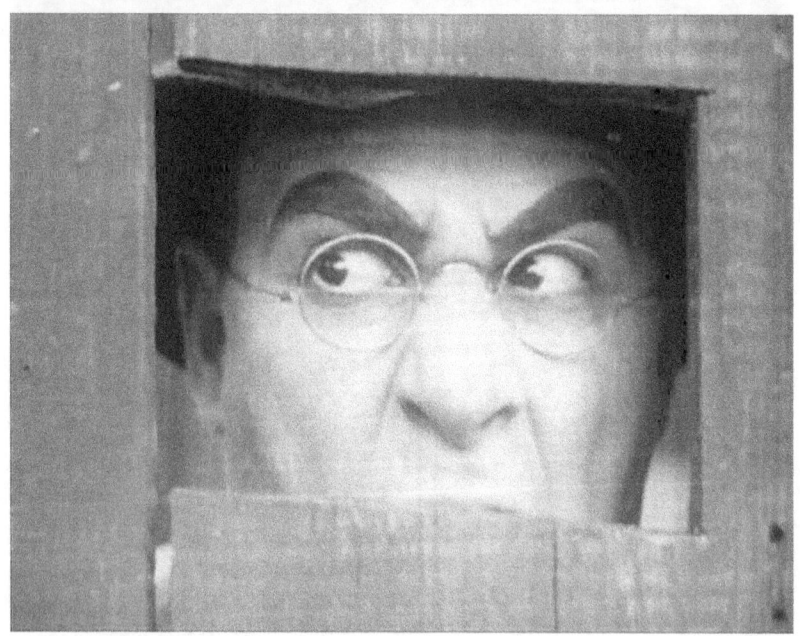

A Thief Catcher
19th February, 1914

Director: Henry Lehrman
Writer: Unknown
Stars: Ford Sterling, Mack Swain and Edgar Kennedy

A Thief Catcher is possibly the oddest entry in Charlie Chaplin's filmography and writing my original review felt strange, given that I'd only seen the first half at the time, as it had only been recently rediscovered and wasn't yet fully available to the public.

As I wrote at that time, at least we know that it exists now and that it does indeed feature Chaplin, in an unusual role as a Keystone Kop. Until 2010, we didn't know that, given that the title had been discounted by all the standard biographers, beginning with the pioneering research of H. D. Waley, the Technical Director of the British Film Institute, which was published in 1938.

The suggestion is that he conflated this title, *A Thief Catcher*, with a similar one, *The Thief Catcher*, which was the reported title for a reissue of *Her Friend the Bandit*, another short film Chaplin made at Keystone Studios in 1914. This is understandable, of course, given that Chaplin made so many pictures that year and they were widely reissued, often under a variety of different names. It's especially understandable here, as *Her Friend the Bandit* has traditionally been the only one of Chaplin's pictures to be confirmed as lost. If *A Thief Catcher* was also lost, there was no way anyone could prove that it wasn't the same film.

It was rediscovered in 2009 by Paul Gierucki, a film historian who currently serves as the head of restorations for CineMuseum, LLC, which has a strong focus on silent comedy. They've restored and released much from this era, including highly regarded box sets like *The Forgotten Films of Roscoe 'Fatty' Arbuckle*, which I can personally vouch for, and *Industrial Strength Keaton*. As I wrote, in 2014, they were finishing up *The Mack Sennett Collection, Volume One*, which included *A Thief Catcher* and was later released by Flicker Alley; on the film's centennial, only the first six minutes were available to the public in the *Chaplin at Keystone* box set, also from Flicker Alley.

It's very possible that, until Gierucki's rediscovery, nobody had seen *A Thief Catcher* since the end of World War I.

He found it in 2009 at an antiques show in Michigan nestled amongst a stack of old 16mm reels. This particular can was labelled "Keystone" but not "Chaplin", so he left it untouched for a few weeks before screening it. When he did, he knew exactly what he had, even though the print is actually of *His Regular Job*, a 1918 reissue by the Tower Film Company of *A Thief Catcher*, which didn't include a mention of Chaplin being in the cast on the company's records.

Gierucki knew what he had for two reasons. Firstly, the quality was decent, even though this was a 16mm print. Secondly, as we can now see, there's just no mistaking this particular Keystone Kop for anyone else. This isn't merely Chaplin playing a Keystone Kop, it's Chaplin playing the Little Tramp playing a Keystone Kop.

We can only guess as to why this happened. Perhaps he was free for a day and put on that famous uniform to help out when Keystone was short of actors, a theory backed up by the fact that one of the other cops is played by Bill Hauber, who had appeared earlier in the film in a short second role as one of the crooks. If Keystone were recycling their crooks into cops within the very same picture, they were surely short on hands when they shot it.

More obviously, Chaplin isn't the star of the film and was still finding his feet. He was still new to Keystone Studios and to the big screen generally. He'd made three pictures before this one, the first of which had been completed and shipped on 14th January, 1914. *A Thief Catcher* reached screens on 19th February, only ten days after his third and still less than two and a half weeks after his first. All told, he'd be on screen in five different movies in February 1914 alone. The world was quickly discovering who he was and what he could do, but they needed some time to do so and there had been precious little of it thus far.

In a twist of irony, the star he supports here is Ford Sterling, who also directed the film. It was Sterling's decision to leave Keystone to start his own company that led Mack Sennett, the studio boss, to hire Chaplin to begin with. Sterling was a huge star for Keystone who, like Mabel Normand, had followed Sennett to California when he left Biograph Studios, and quickly became a key player. He was the original leader of the Keystone Kops, for instance, playing Chief Teeheezel.

As is made obvious in this film, Sterling belongs emphatically to the old school tradition of silent comedy, full of gestures and flamboyance to compensate for the lack of speech. Surprisingly, for anyone who has seen him in a silent movie, he successfully made the transition to sound films and continued to make them until 1937. For instance, he played the White King in the star studded 1933 version of *Alice in Wonderland* (other Keystone alumni like Louise Fazenda, W. C. Fields and Polly Moran also starred, as did a young Cary Grant, in only his second year on the screen). He even returned to Keystone to reprise his old role as the Chief of Police in 1935's *Keystone Hotel*, four years before his death at 55 of a heart attack, led on by diabetes.

He plays another man with a badge here, though we don't realise that initially. He's only a bystander when we first see him, though, walking his dog and stumbling upon a trio of what the intertitles call "yeggmen", an antiquated term for safe-crackers, witnessing two of them disposing of the third over a cliff. This startling scene

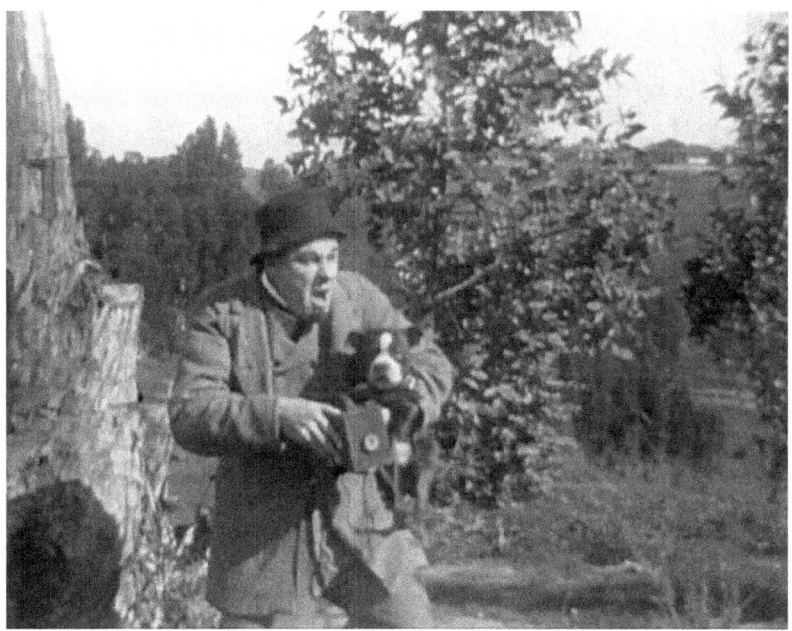

is easily the best one shot in the entire picture, because it looks completely fake until movement shows us that it's as real as any other location in the picture. It's a neat bit of illusion.

Being a cowardly soul, he hightails it out of there, pausing only to snap a quick photo of the murder on something like a box brownie, and the yeggmen pursue him. After a few capably shot but entirely predictable slapstick gags, he finds himself out in the sticks where, in a quintessentially slapstick slice of conveniently bad judgement, he hides out in the yeggmen's very own hideout. It's as he's about to enter this building that we realise that he's actually a lawman, not a Keystone Kop but perhaps a rural sheriff.

If you've ever seen a silent comedy, you can imagine where this setup will take us and you won't be far wrong. The lack of any real surprises (except for Chaplin's appearance) are countered by some imaginative little touches that demonstrate how thought went into even the quickest shoots at Keystone.

Most of these touches revolve around the palpable nervousness of Sterling's character, described in an early intertitle as Suspicious John. At one point, he's so fearful that his fingers lock together, as if

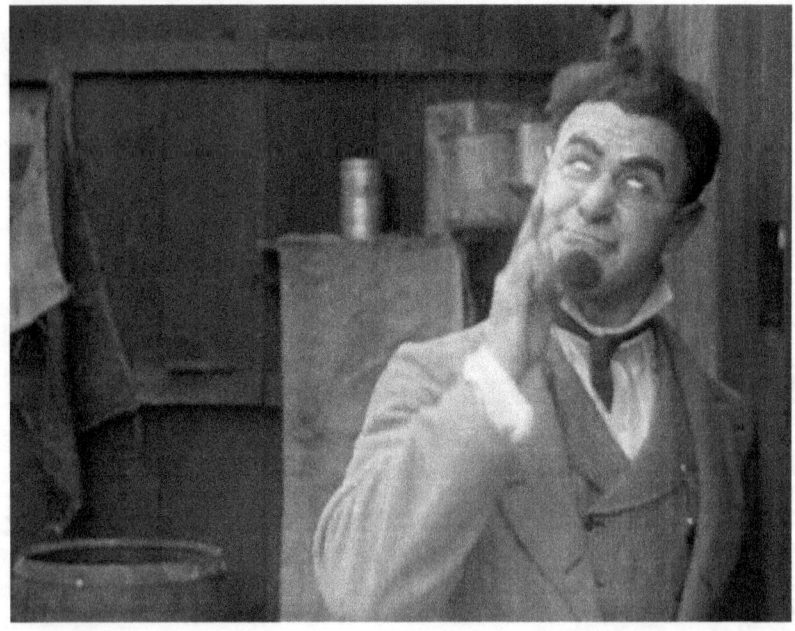

they were trapped in Chinese handcuffs; he has to use his knee to break them loose. He's eventually discovered while hiding behind a coat because he's shaking so much that it moves, even hanging on a peg. During a rather brutal scene where he spies on the yeggmen through a hole in the wall and sees them toss a coin to see which of them will be the one to shoot him, not only once but in a "best of three" sort of scenario, his hair begins to reach for the ceiling; it's quite literally a hair-raising experience for him.

The negative side is in how they do it. While Mack Swain and Edgar Kennedy, playing the yeggmen, have more subtle moments, like the coin tossing scene, all three of them pantomime far more than they act. This was silent movie tradition, because if characters got their point over with gestures, then intertitles weren't needed and the action sped up considerably. When Sterling first tries to get out of his hideout and sees the yeggmen outside, he points at them, then to himself and then to the room he's stuck in; we don't need an intertitle to tell us the situation he's got himself into.

Sterling was capable enough at this to have grown into one of Keystone's biggest stars and Swain and Kennedy were also greatly experienced hands at Keystone. The catch is that, to our jaded eyes with a hundred years of hindsight, they're dated beyond belief. It isn't the lack of sound, as recent silent movies have demonstrated, up to and including the Academy Award-winning *The Artist*, it's in the chewing of scenery with reckless abandon and the telegraphing of things that ought to be obvious. While the scene above is fair enough, his hair-raising scene certainly isn't. We can see his hair moving; we don't need him to point at it through the fourth wall. It is funny, but it's a very dated sort of funny.

Ironically, the movement away from that sort of overacting in American comedy came with the arrival of Charlie Chaplin and that is recreated in microcosm here. When the highly recognisable form of Chaplin arrives five and half minutes into the picture in the even more recognisable form (at this time) of a Keystone Kop, things do start to settle a little.

It's utterly impossible not to compare his subtle and controlled movements with their flailing around, even during this first scene. Chaplin is menacing here, shorter and thinner than either of the crooks but believably able to push them around. There's purpose to what he does, something that was rarely apparent with Keystone Kops. We see a group of them later in the film, after Suspicious John ties a message to his dog and sends it off to the station. They chase to the cabin and join the story, but they do so through a sort of herd mentality. Nobody directs them, they just move and each of them follows each other until they end up somewhere. How they ever get where they're going, I have no idea. Chaplin's cop, even in such a recognisable outfit, is very much his own man.

He gets a little more screen time, entering the hideout to see who else is in there and getting a spade to the face from Sterling for his troubles. Less than a hundred seconds of screen time after he shows up, though, he's gone again, in a variation of the routine we saw in *Mabel's Strange Predicament*. Of course, he's merely dazed here from the spade. He shows up once more to join in the final shot.

It's good to see such contrast in these early films. It ably shows how Chaplin was doing his own thing instead of aping the style of those around him. He just wasn't interested in doing what everyone else was doing. It also ably shows how those other actors hadn't yet responded to his new ideas. Many of them would, of course, once it

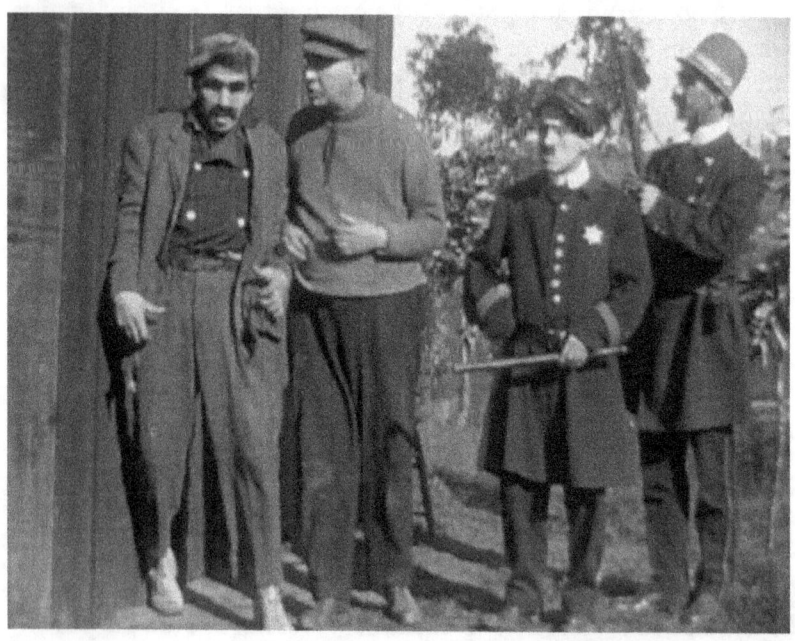

proved to be the right way forward, but it took time and how that evolved is a good part of what made my approach to watch these Keystone films on their centennials such an interesting one.

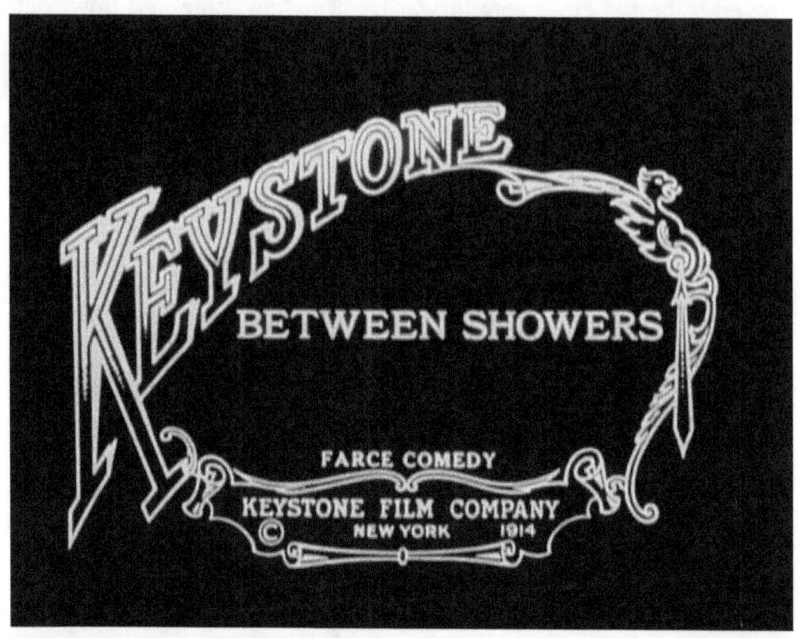

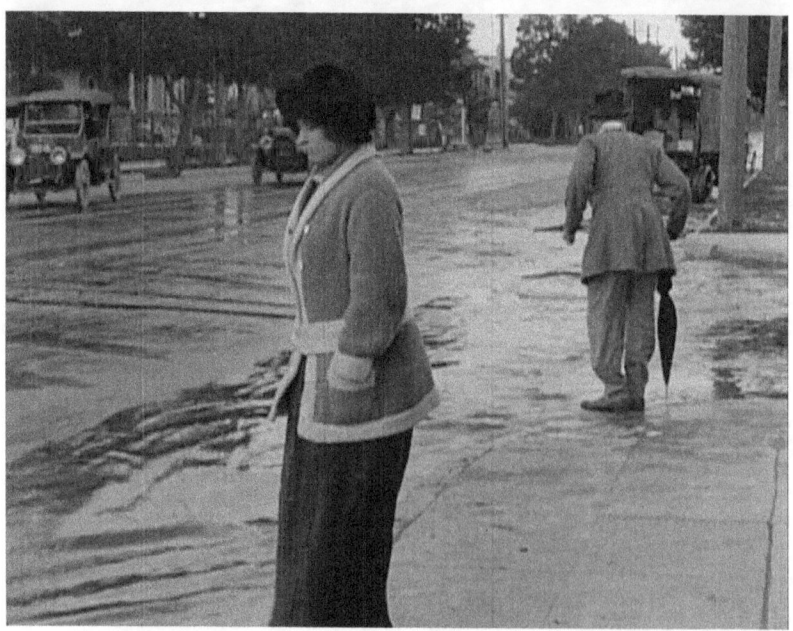

Between Showers
28th February, 1914

Director: Henry Lehrman
Writer: Henry Lehrman or Reed Heustis
Stars: Ford Sterling and Charles Chaplin

Between Showers, the fifth and last film in Charlie Chaplin's busy debut month, screams transition in various ways, each of which highlight both the evolution of his Little Tramp character and his growing importance at Keystone Studios.

Like *A Thief Catcher*, it's a Ford Sterling picture, but Chaplin's part in it is elevated from his minor supporting role there as a Keystone Kop, just helping out on a day when the studio was short of actors, to Sterling's co-star here. In fact, if we didn't know that Sterling was preparing to leave Keystone to form his own studio, we might be forgiven for seeing this as the beginning of a new double act.

At just over fourteen minutes, it's the longest short Chaplin had yet made, though it was still only a one reeler; it would remain the longest until his first two reeler, *Mabel at the Wheel*, six films away in mid April.

It's also the last of his films directed by Henry Lehrman, who left Keystone after this picture to form L-KO Studios. Lehrman had directed four of Chaplin's first five films, just as his replacement, George Nichols, would direct four out of his next five.

The framework of the story is as hilariously flimsy as Keystone stories got and it highlights well just how quickly they made films. Hollywood had been experiencing torrential rain in early February 1914, so Mack Sennett, producer and studio head, had an unknown writer conjure up a comedy around it.

The British Film Institute says the writer was Lehrman himself, while other sources list Reed Heustis, a name attached to many early Chaplin pictures as a scenario writer. Whoever this writer was, he did his work quickly enough that the production could use a particularly large puddle at the side of a road as a prominent prop. That's not entirely surprising given how little there is in what passed for a script at Keystone, which were often a string of gags scrawled down by Sennett and passed over to a director to translate onto the screen.

The story arc follows an umbrella, which Sterling's character steals at the beginning of the film, daringly from a Keystone Kop. He leaves it with a lady in distress, whom he's eager to help across that prominent puddle, only to find that retrieving it from her again is a tough proposition, one complicated by the involvement of Chaplin's Little Tramp, who also wants to help this lady. As was usually the case in Keystone shorts, slapstick comedy is improvised until the umbrella is reunited with its rightful owner through a particularly dumb move by the thief.

And, of course, the umbrella is we might call today a MacGuffin, an object that drives both the characters and the plot but has no importance to the audience whatsoever. This particular McGuffin dates to a couple of decades before Alfred Hitchcock popularised the term, but it had other names back in the silent era; Pearl White, "the Queen of the Serials", for instance, called it a "weenie".

We don't care about the umbrella at all, but we're very interested in the shenanigans that the characters get up to in order to have it,

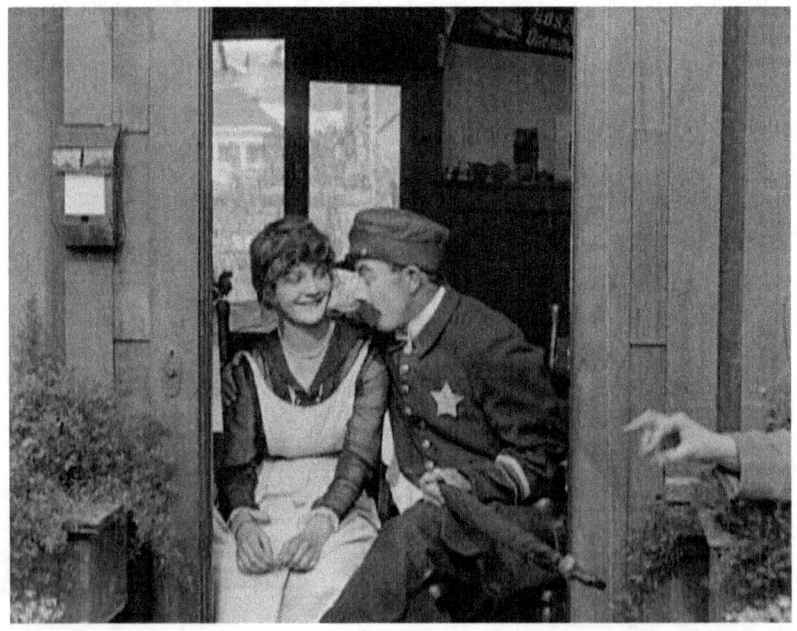

starting with Sterling's antics as the picture begins. He wants the thing because he knows more rain is due and his own umbrella is shredded and useless. Given that he's a thief, Mr. Snookie by name in the print I saw, he's happy to steal one and there's one close by in the hands of a cop, who is being distracted by the attentions of a pretty girl. The cop is Keystone regular Chester Conklin, who has little to do here, and the lady is Sadie Lampe, who decorated the screen nicely in a few small supporting roles in a few early Chaplins. Sterling dominates this scene though and it's interesting to see how.

Sterling was a pantomime artist, the sort of actor people see in their mind if they're asked to think of a silent screen comedian. He never stops moving, even when he's unable to go anywhere. His very expressive hands are always in motion, just like his mouth and the rest of his face. He telegraphs every move with flamboyant gestures and indulges in overt internal conversation to get that across, as if he's explaining himself to an imaginary companion. If this was animation, there would be a little devil on his shoulders, goading him into a heinous act, and a little angel making a mild effort to stop him before it's too late. He doesn't walk; he creeps portentiously. Later in the film, as the action speeds up, he jumps in the air before running, just as he did in *A Thief Catcher*. Earlier, he runs on the spot for effect before making his escape, just like we might expect a *Loonie Toones* character to do. Oddly, we never see him in the same frame as the cop and his lady friend; just his hand in their shots and the end of the umbrella when he's on screen. It helps to highlight how this is all about him.

And so to the vast puddle, where he measures its depth with the umbrella and wonders if he can manage to cross the road without getting soaked. Before he tries it, a young lady shows up, played by Emma Clifton, who wonders the same thing; our thief is instantly smitten. He goes in search of a plank to use as a bridge, only to discover that during his absence, the Little Tramp has shown up to run through exactly the same set-up. Now they are rivals for this young lady's affections, but both of them lose out to a helpful policeman who politely carries her over the road.

He's played by Eddie Nolan, a lesser name at Keystone Studios who had debuted alongside Chaplin in *Making a Living*; his first five films were all Chaplin shorts and he'd play a number of roles in their shared first feature, *Tillie's Punctured Romance*. Nolan's acting style is surprisingly even more realistic than Chaplin's, but it's a lot more limited. He may be subdued and comfortable in his actions, but he doesn't have the expressions of the lead comics; he served best as a tall prop for them to work off.

Five minutes in, Sterling and Chaplin return to the puddle with their respective planks to interact for the first time. We've already contrasted them in our minds, as their styles are utterly different, but we can't fail to do so afresh as they finally share a screen.

At the time, the most obvious contrast may have been between Sterling's goatee and Chaplin's toothbrush moustache, Keystone always keen on having their leading comedians develop their own iconic facial hair to aid in delineation, but today it's between styles, the old one that Sterling did so well and the new one that Chaplin was pioneering.

Like Sterling, Chaplin never stops moving, but his movements are all small ones, much more restrained. Instead of jumping up and down, he merely shuffles on the spot. Instead of flailing around, he just gestures calmly and builds his portfolio of personal tics. He interacts with the other characters rather than imaginary ones for our benefit. As the pair share both screen and gags, it's impossible not to see the difference between them. Only in more active moments does Chaplin imitate a lighter version of Sterling.

Another major difference that becomes more and more apparent as the film goes on is in the tone of their characters. Both play "mashers", an archaic term for men who make advances to women they don't know, usually improper ones, but they do so in utterly different ways.

Mr. Snookie is a long way from the lovable rogue that the Little Tramp was starting to become; he's an angry and violent would be rapist, literally hopping mad, attacking the young lady who won't return his stolen umbrella. He orders her around, grabs her by the hair and even bites her nose! Biting was part of the Sterling schtick, as we saw in *A Thief Catcher*, when he tries to take a chunk out of one of the yeggmen's thighs to avoid being shot. By comparison, Chaplin uses subtlety to woo the young lady instead, gently guiding her elbow and tipping his hat, and offering the protection that she doesn't need.

It's notable that women are strong in this short. The cop's lady friend at the beginning emphatically sends him packing when she sees the broken umbrella Mr. Snookie left him. This former lady in distress proceeds to save herself, belting her assailant, pushing him around and then knocking him down, all while two other women applaud in the distance. Emma Clifton clearly had a lot of fun making *Between Showers*!

Chaplin copes decently in the slapstick fight scenes, but his most memorable moment is instead a charming one that helps to build his pixie-like anti-establishment character. Both mashers face off against the gallant cop who carried the object of their affections over the road and both inevitably lose out, but how they do so is very telling.

Sterling looks threatening but backs off like a coward when the cop slowly draws out his truncheon; their scene is over quickly and promptly forgotten by the character. Chaplin, however, dominates his scene even with his back to the camera. He's just as wary and he doesn't back down but he never threatens, so the cop doesn't need

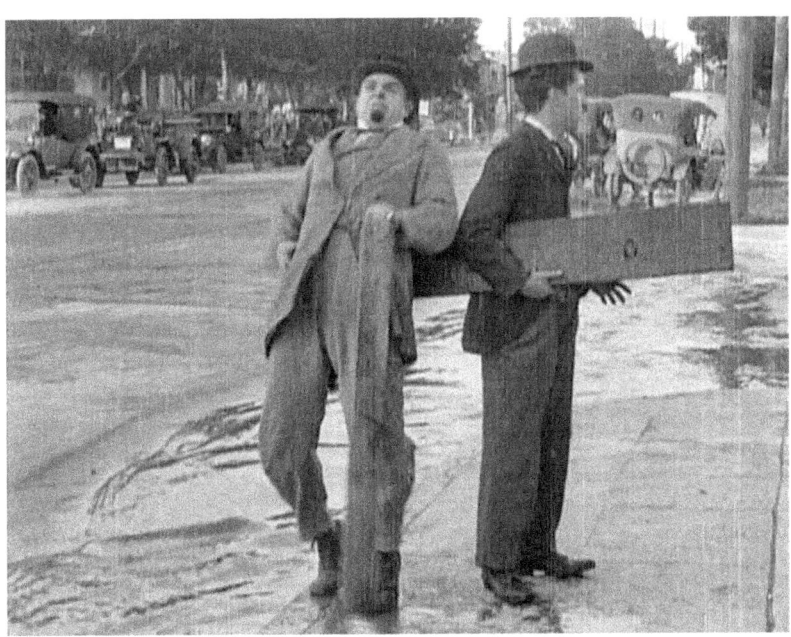

to react. He also maintains control after the cop leaves, as his arms record the story of what he'd like to have done. He cocks a snoot at the departing cop, then breaks the fourth wall and grins a cheeky grin to the audience, sharing the event with us before covering that grin with his hand as if embarrassed by his thoughts. It's charming and infectious and it makes the scene meaningful.

Audiences at the time didn't know it but we'd see this movement repeated a lot in future Chaplin pictures, along with a number of others that he makes here.

Some might have looked familiar even at this point, such as the way he twirls the umbrella and knocks himself in the head; he did this a couple of times with a cane in *Mabel's Strange Predicament* and he would return to it again and again in later films. The well known Chaplin run is debuted here, as he skids into turns and makes them balanced on one foot. He'd get better at it later on but it arrived fully formed here. These are quirky little character depths that are so much more memorable than the inevitable slapstick antics that populate the fights and pratfalls, because that's what Keystone did up until his arrival. Yes, the Little Tramp literally kicks Mr. Snookie

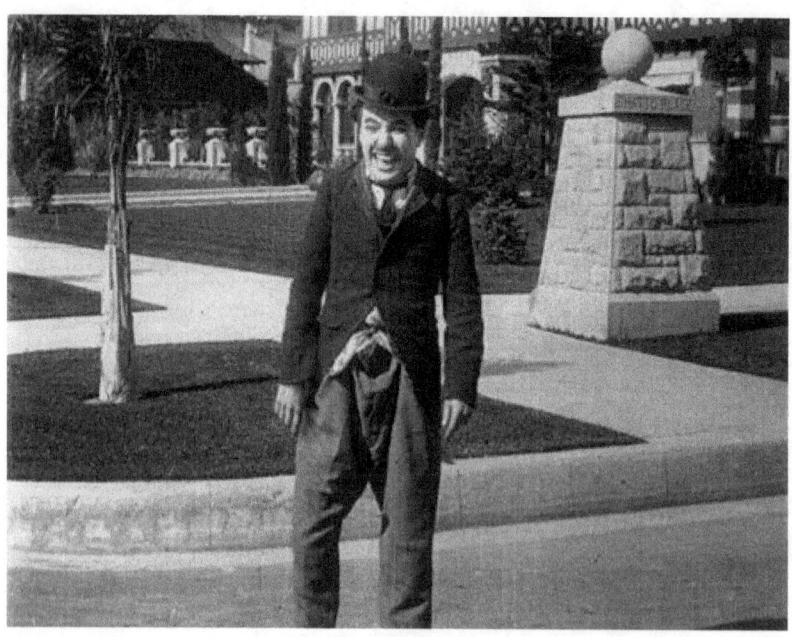

in the ass and both of them are knocked down to the ground more than once.

Between Showers is far from a great film, but it's a surprisingly decent one that serves well as a hint of the future. The Little Tramp was clearly coming into his own and it's not surprising in the least that audiences responded well.

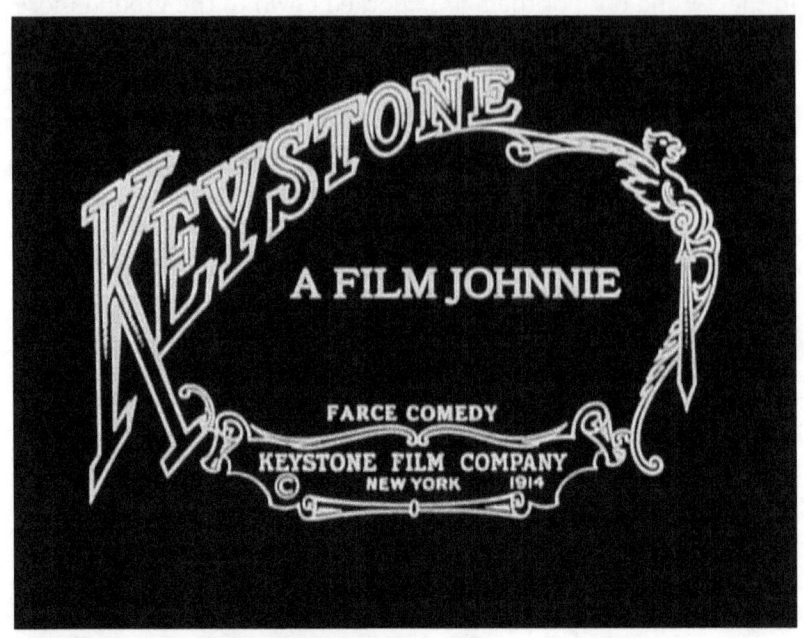

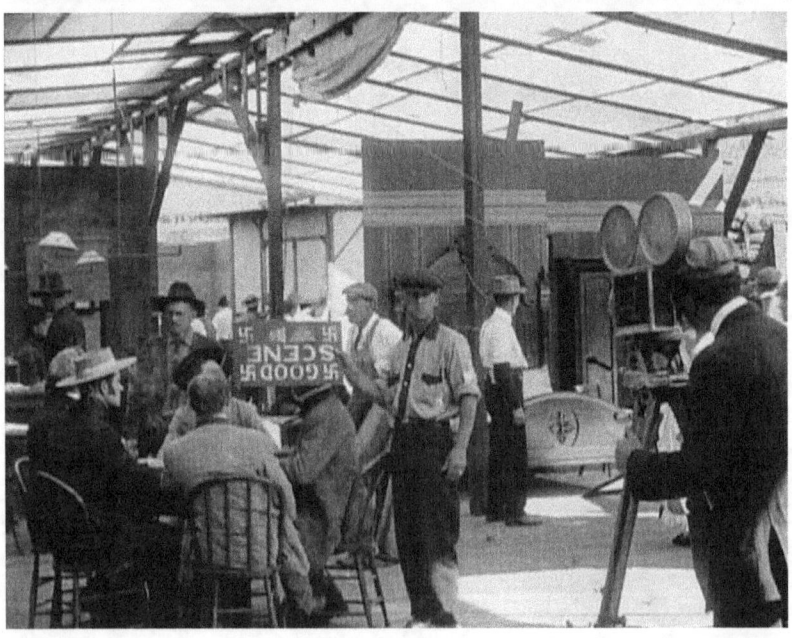

A Film Johnnie
2nd March, 1914

Director: George Nichols
Writer: Craig Hutchinson
Star: Charles Chaplin

A Film Johnnie was Charlie Chaplin's sixth film, released only two days after his fifth, *Between Showers*, on 2nd March, 1914.

I found dates fascinating as I worked through Chaplin's early films, for a variety of reasons, not only because Keystone Studios churned out these farce comedies at frenetic speed. For instance, this was the first of Chaplin's pictures to see release in March 1914, a new month, as all five of its predecessors were first screened to the public in February of 1914.

What's perhaps most amazing to modern day audiences who might be used to the concepts of teaser trailers, test screenings and social media campaigns is that *A Film Johnnie* began shooting on Sunday, 1st February, one day before *Making a Living* opened in theatres. In other words, by the time Chaplin's first picture was first seen by the public, he had already begun work on his sixth.

Shooting began on the 1st and wrapped on the 6th, while post-production was complete by the 11th and the negative was in the post for New York the same day, to meet a release date of only a month and a day after the whole process began. This sort of speed was typical at Keystone: the average film was shot in under a week, on the road a week later and on theatre screens three weeks after that. Sometimes the longest wait was for the reel to make its way across country: here, it took six days to shoot and five to assemble but seven to get to New York.

It was surprising to me that *A Film Johnnie*, which would be called a "meta movie" today, could have been made so early in Chaplin's career, his first lead performance before the public knew who he was. Sure, *Kid Auto Races at Venice, Cal.* was all about him, but it was a simple gag not a story based movie. *Mabel's Strange Predicament* was framed around him and he had the most screen time, but the lead was Mabel Normand. In *Making a Living*, he's firmly playing support and *A Thief Catcher* was an even briefer role for him. Even *Between Showers*, which he dominates, tasks him only to co-star with Ford Sterling.

In *A Film Johnnie*, he's clearly the lead actor and the only major character, in a picture with a real story, or at least what passed for one at Keystone. What's more, his antics unfold against a Who's Who of Keystone talent, sourced from either side of the camera, including the established stars of the day. Of course, he was hired to replace Ford Sterling as the studio's star, but the only conclusion that can be fairly drawn is that, after only a month, it was becoming obvious just what a talent Keystone suddenly had.

It's a fascinating film today, one of the more fascinating of the historic early Chaplin pictures, as it shows us something of what it was like to actually be on a Keystone set. What's more, it shows us, using exaggerated fiction, something of what Chaplin might have been feeling only a couple of months earlier, during his earliest days at the studio.

He arrived at Keystone in early December 1913 but wasn't put to work for a month, starting for real in early January 1914. While he was generally kept frantically busy during his contracted year, working long hours six days a week to make his 36 pictures, that schedule hadn't ramped up during his initial month and he must have felt particularly out of place. As Simon Louvish phrased it in his book, *Keystone: The Life and Clowns of Mack Sennett*, "Chaplin's problem was a familiar one of stage training, longing for the linear continuity of acting, building the pantomime gag and following it through without interruption, as against the stop and start of the films." I wonder how much frustration he foresaw during that first month and what he imagined to counter it.

This film opens with the Little Tramp outside a nickoledeon, looking at the enticing posters on display. These aren't imaginary, they're real pictures from 1913: *The Open Door* from the Broncho Film Company and a couple more from the Reliance Film Company, including *The Alternative*. However, the Little Tramp only has eyes for the leading lady who decorates the poster for *The Champion Driver*, a Keystone picture that is surely what IMDb lists as 1913's *The Champion*, though this one is a war movie rather than a motor racing picture.

You see, he's infatuated with "the Keystone Girl", supposedly played here by Virginia Kirtley (and more on that later), enough to blow soft kisses at her poster and go all moon-faced right there in the street. Kirtley was an odd casting choice, not because she wasn't up to the task but because she plays an imaginary Keystone Girl in a picture that tasks her with acting alongside the real Keystone Girl, Mabel Normand, who appears as herself, or at least as her regular character, Mabel. The fake Keystone Girl had even acted with the real Keystone Girl in a few other pictures, so audiences knew the difference. And, just to add to the strangeness, that poster for the film within a film, was for a Mabel Normand picture, which here stars Virginia Kirtley. Are you confused yet? No wonder the Little Tramp is all in a tizzy. And no wonder we're not even sure if this is Virginia Kirtley, as I believe it's actually Peggy Pearce instead.

After a brief but hilarious scene inside the nickelodeon, in which Chaplin effortlessly causes chaos with his accident-prone nature and his inability to distinguish between fantasy and reality, he's thrown out on his ear. What else could a love-stricken fan do but hightail it out to the Keystone studios to catch a glimpse of his

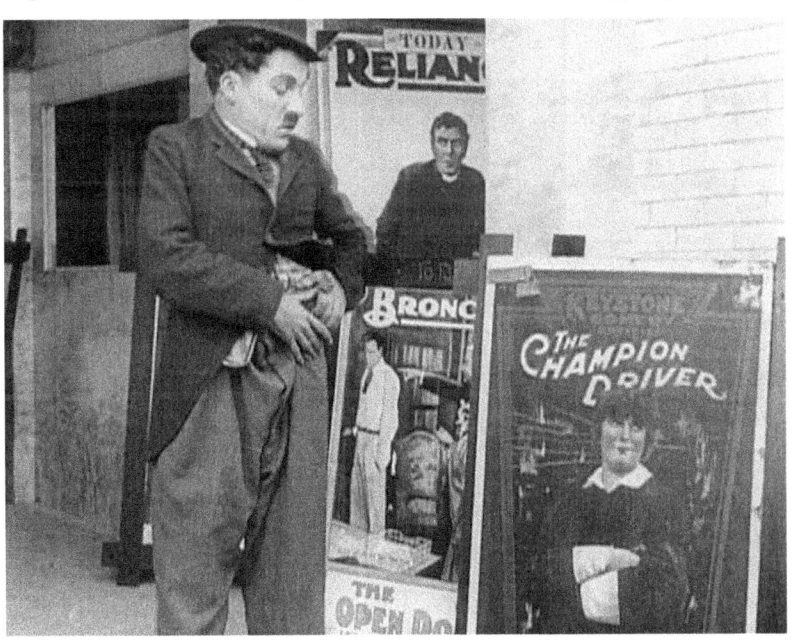

dream girl for real?

As he does so, he meets many of the leading Keystone lights as they arrive for work, not least Roscoe "Fatty" Arbuckle, from whom he cadges a coin, and Ford Sterling, sans trademark goatee, who promptly steals it back.

Here's where the film's title finds some meaning: a "stage door Johnny" was a man who hung around the stage doors of theatres to meet to attempt to pick up stage actresses (more likely succeeding with chorus girls). This merely adapts the concept to film, a good idea for Keystone, whose studio front looks very much like the sort of stereotypical Californian money we imagine behind Hollywood, even if it turns out to be more workmanlike inside. And, of course, being the Little Tramp, Chaplin doesn't just hang around outside, he follows the girls right on in.

As you can imagine from the speed that Mack Sennett's studio churned out movies, the Keystone set that we see in this film is a notably busy place, both in the amount of action and in the amount of distraction. The Little Tramp is presumably so stunned by what he sees that he disappears from the frame and we watch what is

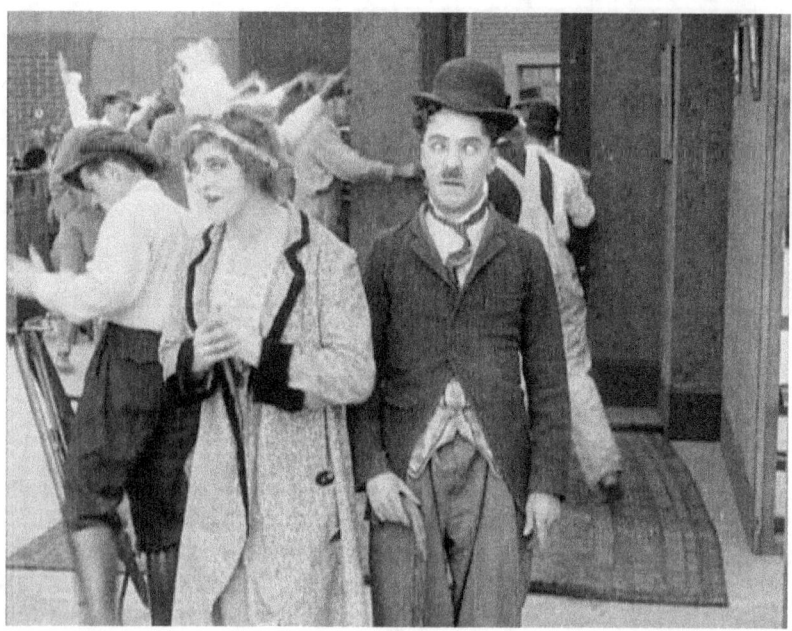

valuable footage of a real Keystone set.

One man carries a board reading, "Pict. No. 148. Sce. No. 36. Munt-Myers." I have no idea which picture this would have been, but it certainly seems to be going well. Another man holds up a board containing the words "good scene" surrounded by prominent swastikas, which in the first decades of the twentieth century were commonplace good luck symbols in the west; the Nazi party didn't adopt them for their more nefarious purposes until the 1920s. A cameraman captures it all, while above his head we see another sign, which appears to be telling extras to keep off the set unless they're in scenes being shot. Clearly the Little Tramp is far too lost in the busy scene to even notice it. Then again, he'd ignore it even if he did.

On this set, nothing can be taken for granted. If you're in the wrong place, as the Little Tramp clearly is, it's the easiest thing in the world to be knocked down by an unfurling carpet or trapped by the closing walls of a set, all of which spring up out of nowhere because fast working Keystone stagehands expect nobody to be in their way. These sets are modular, designed to be assembled and populated with props in no time flat. With everything kept close at hand, a wall to lean on might not be a wall and it might be needed somewhere else entirely very shortly; the same goes for other props as simple as chairs.

Chaplin, who was a seasoned vaudevillian, understood this sort of stage work, but would have been just as struck as we the viewers by the sheer chaos of the studio. In a regular theatre, everything is backstage until it's needed on stage. If these scenes are believable, it's difficult to tell what is a Keystone set and what isn't at any point in time. No wonder the Little Tramp is crosseyed by the time he discovers the Keystone Girl standing right next to him!

And, of course, the source of all his problems in this film is his abiding inability to distinguish between what is real from what is only staged for a movie. Naturally, once the camera rolls on the set that magically appears out of nowhere, he gets caught up in the action himself, just as he did back at the nickelodeon, but instead of interrupting the enjoyment of fellow filmgoers, here he interrupts the actual film itself, leaping into the fray to save his dream girl from the hands of a typically moustachioed Keystone villain.

Needless to say, the chaos he wrought inside the nickelodeon is nothing to what he wreaks here, especially with the aid of a gun grabbed from the prop department, and he isn't done yet because we're about to learn something else that Keystone did: react to situations just as quickly as they built sets. Offscreen, we discovered this with *Between Showers*, a picture which was only created as a reaction to torrential rain hitting California, but we actually see it happen here, as a man spies a fire and promptly notifies the studio. "A fire!" reads the intertitle. "Just what we need to finish the picture."

And so we chase into act three, with the Little Tramp reprising his studio antics once again as the filmmakers transition over to a guerrilla-style shoot at the fire location. The action is too fast paced for the audience to even consider the morals in play, as we only see the man who found the fire calling the studio and we never see the film crew calling anyone. Presumably somebody had the decency to call the fire department too, as they show up and join in the fun.

It's all capably done, but the real shots here are the last ones. The Keystone Girl is more than a little unhappy about the Little Tramp's

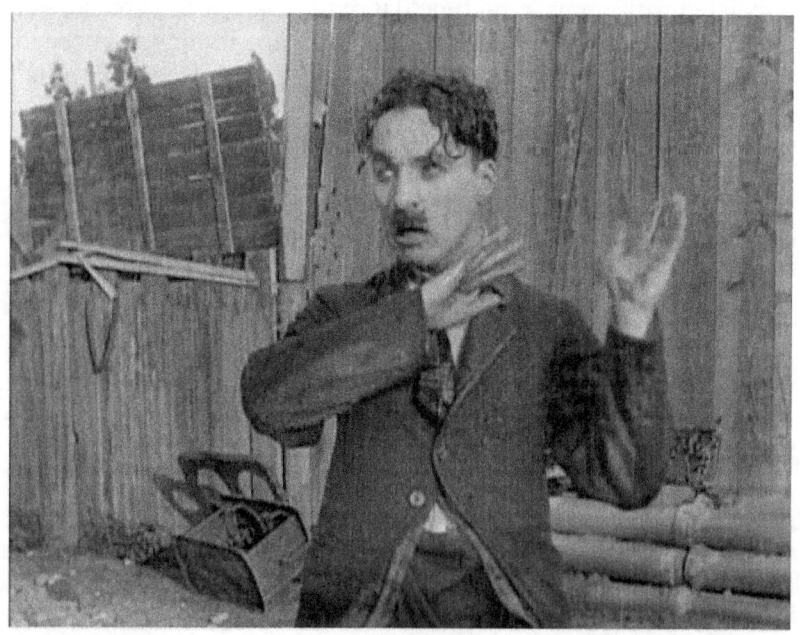

selfless interventions on her behalf and she demonstrates to him in no uncertain terms just how unhappy. By the time she's finished with him, he's surely as devastated inside as he is outside, courtesy of a well aimed firehose. The film ends with the bedraggled tramp breaking the fourth wall and showing us how fed up with the whole thing he is.

Goodbye to the movie business, he tells us, but ironically, at precisely the same time, his first pictures hit theatre screens so that he could emphatically say hello.

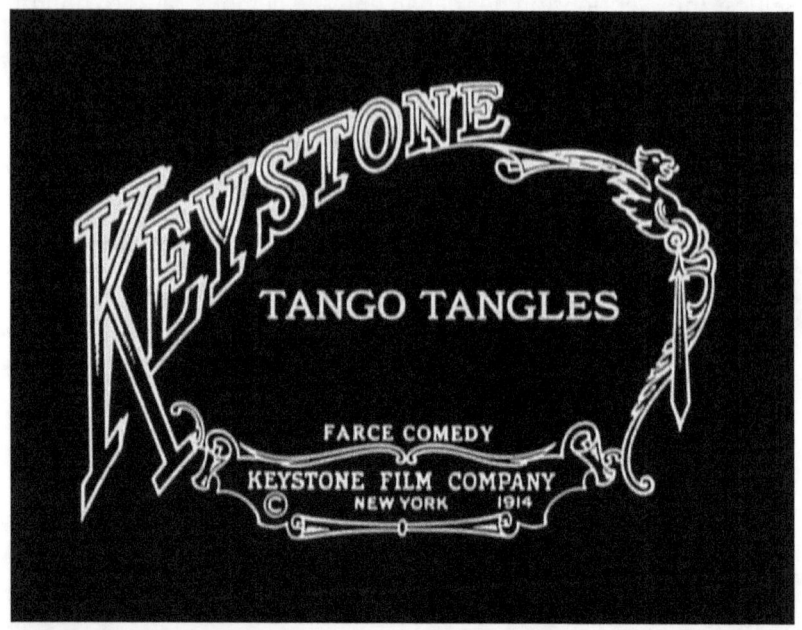

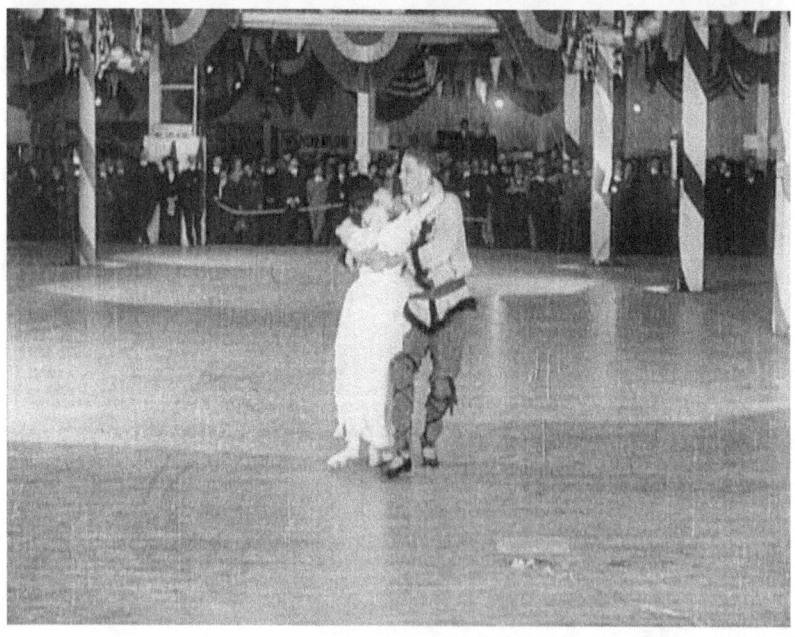

Tango Tangles
9th March, 1914

Director: Mack Sennett
Writer: Mack Sennett
Stars: Charles Chaplin, Ford Sterling and Roscoe Arbuckle

Even seven films in, we're still at the beginning of Charlie Chaplin's career and it's even more clear in this one than its predecessors that he was still experimenting with his character. Either that or there was some sort of bizarre bet going on at Keystone Studios in early February 1914, because that Keystone perennial, facial hair, is notable only by its absence.

It's an utterly surreal experience today to watch Chaplin without his toothbrush moustache, which had been firmly in place for the first four films he made as the Little Tramp and, as we well know from a century of hindsight, would remain firmly in place for most of his career. He isn't the only one to lose his facial hair either, as Ford Sterling appears without goatee, as recognisable a trademark for him as the toothbrush moustache was for Chaplin, one that was far more established at this point in time. Roscoe Arbuckle was a rare Keystone comedian to not need such things to stand out, as his rotund frame was iconic enough. Surely if he'd had facial hair, he'd have lost it here too. Why, we don't know.

Tango Tangles was another location picture, for the most part, though it's less tied to opportunity than *Kid Auto Races at Venice, Cal.* or *Between Showers*. Mack Sennett explained the thought: "We took Chaplin, Sterling, Arbuckle, and Conklin to a dance hall, turned them loose, and pointed a camera at them. They made like funny, and that was it."

This particular dance hall was the Venice Dance Hall on Abbot Kinney Pier in Santa Monica, part of a concerted attempt by Kinney, a noted American developer, to create "a Venice of America". The pier was built in 1904 and the 14,560 square foot dance floor added two years later in a mere seventeen days, rushed to meet a 4th July opening date. Perhaps Sennett chose the location because Kinney had spent $100,000 on improvements in 1914, but, if it was aimed at being publicity (and there's a short clip of real dancers on the floor before the fictional side of the film kicks in), it didn't help for long, as the mostly uninsured pier burned down in 1920 with damages totalling over a million dollars. It was never rebuilt.

Keystone scripts were never complex affairs, though as scholars start to work through the Mack Sennett papers at the Margaret Herrick Library, funded by the Academy of Motion Picture Arts and Sciences (the one that hands out Oscars), we're discovering that they were often less improvised than early historians have led us to believe.

This one feels scripted during the first section, but then clearly improvised from then on as the top comedians at Keystone traded whatever gags seemed appropriate to reach the final desired scene in a similar way to how professional wrestlers trade moves from their respective portfolios until the predestined moment of truth when one pins the other. The camera just sits back and captures it all, leaving only a little work for an editor to piece the important bits together into a usable form to be shipped out to theatres. The furthest this one goes to a story is to have Sterling and Arbuckle

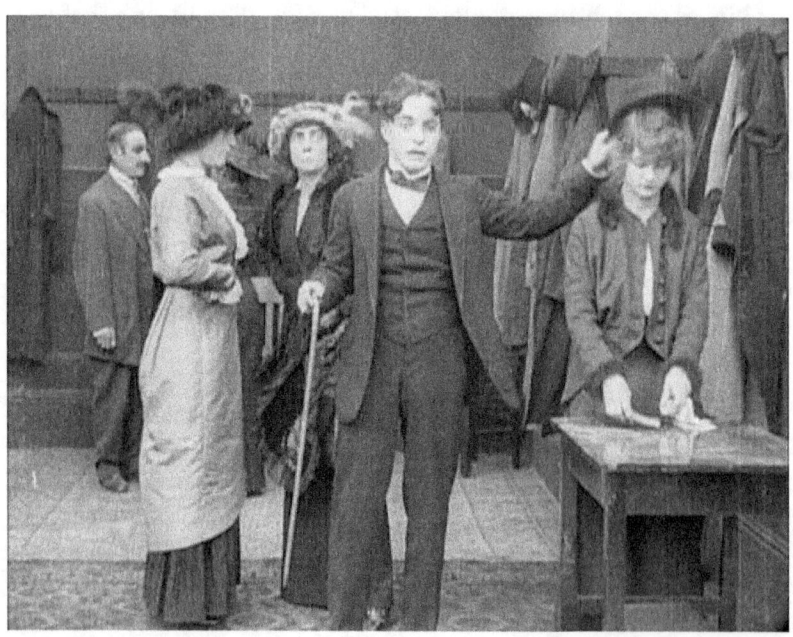

play together in the same house band. Chaplin merely stumbles in "a little the worse of wear". From there, it's just minor set-up to get them onto the dance floor to scrap.

That minor set-up revolves around Sadie Lampe playing a hat check girl who finds herself the centre not of a love triangle but of at least a love rectangle or a love pyramid, however we should work the mathematics on that. It apparently wore her out, as it appears to mark the end of a short career that spanned four of Chaplin's early films for Keystone.

It's a toss up between this one and *Between Showers* as to which contains her finest moment. In the latter, she was the housemaid who enthralled Chester Conklin capably enough for him to fail to notice Ford Sterling's sneaky replacement of his umbrella and thus sparking the plot. Here, she's enough of a vision to make the story viable but not enough of an actress to steal our eyes back from the trio of stars who literally duke it out for her attentions, especially with Chaplin agreeably drunk, Sterling outrageously manic and Arbuckle impressively energetic. The likelihood of anyone today remembering this as a Sadie Lampe picture is nonexistent, though she does steal one moment from Chaplin by apparently laughing for real when he drunkenly misses a table.

She smiles engagingly for what seems like everyone in the film. Initially she smiles engagingly for some random patron to whom we're never introduced. She steps forward to smile engagingly for Sterling, who pantomimes his strong feelings overtly with his hand literally on his heart. Soon, she smiles engagingly for Arbuckle, who storms onto the scene, angered at Sterling taking advantage of his absence. "Keep away from the girl," he demands in a pointless intertitle.

Eventually, of course, she smiles engagingly for Chaplin and the story is in motion. At least Lampe is good at smiling engagingly; she certainly isn't good at cringing in horror when Arbuckle literally lifts another random patron up over his head as if he weighed only a few pounds. I was rather stunned when I first saw this scene. I knew Arbuckle had moves but this is so effortless that today we'd expect it would be done with wirework; he just had muscles and either a talented stuntman or an unfortunate extra to whirl around above his head and then let go, apparently without warning.

No wonder Sterling runs from the scene, in the familiar style that involves him jumping in the air before moving forward. It's little details like this and a later episode of nose biting, which he also demonstrated in *Between Showers*, that render his quick slide into obscurity unsurprising, firmly shifted into the capable shadow of his replacement at Keystone.

He doesn't have a lot of opportunity to evade Arbuckle in this picture, given that they both play in the same band. Sterling is the bandleader, with a trumpet that keeps getting the better of him; at one particularly flustered point he even tries to play it backwards by mistake. Arbuckle wields a clarinet with a more realistic air; his character is obviously playing rhythm in this scene while Sterling plays a lead solo, and that comment holds true whether we read it literally or metaphorically.

Eventually, of course, they both have to notice that while they're fiddling, so to speak, Rome is burning. Chaplin has returned to the hat check girl and coaxed her out for a spin on the dancefloor.

It may be that *Tango Tangles* features no actual tangos, though I'm far from an expert on dance and the terpsichorean art is hardly the point here. The title was primarily meant to play alliteratively on words and cash in on the new dance craze that was sweeping the nation: the tango.

Originating in the 1890s on the border of Argentina and Uruguay, the tango found its way to New York in 1913 via Europe. The ever-receptive and exploitative cinema of the day responded straight away. The 1913 Essanay picture, *A Tango Tangle*, appears to have nothing at all in common with *Tango Tangles*, released only a year later, except for dance; the same goes for a 1914 British film also named *A Tango Tangle*. Other foreign films seem to have jumped on the same bandwagon, but that high wave quickly dissipated; after three titles in two years, there seems to have been nothing similar since.

Even if there are no tangos to be found, there are certainly plenty of extras dancing around behind the stars and clearly having a ball, pun very much intended, until they decide to stop and watch the action instead.

And it's the action that Sennett was most interested in: the centerpiece of the film being the Sterling vs. Chaplin fight. Today it's not great because it looks, rather bizarrely, like Buster Keaton fighting Harold Ramis doing an *Eraserhead* impression. Back in 1914, it wasn't great because Chaplin plays down to Sterling's style rather than Sterling playing up to Chaplin's (or maybe vice versa).

Perhaps the thinking was that Chaplin, removed from his Little Tramp outfit, would take on a completely different character and adopt a completely different style. If so, the experiment mostly fails because this particular drunk remains a broad exaggeration of the Little Tramp, who was becoming so popular through subtleties not just a costume. Without those subtleties, he's less interesting and less engaging.

Of course, he's still the side that we're probably all rooting for because, hey, at least he isn't biting his opponent's nose! It's one thing to build a character out of a healthy disrespect for authority, as Chaplin did, but it's just not cricket to resort to nose biting. What sort of cultural background does that have in early America?

It's much more interesting when the battling pair end up back in the cloakroom, where they attempt to put on the same coat at the same time, managing to get in one arm each. The resulting chaos is

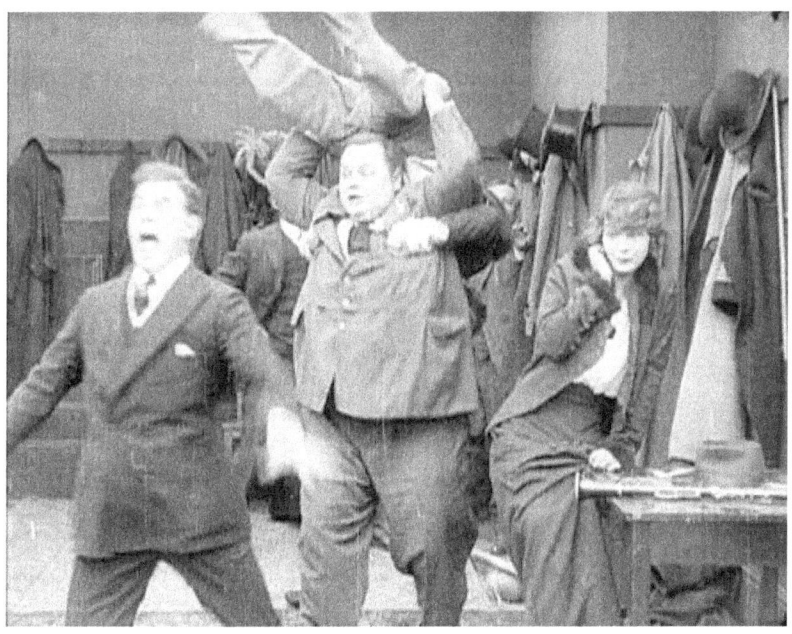

far from inspired, merely more routine destruction until that final move where they collapse in unison.

One interesting note is that, in the film, Lampe ends up with Roscoe Arbuckle, whose real life wife, Minta Durfee, is one of the dancers (not, as some accounts would have it, the hat check girl). Durfee would stand by her husband throughout his notorious trials, even though they were separated at the time.

Another interesting note is that Jeffrey Vance has suggested that the fight choreography used here was sourced from the Inebriate character which Chaplin played in the *Mumming Birds* sketch while touring the vaudeville circuit with the Fred Karno Troupe. If that's true, which is entirely believable, Chaplin was looking backwards rather than forwards here, an odd decision when set against the forward looking framework of most of his other early pictures. But much more on that later!

Finally, it's notable that the director of *Tango Tangles* was Mack Sennett himself, head of Keystone, taking the helm of a Chaplin picture for the first time. Chaplin had made four films under Henry Lehrman and was one into the four he'd make for George Nichols;

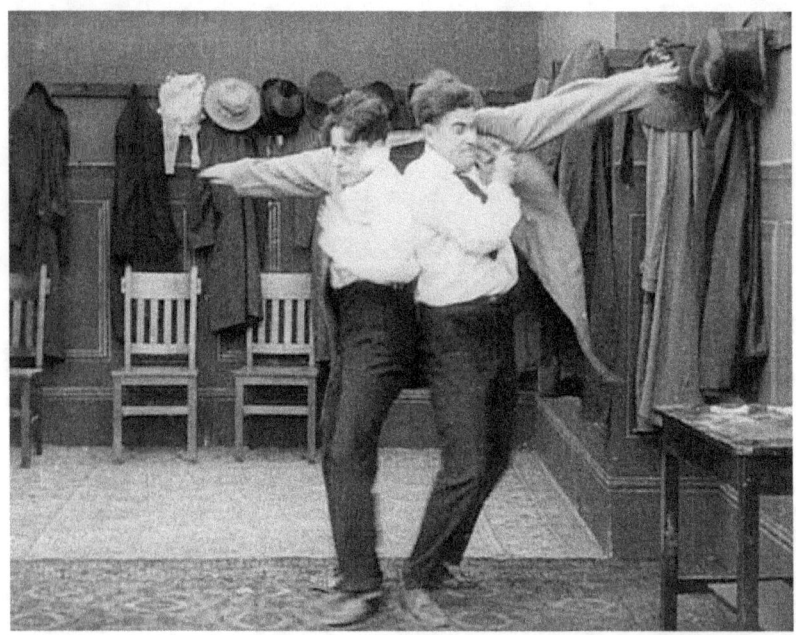

the only exception thus far was *Mabel's Strange Predicament*, directed by its nominal star, Mabel Normand.

If accounts are true, Chaplin didn't get on with any of these directors, whom he saw as either stuck in an obsolete mindset or responsible for ruthlessly editing down his footage and thus his impact. He was already seeking the opportunity to take over that role himself, and he finally got there in April 1914 when he wrote and directed the one reel comedy, *Caught in the Rain*, though he did get his feet wet a couple of weeks earlier, when co-directing *Twenty Minutes of Love* with Joseph Maddern.

Surely Sennett's guiding hand on this film was very different from his predecessors, but it was still heavy handed and perhaps most interesting for the lack of facial hair on show. And that's not a good reason to remember a movie.

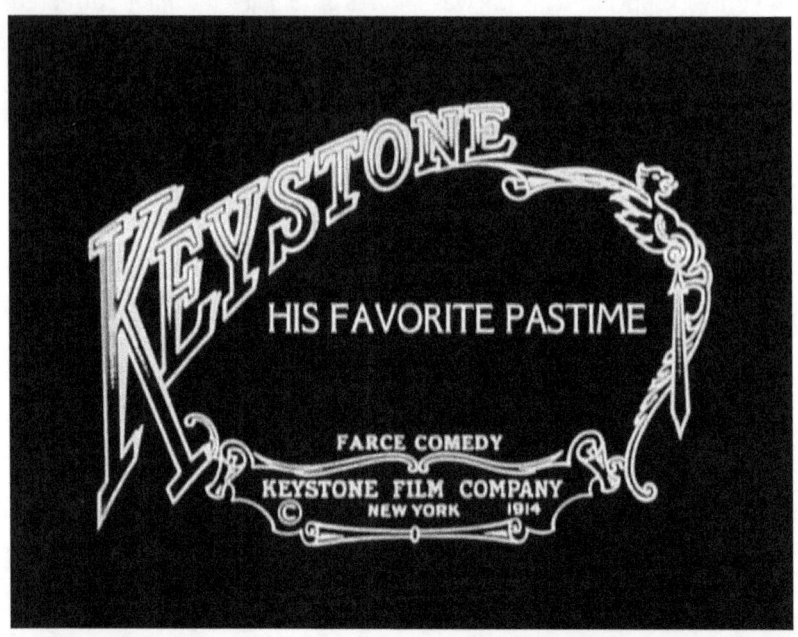

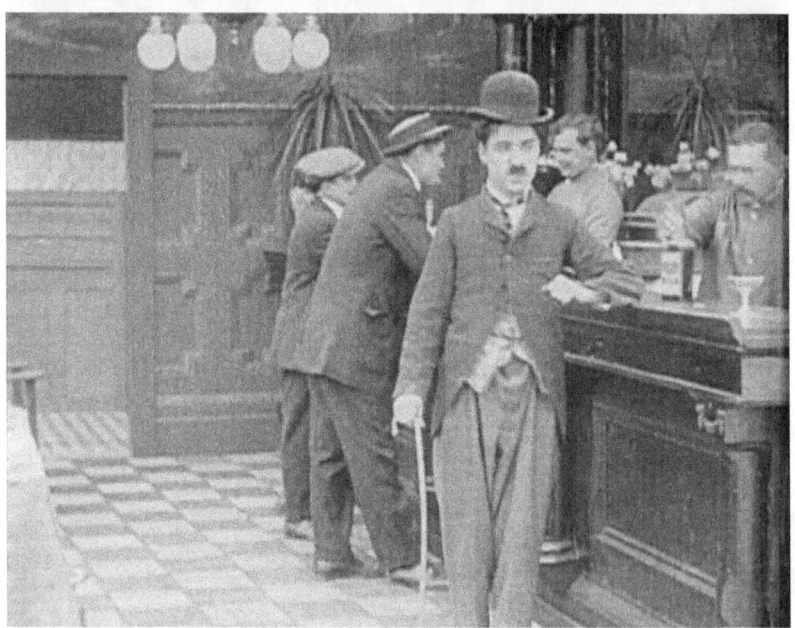

His Favorite Pastime
16th March, 1914

Director: George Nichols
Writer: Craig Hutchinson
Stars: Charles Chaplin, Roscoe Arbuckle, Velma Pearce and Frank Opperman

Not the worst film Charlie Chaplin had made thus far, *His Favorite Pastime* may be however his most inconsequential. Each of his first seven pictures brought something new and interesting to the table, even if it was just a brief slot as a Keystone Kop, but this one doesn't really add anything. The only thing that comes near is the idea of the Little Tramp veering a little further down the sliding moral scale from anti-establishment rogue to just rogue, pure and simple.

He's pretty obnoxious in this one, doing nothing except torment a growing parade of innocents, beginning mildly by teasing a fellow drunk who's run out of beer but progressing as far as to hoist his unwanted attentions onto a married woman in her own house, into which he isn't invited. It isn't quite as morally dubious as it's been made out over the years, mostly because the characters in blackface have been seen out of context, but I'd challenge anyone to argue that it isn't morally dubious. Uno Asplund, in *Chaplin's Films*, calls it "the prototype of the 'unpleasant' tough film" in his early career.

None of that suggests that *His Favorite Pastime* is without merit, because we can at least see further progression to some of Chaplin's regular gags, there are some neat acrobatic moments and there's a strong battle with a swinging door in a restroom, but it's weaker than its predecessors and feels more like it was knocked out in no time without much care and attention, as it perhaps was.

To be fair, much of that comes through the post-production, such as the notably intrusive editing, which is brutal, but some of it may have arisen from another clash in overall vision, this time between Chaplin, now a growing star at Keystone, and George Nichols, yet another director with whom he did not see eye to eye.

It's possible to read Chaplin's progression through 1914 just by looking at who directed his pictures (as indeed I did here with my contents page) as, with minor exceptions, it breaks down into easy sections. He started out with Henry Lehrman, with whom he didn't agree, so Lehrman was replaced by Nichols, with whom he didn't agree either. After a brief period featuring a collection of different directors, studio head Mack Sennett took over for a while until he finally let Chaplin direct himself, something he'd been wanting to do almost from the very beginning.

So what we find here is Chaplin attempting to build gags into more clever and complex routines, while the picture keeps stealing him back into a traditional setting. Perhaps the best example of this approach from Chaplin is the single take opening scene which pits him against Roscoe Arbuckle.

It's easy to see why Chaplin plays a drunk, because that's what he was doing when Sennett and Mabel Normand first saw him perform on the vaudeville stage with Fred Karno's troupe and why they felt he was someone Keystone Studios ought to hire as a replacement for their departing star, Ford Sterling. He does it effortlessly, with a good eye for detail, and he's consistent enough for us to completely believe that he's in his cups. Arbuckle is fair, though clearly not up

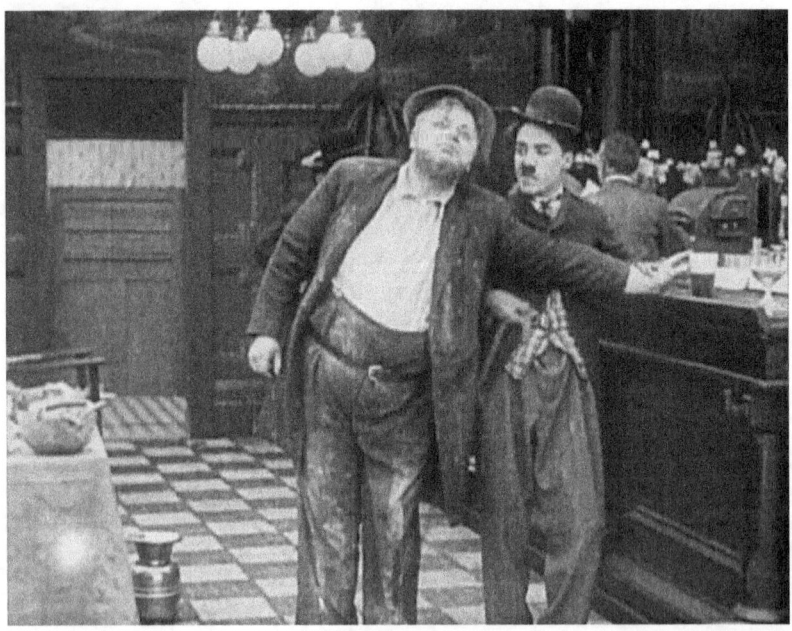

to the same standard, and the two have a fine altercation. Chaplin has a half full glass of beer, while the unshaven Arbuckle is dry and cheeky enough to attempt to steal it, so Chaplin plays with him for a while, letting him think he has a chance, until it's all gone and Arbuckle didn't get a drop.

Sadly Arbuckle exits the film at this point, because it's clearly never about him. In his place enters the leading lady, known today as Peggy Pearce but at the time under her real first name of Velma. Chaplin, describes her in his autobiography in glowing terms, as "an exceptionally beautiful girl with delicately chiseled features, a beautiful white neck, and a ravishing figure," and confesses that she was his "first heart-throb". They met some time during his third week at the studio, which puts the moment around the turn of 1913 to 1914, and, as Chaplin saw it, they "ignited; it was mutual, and my heart sang."

Standard filmographies list *His Favorite Pastime* as the only film they made together, before Pearce left for Henry Lehrman's new L-KO studio, but there's a lot of confusion as to whether she was also the Keystone Girl in *A Film Johnnie*. Keystone films at this time had

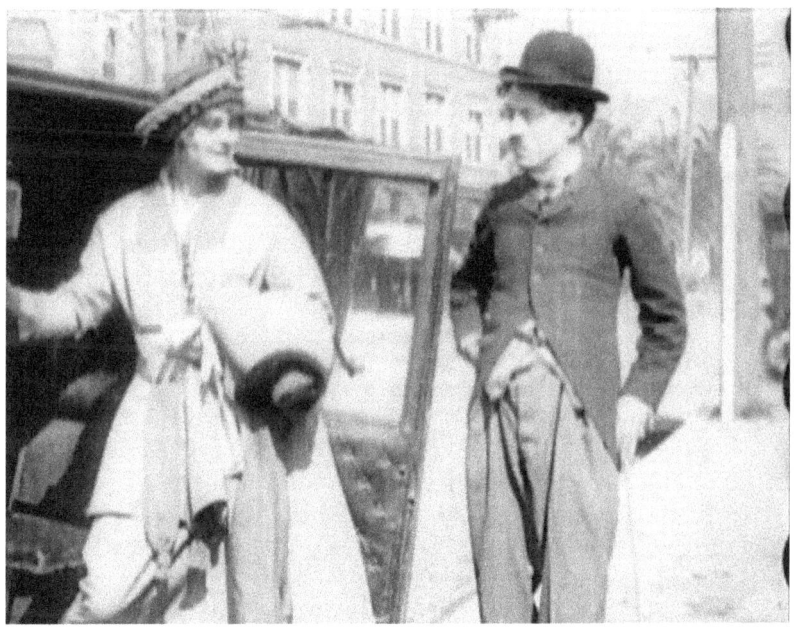

no credits, but official lists suggest that Virginia Kirtley, who played the daughter in *Making a Living*, took that role. Comparing all three films in their restored versions, my vote is with Pearce, meaning that she made two films with Chaplin rather than just one.

Here, as the ham fisted editing sets up, she's standing by her car waiting for her husband. The Little Tramp, as soused as he is, is instantly besotted and promptly shows off by turning his bowler hat into a homburg with a hit of his cane. Her husband, of course, won't have any of it and so back to the bar goes the tramp for some less sophisticated slapstick, at least for now.

After he causes too much trouble there, including for the lady's husband, he decides to pursue her afresh. What he fails to notice is that, as her car drives off, she's walking away in the other direction, so it's really her servant that he pursues with notable vigour.

Missing the car and taking a tumble into the street, he leaps onto a moving trolley car and eventually off it again. His most ambitious tumble, though, comes inside the lady's house, as he falls over a bannister to land on the couch underneath, nonchalantly following up by lighting a match on the sole of his boot as if nothing had happened. It's not as polished as his movements would become in future films, but it's impressive nonetheless.

Less impressive is the use of blackface, the process by which white actors played black characters, as perhaps still personified by Al Jolson in *The Jazz Singer* or the BBC's popular *The Black and White Minstrel Show*. Jeffrey Vance explains in *Chaplin: Genius of the Cinema* that Chaplin used this convention less often than the other great silent comedians, adding a quote to back it up. "I never laugh at their humour," Chaplin explained. "They have suffered too much to be funny to me."

At this point of his career, Chaplin was contributing material to what passed for Keystone scenarios but, as he was hardly in charge of the finished product, it's no stretch to cut him a little slack. I see nothing overtly racist here, though some have applied that epithet to the interactions he has with each character in blackface.

Firstly, he leaves the attendant in the bar's restroom, played by Billy Gilbert, a lit cigarette for a tip, a nasty trick to be sure but one probably more due to the tramp being skint than the colour of the attendant's skin. Secondly, he gives an overblown reaction to the discovery that he's been following the lady's black maid rather than her. Both of these seem eminently explainable merely as gags, not racist ones.

Another factor in this judgement call is that Chaplin gets the worst of most of his encounters in this film and deservedly so, which hardly underlines him as the hero of the piece. He's too obnoxious to be a real villain here, which at this point in time was someone with deliberate evil intent, but he's far from a hero. He's a sort of proto-stalker, though to be fair, he has no conception of who the lady is, just that he likes her and, as under the influence as he is, he can't believe that she won't like him too.

He gets walloped hard by everyone here, however well and often he manages to duck; even the black maid gets in more than a few shots before he escapes to the next hiding. In one of the best scenes in the picture, even a swinging door has it in for him and it's only very careful positioning on Chaplin's behalf that ensures he keeps all his teeth. It's easy to see how he did it when watching frame by frame, but at regular speed it's highly effective, enhanced by the fact that he continues to play outrageously drunk throughout the

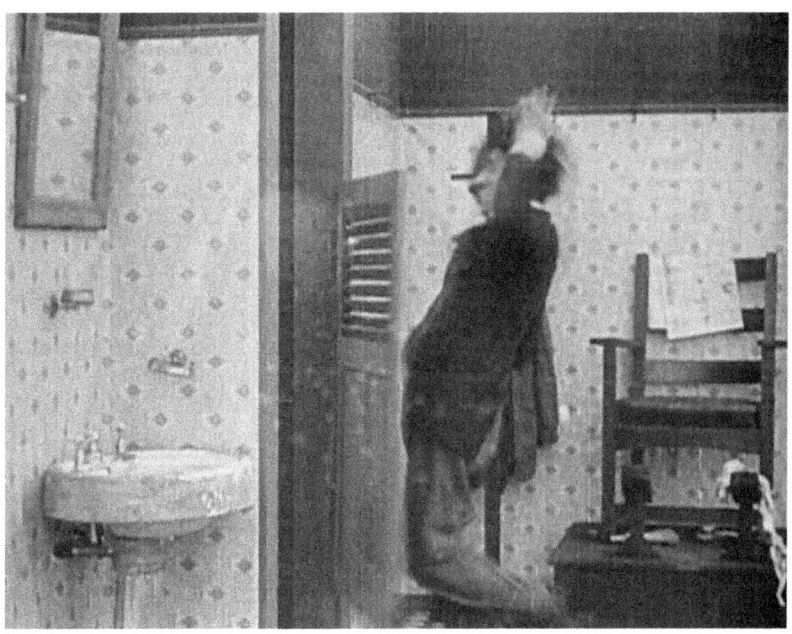

entire picture.

Masterful choreography was one of the skills that was helping Chaplin stand out from what passed for the crowd at this point, as the other household names of silent comedy hadn't really arrived yet. Harold Lloyd technically beat Chaplin to the screen by a year but by this point he was still doing bit parts in odd films like *The Patchwork Girl of Oz*, coincidentally in blackface as a Hottentot, while Buster Keaton's first films were still three years away in 1917.

The famous names at this point were mostly Chaplin's peers at Keystone Studios, such as Roscoe Arbuckle, Mabel Normand and Ford Sterling, none of whom had anywhere near the precision that Chaplin was already demonstrating, however talented they were.

Their routines were more like the larger tussles here, with lots of swinging arms and falling over, including more jumping in the air and, in Sterling's case, his inexplicable nose-biting habit. Arbuckle's more restrained moves were a better fit with Chaplin's, but it's not difficult to see who had the better control in this film. I wonder who was learning more from whom at this point.

That's not to say that Chaplin wasn't still learning because he

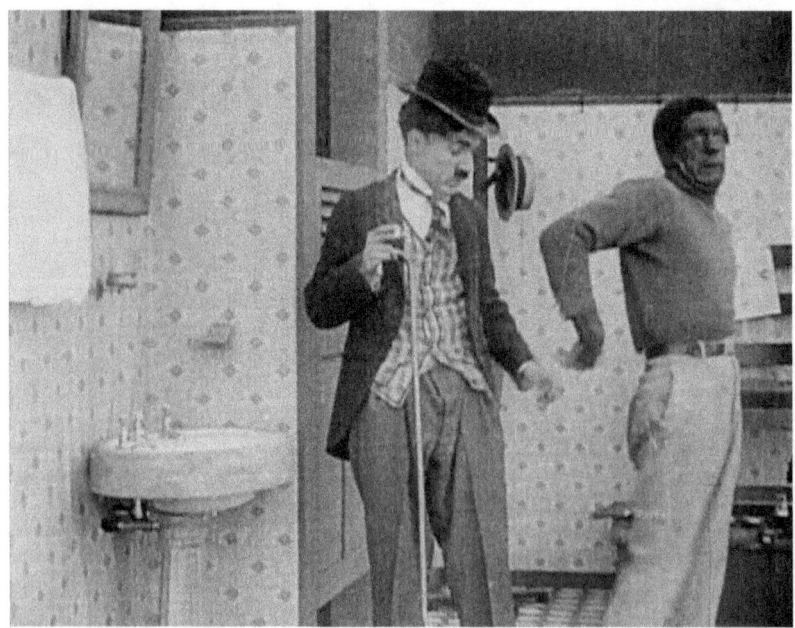

was soaking up everything around him like a sponge. Clearly, given the change in style of *Tango Tangles* and the tonal shift of *His Favorite Pastime*, he was also still experimenting with the medium of film and his next few pictures would underline that. That he had reached his eighth film suggests he was becoming experienced, but those eight pictures were shot in as many weeks and we can only imagine how frenetic the Keystone factory was by watching titles like *A Film Johnnie*.

As we know, the Little Tramp became a lovable character but he certainly hadn't got there by this point and we occasionally wonder with our hundred years of hindsight why he didn't get there sooner than he eventually did.

Today, we tend to think of the Little Tramp as a sad, endearing character, a more grounded version of the roles that Lon Chaney had come to epitomise throughout the 1920s. Chaney specialised in playing outright villains who tormented people until discovering redemption through a self-sacrificing act late in the picture, often a searing one. Chaplin often did similar things, but he did them with pathos rather than the grotesque. He was an outsider rather than a villain, anti-establishment rather than twisted or evil. He was the silent screen's everyman, morally inconsistent like the best of us, fighting for survival and dreaming of love but rarely finding both.

At this point in time, that was still very much in the future. He was endearing to different degrees in a few of his early films, but he just as often found himself playing an obnoxious character who we have difficulty sympathising with, let alone empathising with.

Having drunkenly hit on women far more endearingly in *Mabel's Strange Predicament* and *Tango Tangles*, here he's more like someone we might call the Keystone Kops on.

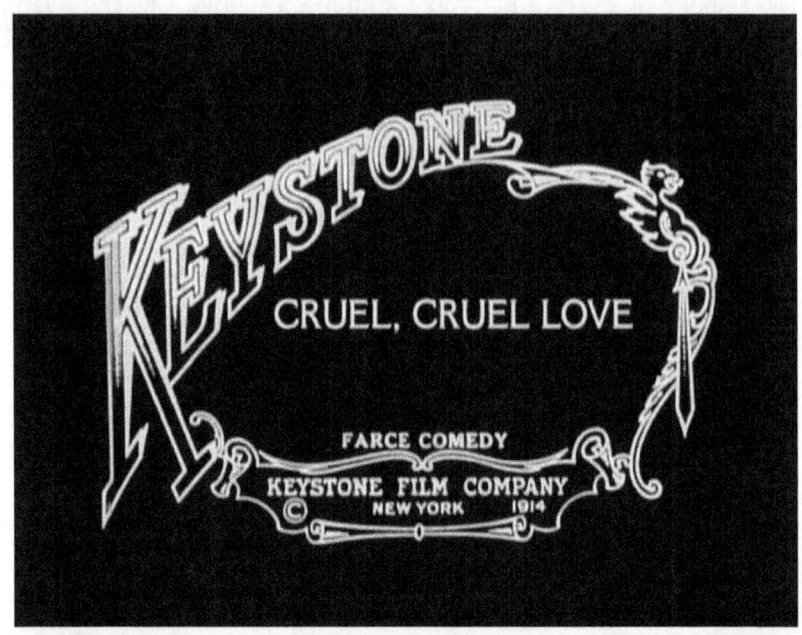

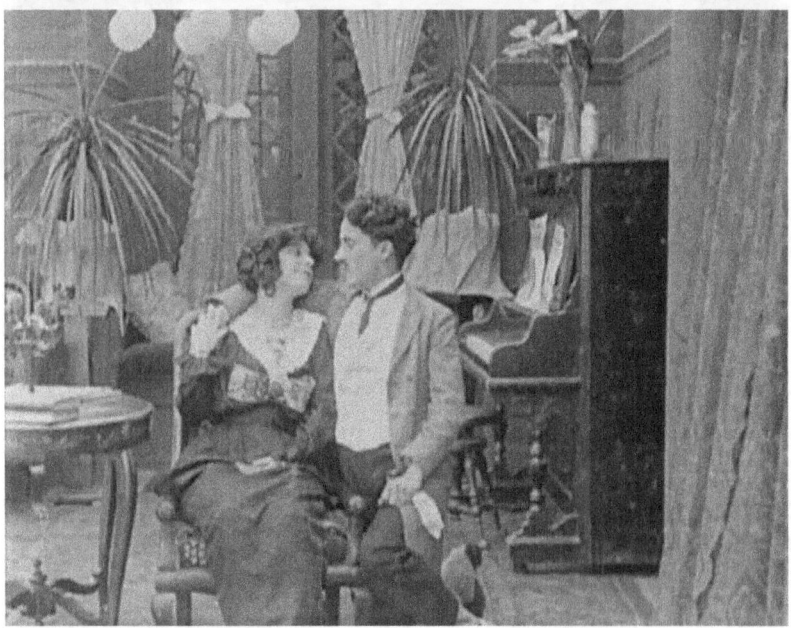

Cruel, Cruel Love

26th March, 1914

Director: George Nichols
Writer: Craig Hutchinson
Stars: Charles Chaplin, Minta Durfee, Edgar Kennedy and Eva Nelson

As if to underline just how much he was experimenting with the cinematic medium at this early point in his career, Chaplin is completely recognisable here in a picture which is otherwise is a real shake up in many ways.

For a start, he doesn't play the Little Tramp at all, though there are some quintessential Little Tramp moments, especially early on when subtle pratfalls bring that character to our minds. Instead he plays a veritable gentleman, a well to do sort with a butler and a much longer moustache than we're used to seeing on Chaplin, though it was trimmed down substantially from the outrageous one he wore in *Making a Living*.

The character is not named in the intertitles, but various sources list him as both Lord Helpus (a glorious name which I will surely adopt myself for some steampunk persona or other) and Mr. Dovey. The former appears to fit much better, as he's the epitome of the overly principled peer whose sense of honour forces him to end his life when his fiancée calls the whole thing off, even when she does so only because of a little misconception which he could so easily have addressed with some basic communication.

The wildest difference to what we might expect comes through the tone of the film, because it's really a melodrama masquerading as a comedy rather than the other way around, and it's assisted by some of the most outrageous overacting that the usually subtle Chaplin ever did.

His Keystone comedies, like all Keystone comedies, were mostly built using a collection of tried and tested routines and gags as building blocks, something that Chaplin was keen to escape, even with only a few pictures under his belt. His keen attempts to find something new and different to bring to the screen are especially obvious in the four shorts which he made for George Nichols, as they couldn't be more different if they tried. *A Film Johnnie* was a meta movie that emphatically equated the Little Tramp with the audience as a sort of everyman character. *His Favorite Pastime* was a trip to the dark side, with an obnoxious Little Tramp in his cups, annoying everyone he could find, and descending so far down the moral scale as to stalk a lady to raise a laugh. *Cruel, Cruel Love* has him overact for effect. *The Star Boarder* was still to come.

Clearly, Chaplin was experimenting and I wonder if this film was original or simply a comedic riff on a more recognisable story, perhaps from a recent, higher profile, film. The way the melodrama escalates has been compared to the work of D. W. Griffith, the most important and influential early film director in America, whose first feature, *Judith of Bethulia*, had been shot a year before *Cruel, Cruel Love* in 1913 but released a mere couple of weeks before it.

While it might seem to posterity that Griffith, the "Inventor of Hollywood", and Mack Sennett, the "King of Comedy", operated at opposite ends of the cinematic spectrum, there are a whole slew of connections which should be highlighted. Sennett honed his craft working under Griffith, for a start, at the Biograph studio, as did many regular faces at Keystone including Mabel Normand. In 1915, Sennett formed a business partnership with Griffith and Thomas Ince to tie their respective autonomous outputs to the Triangle Film Corporation in order to control distribution. In 1919, Griffith founded United Artists, with Mary Pickford, Douglas Fairbanks and... Charlie Chaplin. At that point, Sennett was no longer quite so important, but Chaplin was.

Whether *Cruel, Cruel Love* riffs off a specific D. W. Griffith film, many of which are lost today, or just a general formula that he used, it certainly feels like it started out as a melodrama and had its comedy shoehorned in.

Perhaps this is mostly because the comedy doesn't stem quite as much from gags as was usual in Keystone farces. Instead, we find ourselves conditioned to laugh merely at the sight of Lord Helpus's butler, played by Edgar Kennedy, who laughs his ass off for the entire running time. Each time proceedings veer a little too close to serious, we're cut back to Kennedy slapping his thighs and splitting his sides, because he knows something that the main characters (and the audience) don't and he's hardly going to let them (and us) in on the joke until the finalé because, hey, what fun would that be?

Because it's a melodrama, this joke simply has to tie to the usual culprits, love and death, and the story arc shifts neatly from the former to the latter and back to the former again in the one reel that the picture ran, just short of nine and a half minutes.

The situational setup has Lord Helpus caught in an innocent but compromising situation to which his fiancée can't fail to react. He begins the film making sweet, sweet love to her (well, in the family-friendly 1914 meaning of the phrase) in her parlour, going so far as to kiss her, though he soon takes her leave with a far more polite handshake. They've been interrupted by the lady's maid, giggling up a storm from her position behind a thick curtain, and it's this maid who sets the scene for Lord Helpus's downfall.

Gossiping with the gardener in the driveway, she twists an ankle and stumbles into his lordship's arms. Of course he has the decency to assist the young lady, but helping her into a garden loveseat to check her injury can't fail to be misinterpreted if noticed and, sure enough, it's noticed. "Take your ring," he's informed with vigour. "I

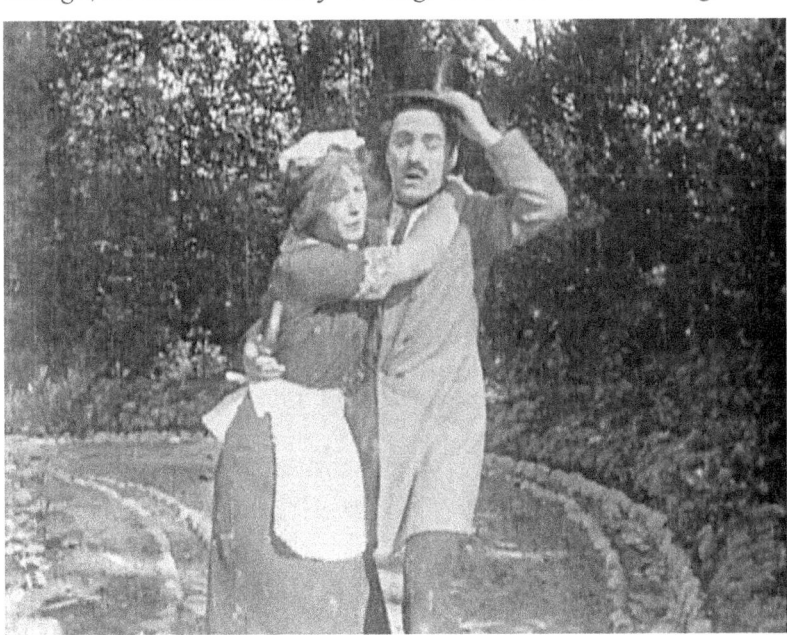

never want to see you again." Ever the honourable gentleman, he doesn't even put his case, merely walks off without a word, goes home and takes poison.

If you can believe it from that synopsis, this is the subtle part of the movie, because it's underplayed indeed compared to where it soon goes!

If its effects are anything to go by, the poison acts on Chaplin more like a superpowered energy drink, prompting him to ham it up for the camera like he never did before. Perhaps he felt he had to because the situation itself has no inherent humour, our laughs prompted far more by his outrageous reaction to imminent death than the fact that he's apparently going to die horribly. Well, that and the fact that Edgar Kennedy's butler convulses in paroxysms of laughter from the outset, just outside the door, because only he knows that the poison is really water.

I grew up with the mystery novel cliché that the butler always did it, but that referred to murder. In Keystone's take on the landed gentry, butlers were apparently more for standing out of sight and laughing up a storm, maybe in the hope that we'd eventually follow suit, if only through peer pressure, no pun intended.

The most overtly Chaplinesque part of the affair comes just shy of halfway in a brief vignette presaged by an intertitle announcing "A Vision of His Destiny". Faced with his imminent demise, Lord Helpus sees himself condemned to the fiery depths of Hell, where he's trapped between the pitchforks of devils and, for some reason, bounced up and down, as if he were on some sort of demonic trampoline. His reaction to taking the poison can't be described as anything less than overblown but it's even more so afterwards, as he exercises enough facial muscles to keep an anatomy class busy for weeks.

And so we're set for the race against time that constitutes the third act, with Lord Helpus gradually destroying his bedroom with histrionics, his butler finding it the most hilarious thing he's ever seen in his life and the rest of the cast, most prominently the lady's gardener, played by William Hauber, attempting to undo the stack of mistakes that have been committed, one by one.

Chaplin is front and centre on this one, as he was with each of the four films he made for George "Pop" Nichols, and he's backed by regular Keystone faces.

Most obvious in this one is Edgar Kennedy, who came to film in 1911 and, over the course of over four hundred films, appeared with almost all the great movie comedians: Chaplin, Normand, Arbuckle, Charley Chase, Laurel and Hardy, Wheeler and Woolsey, Our Gang, the Marx Brothers and Harold Lloyd, among many others. He built his reputation at Keystone, but became best known working for Hal Roach, Sennett's biggest competitor in short comedy, who became a producer in 1915, as well as for a series of R.K.O. shorts entitled *Average Man*, which presaged television situation comedy; he turned out six *Average Man* shorts every year for seventeen years. It was for Roach that he developed the technique that brought him his professional nickname of "Slow Burn", as he attempted to keep his temper in check by rubbing his hand over his bald head and across his face. By that point he had become the screen archetype of the frustrated everyman.

The other major name worth mentioning here is Minta Durfee, playing Chaplin's fiancée, especially as she, through her hotheaded and faulty reaction sparks the entire plot. Like Kennedy, Durfee was

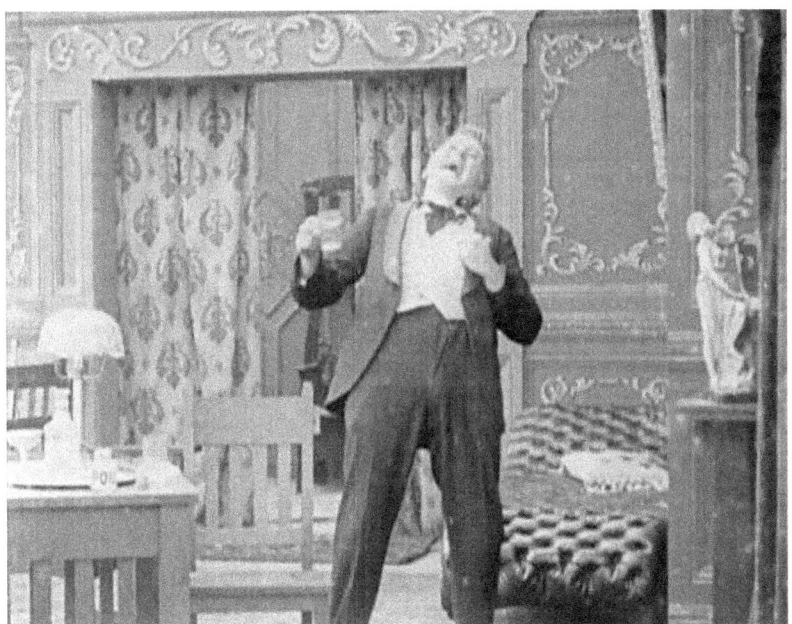

a Keystone regular whose face is easily recognisable in many of Chaplin's early pictures; in fact, she was right there when he began, in *Making a Living*, as the mother of the girl with whom he flirts. She made comparatively few pictures for an early silent star, just over a hundred in a film career that ran almost sixty years, from 1913 to 1971, and forty of them were released in 1914 alone, making her even more prolific that year than Chaplin was.

That long career outlasted that of most of her contemporaries, including her only husband, Roscoe Arbuckle, whom she had married in 1908. They didn't divorce until 1925, but they were separated before the infamous scandal that rocked Hollywood in 1921, when Arbuckle suffered through three trials connected to the death of Virginia Rappe, the fiancée of Chaplin's first director, Henry Lehrman. The ensuing distance of a century has allowed history to come down squarely on Arbuckle's side, whitewashed as he was by a rampant press, but at the time Durfee was one of the few to stand by him, even while separated.

Cruel, Cruel Love has a reputation of standing alone in Chaplin's early filmography, very different from the regular films he was

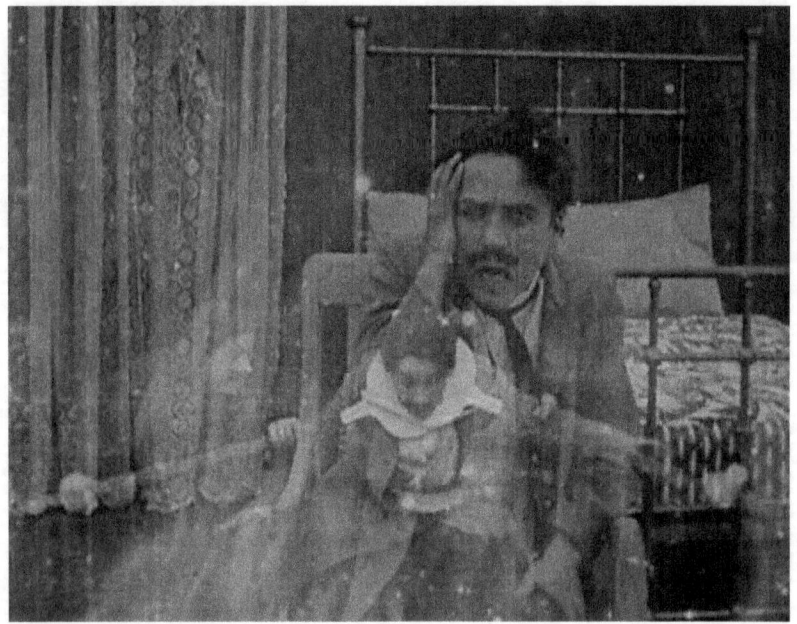

quickly turning out. However, working through them in order, at the speed they were released, it's clear that it was part of a strong experimental phase in his work that is particularly fascinating to hindsight.

Chaplin, who quickly formed his own ideas about how his movies should work, famously didn't get on with his directors, but it was Lehrman who has borne the brunt of criticism over the years, for running roughshod over his suggestions and even editing out his funniest bits. Nichols is often lumped in with Lehrman as the sort of overly traditional director who couldn't understand why comedy needed to change and mature. What I found, while progressing through this project, is that Chaplin's films for Nichols are actually some of his most ambitious: if they fail to define the future of comedy, they do at least involve heavy experimentation in a clear attempt to search for it.

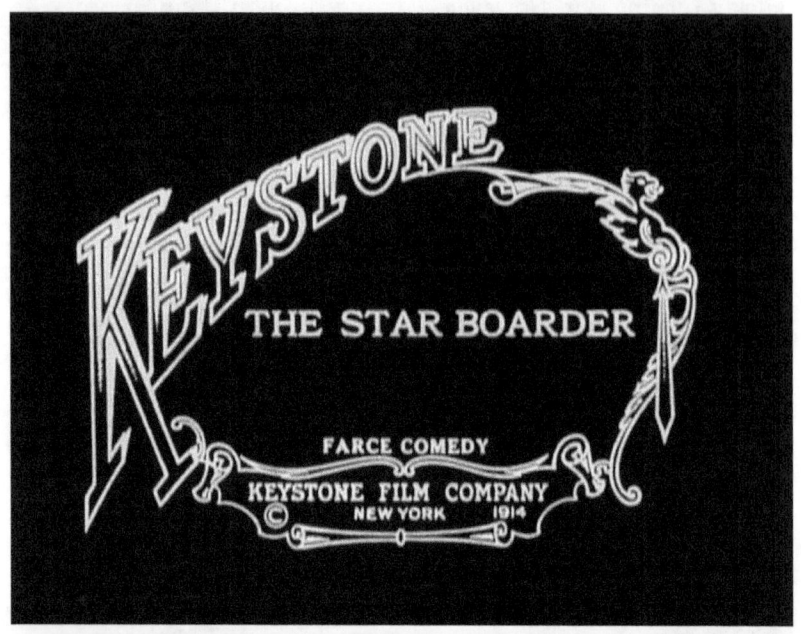

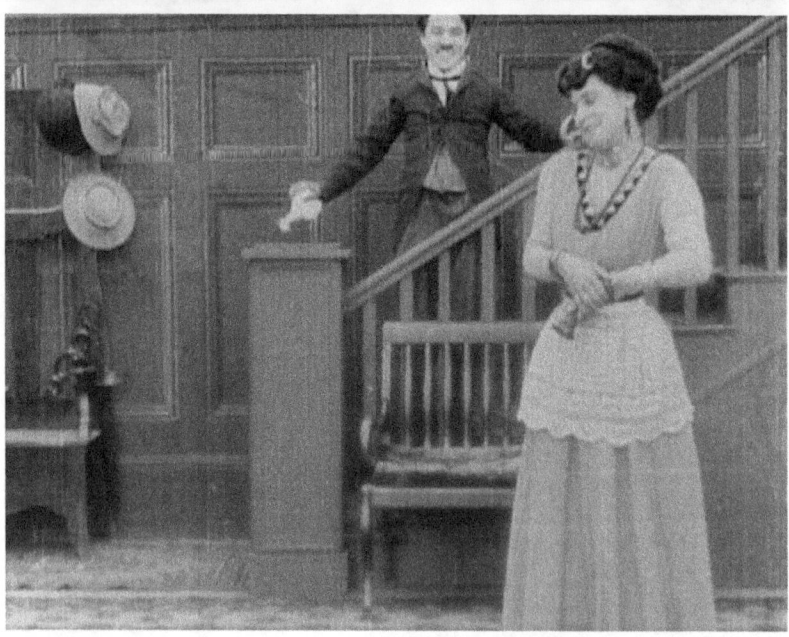

The Star Boarder
4th April, 1914

Director: George Nichols
Writer: Craig Hutchinson
Stars: Charles Chaplin, Edgar Kennedy, Minta Durfee and Gordon Griffith

The last of Chaplin's four pictures for director George Nichols, *The Star Boarder* is by far the most conventional. It could even be considered unrushed, a description that's hard to imagine applied to a Keystone picture, but it does speed up considerably towards the end and even feels like it wants to ramp up to Benny Hill levels, aided magnificently by a new score from Frederick Hodges which mirrors the pace well. Initially that score is an elegant creature, as the scenes are set and the characters established, but it gradually gets more and more frenetic until we wonder if the pianist's nimble fingers are going to drop off.

Maybe the experiment here was to play with control, to set up the jokes and build them, all the while refusing to allow the usual descent into chaos until the time is absolutely right for it. If so, *The Star Boarder* may have been just as experimental a piece at the time as Chaplin's other three films for Nichols, but merely feels less so today because it succeeded in nailing the future much better.

All the primary cast return from *Cruel, Cruel Love*, though they're shuffled around somewhat. Minta Durfee still has influence here, with Charlie remaining attentive to her every word and deed, but they're not lord and lady this time out; she runs a boarding house with her husband and he's one of the guests, the star boarder of the title.

I should add that there's no apparent reason for what appears to be a nautical pun, but perhaps this title riffed on some pop culture icon of the time, as it's one of two pictures of the same title released in 1914 alone, with another four of them following as the decade ran on. All, however, appear to have unique stories.

Edgar Kennedy is promoted from a mere butler to the man of the house, but he's under the thumb of his wife who clearly rules the roost with an unerring eye for any divergence from her preferences and a withering glance to ensure that he does what he's told. He's relegated to being the man in the outrageous moustache, which is a doozy even given Keystone's well known facial hair fetish. His first scenes are spent manipulating it for laughs.

After spending *Cruel, Cruel Love* away from it, Charlie is back in his familiar Little Tramp outfit but he's apparently rather comfortable for a change. He's a paying customer and the apple of the landlady's eye. Chaplin's films usually had a whole slew of titles for their many reissues and one of them highlights his situation even better: not only is he *The Star Boarder* but also *The Landlady's Pet*.

Initially we might believe that he plays up to her in order to get the first or the largest plate of food, but he persists beyond that, so we can only assume that he's flirting outrageously with a married woman at a time long before Production Code rules against such immoral behaviour were put into effect. Another reissue title was *In Love with his Landlady*, which is a little too much emphasis but does make the relationship crystal clear.

Whatever the reason for his status, the landlord is aware of it and

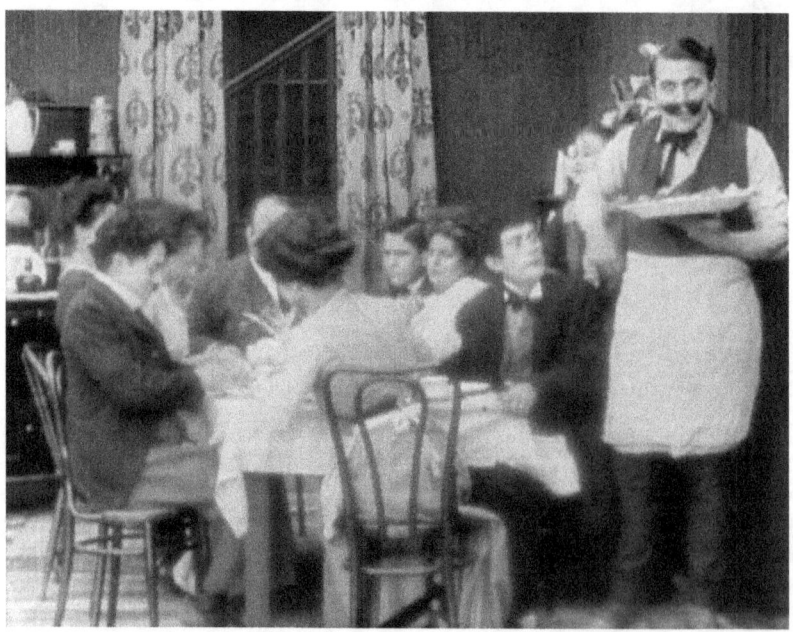

far from happy, but his wife's withering glance puts him back in his place each and every time he attempts to enforce his position and Charlie continues to get preferential treatment.

If Chaplin was the uncharacteristic chewer of scenery in *Cruel, Cruel Love*, he emphatically hands that role back to Edgar Kennedy here. Kennedy bristles and roils and looks menacing, all the time exercising his facial muscles to keep his moustache moving far more than must have been comfortable. It's so large that it's like a pair of caterpillars mating on his top lip and it's so active that it could have had its own credit, had Keystone got round to using them by this point.

By comparison, Chaplin is back to being the Little Tramp, better off than usual but still the inveterate drunk, as is underlined by an odd scene where the story is put entirely on pause so he can drink the kitchen dry for no apparent reason. Perhaps it's to allow him to build the routine from what he performed in vaudeville and in early Keystone films like *Mabel's Strange Predicament* or *Tango Tangles* into something a little more substantial. At least there's a clever scene immediately following that one, which tasks him with hiding everything he spirited out of the kitchen from another guest.

While there are some laughs here for the drunken tramp and a few earlier on too, as he's clearly hung over when we first see him, trying to simultaneously charm his landlady and not fall over the stairs, it's the more sober scenes that work best here.

Much of the fun is built out of the same gag, repeated over and over again in different settings, namely Charlie's attempts to get somewhere with his landlady and her husband's consistent ability to show up just in time and spoil his fun. These start at home, but soon head out for the tennis court and the park.

The tennis match, which is so brief that I'm not convinced a ball ever crosses a net, isn't much but Jeffrey Vance highlights that it marks the first time that Chaplin crossed paths with the game of tennis. It would become a lifelong passion for him, at least until a broken ankle and a series of strokes towards the end of his life prompted him to hang up his racket. Here it's just an excuse for him to spin around and fall over, a move used so often that we want to mimic it.

What elevates *The Star Boarder* from a set of moustache twitching reruns of one gag is the welcome addition of another character to spice things up. No, this isn't a fourth wheel, though one of those is hinted at; this is the landlady's young son whose hobby is to take highly embarrassing, often highly misleading, photographs with his clunky 1914 camera to then project during a free magic lantern show for the assembled guests of the boarding house.

It isn't rocket science to figure out what reactions that's going to prompt here, especially given that the boy has a strong talent for capturing the precise moments that his subjects don't want to be captured. The bonus for us is that young Gordon Griffith was an infectious actor whose many cries of joy at being in the right place at the right time to snap the wrong picture soon find their way to our lips too. He's an absolute joy and we laugh along with him, even as he's getting the expected spanking at the end of the picture.

Griffith hadn't even turned seven years old when he shot *The Star Boarder*, but he had already become an experienced actor, closing in on his twentieth picture. He'd started his screen career at Keystone in 1913, a year before Chaplin, and found himself often paired with Billy Jacobs, who was younger still. Jacobs began his career at three and was given his own film series, the *Little Billy* series, when he was four. Amazingly, he retired at the ripe old age of eight, with almost sixty films behind him. Griffith started later but lasted longer, appearing in serials such as *The Amazing Exploits of the Clutching Hand* as late as 1936, before switching to production and direction. This was the first of a number of films he made with Chaplin in 1914, before he landed his most famous role as the very first screen Tarzan, as he played the junior version of the lord of the jungle who appears throughout the first third of 1918's *Tarzan of the Apes* before handing the reins over to the barrel chested 29 year old, Elmo Lincoln. Griffith also played the screen's first Tom Sawyer and his charisma here explains why.

In fact, Griffith is far more watchable here than most of the cast. Minta Durfee is strong as the landlady, working well with Chaplin and successfully toning down her performance enough to match. They turn out to be a pretty decent double act, hindered only by the stereotypical scenery-chewing of Edgar Kennedy, whose talents as a capable actor are utterly not on display here. He's so out of tune with the rest of the leads that he's almost acting in a different movie, perhaps even an animated one.

In other circumstances, we might call him the comic relief, but we never find ourselves laughing at Kennedy; instead, we laugh at the double act of Chaplin and Durfee and at the contagious mischief of Gordon Griffith. It's somehow odd to see Durfee such a natural foil to Chaplin on screen, given that she was married at the time to Roscoe Arbuckle off it, but she got to play his wife or sweetheart on screen often enough too, even in later Chaplin pictures. They made thirteen of them together at Keystone in 1914.

Of course, the large Keystone output and small Keystone roster meant that actors appeared in the same pictures all the time. It becomes something of a surreal experience to watch a lot of these films close together, especially as the characters rarely have names to delineate them and, when they do, they're often the same ones.

Chaplin was Charlie most of the times he ever had a name, just as Arbuckle was Fatty, Mack Swain was Ambrose and Chester Conklin was Walrus. So in one film, Durfee would be Chaplin's wife, in the next a girlfriend, then a mere flirtation and finally someone else's wife entirely.

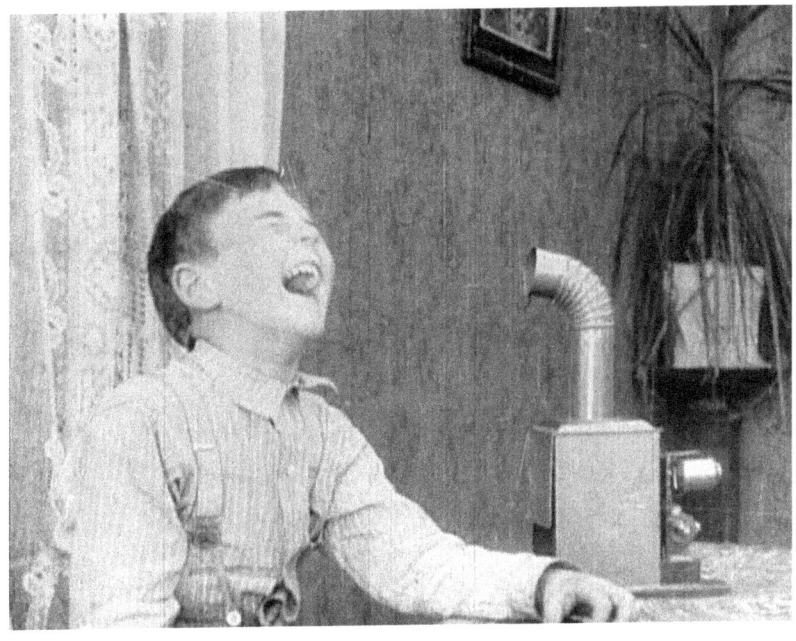

It often feels less like the stock company that a filmmaker might foster and more like a theatrical troupe of stage actors who swap costumes three times a day for different performances. In a way, that's exactly what they were doing, swapping roles until they found the ones that suited them best, at which point they tended to land their own series in which they could continue to build their new personae.

Charlie is still a little on the obnoxious side here, albeit a lot less so than he was in *His Favorite Pastime*, but Chaplin's experimentation under George Nichols may have got him closer to the Little Tramp we know today than he had previously managed.

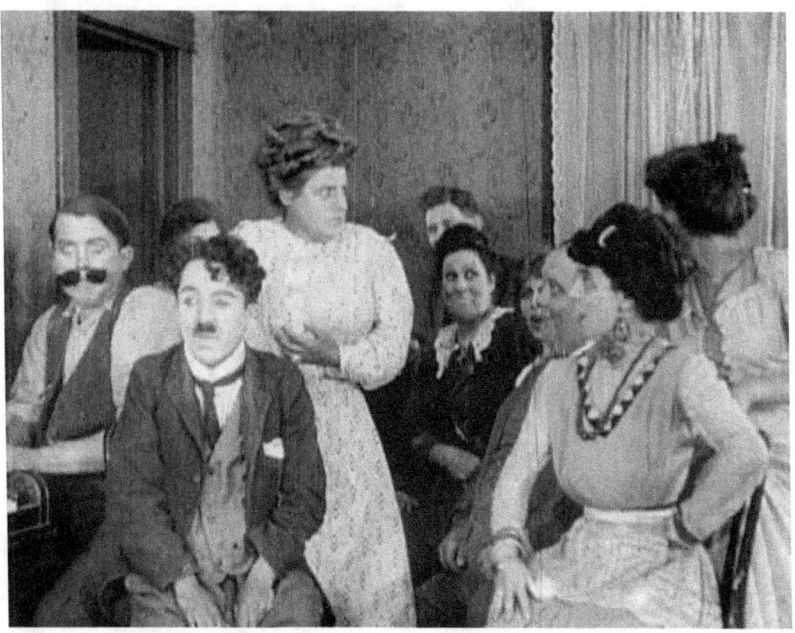

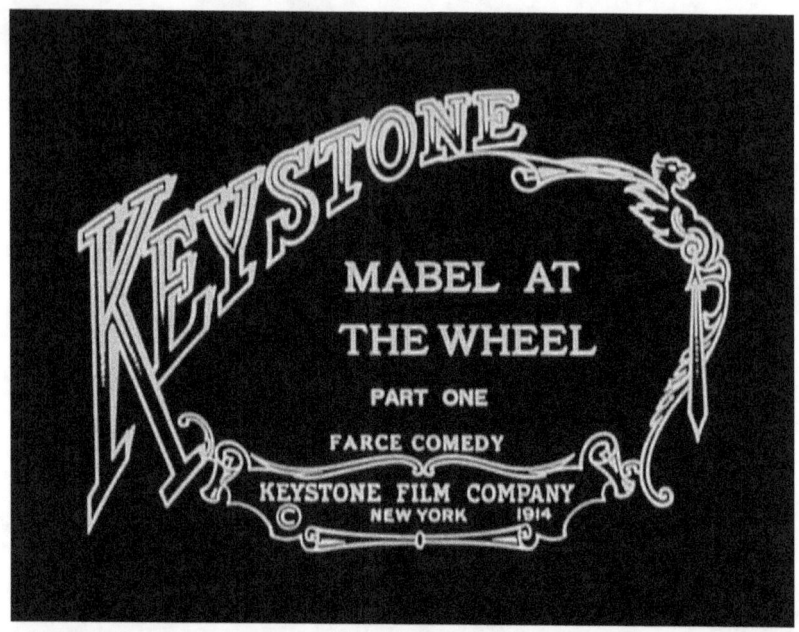

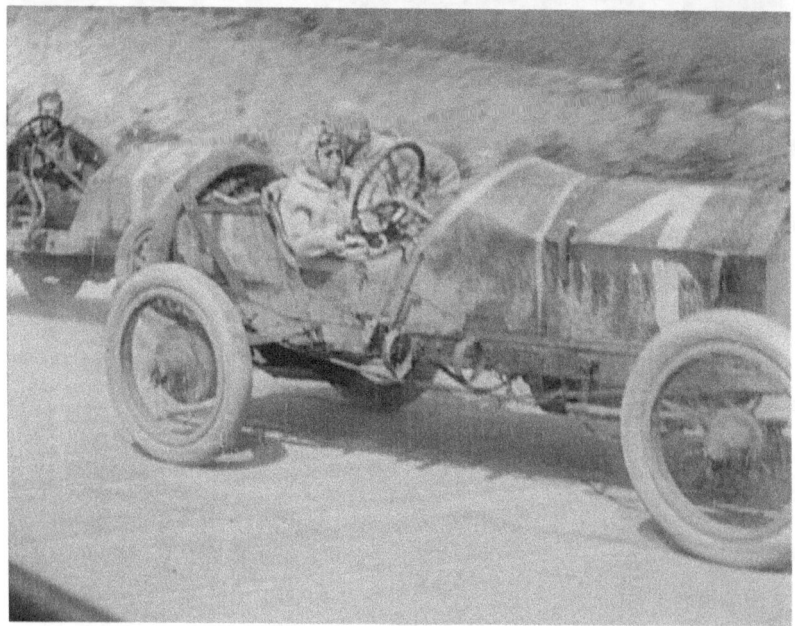

Mabel at the Wheel
18th April, 1914

Directors: Mabel Normand and Mack Sennett
Writers: Mabel Normand and Mack Sennett
Stars: Mabel Normand, Charles Chaplin and Harry McCoy

Charlie Chaplin made 36 films in his debut year of 1914, steadily building towards the lofty status of the most recognised man in the world. If the legend is to be believed, though, his career almost ended in premature fashion after his eleventh picture, *Mabel at the Wheel*.

He was still young, having reached a quarter of a century only two days before this picture reached theatre screens, and he was still inexperienced, having arrived at Keystone a little over four months earlier, even if he had already churned out ten movies in that time. However he had firm ideas about the directions he wanted his screen character to take and he was finding that his ideas rarely matched those of his directors. In fact, he'd learned this before ever making a movie himself, just by watching them be made on the Keystone set. The studio's standard methodology was to build gag on gag until they reached the point where they became a chase, something that Chaplin realised was highly limiting. He mentions in his autobiography that, "little as I knew about movies, I knew that nothing transcended personality."

He famously failed to get on with the first director that Keystone assigned him, Henry Lehrman, who "used to say that he didn't need personalities" and he failed to get on with his second regular one too, even though his four films for George Nichols proved to be a surprising burst of creative experimentation. "He had but one gag," Chaplin later wrote, "which was to take the comedian by the neck and bounce him from one scene to another."

Compared to these two directors though, he really butted heads with Mabel Normand, not merely the biggest star at Keystone (and, not incidentally, the lover of studio head, Mack Sennett), but also one of the earliest female directors. The technique she showed on *Mabel at the Wheel* depressed Chaplin immediately and her disregard for his comedic suggestions prompted "the inevitable blow-up."

While he claims to have "secretly had a soft spot in my heart for her," he emphatically refused to continue with this picture. "I'm sorry, Miss Normand," he explained, without pulling any punches whatsoever. "I will not do what I'm told. I don't think you are competent to tell me what to do."

That clearly wasn't going to help him. Extras apparently wanted to slug him, but Normand kept them at bay. They retreated to the studio where Sennett blistered at him. "You'll do what you're told," he told Chaplin, "or get out, contract or no contract."

Chaplin understandably wondered if he'd been fired, but the next day, the tone was completely different. Now Normand and Sennett were calm and composed, eager to hear his gag ideas. *Mabel at the Wheel* was a go. What prompted the change? Well, Chaplin didn't have a clue at the time, but he does claim that he discovered the reason later and duly outlined it in his autobiography.

He was indeed about to be fired, he explained, but the very next morning, Sennett "received a telegram from the New York office telling him to hurry up with more Chaplin pictures as there was a terrific demand for them." Now, while Sennett was many things, he was a businessman above all and he knew what sort of money his new star was starting to generate. His average picture warranted twenty prints, while Chaplin's were reaching forty and growing. This is a convenient explanation from Chaplin, but it's far from an unbelievable one.

Whatever the reason for the bust up and the reconcilement, it's clear that this is far from the pictures Chaplin wanted to make. He may not have got on with Nichols, but he was able to play a varied set of characters and explore a number of possibilities in the four films they made together. This must have felt like a backward step, even though it was his first two reel film.

He portrays what can only be termed a serial villain, a proto-Dick Dastardly character. He's not the Little Tramp, of course, dressed instead in a top hat and with an odd goatee that resembles a pair of demonic horns sprouting from his chin. The character was clearly based on his predecessor at Keystone, Ford Sterling, but there's much that's taken from the sharper he played in *Making a Living* too.

Yet, even hindered by a poor character, Chaplin dominated both

Mabel's Strange Predicament and *Mabel at the Wheel*, regardless of the supposed star announced in their titles. We can hardly believe these are Normand films in hindsight; the former saw her flail around as if pleading for laughs, while here she doesn't even really aim for any at all.

She's less a comic lead in this picture and more of a heroic one, as well as being the love interest who drives (pun not intended) the plot along. You see, Mabel has two admirers and that could well have been the entire set-up for the story.

One is her boyfriend, in the form of Harry McCoy, moving up from being merely her admirer in *Mabel's Strange Predicament*. He's not just her boyfriend in this picture, he's also a race car driver and with 1914 vehicles that means a true daredevil indeed. He plays a decent, all-American, nice guy, daredevil race car driver, which may have led to further roles as her sweetheart in both *Mabel's Nerve* and *Hello, Mabel*. However, he soon descended once more to bit parts in later Mabel pictures like a hot dog thief, a man in a bar or even, in 1915's *Fatty and Mabel at the San Diego Exposition*, a Charlie Chaplin impersonator. That's ironic because here an atypical Chaplin is his

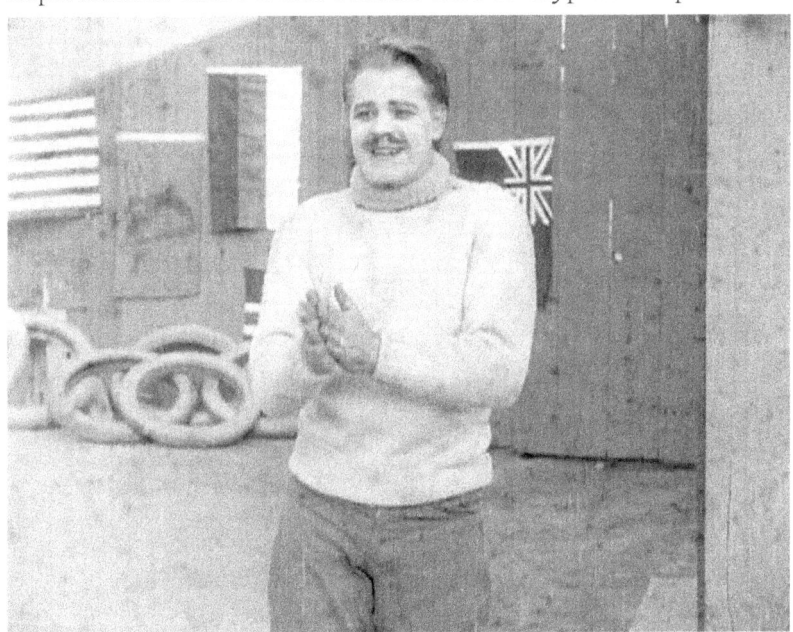

competition for Mabel's attention and he's a dastardly competitor who will stop at nothing to wreck McCoy's chances.

In fact, he'll stop at nothing to wreck McCoy, period. This is an odd Keystone comedy in that it seems to forget that it's a comedy for the majority of its running time and seems content to play up the villainy angle instead against the backdrop of another real event, clearly a common setting for Keystone pictures.

Here it's the Vanderbilt Cup road race in Santa Monica, the adult version of the soap box derby event at which Chaplin debuted the Little Tramp in *Kid Auto Races at Venice, Cal*. Documenting the race constituted the first day of the shoot, on 26th February, but they continued on until 16th March to add in all the dastardly deeds that Chaplin's villain could conjure up.

He starts simply with a pin, in order to deflate one of his rival's tyres outside Mabel's house and guarantee that she'll ride to the track on the back of his motorbike instead; that pin promptly finds its way into a substantial proportion of the backsides that present themselves during the film. He escalates quickly though, to the degree of kidnapping McCoy the race car driver and so prompting

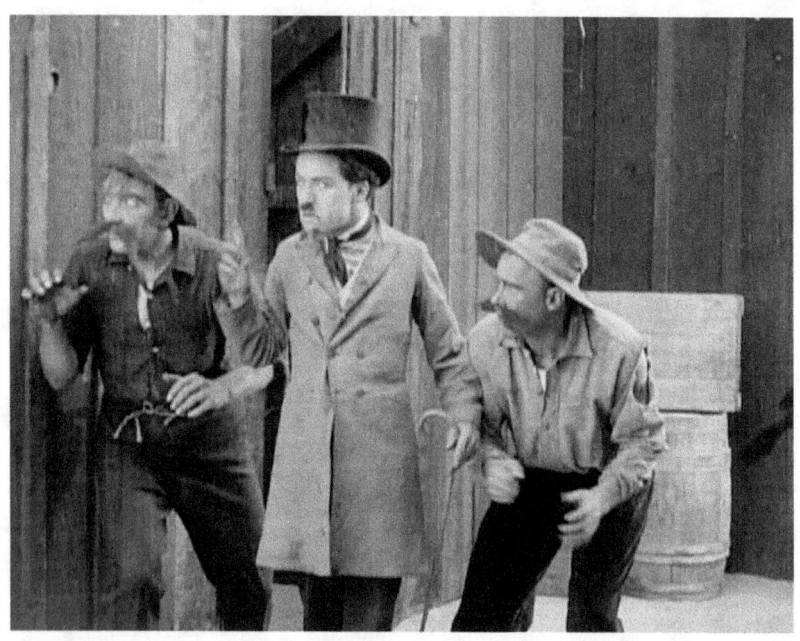

Mabel to take his place in the race.

Chaplin is a very deliberate villain here, confident enough that he wears his villainy on his sleeve. He gesticulates, glowers and gibbers his way through the entire first half of the picture, posing outrageously at every single opportunity as if we might forget how emphatically he can't be trusted. As if that wasn't enough, he has a dubious pair of henchmen with outrageous walrus moustaches to back him up.

Fortunately, the evil edge is tempered a little by his general lack of success. He may succeed in kidnapping his rival but he has a hard enough time taming his heavy 1914 motorcycle, let alone another human being. After he falls off the thing at one point, he needs help from a passerby to just get back on. He's also outnumbered in a rock fight, which looks very painful indeed. That magnificent invention of Mack Sennett, the pie fight, wouldn't have fit in this scene, so they go at it with rocks instead. I'm sure they were really beanbags or some such props that merely looked like rocks, but these actors really knew how to aim and they hit square in the face more often than not. I don't buy into the suggestion that they did take after take to get their aim right, as Keystone didn't mess around. They just knew how to throw.

If the early scenes play up the pain, Normand getting in on the act too with a tumble off the back of Chaplin's bike into a puddle, the later ones finally play up the comedy. The catch is that these scenes aren't particularly funny, with the height of sophistication revolving around the villain spraying oil onto the track so that Mabel spins out and drives a lap in reverse, only to spin out again at exactly the same spot and, in doing so, restore her car to the right direction.

While Dick Dastardly was clearly based on Terry-Thomas with a side of Jack Lemmon's character in *The Great Race*, that role was just as clearly based on the sort of villains in silent movie serials who tied damsels in distress to railway lines. What might be surprising and worthy of note here is that famous serials like *The Perils of Pauline*, also shot in 1914, didn't actually have any such scenes; one of the earliest that did was Barney Oldfield's *Race for a Life*, a 1913 picture made at Keystone with Mabel Normand as the damsel and Ford Sterling as the villain. This would then seem to be an early addition to a Keystone invention which still abides today, even if mostly in cliché and people's erroneous assumptions that each and every silent movie has a pie fight and a damsel tied to a railway line to be rescued by a hero.

Rewatching these early Chaplin pictures, this sort of quandary keeps on showing up. On one side, the comedy on show is hardly sophisticated, Mack Sennett and his directors content to recycle both old stories and the gags that populated them again and again. Yet on the other, they were by far the most successful comedy studio in the business, churning out films that made audiences split their sides, in the process inventing so much that would come to be taken as routine.

This one doesn't feel like it's either original or funny, so Chaplin was very likely correct when he suggested that the 22 year old Normand wasn't a competent director but he was only three years older and was about to get his own chance to prove himself in the director's chair.

And that was the deal he struck with Sennett; if he completed this film how Normand wanted, he'd be able to helm his own. He'd

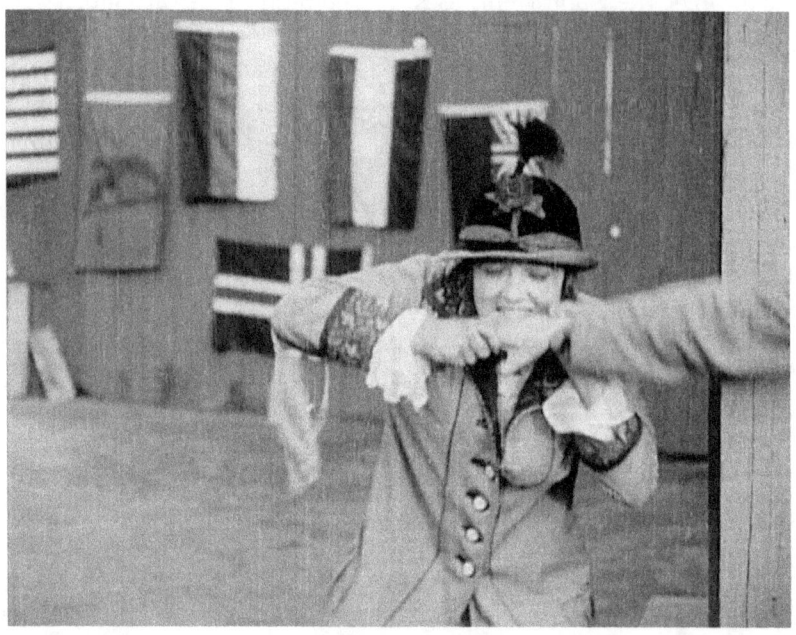

dabble in direction on his next film, *Twenty Minutes of Love*, and go solo on *Caught in the Rain*, two pictures after that. By July, he'd be his only director, helming every remaining short film in which he would appear during the remainder of his time at Keystone.

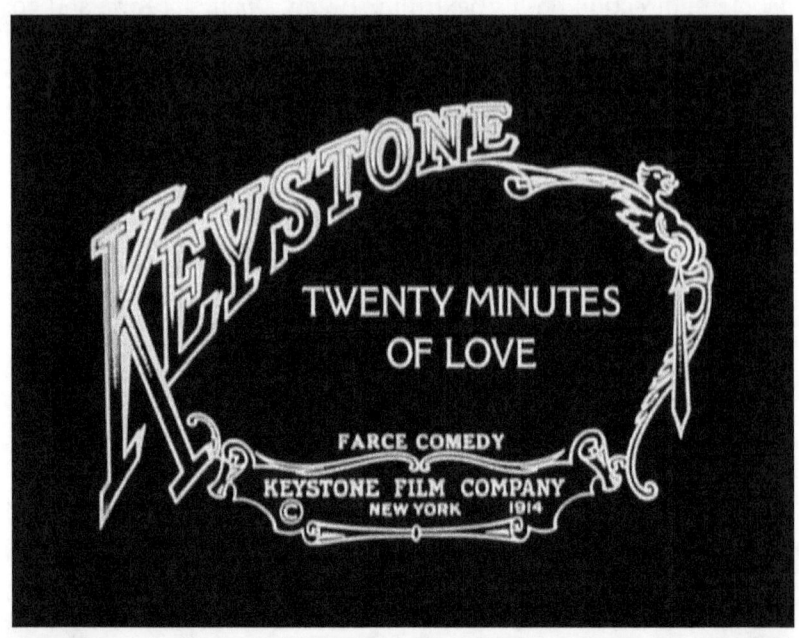

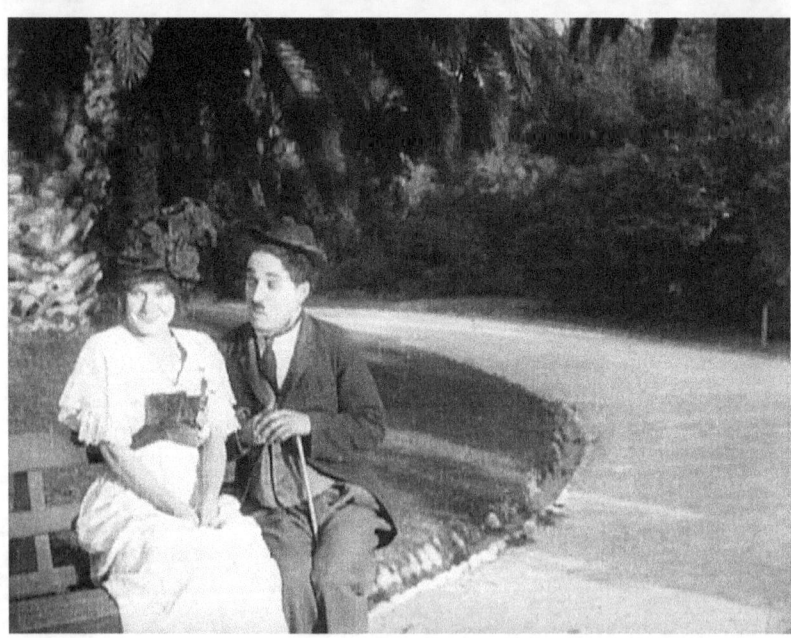

Twenty Minutes of Love
20th April, 1914

Directors: Joseph Maddern and Charles Chaplin
Writer: Charles Chaplin
Stars: Charles Chaplin, Chester Conklin and Eva Nelson

If *Mabel at the Wheel* was twenty minutes of outrageous villainy, *Twenty Minutes of Love* is ten minutes of relatively mild situation comedy, but it's still an important entry in Chaplin's filmography because it represents the first time he was truly able to contribute something beyond acting to one of his movies.

The power struggle that played out behind the scenes during *Mabel at the Wheel* ended with him able to take on more creative control because, after eleven pictures in under three months, he had become firmly in demand. He may still have been relatively new to the silver screen and he was obviously still developing the Little Tramp's character, whom he hadn't even portrayed in his previous film, but his star was already starting to eclipse that of Ford Sterling, whom he had replaced. That popularity gave him some clout, so he felt that it was long overdue for a Chaplin picture to feature his writing and his direction as well as his acting. *Twenty Minutes of Love* is the first time that happened.

Now, how much of that direction is evident in the finished movie is very much up for discussion as most sources also list Joseph Maddern as a director of this film.

Chaplin's very own words in his autobiography claim *Caught in the Rain*, two films and two weeks away, as "my first picture" as a director. However his handwritten filmography, as reproduced in David Robinson's biography, *Chaplin: His Life and Art*, lists this one as "my own". That rather vague term has been interpreted to mean movies that he directed as well as acted in, but he also claims *Mabel's Married Life* there, which is more often attributed to Mack Sennett. Perhaps it meant a film to which he felt he contributed in a more substantial manner than merely an actor, as most sources agree that he did at least write *Twenty Minutes of Love*. As he also claims in his autobiography to have made this film in a single afternoon but records suggest a six day shoot, perhaps the truth is that the single afternoon comprised his directorial contribution. We may never know.

However the responsibilities were split, the key is that this film served as a new beginning: Chaplin was finding some control over his work and he clearly felt that was immensely important. He doesn't devote much space in his expansive autobiography to his year at Keystone, surprisingly as it was also his first year in the film industry, but what he does allot mostly covers this particular point in time.

For instance, while most of his Keystone pictures aren't even mentioned by name and those that are get mere sentences, he describes how he managed to convince Sennett during the *Mabel at the Wheel* brouhaha to let him direct as conversation. His boss was pleading with him to just get along with Mabel Normand when he suggested, "Listen, if you'll let me direct myself, you'll have no trouble." Sennett asked who would pay for such a film if it wasn't viable for release. "I will," Chaplin replied. "I'll deposit fifteen hundred dollars in any bank and if you can't release the picture you can keep the money." That idea, along with Chaplin's finishing *Mabel at the Wheel* under Normand's direction, was it. The very next movie up, he was behind the camera as well as in front of it.

There's another telling line in Chaplin's autobiography that's worthy of mention here too. Later in 1914, as Chaplin's contract with Keystone was coming up for renewal, he asked Sennett for a thousand dollars a week. "But *I* don't make that," Sennett famously replied. The argument proceeded with Chaplin highlighting that it was he whom people queued up to see and Sennett responding that it took the support of an organisation such as Keystone to make that possible. Finally, in an appropriately oft-quoted rejoinder, Chaplin memorably suggested that, "All I need to make a comedy is a park, a policeman and a pretty girl."

He probably didn't specifically have *Twenty Minutes of Love* in mind as he said that, because a great deal of his Keystone pictures fit that general set up, not least the earlier *Between Showers*, which started out in the flooded streets of Hollywood but surely enough found its way to a park containing a lake that had no purpose other than to become the eventual recipient of a number of characters.

However, this is a prime example of the formula as there's very little here to speak of except Chaplin, either Westlake Park or Echo Park, two policemen and a few pretty girls.

Given the circumstances around its creation, it's impossible not to watch *Twenty Minutes of Love* without attempting to figure out what Chaplin personally brought to it.

Certainly there's Chaplin-esque whimsy from the outset, as the Little Tramp mimics the flamboyant antics of a pair of park bench lovers in parody by breathlessly embracing the nearest tree. This couple, portrayed by Minta Durfee and Edgar Kennedy, promptly become about as static as that tree by effusively throwing their arms around each other and locking themselves in a long kiss, a rather chaste one that involves almost no movement whatsoever.

That could easily be a Chaplin touch too, as they're no more than a background for him to act against or a prop for him to use. While they're playing at being statues, he shows us no end of movement, wandering over to them, examining them, sitting down next to them, highlighting their heat, ignoring them and eventually, of course, interrupting them. Only then do they get to move, and in

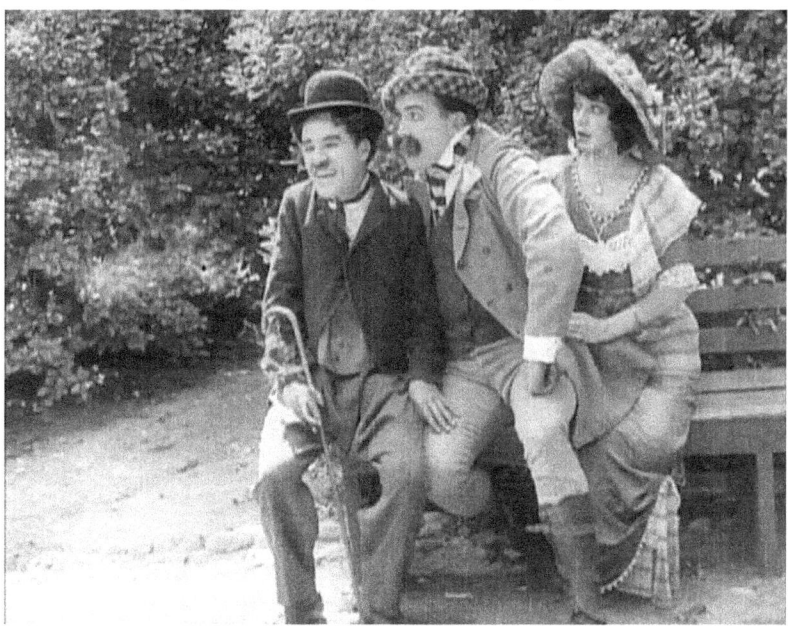

Keystone style too, given that much of that motion is exhibited by Kennedy's outrageous walrus moustache.

There's some well timed slapstick here, as Kennedy prominently inserts himself between his girl and the interloper with the intent of bumping him off the bench, only to be set up to bump himself onto the ground in return.

It's a traditional Keystone scene, though there is one subtle moment here too that could well be another Chaplin contribution: while he sits there, enjoying the results of his interruption, Edgar Kennedy puts his head so close to Chaplin's that his moustache literally tickles his ear. The phrase "he bristled at him", one that could be applied to many Keystone moments, has never felt quite so appropriate as it does here.

That Chaplin is promptly done with these two well known and thoroughly established Keystone stars in one early and relatively meaningless scene in favour of the story he's about to kick off could easily be read as meaningful in itself: a rejection of the unsubtle facial hair approach to screen laughter in favour of an intricate situation comedy with characters that feel more real. Of course,

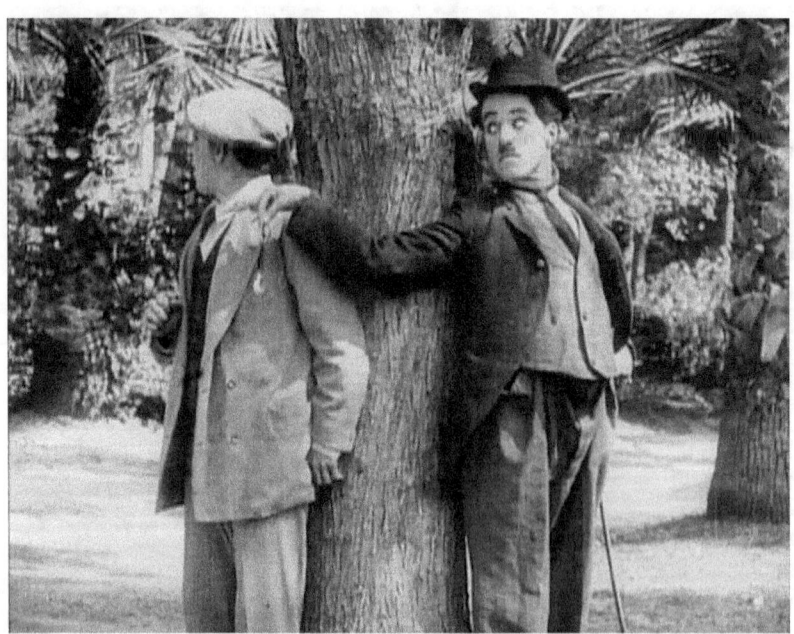

maybe that's just hindsight talking.

That story proper revolves around a pocket watch which is a perfect MacGuffin. Another girl on another bench won't accept her deadbeat admirer's love without a token to prove it, so he picks a pocket watch from the pocket of a sleeping man to give to her. Coincidentally Chaplin takes a fancy to the very same girl, so picks the pocket of the pickpocket to give the pocket watch the pickpocket picked to her himself. Whew! Say that ten times fast!

Of course, you can see where this is going, even if you haven't seen *Between Showers*, which ended up in a very similar situation, merely with an umbrella instead of a pocket watch. Just as the policeman from which the umbrella was stolen ends up being the arbiter of the eventual fight over it, here the Little Tramp attempts to sell the watch back to its original owner, which merely includes more players in the ensuing chaos. There's very little that's new here and those who have seen *Between Showers* can't fail to notice the deep similarities, but it's a well constructed piece that plays out confidently and effectively.

The acting is still the weakest link at this point, because many of these actors are still firmly adhering to the old pantomiming ways. When Chaplin wrote, "There was a lot Keystone taught me and a lot I taught Keystone," he clearly saw the latter category as including things like technique, stagecraft and movement. His peers "knew little about natural pantomime" and "dealt little with subtlety or effectiveness," something very obvious here.

Just compare the two instances in which the pocket watch is lifted and you'll see the massive differences. Chester Conklin, the original pickpocket, lifts it from its owner capably enough but pantomimes what he's about to do before he does it and proves almost unable to to keep his fingers off it from that moment on. Chaplin does the same when he lifts it from Conklin, but with a much quicker and smoother action. We can't fail to realise that Conklin only succeeded because his victim was asleep at the time; he's far more believable when he becomes a victim himself. No wonder Chaplin said that his own skills "stood out in contrast" when audiences inevitably compared the actors.

Like Chaplin's pocket picking over Conklin's, *Twenty Minutes of Love* itself is far smoother than the earlier version that was *Between*

Showers, but its unoriginality sinks it. Chaplin's first shot as a writer highlights that he really did know where he wanted to go with his character and the stories that he would be part of, but was only beginning to learn how to get there. "Like a geologist," he later wrote, "I was entering a rich unexplored field."

If it wasn't a bad pun, given how almost every character ends up in this film and the many others like it, *Twenty Minutes of Love* could easily be seen primarily as a chance for Chaplin to get his feet wet as a director. Two films later, he'd be given the opportunity to dive in fully, to write and direct the most Chaplin of Chaplin pictures up until that point, *Caught in the Rain*.

When this nascent director wrote that, "I suppose that was the most exciting period of my career, for I was on the threshold of something wonderful," I firmly believe that he was talking not only about his year at Keystone in general, but especially about the single month between mid-March and mid-April when he made these two films and the pendulum of control finally swung his way. If Chaplin's middle name hadn't been Spencer, it could easily have been Control and his Keystone career is easily compartmentalised

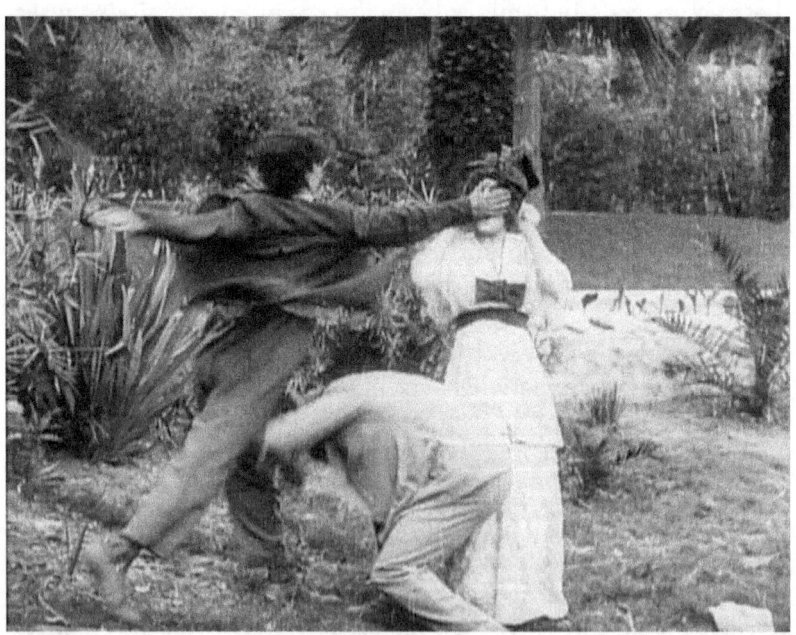

between what he controlled and what he didn't.

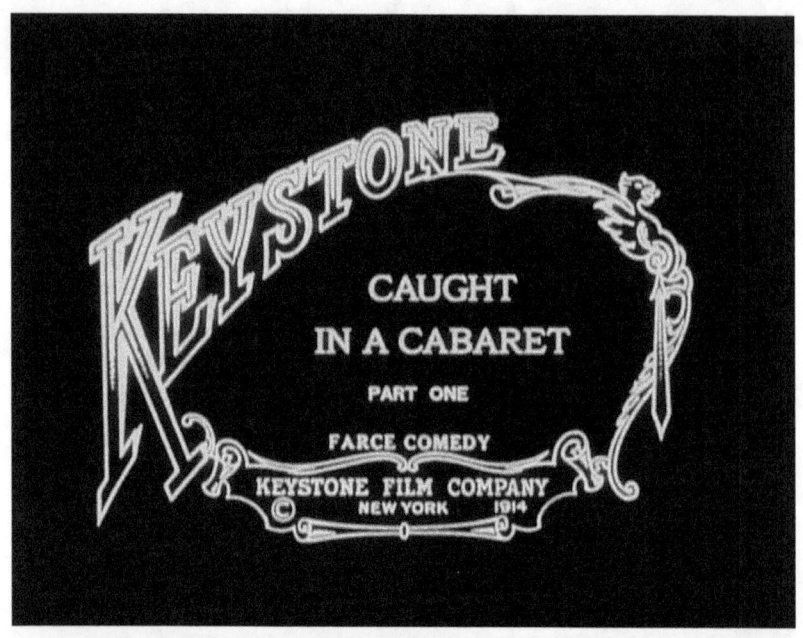

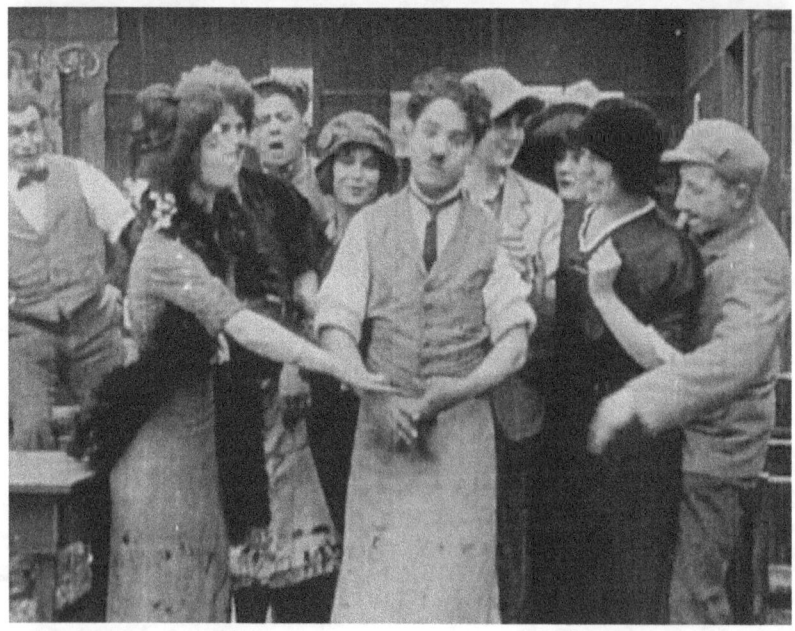

Caught in a Cabaret
27th April, 1914

Director: Mabel Normand
Writers: Mabel Normand and Charles Chaplin
Stars: Charles Chaplin, Mabel Normand and Harry McCoy

Chaplin's first two reel film was *Mabel at the Wheel*, during which he rejected Mabel Normand's direction and caused a major spat with Keystone Studios head, Mack Sennett. If Chaplin's account of why he didn't get fired over this is taken as gospel, it's because his popularity was soaring and it's easy to see that state of affairs backed up here. After he debuted as a writer with *Twenty Minutes of Love*, he made his second two reeler, *Caught in a Cabaret*, again under Normand's direction but with the writing split between them.

Not only is this clearly a Chaplin picture with Normand little more than a love interest, it doesn't even feature the name of her character in the title of the film. Normand was the biggest star at Keystone at the time, a personal favourite of Sennett, with whom she was, shall we say, romantically entangled, and the titles of most of her pictures clearly stated who they were about. Even those in which Chaplin guested before this one followed that standard: *Mabel's Strange Predicament* and *Mabel at the Wheel*, so it's more than conspicuous that this one isn't, say, *Mabel Caught in a Cabaret*.

Comparing it directly to the previous two reeler, we do see some similarities. Charlie has the hots for Mabel again, who is attached in some manner to an unnamed character played by Harry McCoy, who gets the worse of it for the duration of the film but nonetheless wins out in the end.

The biggest difference is that this time Chaplin isn't playing a villain, let alone such an outrageously stereotypical Dick Dastardly prototype; instead he's a sympathetic character who goes a little beyond the boundaries he's been given.

Here, that throws him into class territory, a topic that would be revisited many times in many Chaplin pictures. The Little Tramp was never going to be high class, at least not truly and never for long, but he could and often would play the part when he could get away with it. That's exactly what he does here, passing himself off to Mabel with a fake business card that identifies him as Baron Doobugle, the Prime Minister of Greenland. With a position like that, it's within the bounds of possibility that he could wheedle his way into, shall we say, other positions.

Of course, he's really the Little Tramp rather than the Prime Minister of Greenland. He is employed here, but only as a lowly waiter at some sort of café and dance hall. It's clearly not a high class establishment, though the various professional ladies who hang around may well be taxi dancers rather than prostitutes. If so, this is an early depiction of an industry that sprang up only a year earlier in the Barbary Coast red light district of San Francisco, but would soon become a commonplace component of the American landscape throughout the twenties. If not, well, they're ladies of the evening and this dive is even more disreputable. The fact that the next door establishment is clearly Chinese may also highlight a low rent neighbourhood in 1914.

Early on, Charlie doesn't appear to be happy with his lot, the beginning of his battle with a swinging door unfolding in a

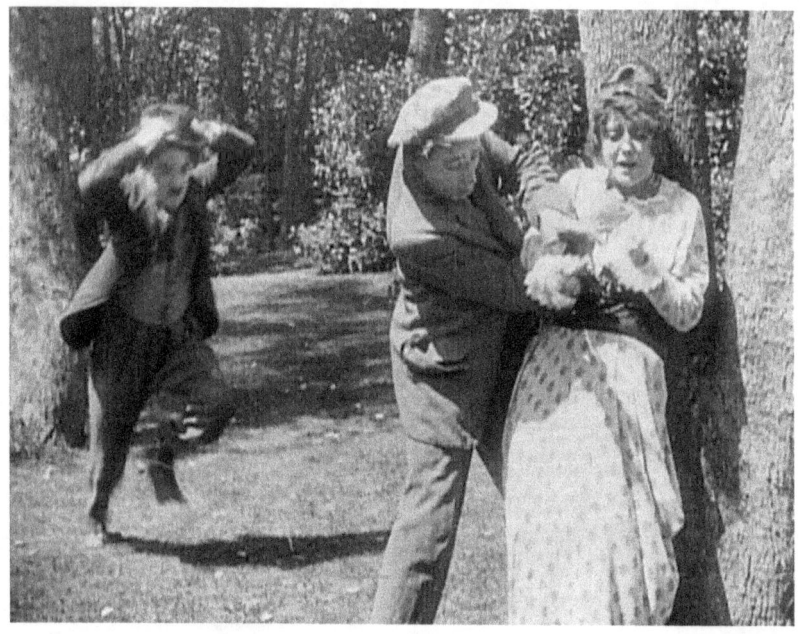

completely blasé fashion, unlike the more violent altercation five pictures earlier in *His Favorite Pastime*. What he's most happy to do is escape and take his little dachshund for a walk in the park.

Given that he only has a ten minute break, the dance hall and park must be pretty close to each other physically, but they aren't remotely close socially. While he fits in well with his customers at work, he's obviously an odd man out in the park. It's perfectly acceptable for high class characters like Mabel to walk up and say hello to his dog, but it's never going to amount to anything more than that.

Well, at least until a crook arrives, that is, in the presumed form of William Hauber, a Keystone stuntman and bit part actor who died while scouting for locations during the production of a lost Edward Everett Horton feature from 1929 called *The Aviator*. The British Film Institute credit him here as a thief but he's more like a kidnapper as he takes down Mabel's lover and then turns on her, but Charlie comes to the rescue, violently and rather effectively. Now when the waiter preens overtly at Mabel, she's willing to pay attention, especially after he hands her his fake business card. Her cowardly suitor, in the regular form of Harry McCoy, no longer gets a look in.

And so we have a story, albeit an easy one to figure out from here. Of course, Charlie is going to play up his newfound attention, while carrying on at his job. Of course, he's going to get found out. Of course, the whole thing will end with slapstick shenanigans. This is a Keystone farce comedy from 1914; what else do you think is going to happen?

What's notable is how it unfolds. The scenes during the middle of the film, as Charlie takes his leave of the lady to run back to work with a new lease of life, unfold much smoother than any scenes I've seen anywhere else in these early Chaplins. The editing is far from sophisticated, but it's quicker and with a better sense of timing than in any of his previous pictures. The fact that the story unfolds over two reels is a step up from those too, where it would have been crammed into a single reel. There's even a dream sequence, which is far more grounded than the visions of Hell which Lord Helpus, Chaplin's character, conjured up in *Cruel, Cruel Love*. In fact, it's shocking to realise that that was only one month and four pictures earlier.

I'd also suggest that Chaplin's subtleties fit here better than in any of his previous films. In those, he was surrounded by old school hands in the silent comedy business, who mostly carried on just as they always had. Here, that approach remains apparent in Harry McCoy's pantomiming that he'll soon get his revenge on the new challenge to his girl's hand, as he apparently didn't understand that subtleties were in. Most of the other actors, though, are slower and less overt as the picture unfolds, adhering a lot more to Chaplin's timing and pace, though it's fair to say that it's less that they match him and more that they keep more out of his way than usual. For Chaplin's part, he feels more confident here, more in control of his picture, even with Normand officially calling the shots. There are scenes full of little details that point to what he'd do in more substantial films to come. In one shot, for example, as he prepares to first leave work, he lets his hitherto unseen dog out of the cupboard, lifts him up with one hand and takes off his apron from under his jacket with the other.

None of this is to say that this isn't obviously a Keystone picture. It surely ends like one, with the first pie that Chaplin ever threw in his career at the studio that invented pie fights. Mack Swain in particular goes wild during this finalé, throwing far more than pies. Are those bricks that he tosses in the vague direction of everybody else?

While the park we see is quite obviously a park, the café we see quite obviously isn't a café; it's quite obviously a sparsely decorated set on the Keystone lot, very apparent even before Swain collapses against it and the walls move to accommodate his considerable bulk. He's not the only one to be wearing the traditional outrageous Keystone facial hair, though even that seems to have been toned down just a little. What's more, even when Chaplin is pretending to be the Prime Minister of Greenland, he still gets drunk and staggers through a good part of the picture. After all, it was his performance as an inebriate on the vaudeville stage that prompted Sennett and Normand to hire him in the first place. Why not milk it?

What this all means is that this is perhaps the point in Chaplin's career at Keystone at which it was most apparent that he was moving forward, both in front of and behind the camera, and even beginning to haul some of his fellow actors along for the ride.

It's quite understandable, given the context. He'd finally been able to experience the power of direction for the first time on his previous picture, *Twenty Minutes of Love*, but he didn't direct all of it. He did, however, write that scenario and he surely built on the experience to contribute to the writing of this one. Given that the story arc is all about Charlie (along with the fact that there is such a thing as a story arc to begin with), while Mabel is given next to nothing to do except react to his hiccups, there's little doubt that he contributed far more to the writing than she did, perhaps as she concentrated on the direction. However, while Normand is usually credited as the sole director for this picture, Chaplin would be firmly in the director's seat for his next one, *Caught in the Rain*. It was all finally starting to happen for Chaplin, making this his lucky thirteenth movie.

The most obvious downside isn't the film itself but its condition today. Even the Flicker Alley box set, *Chaplin at Keystone*, which brought us remastered editions of these films that are in an entirely different league to the public domain copies we've been watching

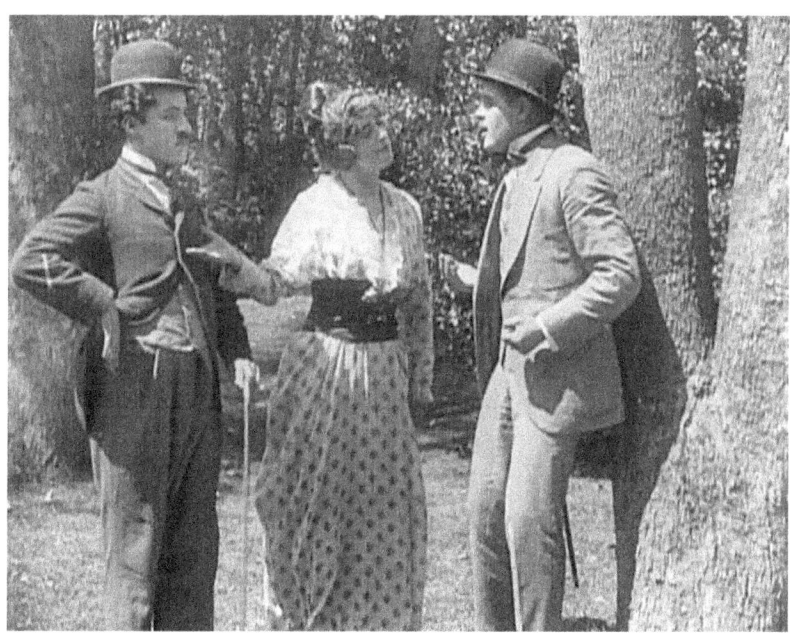

for years, can't do much with the extant prints of *Caught in a Cabaret*. It claims that all surviving copies are fragmentary and of poor quality. What they include in the box is a composite of three prints, including the nitrate dupe negative at the B.F.I.'s National Archive in London which is apparently the most complete. The original intertitles are believed to be lost, so what we see here are taken from what is presumably a reissue. Certainly the versions easily available online at the usual places use different intertitles written much later on by Chaplin's half-brother, Sydney. And so what we can see of *Caught in a Cabaret* doesn't have the picture quality of the other restorations, which is a shame. Of all the films in Chaplin's Keystone year that I'd watched thus far, this is the one I'd most like to see in pristine condition.

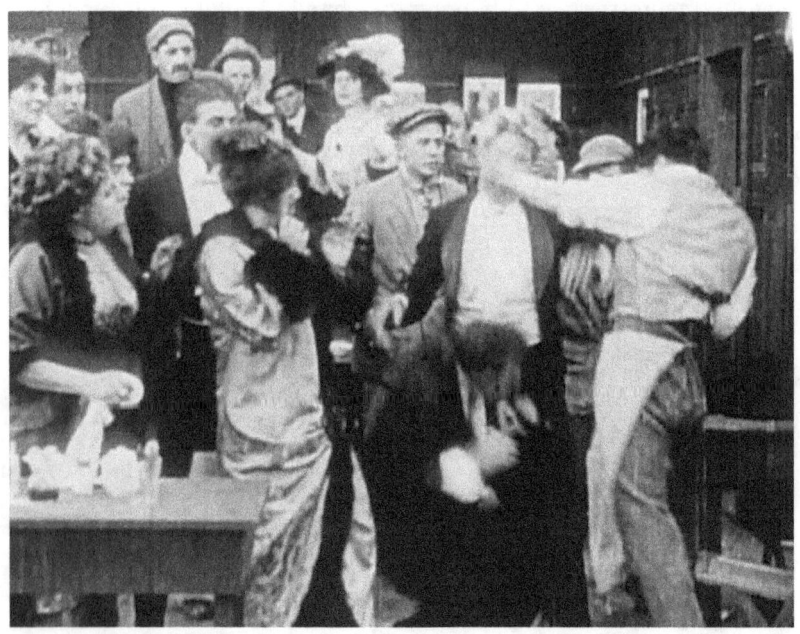

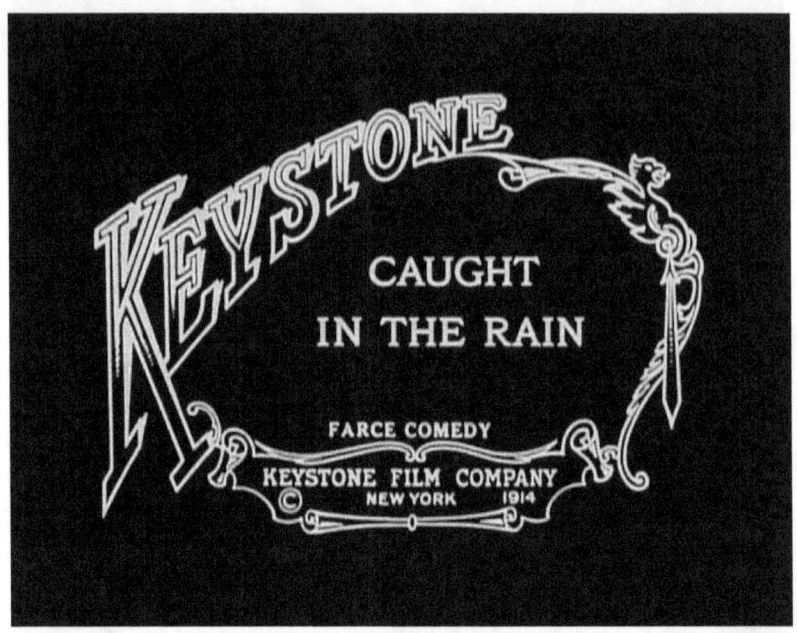

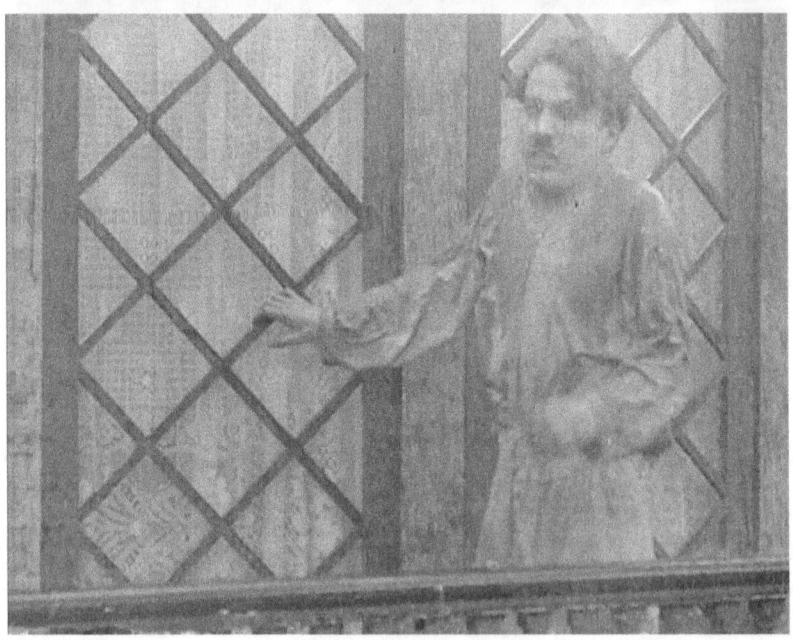

Caught in the Rain
4th May, 2014

Director: Charles Chaplin
Writer: Charles Chaplin
Stars: Charles Chaplin, Mack Swain and Alice Davenport

Looking back with a century of hindsight, we know that Charlie Chaplin was one of the most versatile of the world's filmmakers. Biographer David Robinson wrote that, "If he could have done so, Chaplin would have played every role" and, in a way he did, acting them all out for his fellow actors to imitate.

His great films, all years away from being made at this point, highlight this ambition well. Beyond merely starring in *City Lights* or *Modern Times*, for example, he also wrote, produced, directed, co-edited and composed the scores. From 1918 to 1952, he shot all his films at the Charlie Chaplin Studios, where he could take as long as he felt he needed and break from production for as long as he wanted. Distribution from 1923 to 1952 was through United Artists, a studio which he had co-founded in 1919 and still co-owned. Rich enough to work only when the muse struck him or his notorious perfectionism drove him, he became the template and the epitome of the sort of filmmaker that the French critics would eventually define as an "auteur".

When he started at Keystone Studios in 1914, of course, none of this was the case. He tried and failed to persuade his directors to change things, but they either couldn't or wouldn't understand what he aimed to do. Only with the spat that followed his refusal to follow direction from Mabel Normand while shooting *Mabel at the Wheel* did he get the opportunity to put his money where his mouth was, somewhat literally, and achieve the sort of control he wanted. Studio head Mack Sennett saw the money coming in from Chaplin's acting and decided to allow him some more creative freedom.

This new trust wasn't immediate but it moved him towards what he wanted over a couple of pictures. He got to sit in the director's chair for *Twenty Minutes of Love*, though Joseph Maddern did too. He wrote *Caught in a Cabaret*, but Normand directed. Only here could he finally play the roles of writer, director and lead actor on the same film, without having to share any of them with anyone else. As such, it's one of the most important pictures of his career, if clearly not one of his best.

Jeffrey Vance highlights how it's "not an ambitious effort" by detailing how it "draws upon past successes". He's absolutely right about the latter, but I'd happily debate the former a little. While it's clearly not ambitious in the risk-taking sort of way, the overriding impression that I got from *Caught in the Rain* is that Chaplin threw everything but the kitchen sink into his first solo picture.

It's like a compilation of everything Keystone did, not only what Chaplin did for Keystone but what anyone had done for Keystone too, with every ounce of fat taken off the bones and then the bones made to dance for the Little Tramp. In a way, it's Chaplin's idea of the ultimate Keystone stew, based entirely on the ingredients he'd seen thrown into the pot during the four months he'd spent at the studio, including those which he had brought with him from the vaudeville stage. Once that heady stew was brewed to what he saw as perfection, he added a few new little spices he felt might add to the mix. With hindsight, those are the tasty bits in a lively, but very familiar, old dish.

Because there are so many ingredients, it's a challenge to provide a succinct recipe. It begins in the park, as so many silent comedies do, whether Chaplin's, Keystone's or both. Mack Swain and Alice Davenport are a married couple, but while he's off buying a box of chocolates for her, Charlie gets in between them by cosying up to the lady, albeit not without her invitation. This sets up a firm spat between the couple which runs through the entire picture.

There are some capable gags and stunts here, though Davenport rather obviously sets up the one with the rose. There's nothing new, though, except perhaps the appearance of the character of Ambrose, which Swain would go on to play for seven years. He isn't credited as such, as there were no credits to these early Keystone films, but I can't find an official debut for the character and this one plays entirely consistently with the others he'd go on to play under that name, starting later in 1914 and often in partnership with Chester Conklin as Walrus. Hey, the moustache seems the same and who can argue with Keystone facial hair?

With the park out of the way, Charlie naturally finds a bar, as he so frequently did. Any excuse for him to play the drunk once more was a good excuse at Keystone and this is little more than an excuse. We don't see him get drunk, just drag himself by the ear into the bar, then stagger out again, through a swinging door, to emphatically light his match on a policeman's jacket. By this point, we're checking off Keystone tropes on a virtual bingo card as those of us paying attention have seen all of these moves before.

What's new can be found in the editing, which has finally become a far more sophisticated creature than I'm used to seeing in these Keystone pictures. What would normally be long, slow scenes are cut down into quicker, shorter ones. They're crosscut too, so that for much of the picture we see two different stories unfolding alternately. The result of these two approaches is that this is a one reel film that contains material enough to fill two or three. Such careful editing speeds up the pace to play so quickly that it causes havoc with taking notes and surely kept contemporary audiences on the hop.

So we've played in the park and Charlie's got drunk, so it's no

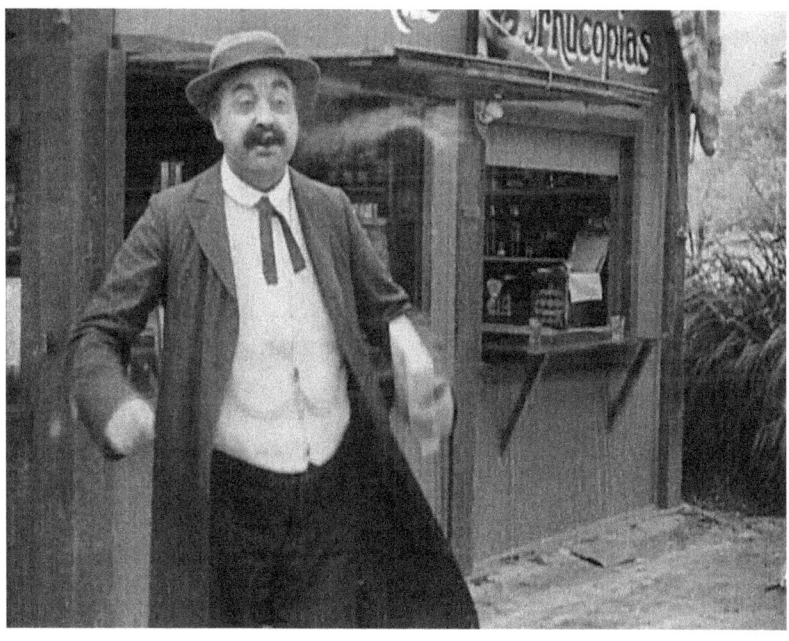

surprise to find that we promptly shift to a hotel, the third in the traditional Keystone triumvirate of locations. The next discernable segment unfolds in a hotel lobby, as did the long opening scene in *Mabel's Strange Predicament*, the first time the world saw what Chaplin could really do.

The bulk of this hotel lobby scene is one of the centrepieces of the picture, as the "tipsy hotel guest", as Chaplin's character tends to be listed, transforms everybody to be found inside this peaceful room into participants in a slapstick routine that runs a short forty seconds. It's relatively simple and, to be fair, the choreography is obvious, but it's handled superbly nonetheless. These folk merely want to go upstairs. Charlie tries it at a run but slides back down again. If one can fail, so can two and four and then, with everyone sober safely out of the way, Charlie can fail once more solo just to highlight how this is all about him. This centerpiece is a good microcosm of the film as a whole. Everything here has been done before, but it's executed well and so quickly that we can hardly blink before we're onto something else.

Of course, with the downstairs scene wrapped up, now we shift to

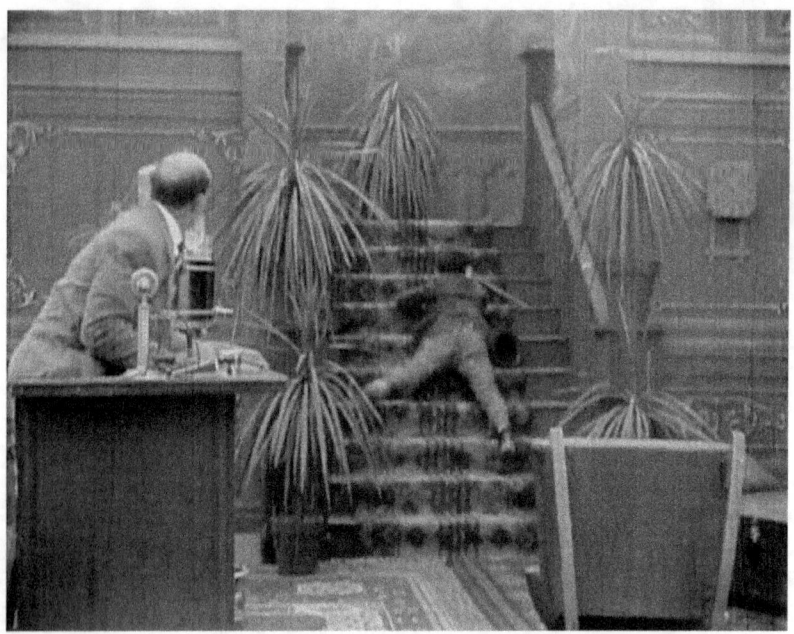

the upstairs scene. As you'll recall from *Mabel's Strange Predicament*, and any number of other Keystone comedies set in hotels, this means a lot of slapstick situation comedy where people end up in the wrong rooms.

Chaplin doesn't merely task one character with sleepwalking for a while, he has two: first himself, maybe more in a daze than a sleepwalk proper, somewhat reminiscent of his exit from *A Thief Catcher*, but the effects are identical, then the wife he tried to flirt with at the beginning. Of course this couple are staying in the very same hotel on the other side of the hallway. No coincidences or plot conveniences are too outrageous for a slapstick short!

You could write most of these scenes yourself, but Chaplin does add some neat touches to them too. One has the couple pause their bickering momentarily while the maid brings in a pitcher of water, only to resume full force as she leaves. Another involves the set up for the final Keystone must have: thrown out of the window onto the balcony, Charlie is mistaken by a trigger-happy passing cop for a burglar.

Enter the Keystone Kops, who have never moved so fast in their lives because the editing has become so rapidly paced that we can hardly keep up with the progressions, even used as we are to the A.D.H.D. editing that became *de rigeur* with the MTV generation.

As I pause to take a breath, I wonder what I might have neglected to mark off the Keystone checklist. When leaving the bar, Charlie is almost hit by a car, so he falls down in the road, the scene over so quickly that if you blink, you might just miss it.

There's a strong scene in which Charlie undresses for bed, in his cups throughout but in progressively fewer clothes. He wipes his boots with his cravat and his forehead with his collar, all while attempting but failing not to fall onto and off of the bed. The Little Tramp isn't living on the streets here but he's still not doing particularly well. A neat touch has him stop at his socks, as there isn't enough of them to remove, and put a boot under his pillow. When Davenport sleepwalks into his room and tries to pick his pocket, he has his trousers join the boot. Another neat touch has him try to open a door with a cigarette, always a handy prop for the Little Tramp.

It's often said that Keystone shorts never had scripts, just a set of gags upon which improvisations occur until the eventual chase, and I've highlighted this traditional understanding a few times already, while talking about earlier films in this book. However, Simon Louvish finally busted that cliché by including actual examples of what they did have in his book, *Keystone: The Life and Clowns of Mack Sennett* and it's abundantly clear that they really were scripts, at least of sorts.

Perhaps we can best describe them as stream of consciousness lists of gags, but they're structured with stage directions in prose that clearly outline what needed to be shot. Before Chaplin came along, these would have worked well as synopses of the films that they would become, but they don't work that way for Chaplin's pictures as he added something less tangible to the mix: they miss out on his nuances of personality that make us laugh even between the traditional gags.

This film would surely have one of the longest synopses of any Keystone one reeler, because it could easily be seen as a "greatest hits of Keystone" sort of picture, merely constructed out of entirely new footage. However those old hits aren't what resonate, it's those

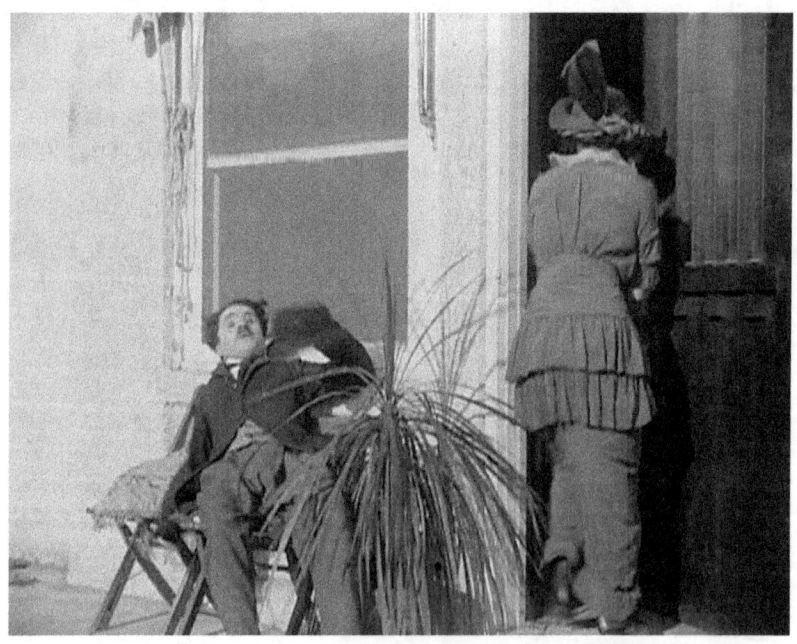

little moments that Chaplin was adding in: the ear, the pause, the socks. To hindsight, his point is clear, but naturally it wasn't that obvious in 1914 and this project aims to discover how much and how soon it became obvious.

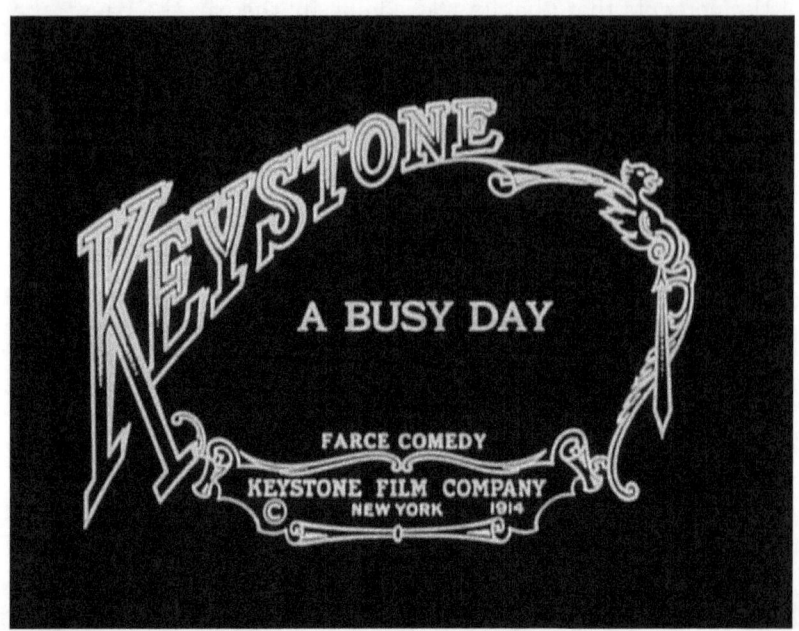

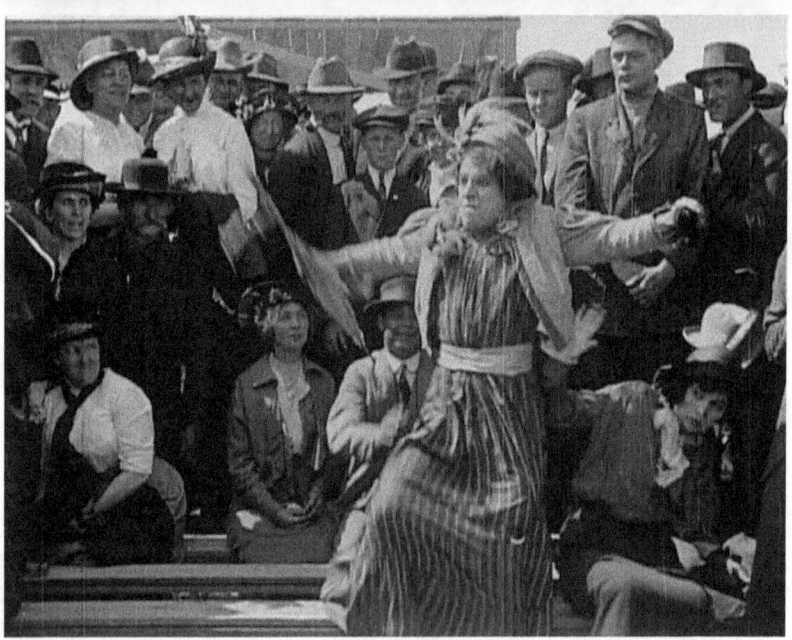

A Busy Day
7th May, 1914

Director: Mack Sennett
Writer: Charles Chaplin
Stars: Charles Chaplin and Mack Swain

At a first glance, *A Busy Day* isn't much at all. It's a split reel film, meaning that it wasn't long enough to have its own reel and so had to share one with another short subject. Clocking in at just under six minutes, it shared its reel with an educational short about the cartoonist Edmund Waller Gale called *The Morning Papers.*

Six minutes might not sound like much, but given how much Chaplin crammed into his previous picture, *Caught in the Rain*, it ought to be more than enough to endow it with some substance at least. Sadly, he wasn't able to endow it with much of anything, merely a love triangle with the unlikely form of Mack Swain in its centre and a sustained burst of slapstick violence.

Most of the picture revolves around Swain's wife in search of her errant husband, beating up cops until she can find both him and the new girl on his arm so she can beat them up too. If anything, that description makes the story sound too subtle, so perhaps I should attempt to resummarise using only words found in action bubbles on the *Batman* TV series. Yes, it's that blatant.

At a second glance, *A Busy Day* still isn't much, but there are things worthy of note. For a start, you may wonder which role Chaplin might be playing if we're here to watch two women fight over Mack Swain. Well, he's the wife, spending the entire picture in particularly garish drag. His outfit is outrageous enough that we can surely be thankful we can only see it in black and white; if it was colorised, he might appear to be playing an entire gay pride parade all by himself. Then again, I've seen drag queens a lot worse than Chaplin and not a one with the industrial quantities of raw energy that he brings to the table; he's like the Energizer Bunny in Doc Martens here. *The Complete Films of Charlie Chaplin* suggests that he was wearing one of Alice Davenport's dresses, but that book is not without its errors, so whether that's true is open to discussion.

Whether it was or wasn't, it's certainly accessorised, the feathers on the hat valiantly remaining in place, at least until the end when they're surely ruined by a notable backflip off a pier into the ocean.

Talking of parades, this is another of those Keystone guerrilla shoots at an organised event, this particular parade accompanying the dedication ceremony to begin the expansion of the Los Angeles Harbor in Wilmington, CA. That may not sound too exciting, surely a lot less exciting than automobile races and perhaps less exciting than the arrival of a huge puddle in Hollywood, but there's a fair crowd, if apparently a smaller one than turned out for the Junior Vanderbilt Cup at which Keystone shot *Kid Auto Races at Venice, Cal.*

That film is the obvious comparison here, not least because it's deliberately riffed on. Chaplin even hauls out some of the same moves to swan around in front of what might even be the same camera, this film being shot a mere three months after the earlier one, even with a full dozen other Chaplin pictures being made in between. We find ourselves in reminiscent territory quickly: the first intertitle explains that the unhappy couple have "gathered to see the parade and hear the band play", but clearly Swain's interest

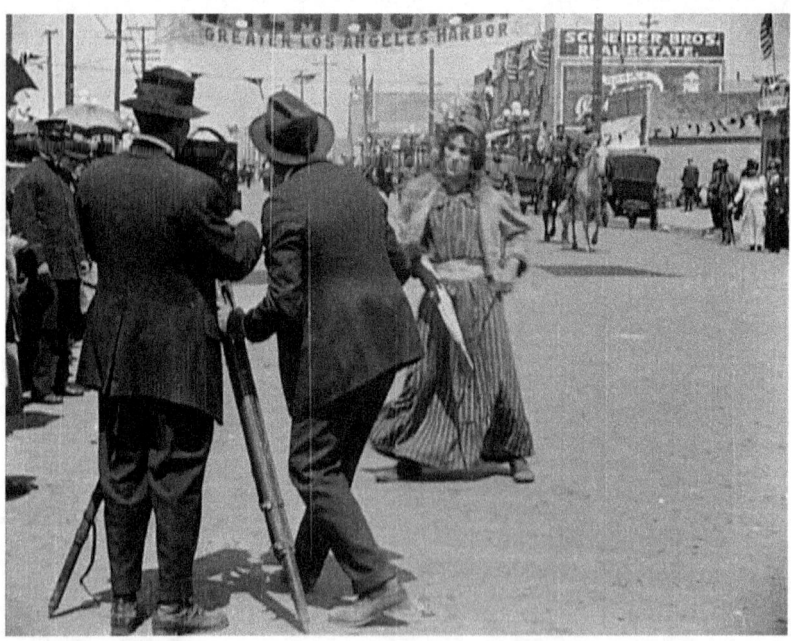

is more in the girl with the come hither eyes next to him, so off they dash, leaving Chaplin to follow them into the parade.

As this happens, we can't fail to see both the similarities and the differences between this and *Kid Auto Races at Venice, Cal.*, especially given the importance of that film in the Chaplin chronology.

For a start, both follow fictional characters at a real event and both start in the audience. The earlier film had the Little Tramp wander around in front of a movie camera annoying the men behind it, while this one has Charlie in drag do the same thing, merely a little more coquettishly. It's a deliberate homage and it's a fair one because it doesn't run on. Chasing her husband, Charlie just finds herself in the right place at the right time and preens herself in the spotlight, before being rudely moved on.

The most notable difference can be seen not in the folk we're supposed to watch but in the folk who are watching the folk we're supposed to watch, there in person while the film was being shot. In the earlier picture, most of the audience watched the races with a few wondering what the strange little tramp was doing, only to gradually shift their attentions during the shooting of the film. By the end they were watching him and laughing hard. Here, some of them obviously know who Charlie is from moment one and they're laughing from the very first frame.

While Charlie showing up in drag is surely the biggest surprise *A Busy Day* has to offer, being about as far from the Little Tramp's outfit as could be imagined in 1914, another is that there's precious little of the event that the cameras came to capture. Perhaps the parade just wasn't as exciting as the soapbox derby in the earlier film, but we get nothing of the ceremony, very little of the parade and only a couple of other shots: one of some battleships and one of some small boats heading out into the harbour. For all the effort they made, they could have stayed home on the Keystone lot and shot most of the same thing.

It's only the crowd who made the trip to Wilmington worth it; I'm sure Sennett could have conjured up enough extras to flesh out a studio shoot, but we'd have recognised their faces. These folk look like regular Joes, almost all of them wearing hats but without any outrageous facial hair. The ironic flipside to that observation is that we can't recognise one of the Keystone actors here: the young lady who conjures Swain away from his wife. Most sources say Phyllis Allen, but that doesn't ring true.

Without much of the event on offer, beyond the laughter of the crowd, and precious little story to capture our attention, we're stuck focusing on the energetic action. It's simple slapstick stuff, more so than usual, as there are perhaps only three moves on show and one of them dominates.

This is the one where one character places their foot on the chest of another and pushes hard, so that their opponent flies backwards, often out of the frame and into a different one, where they fall over, usually with their legs in the air. It's hardly a new move, but its dominance here and the frequency with which it's used make it seem like it's an Olympic sport and we're watching the highlight reel. Usually the dominant move in these 1914 pictures is the one where a character takes hold of another's face and pushes them over, but that's relegated to a rare spectacle in this one. Even rarer is that good old favourite, the kick in the ass, demonstrated on Chaplin in *Kid Auto Races at Venice, Cal.*, but here by Charlie on a cop. The police don't come out well in this picture.

As the title suggests, *A Busy Day* was shot in a single busy day: Saturday, 11th April, 1914, partway through the shoot for *Caught in the Rain*, which ran around it from the Tuesday to the Monday. Apparently, when an event cropped up on the calendar that could provide useful footage, a Keystone crew just loaded up and trucked out to shoot it. Perhaps someone even rang the studio on the day to let them know and they reacted to it like their fictional equivalent reacts to a fire in *A Film Johnnie*.

A few available actors were a bonus and, hey presto, Keystone had a movie with a fresh background that could fill up a slot in their delivery schedule. It didn't have to be any good, as we find here where sustained action is about all that makes up for the lack of almost anything else. There are precisely two reasons to watch A Busy Day and neither of them has a thing to do with the parade that half-heartedly provides a background. One is the sight of Charlie Chaplin leaping about in drag, sometimes quite literally; he even does the recognisable Ford Sterling leap before running at one point. The other is the sheer level of violence, which is strong and sustained.

Under normal circumstances, I might suggest that this makes the film play out like what 1914 audiences were discovering was called an animated cartoon. Like most things in the cinema, this began in France during the last decade of the previous century, but the first true character animation had only shown up a few months earlier, the debut of Gertie the Dinosaur trailing Chaplin's by only six days.

These aren't usual circumstances though, because Chaplin in drag is very reminiscent to me of an older character, namely Mr. Punch (or, more accurately, his wife). I'm used to watching early American films and missing their cultural connections because I'm English and don't share them, so prompting research, but Chaplin was an Englishman too and the Punch and Judy puppet show is a quintessentially English cultural event, even if its origins are in Italy with the *commedia dell'arte* of the 16th century. Punch and Judy shows have played in England since 1662 and, traditionally, Punch celebreated his birthday on 9th May, only two days after this film was released.

Could this be Chaplin's homage to Mr. Punch? His character here is clearly outrageous and over the top, believably descended from

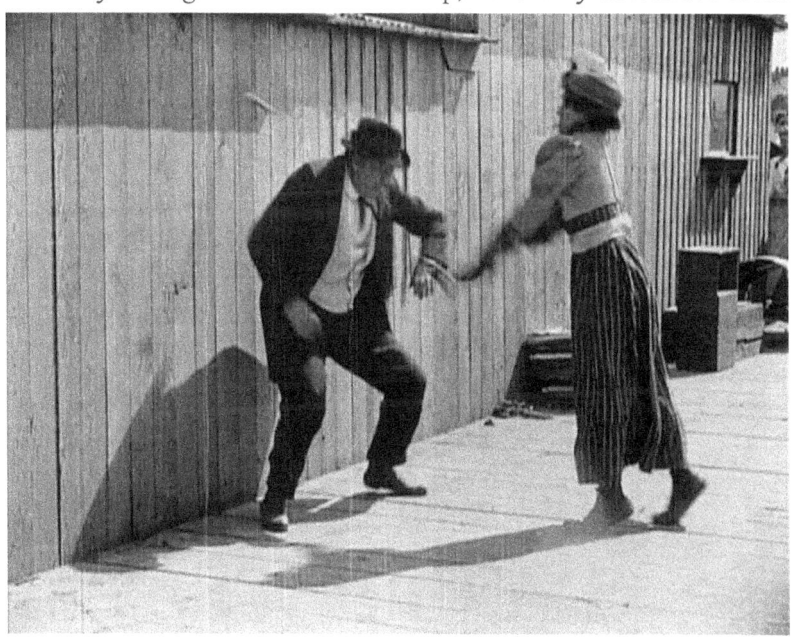

the same trickster gods, so ladylike that she blows her nose on her dress. As politically incorrect as it gets, Mr. Punch spends most of his time beating up his spouse, a constable and whichever other characters joined the highly changeable cast list of a Punch and Judy show, and that's precisely what Chaplin does here, merely in the role of the wife rather than the husband.

The most obvious other differences are that there isn't a baby to be found to treat horrendously and turn into sausages, though even slapstick comedies had their limits, and no crocodile either, but how they could have had that show up in the Los Angeles harbour, I have no idea. So what we have is what Chaplin could adapt from the traditional Punch and Judy story into the framework of a one day Keystone reality shoot. I'd almost buy that the handle that breaks off the umbrella Charlie hits her husband with was a deliberate homage, but that's a stretch, I admit. I've heard worse explanations for this one, though, trust me.

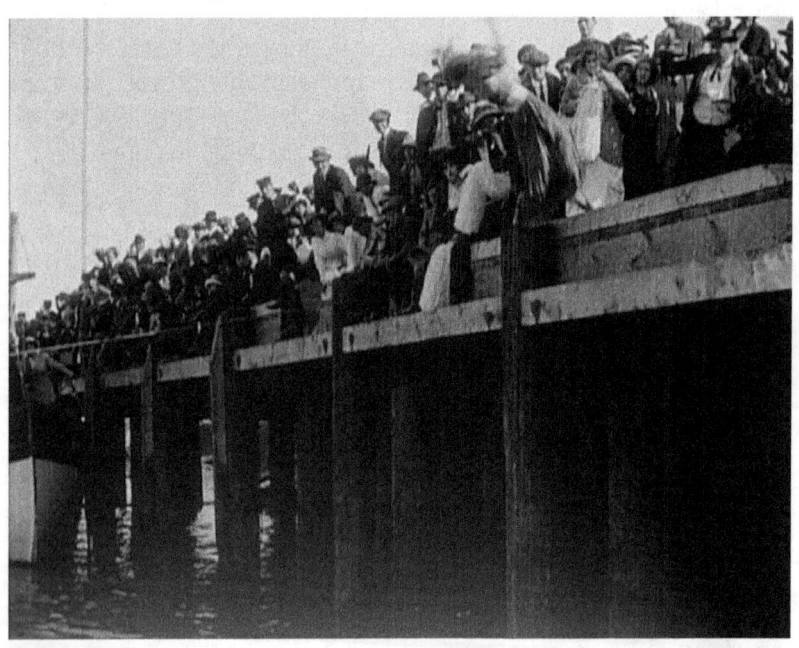

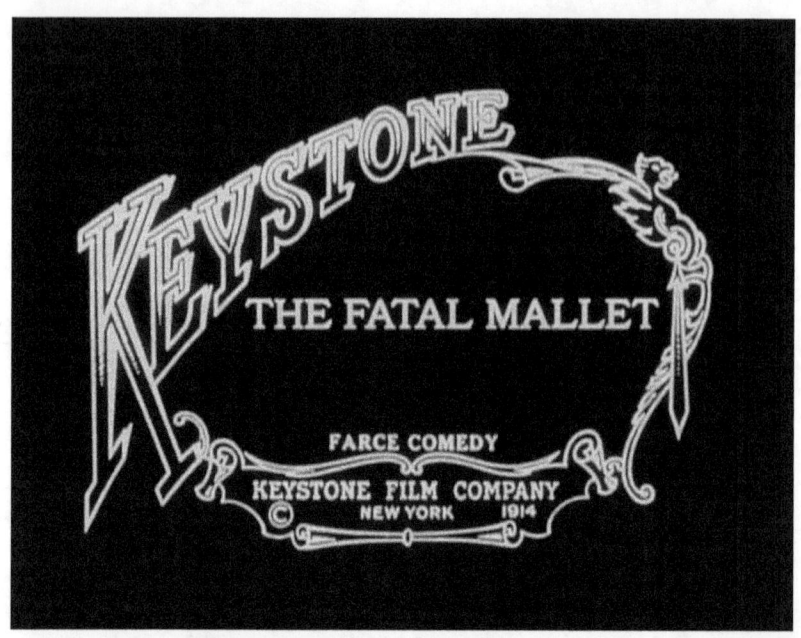

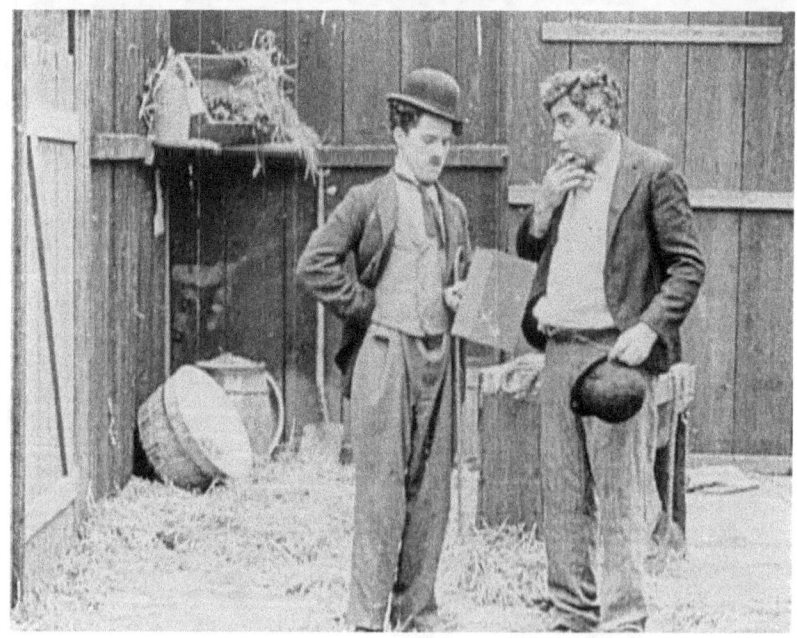

The Fatal Mallet
1st June, 1914

Director: Mack Sennett
Writer: Mack Sennett
Stars: Charles Chaplin, Mack Sennett, Mack Swain and Mabel Normand

To suggest that Keystone Studios made Charlie Chaplin a busy man during his year there in 1914 is an outrageous understatement. They released five Chaplin pictures in February alone, four more in each of March and April and, eventually, the staggering total of 36 for the year. Yet, the first screenings of *The Fatal Mallet* on Monday, 1st June marked the end of a 25 day drought since the release of *A Busy Day*.

At this point, the public had never had to wait for a Chaplin picture for more than a fortnight, but studio head Mack Sennett had decided that the time was right to make a feature, the very first American feature length comedy, *Tillie's Punctured Romance*. And you expected a holiday, right?

Shooting on *Tillie's Punctured Romance* began on 14th April, the day after Chaplin had wrapped on *Caught in the Rain*, his solo directorial debut, and continued until 9th June. Chaplin worked on nothing else for a month, but then made rapid amends for his lack of new material on theatre screens by churning out four short films in just over two weeks. *The Fatal Mallet* was the first of them.

The strange thing is that this is far more notable as a Sennett picture than as a Chaplin picture. Not only did Sennett produce, direct and write the film, he also starred in it and as a lead actor too, functioning as the other half of a double act with Chaplin for most of its running time. In so doing, he kept more screen time for himself than he had done before in any Chaplin film and I can't help but wonder why.

Sennett's substantial contributions to the art and science of American screen comedy cannot be overstated, but none of that comes down to his talents as an actor; even his biggest admirers would admit that he was one of the weaker actors on the Keystone set and, as we've found, many of the actual actors weren't exactly actors either, at least to our modern sensibilities. It could just be that Harry McCoy was sick but, perhaps, after considering feedback from each of Chaplin's directors, all of whom had struggled with the studio's new star, Sennett wanted to experience him first hand for a few pictures before letting Chaplin loose to consistently direct himself. Certainly, he was done giving him to others; from *A Busy Day* until his very last day at Keystone, Chaplin only had to take direction from Sennett or himself, except for his guest appearance in the Roscoe Arbuckle short, *The Knockout*.

Whatever the reason for Sennett's prominence on screen, his contributions can't be ignored and certain decisions ring down the years with the power of hindsight. Initially he's Chaplin's rival for the attentions of Mabel Normand, but with the arrival of a third suitor, played by Mack Swain, the two team up to take down the bigger man. Normand was a lovely young lady, who had been one of Keystone's biggest draws long before Chaplin was hired and would remain so after he had left the studio, but she's remembered more today for her relationship with her boss than for her actual acting.

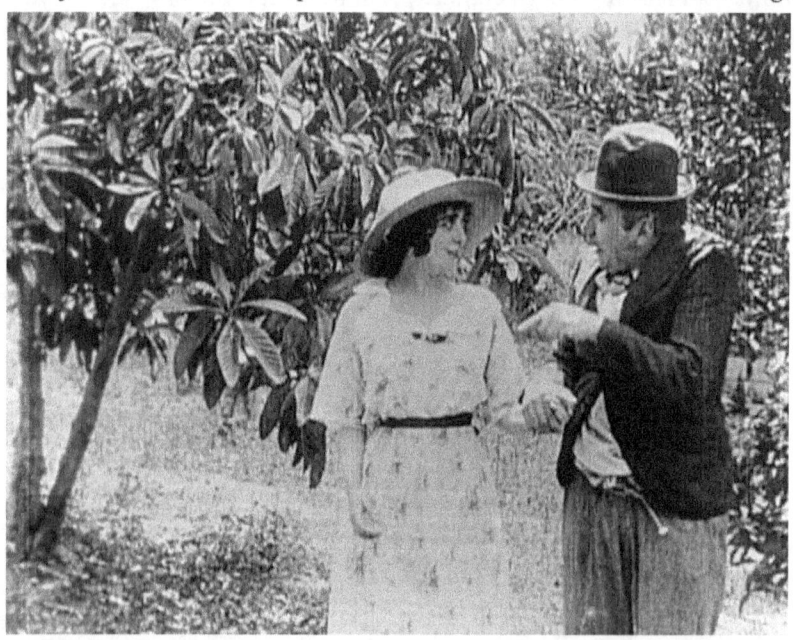

Mack and Mabel were a couple, but their ride was never an easy one and Mack's inability to put a ring on Mabel's finger is surely why Sennett never married. For his part, Chaplin tried but failed to start a romance. "We remained, unfortunately, only good friends," he reminisced in his autobiography. He admits a mutual kiss but sadly reports that attempts to build upon it failed: "No, Charlie," she said good-humouredly, "I'm not your type, neither are you mine."

Most of my reviews of Chaplin's Keystone pictures thus far have highlighted how he was bringing change to the studio's comedic style, introducing subtleties and emotions that he knew well from the vaudeville stage to a studio that was, admittedly successfully, doing what it had always done with no will to do otherwise. Thus it can't come as much of a surprise to find that *The Fatal Mallet*, as close to being a solo creation of Mack Sennett's as any of Chaplin's pictures and very possibly of any film made at Keystone, is what Jeffrey Vance appropriately described as, "One of the crudest of the Chaplin-Keystone comedies," though he did add a further comment that, "it nevertheless fascinates for the extended comic interplay between Chaplin and Sennett."

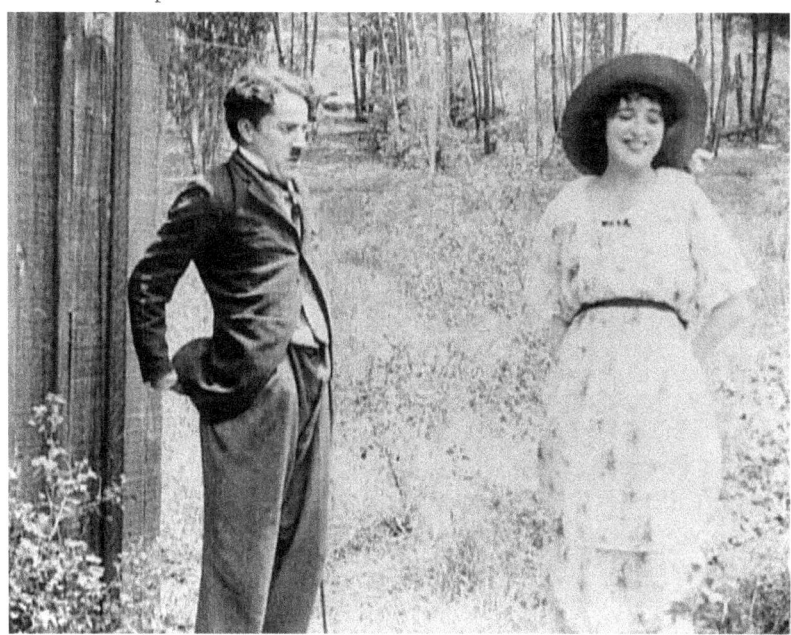

The underlying concept is simple: everyone wants in Mabel's pants. There are only five characters on screen: Mabel, three suitors and a young boy who wants Mabel as well, if perhaps in a different way. Only one can win out, so the title card could easily have read, "Let battle commence!" That it immediately does, with almost the entire running time built out of kicks, shoves, thrown bricks and swung mallets.

Initially Sennett appears like a junior version of Chaplin. He's another tramp, as evidenced by the string holding up his trousers. He has a similar hat and a similar jacket, later seen fastened in a similar way to Chaplin's, with a lone button straining to keep the garment closed. However, where Chaplin is crisp and assured in his movements, Sennett is not; they're generally slow and overdone. Given that he obviously kept laughing throughout the entire three day shoot, the constant half smile on his face makes him look idiotic, a visage that Yorkshiremen would call "gormless". As the picture moves on, he seems more and more like Tweedledee or Tweedledum; maybe we could call him Tweedledumber. He has Mabel's attentions at the outset, to give a great example, but it doesn't take much for Chaplin to woo her away from him. He just pulls the old "look over there" trick. Sennett's response, once he's caught up with what just happened to him, is just as old: he kicks Chaplin in the ass and runs away.

What follows is exactly what you might expect, hereft of pretty much anything in the way of subtlety, in fact just the least subtle parts of *Caught in a Cabaret* expanded out to be the entire picture. The bricks thrown during the finalé of that film are thrown during the majority of this one, and the large mallet that Chaplin uses to knock out Mack Swain there may just be the very same mallet he uses to knock him out again here. Keystone was all about reusing gags that worked; if one got an audience to laugh, it would surely do the same thing in the next twenty pictures it got hauled out for.

Here, Sennett throws the first brick at Chaplin, but it merely prompts a brick throwing war between the two rivals, growing in intensity as Swain arrives on the scene and Mabel escapes her twin suitors to preen for a third. By this point, they've descended to what could only be described as animalistic territory protection, Chaplin hopping at Sennett in a threatening manner that involves an outrageous pelvic thrust to emphasise his intentions. It's like they've become a couple of baboons.

Why this film was called *The Fatal Mallet* I have no idea, because not a single character dies in this movie, whether by mallet or any other instrument. Its working name was *The Knockout*, but perhaps that got changed when it became clear that the title would work better for the Roscoe Arbuckle boxing short which began filming the day before this one wrapped, with Chaplin making a guest appearance as a referee. Beyond making more sense there anyway, that was also a two reel picture so surely took priority over this one reeler. If we factor in how incredibly empty this one is, it must have felt like a no brainer. If Chaplin had crammed into the one reel of *Caught in the Rain* enough material to fill three, here Sennett really only had enough to make a split reel feel weak. I actually prefer one of the reissue titles, because *Hit Him Again* sums up the picture magnificently, certainly more emphatically than *The Rival Suitors*, which is accurate but far too genteel, or *The Pile Driver*, another title that makes no sense whatsoever, whatever meaning of the term might have been suggested.

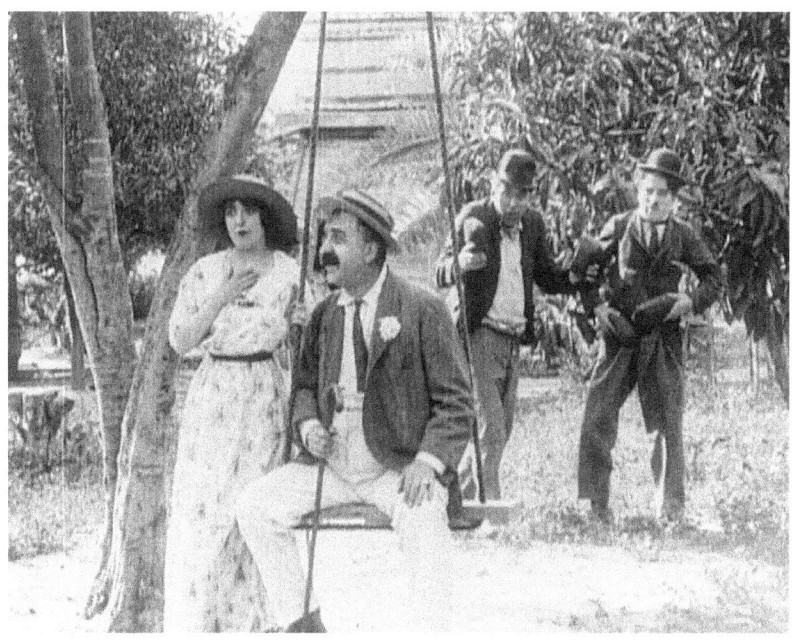

To give him some credit, Chaplin does make an effort, but there's so little framework here that it's clearly a struggle, especially if we factor in who he's stuck working with. Working a double act with Sennett would have held anyone back and he'd done well opposite both Ford Sterling and Roscoe Arbuckle in earlier shorts, not to mention quite a few of the Keystone ladies. What the Little Tramp does manage to achieve is obvious in any scene featuring the pair of them, none of which could fail to stand witness as a comparison in Chaplin's clear favour.

With Swain stuck in the same brick throwing rut as everyone else, he doesn't get much of a chance to elevate things either, if he indeed could, which leaves Mabel Normand, the focal point of *The Fatal Mallet*, with her best opportunity in a Chaplin picture thus far. She does far better than I'm used to seeing her do in these films, even the ones with her name in their titles, taking bricks and kicks better than her boss but also smiling agreeably and adding some charm to proceedings. Chaplin soliloquised of "full lips that curled delicately at the corners of her mouth, expressing humour and all sorts of indulgence." Stuck in a role that could easily be described

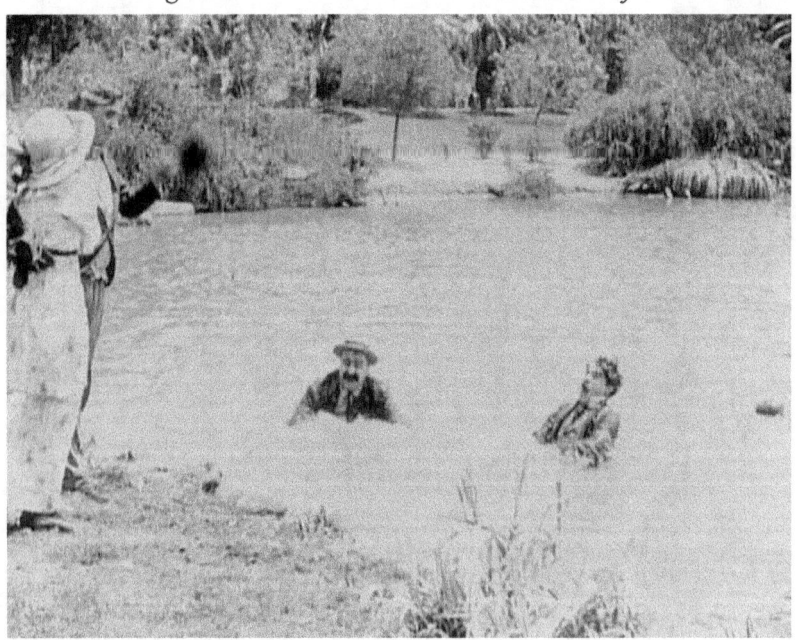

as the MacGuffin, those attributes are very much on show.

And really, at the end of the day, it's Normand who manages to walk away strongest from this one. Given that the entire film takes place in a park, anyone who's been paying attention to my previous Chaplin at Keystone reviews will know precisely where the majority of the characters will end up and precisely how it will happen as well. Yet Mabel, for all that she's spent the picture being clobbered in almost every way, from accidental fists to unearned kicks via a careless run in with a swing and never forgetting those wayward bricks, she isn't among those left floundering in the lake, instead walking away arm in arm with her boss, lover and co-star, Mack Sennett.

I couldn't help but remember Howard Hughes, secluded away in his later years, screening *The Conqueror* over and over, so aiding his mind to conquer Susan Hayward, his former lover, again and again. *The Fatal Mallet* has a dream ending for Sennett, clearly getting the girl he cared about most but wasn't able to wed. He outlived her by thirty years and I wonder how often he screened this to remember.

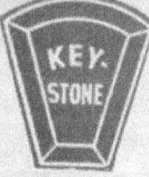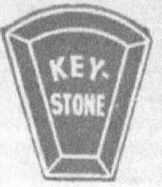
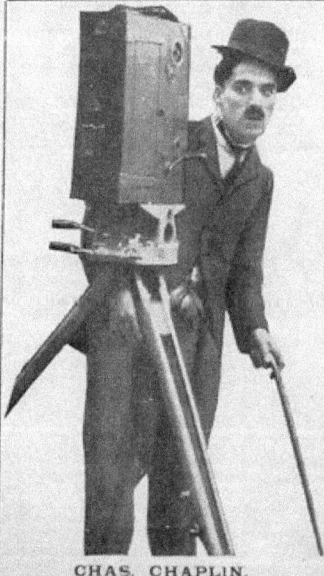

Her Friend the Bandit
4th June, 1914

Director: Mack Sennett
Writer: Charles Chaplin
Stars: Charles Chaplin, Mabel Normand and Charles Murray

When I worked through each of Charlie Chaplin's films from his debut year of 1914, this was the shortest of the reviews I posted, for one very good reason: *Her Friend the Bandit* is considered a lost film.

Now, we can all cross our fingers and hope that maybe one day it'll show up somewhere. After all, *A Thief Catcher* was rediscovered as recently as 2009 at an antiques show in Michigan, and that wasn't merely considered lost, it was also considered to have never even existed, a sort of mythical beast referenced only in a memory of Chaplin's that he had once played a Keystone Kop. In reality, it had over time become conflated with this picture, which was later reissued under the title of *The Thief Catcher*. So, who knows if some film fan will one day turn up a copy of the final remaining lost Chaplin picture, *Her Friend the Bandit*. Here's to hoping.

Without being able to see the film today, we're stuck looking at contemporary reviews, which I've found to be rarely helpful. For a start, tastes were wildly different in 1914, leading to reviews like the one in *The Cinema* that said about Chaplin's threadbare second picture, that "*Kid Auto Races* struck us as about the funniest film we have ever seen." Sometimes, however, it almost feels like reviewers watched completely different films. For instance, the *Syracuse Post-Standard* review of *His Favorite Pastime*, as quoted in *The Complete Films of Charlie Chaplin*, focused on the final scene in which Charlie is stuck at the top of a telegraph pole lowering a chunk of limburger cheese to drive off his enemy who's loitering below with an axe. No known print of the film contains this scene and it wouldn't seem to remotely fit with the rest of it. Perhaps the cheese scene was tacked on from another source for a reissue. More likely, the reviewer just confused it with another film, "Charlie's India rubber countenance" sounding far more like Buster Keaton than the Chaplin of 1914.

The synopses that we have suggest that Charlie shrugs off the costume of the Little Tramp once more, which he did for a number of films in 1914. This time it's so that he can play a bandit, perhaps an elegant one, as some accounts have it.

He's already had a flirtation with Mabel, naturally played by Mabel Normand, so could be forgiven for attending a party at her house. However he attends it while masquerading as a French nobleman, Count de Beans, and his inability to mimic the etiquette required to prove that he's a member of high society brings him down. In other words, his constant and presumably highly comedic faux pas shock the guests until the Keystone Kops are called and we finish up in the usual chase scene.

This sounds like a rather interesting new approach for a Chaplin picture, while never straying too far from the traditional mechanics required for the usual Keystone slapstick. That Chaplin wrote the picture himself promises much, but it was also directed by Mack Sennett, so may have inevitably remained closer to the routine.

Most of the cast are unverified, but confirmed in support to Chaplin and Normand is Charles Murray as the real Count de Beans. Older than Chaplin by seventeen years, he only debuted on screen in 1912, a couple of years before his rival here, but he had churned out over eighty films before this one and had also established a regular character, Skelley, at Biograph. This was his first picture with Chaplin, though he would be back for *Mabel's Married Life*, *The Masquerader*, *His New Profession* and, like everyone else at Keystone, the feature length *Tillie's Punctured Romance*.

Normand, of course, was a Keystone regular who had appeared in many Chaplin pictures, as he had also appeared in many of hers. Having so recently brought a little feminine charm to *The Fatal Mallet*, this would seem to be a great opportunity for her to play an elegant hostess, Mrs. de Rocks. Sadly we may never know, because at this time, as far as we're aware, nobody has yet turned up a print of this picture.

Check your attics, folks!

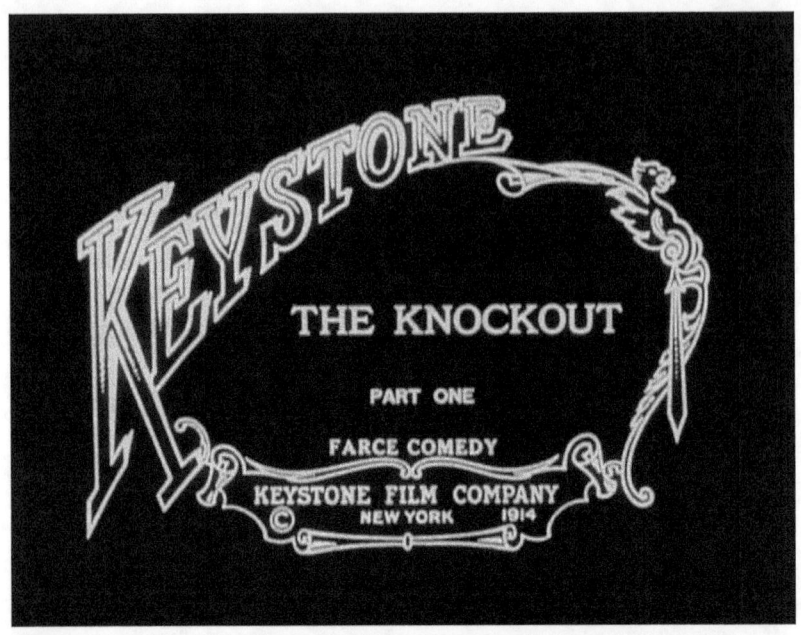

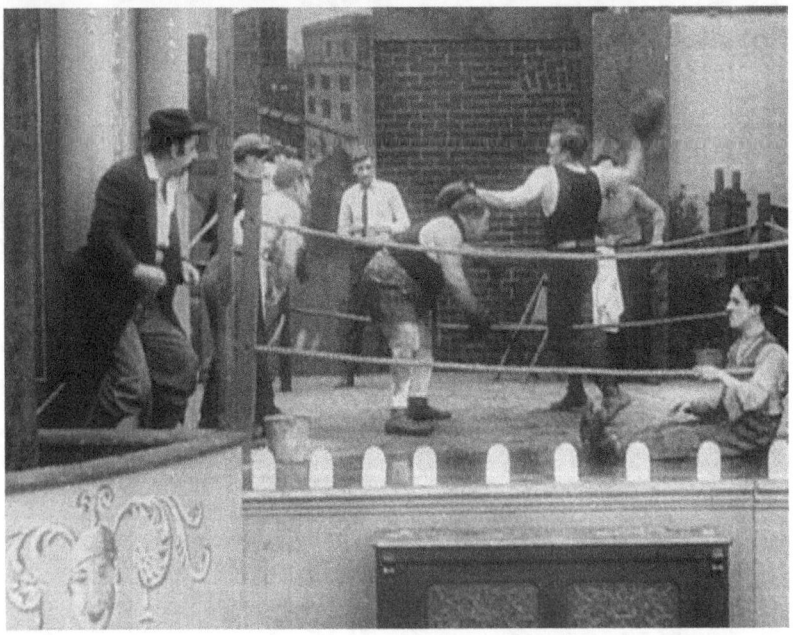

The Knockout
11th June, 1914

Director: Charles Avery
Writer: Unknown (possibly Charles Chaplin)
Stars: Roscoe Arbuckle, Minta Durfee, Edgar Kennedy and Charles Chaplin

Even as a new face on the Keystone lot, Charlie Chaplin was thrown in at the deep end as a leading man. Most of the films he made were Chaplin films, pure and simple, beginning with his first, *Making a Living*, and especially with his second, *Kid Auto Races at Venice, Cal*. When he made a guest appearance in a another star's picture, such as *Mabel's Strange Predicament*, the first of various Mabel Normand films in which he appeared, it generally turned into a Chaplin film anyway by sheer force of his performance.

We rarely think of him being a minor cast member, whether in a cameo role or really filling a supporting role as a guest, mostly because it rarely happened but perhaps also because the finest example of this is the one we didn't have until recently. Chaplin's brief performance as a Keystone Kop in *A Thief Catcher* was, for the longest time, regarded as a faulty memory on his part until the picture was rediscovered in 2009. Until then, *The Knockout*, clearly a Roscoe Arbuckle vehicle, was the best example we had.

It's Arbuckle we see immediately and who dominates the film throughout, whether that be as the large presence on screen during the first reel or as what can only be described as the force of nature blitzing through the second. Chaplin doesn't show up until that second reel, officiating (if that term can remotely be applied here) over a boxing match between Arbuckle and Edgar Kennedy.

Until that point a relatively slow and not particularly interesting Keystone picture, this is when it speeds up substantially and grabs our attention, Chaplin's contributions surely being a large part of that. Initially I felt like the two thoroughly different reels played like two thoroughly different, albeit linked, films, as their tones couldn't be more out of whack. However, with more thought, I realise that the boxing match plays like a long finalé, wrapping up a consistent story arc before *The Knockout* descends into the chaos for which Keystone were rightly known, with the subsequent chase marking the real departure, somewhat like a tacked on extra.

Ironically, it's the entire second reel, the boxing match finalé and the insanity fuelled chase scene that follows it that resonates today. I couldn't help but be reminded of the famous ending of *Blazing Saddles*, in which a sprawling fight scene in an admittedly already unconventional western bursts, quite literally, through the walls of the studio in which it's being shot and, in so doing, transforms the film entirely. This doesn't quite go that far, though there is a neat scene earlier in which Arbuckle ventures into this sort of territory, having the cameraman temporarily point the camera away from him while he gets changed for his fight. Even if it doesn't escape the confines of the film, this chase scene, as sprawling as the brawl scene in *Blazing Saddles*, does veer away from its story arc and spills over into others, which are never explained, such as a fancy party in a mansion. While this mansion could be an unrelated building in town, it could easily have been seen as another movie set if only they had broken one more rule.

Who was responsible for *The Knockout* is surprisingly unclear to us today. Historically it's been regarded as a Mack Sennett picture, whether he's listed as the film's director or after a more vague credit like "made under the supervision of". More recently, Charles Avery's name has been associated with *The Knockout* as its director, by as reliable a source of record as the British Film Institute though for as unreliable a reason as an unsupported claim at Wikipedia that Avery directed 35 of Arbuckle's pictures at Keystone.

Similarly, who wrote the film is open to debate. Some sources say that Chaplin was responsible for the story, though it doesn't ring true. It's far too wild and inconsistent, not to mention traditional for Keystone, to be entirely his, though anyone watching the scene he's in can't fail to recognise that he must have contributed in a major way to that part. Jeffrey Vance highlights that it "borrows from bits in Karno sketches", namely *The Yap Yaps* and *Mumming Birds*, the latter of which Chaplin performed and the former of which he certainly knew.

And so we're left with what's on screen, which is quite a bit in a long two reeler that runs thirty minutes, the longest film Chaplin had been in thus far except for a feature, *Tillie's Punctured Romance*, which wouldn't be finished for another six months.

Most of the enjoyment is sourced from the second frantic reel, because the first is slow and poor. Arbuckle portrays a character named Pug rather than Fatty, surely a hint at the pugilism he'll soon be getting up to, but for now he just eats a burger with his dog and flirts with his girlfriend, played by his real life wife, Minta Durfee. Incidentally, keeping it further in the family, his nephew, Al St. John, reportedly plays three bit parts in the film too.

One of them starts the action, as the leader of a gang that hones in on Pug's girl, who was therefore his aunt in real life. After Pug leaves to get more cigarettes, his attentions escalate in his absence and turn into a full fledged fight after his return, with Pug proving victorious over a gang of four, even with bricks flying every way the wind blows.

His success against such odds becomes how he connects to the main plot, which revolves around a pair of new conmen in town setting up a fake boxing match. Spying a theatre with a *Caught in a Cabaret* poster on display, they talk the owner into letting Cyclone

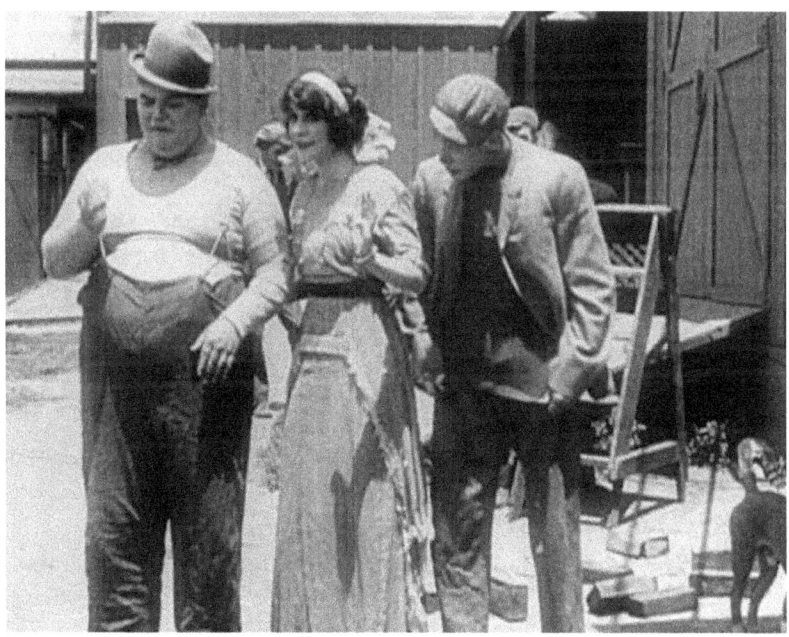

Flynn take on all comers and Pug soon becomes the first of them.

Pug's size leads to complications, but it's the arrival of the real Cyclone Flynn which really stirs it up. Arbuckle looks laughable in his short tank top, shorts, tights and girly belt, more like a poorly dressed drag queen than a boxer. Flynn, however is played by Edgar Kennedy, who had serious experience in the ring, to which he gravitated after school. In his 1948 obituary, *The St Petersburg Times* reported that he'd once gone twelve rounds with Jack Dempsey, eventually losing by decision rather than knockout. Only a single picture for Selig separates his boxing career from his much longer career in film comedy, which began at Keystone Studios with a 1912 picture called *Hoffmeyer's Legacy*, playing a Keystone Kop.

He certainly looks completely at home in the ring, unlike Arbuckle and especially Chaplin, who breezes onto the screen just before the twenty minute mark to officiate in a suitably inept fashion. He retains his toothbrush moustache but otherwise doesn't seem to be an incarnation of the Little Tramp, being neatly dressed in regular sized clothes.

In reality Chaplin knew the ring very well, not as a boxer but as a regular at prizefights in Los Angeles. He'd play a fighter in future films but here he restricts himself to fighting in a set of highly inappropriate ways, both taking and giving as many punches (and kicks) as he would if he was supposed to. Even guest referees in W.W.E. title bouts don't get caught up in quite this much action!

The choreography is clever, because it's clearly dangerous to walk in between two fighters, however carefully you might do so, but Keystone was always strong on choreography. It was less strong on cinematography and there were odd decisions made here on that front that aren't all easily explainable.

I can understand shooting the audience separately to the ring, because they were using a fixed camera. It's easy to shoot the two angles separately and edit them together later, even linking them through our perception by having Pug's mouthful of milk spray the guy in the front seat of the audience. I'm less on board with why they chose to shoot the ring from such a bizarre angle. We're not close to it, for a start, but we're also far enough off to the side that it's condensed into what must be about only half of the screen's available real estate.

The only reason I can see for this choice is so that we can also watch Mack Swain's western style gambler sitting in his box to the left of the ring. He's only just been brought into the story but he has a crucial part to play in it. Quite why he couldn't have stayed off screen throughout the fight until the moment he's needed, I have no idea. *The Knockout* certainly followed that approach elsewhere, as a Keystone Kop walks on screen at one point only to be hit by a flying brick and knocked into a horse trough.

In the absence of nuanced decisions in these matters, it falls, as always, to Chaplin to throw in many of the little touches that light up the second half of the film. At one point, the ring becomes soaked, maybe to wake him up from one of his periodic knockouts (only the referee gets knocked out in *The Knockout*), so he hauls himself along on his backside using the bottom rope. Another instance has him look up to the roof and pray for God's aid in dealing with these two monsters.

Compared to what Chaplin gets up to in the ring, the ensuing chase across the rooftops is merely blatant, fuelled by a pair of pistols that can somehow be easily held and fired by a man wearing

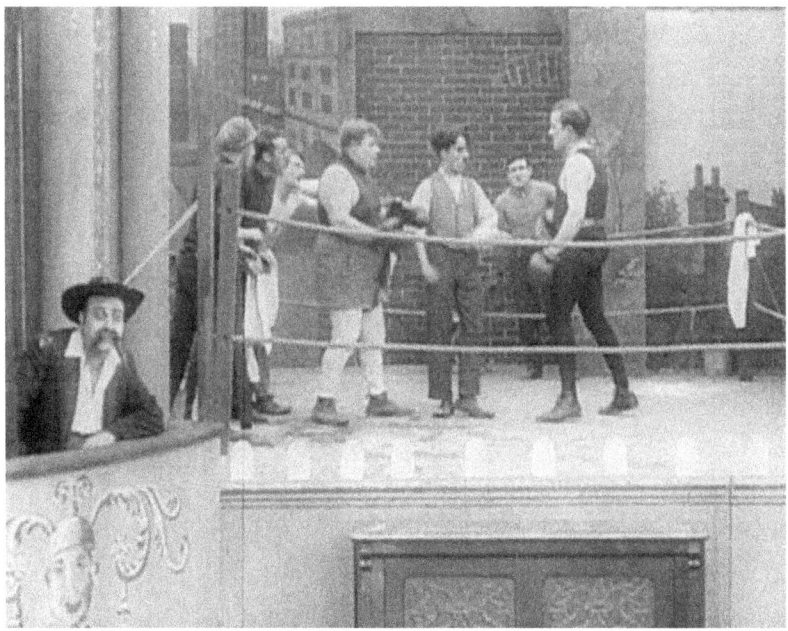

boxing gloves. Needless to say, its almost endless supply of bullets is almost glossed over. This is a great chase sequence just for Arbuckle and Kennedy, who is reminiscent at points of a swashbuckling hero, but the Keystone Kops inevitably join in and make it still more fun. It's thoroughly enjoyable, just not for its subtlety. It wins out in the end through sheer exuberance.

At this point, it's almost unbelievable that the second reel follows the first. Where that was slow and plot driven, for the most part, this is traditional mile a minute Keystone insanity but with more imagination than usual. It's also where the real ingenuity comes into play, not only through Chaplin's brief segment.

Arbuckle, never a small and insignificant flower, is a force of nature here, a behemoth who successfully takes on half a dozen Keystone Kops at once, not in a fight but in a bizarre tug of war. One manages to lasso him, but he carries on regardless. And on and on, hauling them, dragging them and swinging them around as if the laws of physics don't apply to him. The subtletly in this film may belong to Chaplin, but the film itself belongs to Arbuckle, whose relentlessness and boundless energy are as infectious as they are

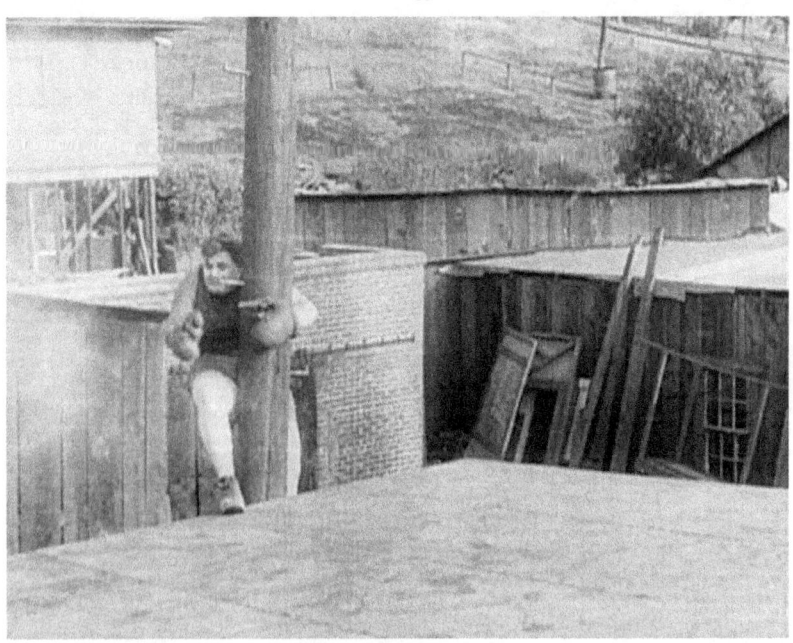

humorous. By the time it was over, I felt like I could challenge Cyclone Flynn myself, after I stopped for a breather of course.

There may well be a full half hour of chaos to found in the half hour that *The Knockout* runs, but it's all compressed into the last fifteen minutes.

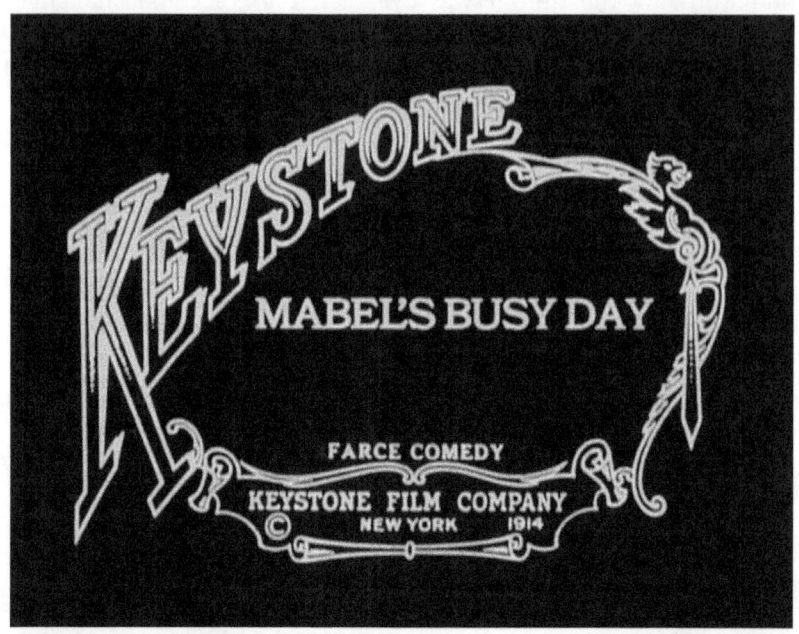

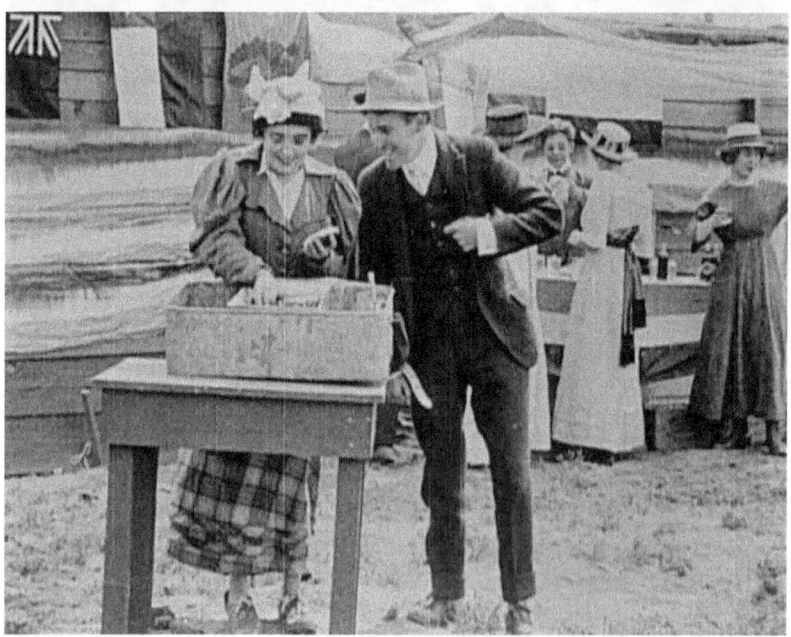

Mabel's Busy Day
13th June, 1914

Director: Mack Sennett
Writer: Mabel Normand
Stars: Mabel Normand and Charlie Chaplin

The title of this picture refers to Mabel, the regular character played by Keystone star Mabel Normand, but, if she was merely having a busy day, Charlie Chaplin was having a busy month.

This was the fourth of his films to reach cinema screens in June 1914 and the month wasn't even half over yet! In fact, it had only been a mere two days since theatre audiences had enjoyed his guest appearance in the Roscoe Arbuckle two reeler, *The Knockout*, but he was back to torment Mabel in another one reeler.

Unfortunately it's a weak film, partly because there's very little in the way of story and next to nothing to elevate it from the other Keystone pictures around it. Mostly, though, it's because of its notably disagreeable tone. This short is a particularly mean spirited comedy, if it's worthy of being called a comedy at all, with Chaplin's usually cheeky and sympathetic shots at authority figures aimed instead at Mabel, in financial straits and trying to eke out a living selling hot dogs. She emphatically plays the sympathy card like her life depends on it but, with Chaplin so mean, she had our sympathy from the outset without trying.

At least he's not playing the Little Tramp this time out, or at least I don't think so. If he isn't, he's much closer to him than any of the other characters he'd played thus far. His toothbrush moustache remains intact but his outfit is much neater and his outlook on life much more ruthless; he's what Jeffrey Vance ably describes as "a shabby scoundrel", a fair description of him, given that there are apparently no lows to which he won't stoop.

Initially his target is that old Keystone faithful, a policeman, but unlike the usual scenario where we're on his side, we're firmly on the side of the cops in this one. They're merely attempting to stop this shabby scoundrel from jumping the line at a racetrack and sneaking in without paying. His response to being noticed is to get immediately violent, a tone which he keeps for a while, beating up the only truly sympathetic cops I've seen working in a Keystone film since the one who helped Emma Clifton across the road in *Between Showers*. If I'd have been in that line, I'd be knocking him down rather than them, an odd feeling indeed. Maybe it's the Little Tramp all dressed up to go out, but I'm seeing him as a different character entirely.

Mabel is far more the sort of character we might expect with hindsight to be in a Chaplin picture, though she does plead rather outrageously for our feelings rather than allow her situation to speak to us on her behalf. She's clearly down on her luck, hawking hot dogs from a tray strung around her neck and her face ably displays how desperately she needs to sell the lot. A few years later we'd have seen a half dozen scrawny kids waiting at home for mom to bring food, but here we just get Mabel.

She's already sneaked into the racetrack too, not to watch the races but to sell her wares, and she made it in through a back gate with the deliberate knowledge of the cop who's on duty guarding the thing, yet again highlighting how far the police are staying on

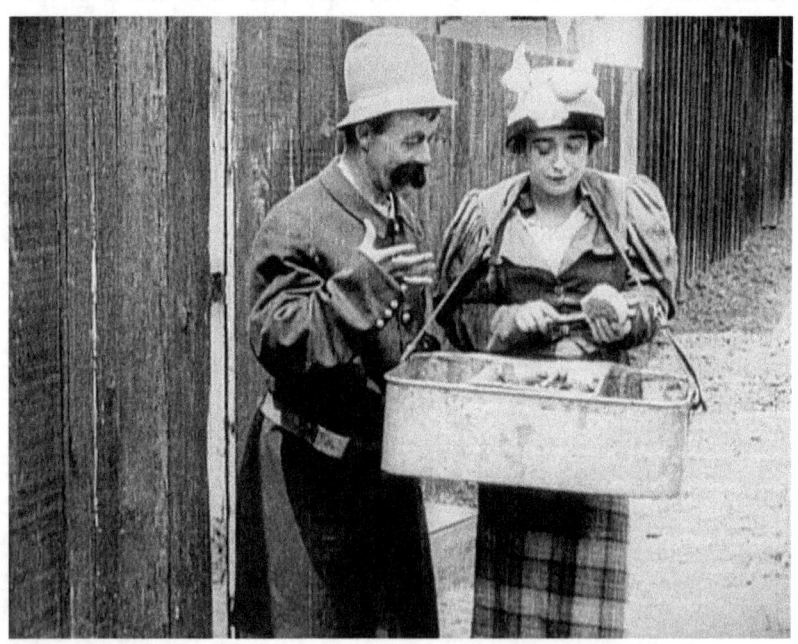

the side of Everyman in this picture, even if it's for selfish reasons. He does get a free hot dog as a makeshift ticket price. How's that for rampant corruption in the hierarchy of authority? He doesn't even get a promise of something else later, you know, the sort of thing that they couldn't show in 1914 comedies but could and often did hint at with a wink.

We do feel for Mabel, however much we wish she'd quit with the overacting. We might find ourselves immune to her charms because we can see how much she's trying, but we feel for her anyway because of how consistently badly everyone in the film treats her. They all seem to want something for nothing and they aren't even nice about it. For a start, the first potential customer thinks it would be a laugh to stick one of her hot dogs in her nose, just to show off to the pair of ladies he's with. She knocks him down for his troubles and sends him packing. The next few just move her on, as if they're offended by her presence, but then, almost in tears at how badly she's doing and possibly losing her voice to boot, she finds some customers. The first initially walks away without paying her, though he does come back to tickle her chin and leave her a coin. The second has a whole wad of cash, but throws his purchase back in her tray when he realises she can't make change. Later in Chaplin's career, we might expect this to be social commentary on class, but here it's just men behaving badly.

Behaving the worst of all, of course, is Chaplin's character. He hones in on a trio of young ladies engrossed in the racing, first walking in front of them, then using one as an armrest and finally opening another's purse in a rather blatant fashion, hauling out what appears to be a wig and using it as a fan. What's most amazing is that, when he's discovered, inevitably because he isn't remotely hiding anything he's doing, he simply turns on the charm and all three of them start grinning like lunatics.

I wonder if this is supposed to be just another extension to the mischief Chaplin's characters often get up to, the charm suggesting that it's all in good fun, however mean spirited it might seem. Alternatively, it could be read as Chaplin coming to a realisation that he could do anything on screen and audiences would still laugh, so he was testing his boundaries to see how far he could go without losing us. I don't buy that in the slightest, thinking more that humour was merely far less sophisticated in 1914, but the thought resonates as he was also clearly exploring the power of sympathy on screen.

The one kindly act he performs here arrives when an obnoxious customer starts hassling Mabel physically. I say kindly rather than altruistic because he has hidden motives. He isn't doing it to help Mabel, he's doing it to show off to those three ladies, and his next action underlines his morality (or the lack of it).

Initially he plays it just like any Chaplin character: he saves the girl by preventing a man from stealing one of her hot dogs, taking him down and sending him packing, then he consoles her, telling her that it's all right. The unexpected coda here is that he then promptly steals one himself and hightails it out of there. Because of the way it's played, how he sets up the contrast, it's the one truly funny moment in the film. Again, I come back to that thought about whether he was manipulating our emotions to see what he could get away with. Just as Catholics believe that sins can be wiped out through confession, does one kindly act in a Chaplin movie cancel out all the horrible actions he's got away with prior to it? If charm doesn't, maybe kindness does? Perhaps he was finding out.

If that was the extent of it, we might be able to buy into his thinking, but it escalates, as Keystone films have a habit of doing. Mabel chases him and elicits the assistance of the cop who let her in, so Charlie does a runner. That makes sense, but here he goes a step beyond, stealing not just another hot dog in the process but her entire tray of them, promptly giving them all away to the first crowd he stops in. Clearly Mabel had pitched her tent in the wrong part of the racetrack, because here she'd have sold out in no time, but, by the time she gets the chance, her stock is completely depleted, except for what he's stolen back from the people who stole from him what he stole from her. Are you following?

As with the three ladies earlier, the fix to this disconcerting state of affairs is to turn on the charm because that's all that's needed in this picture to make everything OK. It's like Chaplin's working on the level of three year olds with boo boos. Let mommy smile for you and it'll all be better, right? That doesn't quite work with "a shabby scoundrel" destroying a young lady's entire livelihood.

Unfortunately, what could easily be the picture's only mitigating factor just isn't there for us today. There is a suggestion that the heart of this shabby scoundrel might be touched by Mabel's tears during the finalé, thus leaving us a positive outcome that wouldn't seem out of place in a Chaplin picture, but this would need an intertitle to back it up and the intertitles are believed lost. If this is the case, they certainly left it late to turn it around, as even Chaplin can't grab our sympathies that quickly. Given all that's gone before, we can't help but see it as another con.

So, with that possible saving grace lost to us, at least at the moment, we're forced to look elsewhere and we don't find much. Perhaps the most notable aspect to the picture today is how the crowds, who are generally kept away from the actors, receive their antics. The restored version of *Kid Auto Races at Venice, Cal.* shows us how the public first saw Chaplin, but there's a progression to that apparent in some of his later Keystone films shot on location, like this one. By this point, the surrounding audience are very clearly laughing at everything Chaplin's doing in scenes like the one where he gets into the racetrack.

In other Chaplin films, the races themselves might be something

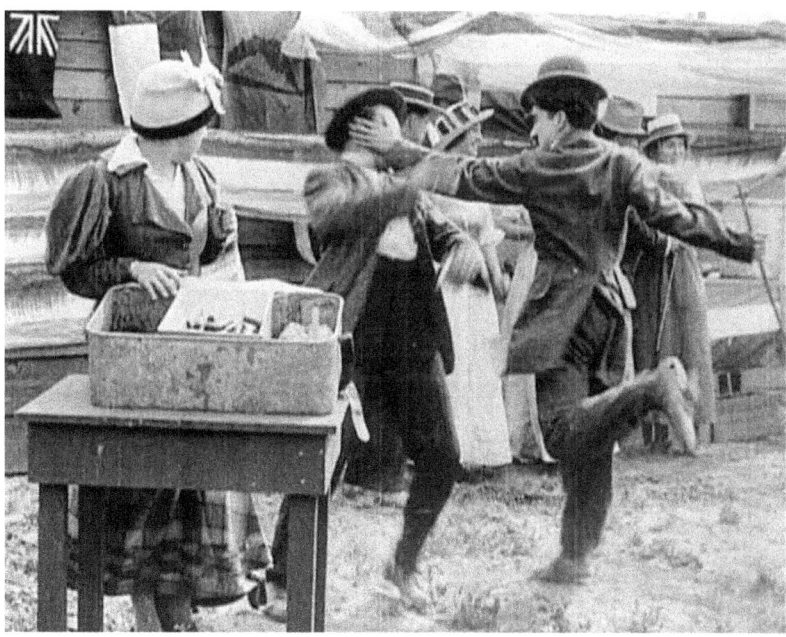

of a draw. Even in something as primitive as *Kid Auto Races at Venice, Cal*, there's an interplay with the location as Charlie nearly gets knocked down by a couple of vehicles and, of course, *Mabel at the Wheel* was built around that interaction. Here, there's nothing of the sort.

The Keystone cast and crew were at the Ascot Park Speedway in Los Angeles for an exhibition race that ran on 17th May, 1914, but they only shot the race with a single static camera positioned on a bend, thus capturing little but great clouds of dust hurled towards it as cars chase around that corner; Ascot Park was unsurprisingly a dirt track. We never see moving cars in the same shot as people, let alone with Charlie or Mabel.

If it wasn't for the reactions of the audience to their antics, this is yet another location shoot that could have been made back at the studio without travel costs. Surprisingly close to the city, Ascot Park was apparently a popular venue not just for racing but for movie shoots, also playing host to the original *Gone in 60 Seconds*, *A Very Brady Christmas* and a few of the Frankie and Annette movies. Sadly we'd be better off watching any of them than *Mabel's Busy Day*.

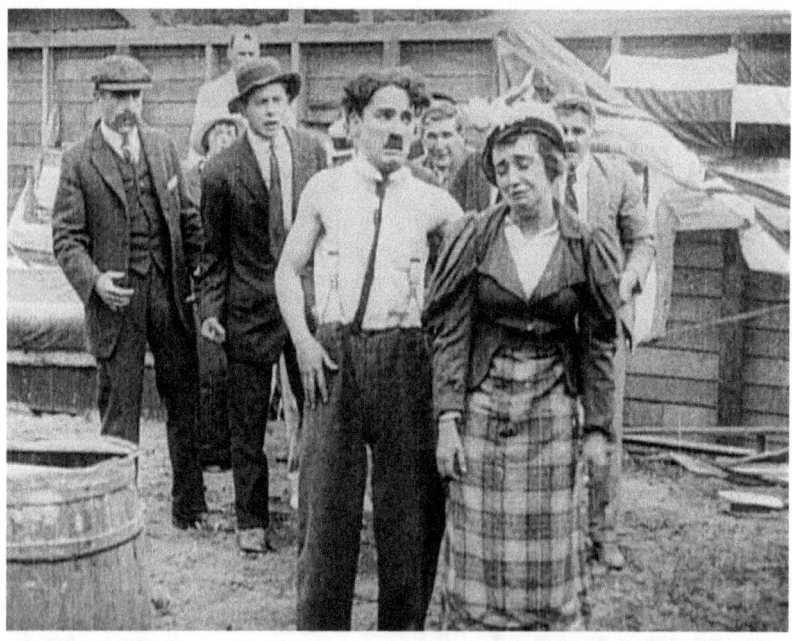

Charlie Chaplin Centennial: Keystone

161

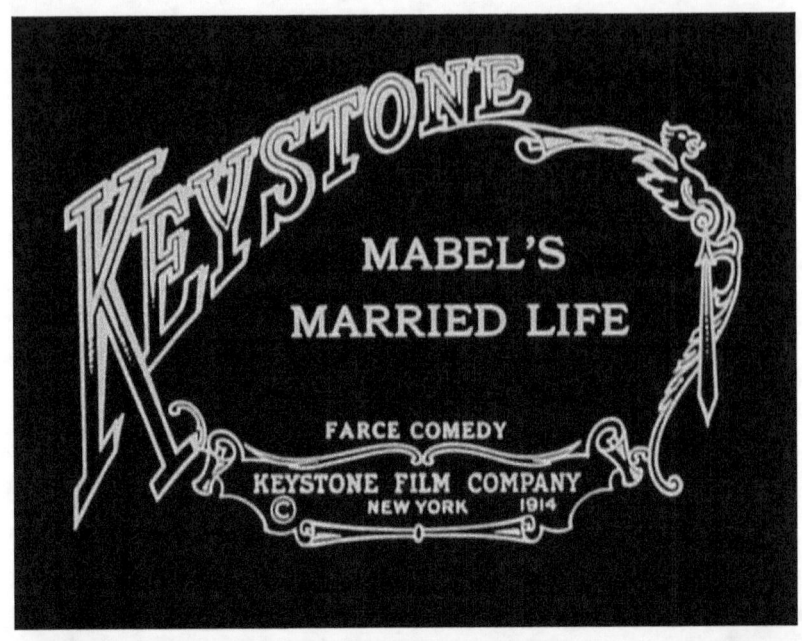

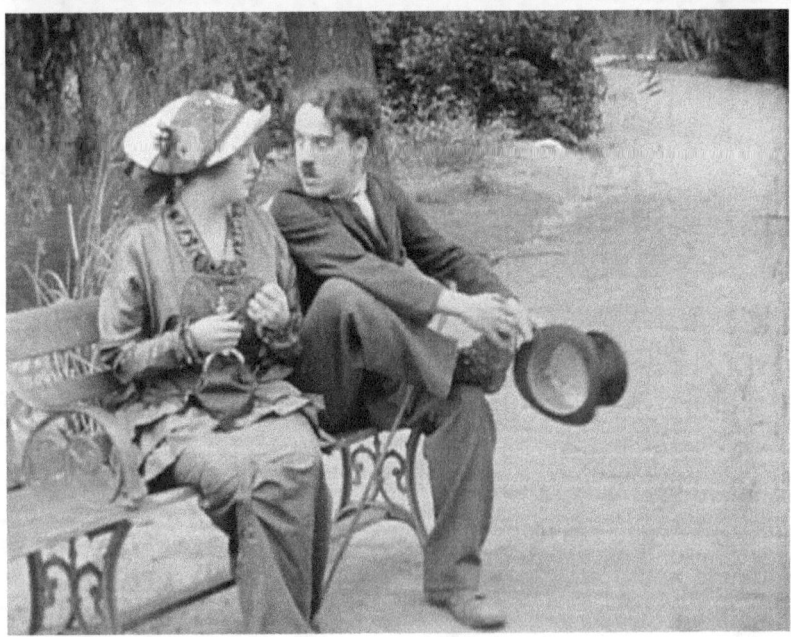

Mabel's Married Life

20th June, 1914

Director: Mack Sennett (or Charles Chaplin)
Writers: Charles Chaplin and Mabel Normand
Stars: Charles Chaplin, Mabel Normand and Mack Swain

Mabel's Married Life arrived at the point where Chaplin was finally beginning to gain a semblance of control over his work. How much, however, is open to debate.

Most authorities list Mack Sennett as the film's director, thus marking the last time Chaplin would appear in a short film that he didn't direct himself, while others, like the British Film Institute, claim that it was Chaplin himself in the director's chair. Chaplin's handwritten filmography, reproduced in image form in David Robinson's biography, *Chaplin: His Life and Art*, lists it as "my own", though, as with *Twenty Minutes of Love*, his first possible foray into direction, this could well mean that he contributed to it as a writer rather than a director; certainly there's no argument that he wrote this with Mabel Normand. There's also little dispute that he took over as his own director as of his next short, *Laughing Gas*, and his only movies still to come which he didn't direct himself are *Tillie's Punctured Romance*, the one feature he made at Keystone, and a few odd others later on, like *Camille* or *Souls for Sale*, which contained Chaplin cameos or guest appearances rather than leading roles.

Certainly this feels far more like a Chaplin film than a Sennett film, because the pace is surely the slowest of any of his twenty pictures thus far and the comedy is light enough that it almost plays out as a drama for much of the running time.

It's firmly rooted in the Keystone standards, but they're often either ignored as mere background or approached from a slightly different way to usual. As Jeffrey Vance highlights in *Chaplin: Genius of the Cinema*, it's yet another Keystone short to be predominantly shot in Echo Park, located only five blocks south of their studios in Edendale, but, however close folk get at points, not one of them ends up in the Echo Park Lake. Another Keystone standard, the kick in the ass, is stunningly ineffective in this picture, Mack Swain able to shrug off Chaplin's very best efforts to distract and provoke him. Mabel Normand gets to spit on her hands and knuckle up and Chaplin gets to visit a bar, getting drunk yet again. He was a dab hand at this but it does start getting tiring after so many close repetitions.

He clearly plays the Little Tramp here, though his usual bowler is swapped out for a battered top hat, but the internal consistency seems a little lost. He's in his regular tight coat, dilapidated shoes and an even more baggy pair of trousers than usual, but he's living in what appears to be decent accommodation and he's married to the title character played by Mabel Normand. Harry McCoy, who played Mabel's boyfriend or husband in a number of 1914 pictures at Keystone, as early as *Mabel's Strange Predicament*, Chaplin's third picture, is sidelined into a bit part as just a man in the bar which Charlie frequents.

Putting Charlie and Mabel together as man and wife on screen isn't merely a combination of the two biggest draws at Keystone, it was also a counter to the antagonism of their last picture together, *Mabel's Busy Day*, in which Charlie destroyed poor Mabel and her fledgling business with deliberate intent. Surprisingly, they're not a bickering couple here. They don't have a happy relationship either, given Charlie's fondness for the bottle, but it's one that he's willing to fight for.

And it certainly seems like he needs to. His opponent here, yet again, is Mack Swain, credited to posterity as "Sporty Ladykiller", which means that he carries a tennis racket and hits on Mabel, even though his own wife is mere yards away on a different Echo Park bench. In fact he rather emphatically hits on Mabel, not remotely taking no for an answer, and, with Charlie getting drunk in a nearby bar, there's apparently not a soul to stop him.

The comedy arrives when Charlie leaves the bar, notices what's going on and drunkenly attempts to do something about it. Here's the inevitable ass kicking scene, because Swain just shrugs him off, using his sheer bulk to keep him away from Mabel. Charlie can't get round him, so resorts to punching, then kicking him in the ass, only to be completely ignored for his troubles.

This isn't a bad scene, because it tries to do something a little different from the norm, even if it's otherwise so reminiscent of scenes in a whole host of other Keystone films of the era. It does show a little imagination, at least.

Light drama then takes over from comedy for quite a while, with laughs present but notably milder than usual, even if we factor in Chaplin's continual attempts to ratchet down the more emphatic slapstick for which Keystone was justly known and introduce more subtle character-infused humour in its place. Eventually though, we find Charlie teaming up with Sporty Ladykiller's wife to rescue Mabel from his clutches.

Whether Swain's screen wife is played by Eva Nelson or Alice Howell, it's certainly clear to everyone involved that she's much more capable of dealing with the situation than Charlie the Little Drunk Tramp. This surely resonates in Mabel's mind, so she buys the boxing dummy on display in front of a sporting goods store to stir things up later.

While we can hardly expect the Keystone prop department to throw things out after a single use, this is clearly the very same boxing dummy that audiences saw Roscoe Arbuckle take on only nine days earlier in *The Knockout*. They could at least have put it in a

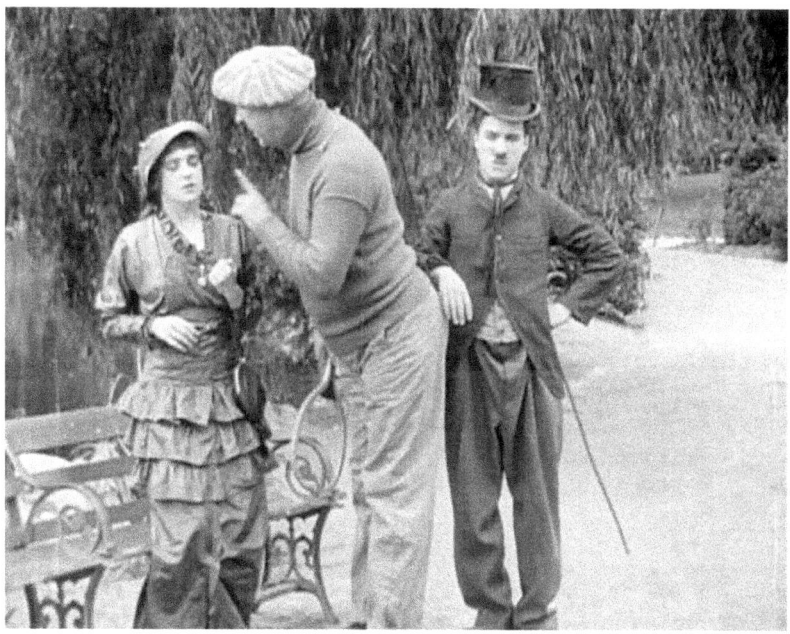

different turtleneck or perhaps turned down the collar.

Given that Charlie has trouble getting through the bar's swinging door, in yet another recurring Keystone gag, it'll be no surprise to figure out what happens next. Yes, he's as drunk as a skunk by the time he gets in and Mabel's already in bed. Perhaps he thought the onions he stole from the bar were a bunch of flowers, but he gets waylaid by the boxing dummy, which... and suspend your disbelief here... he mistakes for Sporty Ladykiller, who surely must have followed her home to stand like a sentinel just inside their front door. I don't want to fall into the black hole of arguing against drunken logic, but this is a stretch.

It's also hardly the most surprising set up for a set of gags, not one moment after she bought the dummy coming as anything close to unexpected, but Chaplin and Normand were both consummate professionals and they played it all out with the sort of pristine timing required. It's a shame they didn't get a better scene to end the picture, which marked the last time they'd act together in a film carrying the name of Mabel's regular character. Otherwise they had a couple of shorts and a feature together still to come.

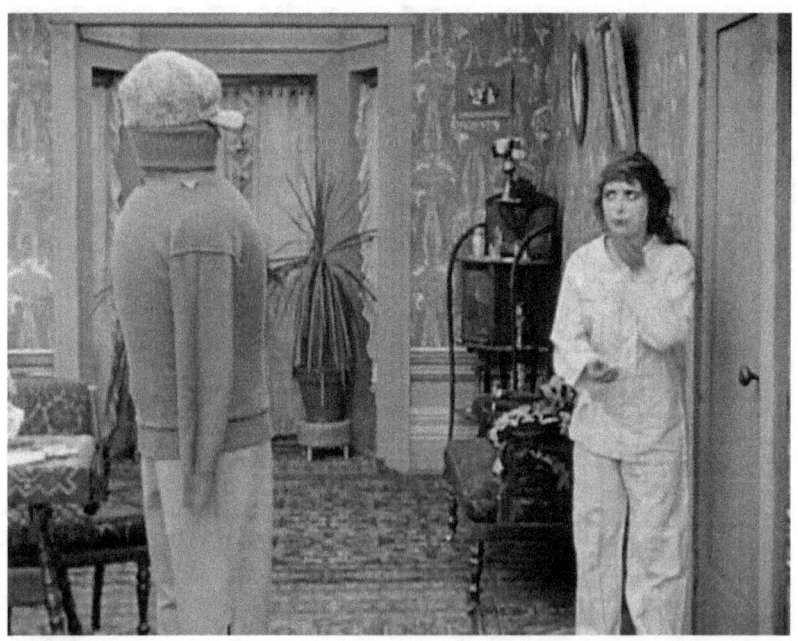

It's telling that there's so little to say about *Mabel's Married Life*. Beyond being made at a rather crucial point in Chaplin's career, it's notably unworthy of note.

Chaplin is capable, but he'd played a drunk so often thus far that we can't fail to realise how routine this was for him. Normand is capable too, especially late in the film, but is given next to nothing to do. She'd taken a surprising back seat to Chaplin from the first moment they appeared in film together, but at least she tried to steal her films back early on. By this point, she'd apparently decided it wasn't worth the fight and let him run the show. She plays her few scenes without him well, but not quite so well as to elevate the film. Mack Swain is on lecherous autopilot and his wife is precisely the crotchetty old spouse that might just be able to have him under her thumb, however large he is. The only other character who gets a moment to shine is a supposed friend who torments Charlie in the bar. He's played by Hank Mann, who, years later, would play a far more memorable foil for Chaplin in the boxing ring in *City Lights*.

Perhaps *Mabel's Married Life* suffered from the sheer speed at which folk were working in mid-1914. After wrapping *Caught in the Rain* on 13th April, Chaplin went straight into work on Keystone's comedy feature, *Tillie's Punctured Romance*, which shot from 14th April to 9th June. He didn't work on a short for a month, then caught up with a vengeance by shooting three pictures in a mere nine days in May: *The Fatal Mallet* from the 10th to the 12th, then *Her Friend the Bandit* and *The Knockout* back to back between the 11th and the 18th. Work began on *Mabel's Busy Day* on the 17th and continued until the 26th. It looks like he took a breather for a few days and then knocked out *Mabel's Married Life* between the 30th and 2nd June, a four day shoot.

In all, five Chaplin pictures reached cinema screens in under three weeks in June, surely an unimaginable pace to us with a century of hindsight. By comparison, there would only be a single one in July, before another five arrived in August, though spread out at least across the entire month from the 1st to the 31st.

No wonder this was hardly a stellar period in Chaplin's career. After a few poor early pictures as he found his feet, he settled into a solid routine of capable comedies that occasionally warranted more attention, like *A Film Johnnie*, *The Star Boarder* or *Caught in the Rain*. However, his previous film, *Mabel's Busy Day*, was surely the weakest he'd made thus far and this is almost the epitome of an OK movie, probably the most forgettable film he'd made yet.

It's notable that this down period corresponds with the presence of studio boss Mack Sennett in the director's chair. However badly Chaplin got on with George "Pop" Nichols, he was able to find a way to experiment in the films he directed. Under Sennett, his only experimentation was to appear in drag in *A Busy Day*, though we don't have *Her Friend the Bandit* to review.

So *Mabel's Married Life* is only notable as a marker at the end of the first phase of Chaplin's career, in which he was directed by others. As of his next picture, *Laughing Gas*, he'd begin to have the creative control he had fought so long for and the list of factors that flavour our understanding of his progression through a year at Keystone become less important.

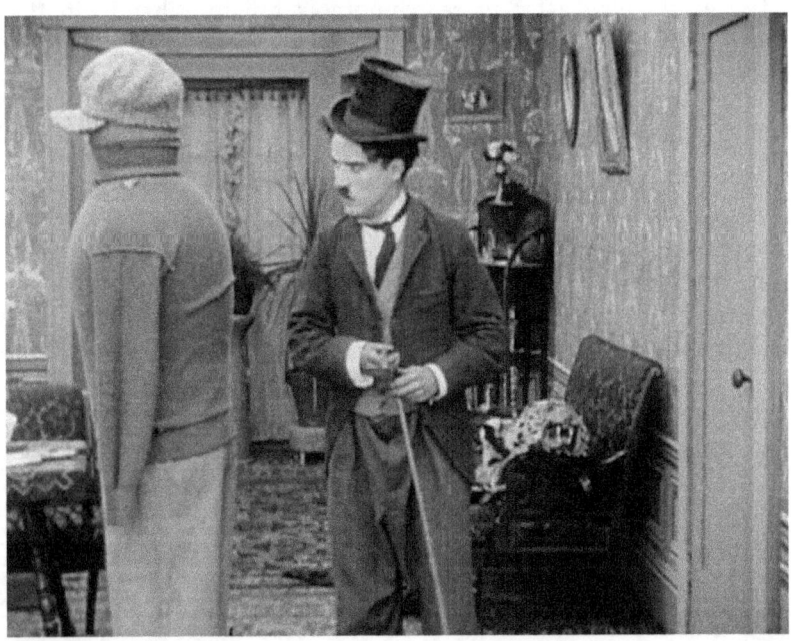

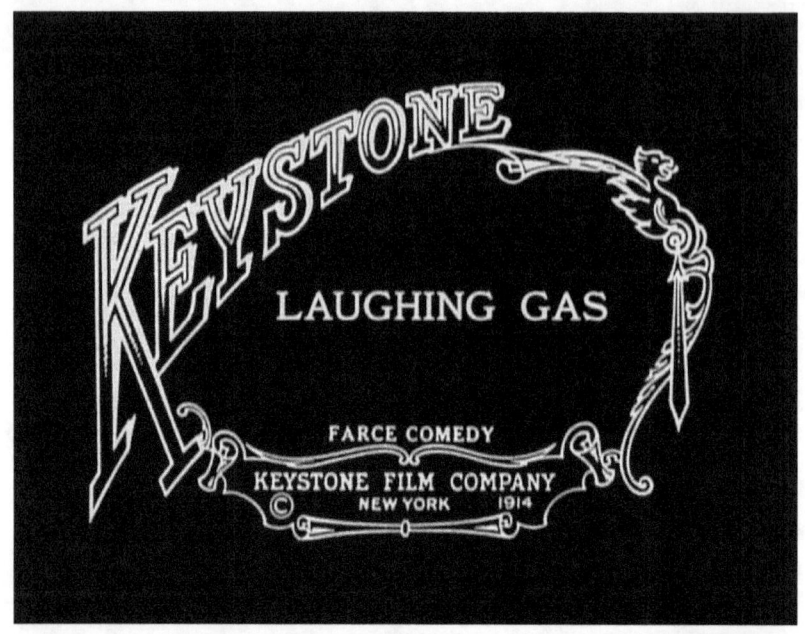

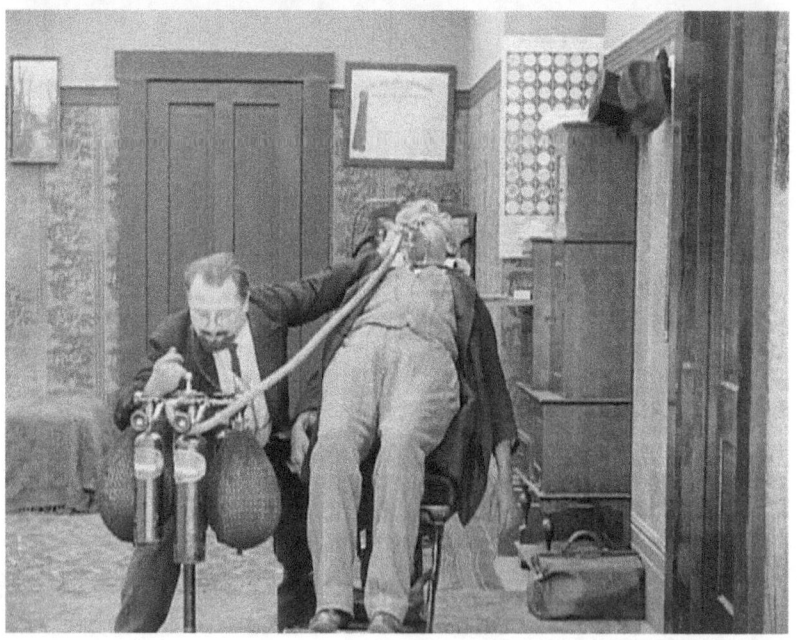

Laughing Gas
9th July, 1914

Director: Charles Chaplin
Writer: Charles Chaplin
Star: Charles Chaplin

However Chaplin experts decide to divide up his early pictures into sections, and there are more than a few ways to do that when over half of them are clearly a first something or other, we can't avoid this one being a pivotal moment of change, possibly the most important picture he made after his first one and his first as the Little Tramp.

His first twenty shorts were directed by a variety of directors and written by a variety of writers, with debate open as to the size and quality of Chaplin's off-screen contributions. He did contribute to his films from the beginning but often not much and what he did bring to the table didn't always make it into the finished product. It took him a dozen films to get the chance to sit in the director's chair, on *Twenty Minutes of Love*, but he had to share that honour with Joseph Maddern. He flew solo on short number fourteen, *Caught in the Rain*, but then Mack Sennett stepped in to direct the next half a dozen. From *Laughing Gas* on though, he would never be directed by anyone else on a short film again.

Already established as an actor and screen comedian, this could be seen as his coming of age picture as a filmmaker, appropriately given that it was his 21st. The credits here start to mirror what we might expect of a Chaplin film, or at least they would if Keystone pictures had credits in 1914. It was directed by Chaplin, written by Chaplin and starring Chaplin, with nobody else really getting much of a look in. While the cast does include actors like Mack Swain and Slim Summerville, both regular names at Keystone, they're firmly relegated to minor roles, as indeed is everyone else. Having played second fiddle in his last three pictures, once to Roscoe Arbuckle and twice to Mabel Normand, there's no mistaking who the star of this movie is, from the very moment Chaplin, in familiar tramp attire, swaggers into Dr. Pain's dental surgery and exudes authority, taking off his hat and gloves as if he expects a servant to put them away for him. Surely he's Dr. Pain himself! No, that's just a setup; Chaplin is playing with us from moment one.

It turns out that he's merely an assistant and not the only one either, as there's another in the back room waiting for him.

I'm not sure quite what this fellow is supposed to be, but if it wasn't for a prominent and strong moustache, I wouldn't have said he had made it to his teenage years yet. Chaplin wasn't a tall man, only a mere 5' 5", but he towers over his fellow assistant by a foot or so. Either the actor, who seems to be a Joseph Sutherland in what may well be his only appearance on screen, was either of seriously diminutive height (though perfectly proportioned with it) or he's really a young lad transparently pretending to be an adult for some reason or other that is never explained.

Your guess is as good as mine, but it seems strange in the cruel days of slapstick comedy that Keystone would not take advantage of attributes so apparent and work them into the script. Physical uniqueness was always highlighted; that's why actors like Arbuckle, Summerville and Swain were so important to the studio: as fat, thin

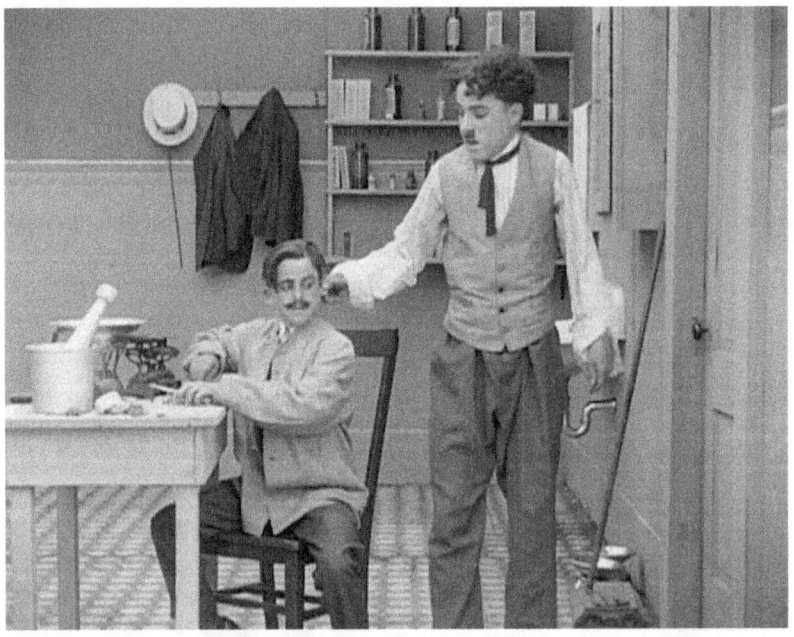

and large actors respectively. Talent was a bonus, but appearance was primary.

Whatever the explanation, we're certainly kept on the hop as *Laughing Gas* gets moving and get moving we do. While the camera is still a static creature and the editing hardly imaginative, this is a smooth ride throughout. Even when chaos erupts towards the end, as was almost compulsory at this point in time, we watch it unfold in a smooth and controlled manner.

While we're used to wild and unpredictable jumps in pictures of this age, it's easy to assume that they were always due to poor quality public domain prints, which had frames or even entire reels missing. However, watching the remastered versions of Chaplin's films at Keystone, even factoring in that we still may not have every single frame, highlights that sometimes jumps were there all along because editing wasn't close to being the art that it would become.

I wonder how much of this was due to Chaplin, who talked in his autobiography about the "primary rules", that "if one exited right from a scene, one came in left in the next scene" and so on. He mentions these before philosophy about camera placement that he learned as he went, so he's treating these as gimmes. Yet his earlier films don't always follow those gimmes, suggesting that some crew members may not have been aware of them or may not have cared enough to follow them.

That's not to suggest that there aren't technical difficulties even here, because there are. Dr. Pain's lobby was constructed cheaply even for a Keystone set, because the books are clearly painted onto what aims to pass for a bookcase and so is the mantel clock on top of it. The Rasputin beard on one patient is more outrageously fake than even the norm at this studio which was renowned for its fake facial hair.

However, there's less to obviously stand out as problematic here and more that just moves on so smoothly that we wonder why this wasn't standing operating procedure for Keystone up until this point. Even Chaplin's moves are clearly getting slicker, his famous stagger as he rounds a corner or bounces to a stop is better and used more here than previously. The inevitable pratfalls as people push others over are handled efficiently, even when there's a foot difference between assistants. Sutherland does well to push Chaplin over, just as Chaplin does well not to castrate the much taller Mack Swain when kicking him in the belly.

Eventually the real dentist shows up, of course, in the form of German-born Fritz Schade in a top hat and monocle and with the overdone acting style that might suggest. This was his first Chaplin picture, though he'd show up in eight of the remaining fifteen. He had a presence to him that lent itself to certain types, but even a quick glance at the variety of roles he racked up between 1913 and 1918 show that he was a versatile addition to the Keystone roster.

It's here that we get down to the sort of dental shenanigans we might have expected from the outset. I expected a lot more of this than we get, as the story is a restless creature that constantly adds new elements without forgetting what it is. Chaplin's script is much more ambitious than the one he wrote for *Caught in the Rain*; that felt like a frantic sprint through every stock situation he'd seen by that point, while this is a more controlled stride through scenarios familiar or not. The familiar sections are generally the more manic ones, while the sensitive ones feel newer.

What's more, *Caught in the Rain* was a very traditional picture in that the inspirations were all taken from previous pictures. Here, there are other sources, as Jeffrey Vance ably highlights in *Chaplin: Genius of the Cinema*.

One key influence was a vaudeville sketch named *The Dentist* that Chaplin knew well from his time on stage with Fred Karno, though he never performed it himself. Of course even this was far from original; as Vance points out, "dentistry and tooth extraction have been a source of humor since the *commedia dell'arte*."

A further influence was personal, as Chaplin apparently had a bee in his bonnet about dentists; in his later years, his family would struggle to convince him to visit them. These sources, combined with much more traditional movie slapstick and ideas that earlier directors might have jettisoned, show that Chaplin was far more confident in his writing than he was only a couple of months earlier when scripting *Caught in the Rain*. Of course, this bodes well for the films he was yet to make at Keystone; let's see how much he grows before he leaves.

The best moments in the film are the ones that revolve around women, unsurprisingly from what we now know about Chaplin's predilections. Sure, he has fun knocking people over and stepping over them, and he gets a good scene with an anaesthetised patient and a mallet, initially using it to wake him up and then to knock him back out again, but it's the scenes with girls that shine the brightest.

One sees him follow a pretty young woman on the street, who he doesn't yet know is his boss's wife, only to slip and rip her dress off on the steps to a building. Alice Howell shines in this physical role, making it no shock to find that no less a comedic name than Stan Laurel listed her as one of the ten greatest screen comediennes. Another strong scene has Charlie flirting up a storm with a patient played by Helen Carruthers, whose twenty-one films in 1914 and 1915 include a dozen with Chaplin. He uses an dental extraction tool on her nose to turn her head towards his so he can steal a peck or two. It's a huge contrast with the scene where he uses it for its intended purpose, naturally with much more violence.

While this is still formative Chaplin, it may well mark the point where he started to benefit from a little more creative freedom than he had experienced previously. There's certainly some classic

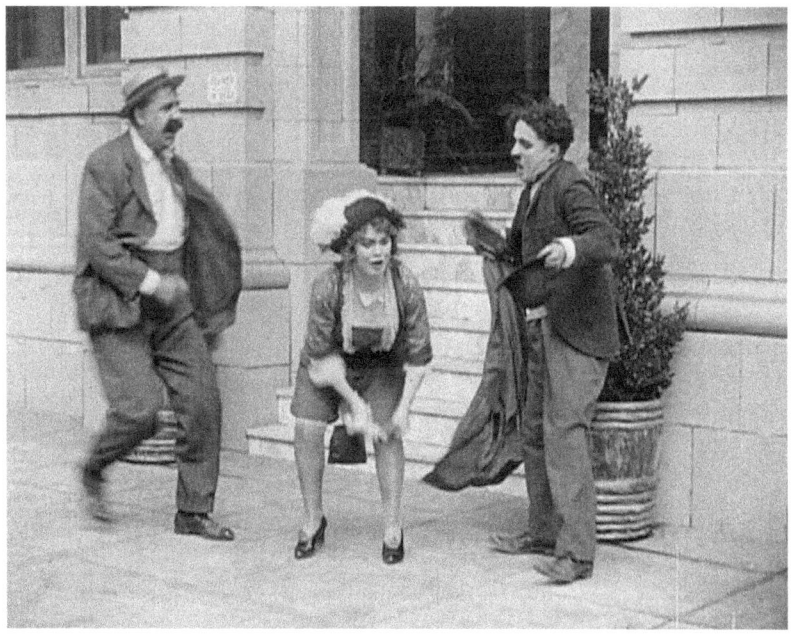

Charlie in here, just packed in tight like sardines with more blatant and traditional material.

Even there I wonder about how some of these scenes were shot. There had been brick throwing battles in a few of Chaplin's earlier pictures, such as *Caught in a Cabaret* and especially *The Fatal Mallet* and *The Knockout*, but as brutal as those battles often are, we don't tend to see blood or damage. Here, with only two bricks thrown, we get teeth conspicuously knocked out of two different faces.

Sure, this is a short comedy set in a dentist's office, so any way in which to damage a tooth is a good one, but it's still a new edge to an old gag and when you work through whole batches of Keystone pictures, a new edge is always a good edge because the repetition can be mind-numbing.

For all its faults, *Laughing Gas* feels somewhat refreshing. Perhaps that's underlined by the scene with Charlie on top of a patient in the chair, yanking a tooth out with force. It's the most expected scene in the movie, but its true value arrives when we realise that it's merely a minor moment.

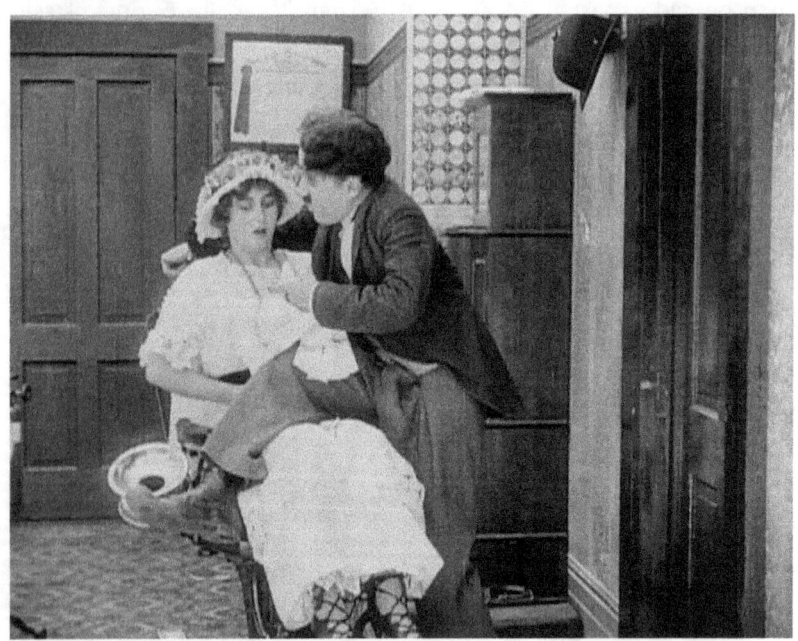

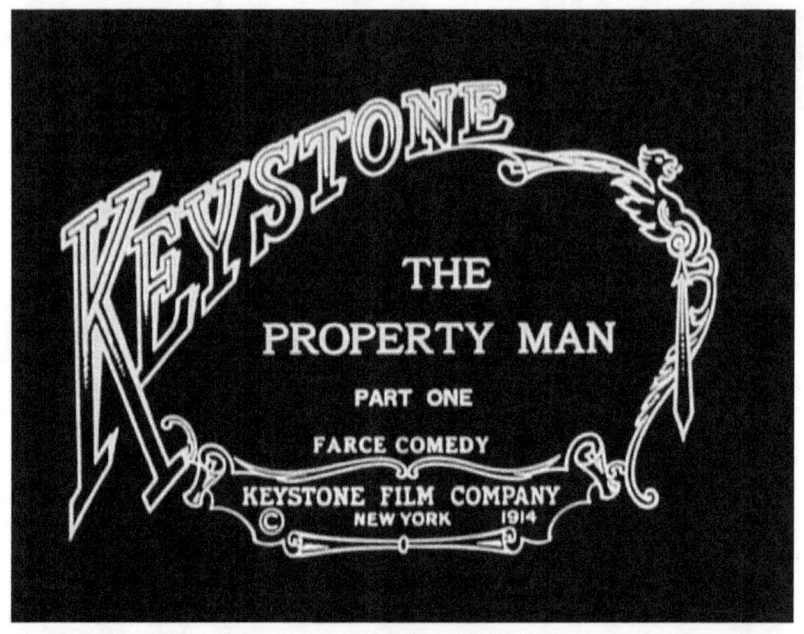

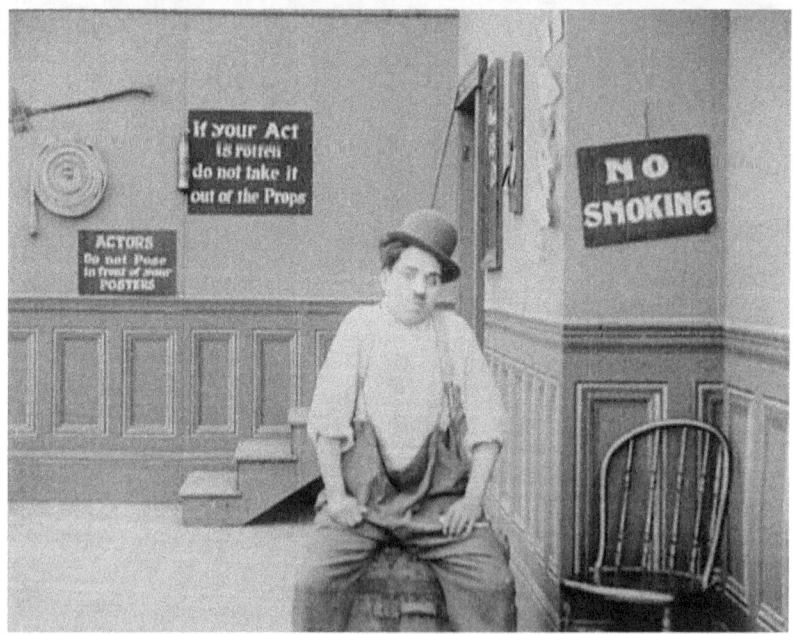

The Property Man
1st August, 1914

Director: Charles Chaplin
Writer: Charles Chaplin
Star: Charles Chaplin

Working through all Chaplin's 1914 films on the days they were originally released ably highlighted just how many of them there were. Each time I reviewed one, my eye was already on the next as it was never far away. It was easy to think back to 1914, as the original audiences saw these films for the first time, watching this funny new face show up time and time again to establish a hold.

His first three films arrived on cinema screens in the span of only eight days and, by 20th June, no less than twenty Chaplin films had been released. Even with an uncharacteristic 25 day gap between *A Busy Day* and *The Fatal Mallet*, that averages out to one picture every 6.9 days, an output faster than a weekly television show today.

Yet his nascent career as a film director started out much more slowly; *Laughing Gas* was released 19 days after *Mabel's Married Life* and *The Property Man* didn't show up for another 23. For the first time in this entire project, his previous picture wasn't fresh in my mind as I watched the new one. At this speed, life started to get in the way.

Part of the reason for this delay is that, while most of Chaplin's earlier films were one reelers that took a week to put together, this was a two reeler that ran 24 minutes and took 16 days to shoot. It's not tough to figure out why, though, as this must have felt like a particularly important movie to him. Certainly, to our century of hindsight, it points firmly towards the future far better than any of the pictures he'd made thus far, but it's also fundamentally rooted in his music hall past, most obviously the famous *Mumming Birds* sketch that he had performed on stage with Fred Karno's London Comedians, the very one that impressed Mack Sennett and Mabel Normand enough to hire him to replace Ford Sterling at Keystone.

The part he played in *Mumming Birds* strongly influenced the characters he would play at Keystone, which is why he shows up

179

drunk so often in 1914. However, *The Property Man* is sourced less from the character he plays in *Mumming Birds* and more from the actual sketch itself.

Mumming Birds apparently grew out of a comedy that had been written to entertain the Shah of Persia when he visited London in 1903, imaginatively titled *Entertaining the Shah*. It reached the music hall stage almost a year later, its name progressing within a couple of months from *Twice Nightly* through *A Stage Upon a Stage* to *The Mumming Birds*. It was still being performed on stage in the forties, billed as "Fred Karno's Greatest Comedy" with the boastful tagline, "The show that made Charlie Chaplin and Laurel & Hardy", as both Chaplin and Stan Laurel had played parts in it to great acclaim.

The concept is one that we would describe as "meta" today, as the curtain would rise to show another stage, with some of the cast taking the role of players and others audience members. In the box to the left would be a public schoolboy and his guardian, with "a drunken swell" on the right, Chaplin's preferred role. A string of performers, all of them incompetent, attempt to do their thing but are constantly interrupted by the audience on stage in increasingly chaotic ways.

No wonder Sennett was hooked when he saw it under its touring title of *A Night in an English Music Hall*, as it sounds like a Keystone picture on stage. Of course, before hiring Chaplin away from Karno, Keystone would never have produced a film version quite like this; *The Property Man* has Chaplin's name all over it, even more here as a writer than as an actor or director, because for him it was never just about a set of gags leading up to chaos, though they do reach that standard goal; it's about how those gags build and feed into others, it's about how better defined characters can render those gags still funnier and it's about how a stronger setting can ground the whole thing and ratched up the comedy even further. While it's far from Chaplin's best picture, it's arguably his best thus far because it's consistent and interwoven. *A Film Johnnie*, *The Star Boarder* and *Caught in the Rain* hinted at this but were each more Keystone than Chaplin. This, finally, is the other way around.

While *The Property Man* is clearly sourced from *Mumming Birds*, it's no direct adaptation. We do watch an audience watching an inept set of vaudeville acts, but the fun is less in their interactions with it and more in how the property man leads the troupe into chaos.

He's played by Chaplin, of course, who is the lowest rung on this ladder except one, and that pecking order is established very quickly. In fact, that's the very basis of this picture, differences in status always serving as a clear parallel to the class differences so often explored in British comedy and drama.

Surely this is how Chaplin expected to find sympathy for his character, though the full century since its release has rendered him rather more unsympathetic. Status is everything here. When a couple of new artistes arrive, he mostly ignores them just because they're new and so his status in comparison to theirs hasn't yet been established. He highlights the "No Smoking" sign, though he's smoking a pipe himself. Yet he doesn't dare do the same thing to the strongman, an established opponent, so he flips the sign over instead.

In turn, this lazy, uncaring and sadistic property man takes out his frustrations on the only character who is lower than him. That's his assistant, who Josef Swickard, for comedic emphasis, depicts as an old man with a long beard who has to walk with the assistance of

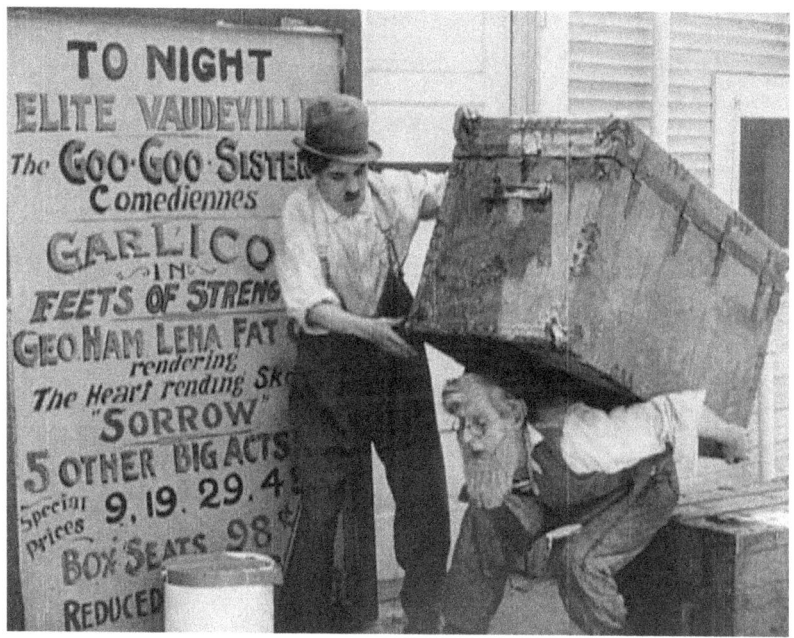

a cane, even when carrying heavy trunks on his back.

Many have called this picture out as an especially cruel one in Chaplin's filmography, starting with *Motion Picture World*, when reviewing the film in 1914. "There is some brutality in this picture," said their critic, "and we can't help feeling this is reprehensible. What human being can see an old man kicked in the face and count it fun?"

I don't buy this take, as the film's tone is notably less cruel than *Mabel's Busy Day* and all the cruelty does serve a firm purpose. Details are either individual components of more substantial gags or help to establish the pecking order upon which all interaction is based. Even those kicks, while admittedly cruel, enforce rather than damage. This old man seems as indestructible as a cartoon which, of course, as a character in a slapstick short, he's a forerunner to.

The scene most frequently called out for criticism finds the old assistant stuck under a particularly heavy trunk that he's carried downstairs. With the exception of a couple of those feet to the face, I found this a great example of an effective gag built out of equally effective smaller ones.

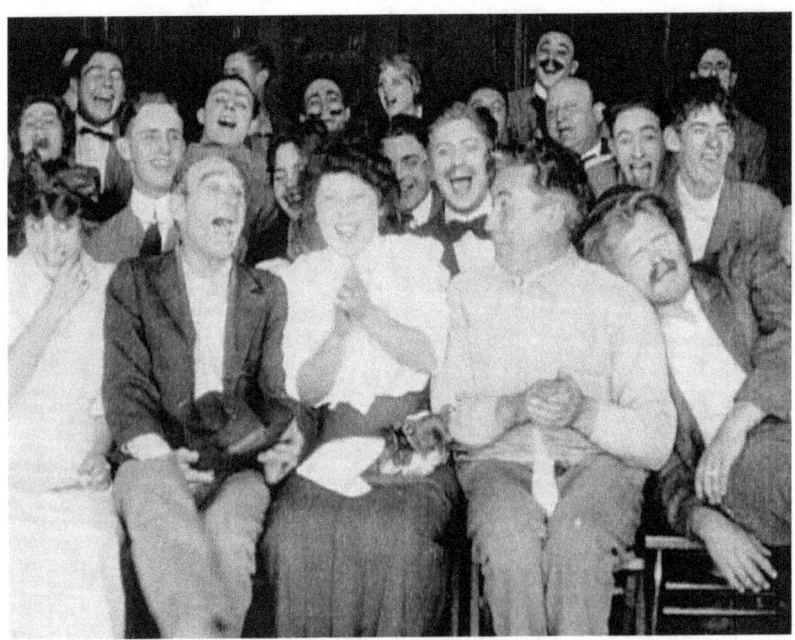

When it happens, Charlie's first act is to strike a match on the trunk in order to relight his pipe, then he clambers on top of it in an attempt to lever it free, though naturally he only makes the situation worse. Getting nowhere, he breaks off at the call of the strongman's wife, with whom he happily flirts for a while. Soon most of the cast are involved in trying to free the old man, all of them getting precisely nowhere until the strongman is called. He takes it as yet another opportunity to show off, easily doing alone what half a dozen couldn't do together, thus reaffirming his position at the very top of the pecking order. Swickard, on the other hand, merely portrays the character at the bottom of it, so any cruelty is really rooted in the inequality of the class struggle.

Even when we get past pre-show shenanigans and the so-called "Elite Vaudeville" performance begins, everything can be easily interpreted as depicting the lower class, in the form of Charlie the property man getting one over on the upper class, in the form of the performers who have more status than him.

The audience loved it, perhaps because they were predominantly made up of the lower class, as is ably depicted in the scenes involving the audience watching the performance. It may never have been a deliberate act on Chaplin's part, but it's telling today that the audience we see in the film is comprised of the old guard at Keystone. That's Mack Sennett himself in the front row, with his goofy grin, and a drunken Harry McCoy frequently asleep on his shoulder, while Slim Summerville and Chester Conklin are there as well. As with *Mumming Birds*, there's a lot of fun in seeing the audience's reaction to bad vaudeville performances or to Charlie inadvertently becoming part of the show, causing chaos or ogling the dancing girls.

While class was clearly the dominant theme of *The Property Man*, there's also a sense of time that comes through hindsight. It's a timely film for reasons beyond it being his first two reeler as a director and the proof that his work was beginning to benefit from the creative freedom that he began to find with his previous film, *Laughing Gas*.

Music hall, or vaudeville in the States, had been the dominant form of entertainment for the masses since the 1830s and, while it would fall into the shadow of cinema and eventually television, it was about to reach its peak of popularity. The First World War broke out on 28th July, 1914, only four days before the release of *The Property Man*, and the music halls would serve as a rallying point for public support and a massively effective tool for the war effort, recruiting many through patriotic songs like 1914's *Keep the Home Fires Burning*. Chaplin wasn't as vocal about the conflict as he would be as the Second World War loomed. "Everyone thought it would be over in six months," he wrote in his biography.

Ironically, given that Chaplin came from music hall and was hired out of vaudeville by Sennett to become his new star at Keystone, his rise in cinema was mirrored by the decline of the music halls and the two ended relatively close together. It has been said that music hall ended with the death of Max Miller in 1963; at that time, Chaplin only had one more film in him, *The Countess of Hong Kong*, made in exile from the U.S. and released in 1967.

As this picture brings to mind an end, it also brings to mind a beginning. While the finalé, in which the property man turns a firehose on both the stage and its audience, was set up for comedic effect, it surely has meaning. The hose is the great leveller, wiping out every difference in status and leaving Charlie firmly in charge; audiences would remember *A Film Johnnie* ending earlier in 1914 with Charlie being drenched by a firehose, so this underlines his elevation in status. It could also be read as an homage to the very first cinematic gag, in which a gardener is drenched by a hose in the Lumière brothers' film, *L'Arroseur Arrosé*, in 1895.

The Property Man was one of the few of Chaplin's 1914 films that I hadn't seen before, so the Flicker Alley box set introduced me to the film rather than just a better quality copy of it. Ironically, it's one of the least consistently restored titles in that box, as the majority looks great but a few scenes are of horrible quality. Presumably this is because it was pieced together from no less than seven different prints in three different countries, but it's annoying to see such an inconsistency. That we can complain about this highlights how absolutely this box set has spoiled us! Most of it looks great though, enough that we can read the bad spelling on a number of signs (such as "Garlico in Feets of Strength") and a host of little details that a cheap print would probably obscure, such as Harry McCoy's drunk seeing the firehose as a good opportunity to both sober up and shower.

While many seem to dismiss this film as an exercise in cruelty, I'd suggest that they read it with the appropriate subtext; if they do that, they may see *The Property Man*, as I do, as the best of Chaplin's pictures thus far.

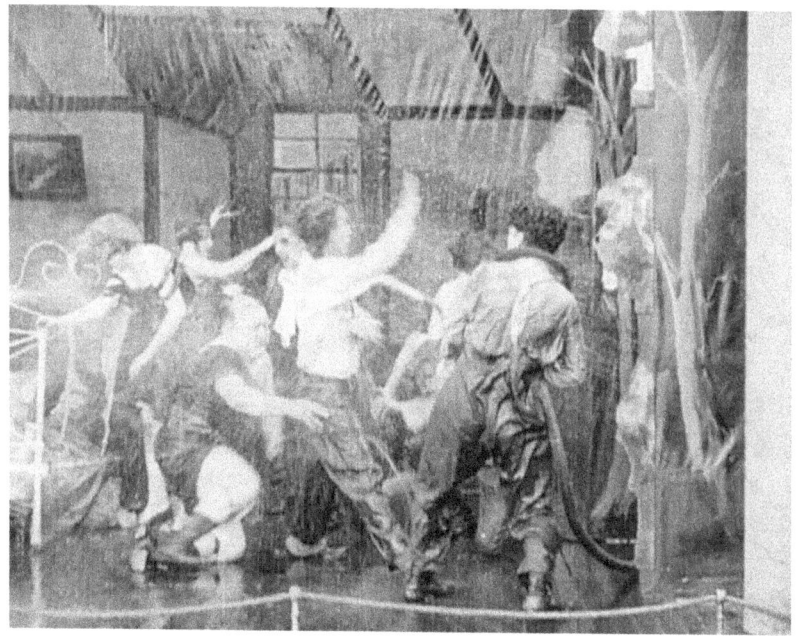

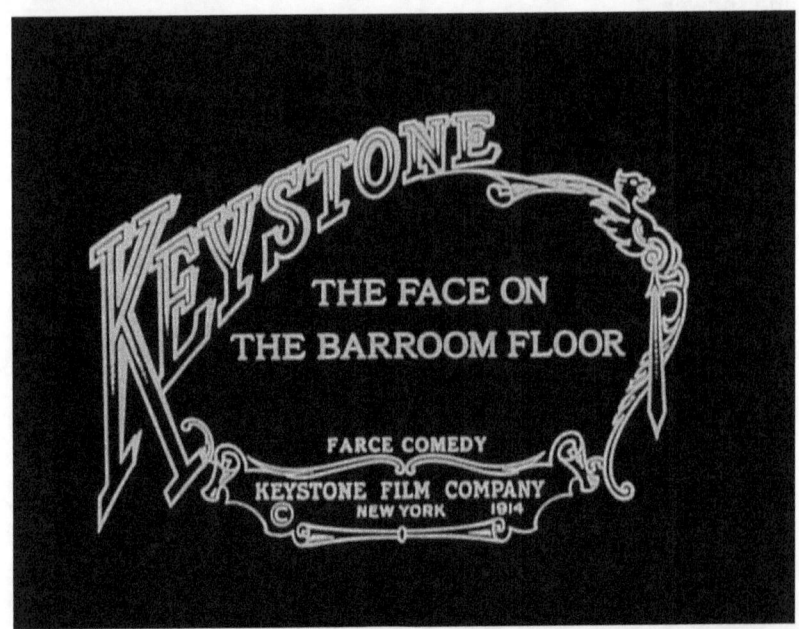

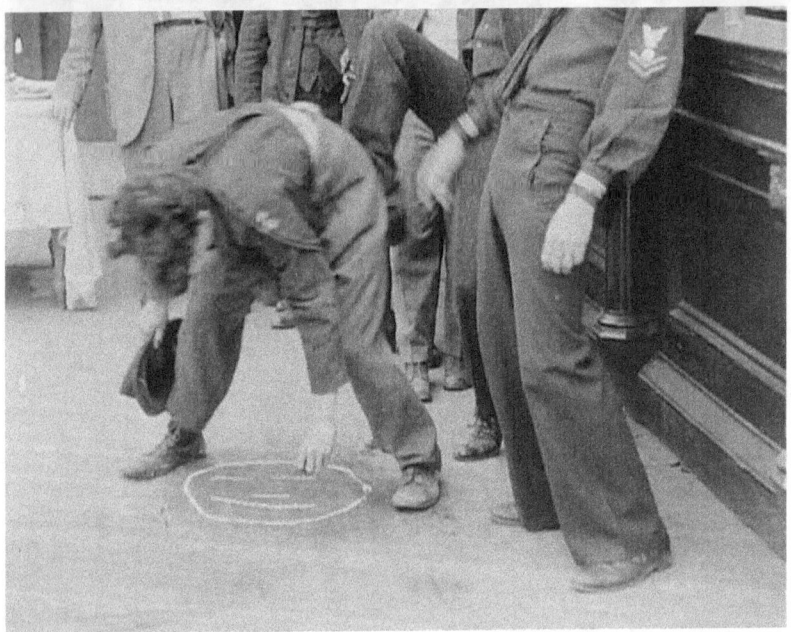

The Face on the Barroom Floor
10th August, 1914

Director: Charles Chaplin
Writer: Charles Chaplin, from the poem by Hugh Antoine d'Arcy.
Stars: Charles Chaplin, Cecile Arnold and Jess Dandy

It has to be said that *The Face on the Barroom Floor* is surely one of Chaplin's weaker films, but it does carry some interest because of what he tried to achieve. For instance, it pays homage to the time-honoured Keystone formula, but without really following it.

Sure, Chaplin plays a drunk for the umpteenth time, but this time he's one with a real story to tell for a change. Things escalate towards the end of the picture with some slapstick fighting, but it could hardly be called a standard Keystone ending, with no chase, no cops and no bricks thrown. It's all familiar material but it's still presented in a completely different way with a completely different framework.

It's a short comedy based on a poem, of all things, which is both interpreted seriously and then parodied on screen, with the very last line transformed into a gag. It seems tailor made for Chaplin's Little Tramp, but it predates him by decades. Perhaps the fact that Chaplin adapted it to the screen soon into the period at Keystone when he had relative creative freedom suggests that it may have been an inspiration for his character.

The poem is by Hugh Antoine d'Arcy, a Frenchman by birth, who came to the United States via England, where he studied at Ipswich University and became an actor at Bristol's Theatre Royal and later in London. However, he gave up acting in the States, becoming instead a business manager, taking care of other stage actors of renown. It was in 1887 that he wrote *The Face Upon the Floor*, a poem in ballad form which saw its first publication that year in the *New York Dispatch*.

While it's far from great literature, it immediately caught on, becoming the title piece in *The Face Upon the Floor and Other Ballads*, a 1890 collection of d'Arcy's work, a year after being anthologised in *Standard Recitations*. Maurice Barrymore, the patriarch of the famed

Barrymore acting dynasty, which was stage royalty at the time and is still notable today, regarded it as a favourite recitation of his. It was also promptly adapted into a song under its current title, possibly in a cunning attempt to evade d'Arcy's copyright, ironic as d'Arcy had apparently adapted his poem from one written in 1872 by John Henry Titus.

The origin of the story is utterly unproved, especially given that little snippet of provenance, but d'Arcy claimed that it originated in truth and, as we were taught in *The Man Who Shot Liberty Valance*, "when the legend becomes fact, print the legend."

As he told it, he was drinking at a bar in Manhattan called Joe Smith's when a bum entered and was promptly evicted. Feeling for the man, d'Arcy followed him to give him a drink and some money and, when he asked what the man did for a living, was told that he was an artist. Thus arrived the inspiration for the poem about an artist who turned to drink because he lost Madeline, the love of his life, to a friend who had also modelled for him.

Quite why it touched a nerve I have no idea, but it prompted a few films, with or without a hyphen in the title. Certainly at least three were based directly on the poem: the first was by Edwin S Porter at Edison's company in 1908, Chaplin's parody followed in 1914 with a lost hour long feature from John Ford arriving in 1923 at Fox. Later pictures also carried the name, but are less likely to be direct adaptations from the poem than melodramas inspired by it and its ironic adoption by prohibitionists.

Chaplin's take on the poem looks relatively standard to us today, but it was a real departure for him back in 1914. He plays the lead, of course, the drunk staggering into a bar and asking for someone to foot him a drink because he used to do that for others. In return he tells them a story, the story of how he came to be in such a state, the story that's recounted in the poem.

What's new is that we see this in flashback, an approach that Chaplin had never used before and, according to Jeffrey Vance, would only use twice more in the future, in 1918's *Shoulder Arms* and in *Limelight*, released an entire era later in 1952. Even within the flashback, things look notably different from anything seen in his Keystone pictures thus far.

We're on a static set, of course, but it's designed with far more elegance than was the norm. It's shot from an angle, for a start, and its shape doesn't follow the usual right angles. There's a staircase at the back of the room, at least some of whose stairs are real, and the set decoration is done with a careful eye.

He's a neat painter, retaining the toothbrush moustache but in a much nicer suit with a bow tie, and he's painting his lady love, Madeline, though her pose isn't what's showing up on his canvas. Then again, the addition we watch him make isn't her at all, but an imaginary urn on a stand in front of her that evolves from her curvacious rump.

There are a few minor gags here but mostly the piece is played straight. When we return to the flashback to watch him paint "a fair haired boy, a friend of mine", the humour comes less from gags and more from the fact that he's played by the rotund and far older Jess Dandy, with precious little hair at all, highlighting both that the idea that Madeline might fall for his "dreamy eyes" is at once ludicrous and still more painful for the lovestruck artist who can't help but compare himself to his former friend and wonder at how he came off second best. Cecile Arnold, who had debuted as one of

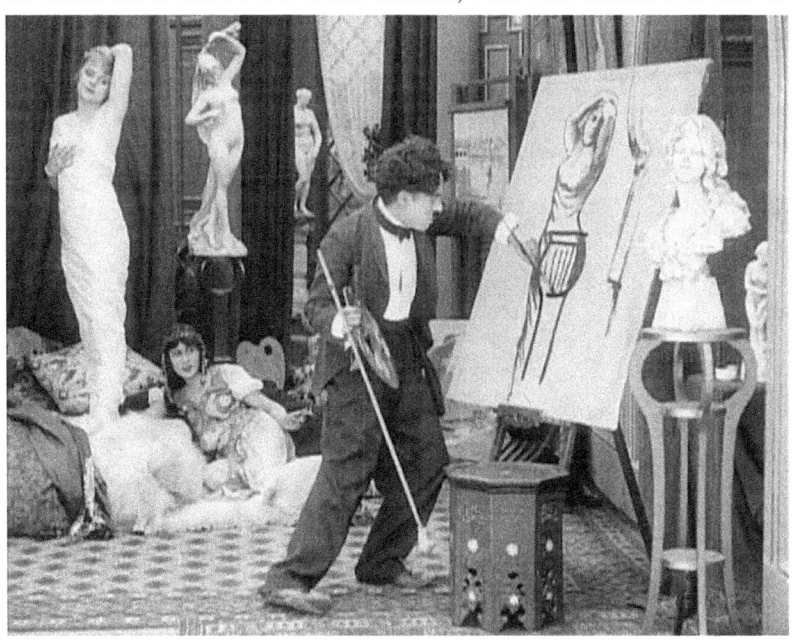

the dancers in *The Property Man* earlier in the month, is easily able to make Madeline look like a Hollywood starlet; Jess Dandy looks like a fatter Hercule Poirot.

I have to admit I got a mild kick out of Chaplin's first attempt at parody. The humour is more subtle and sophisticated than anything else Keystone was turning out, pointing the way firmly towards the future. Even though the Little Tramp is a tramp for less than half of the picture, his character is carefully designed to ensure at least as much sympathy as laughs from the audience, if not more.

While there's always another laugh about to arrive, there's a lot more drama here than we're used to in these Keystone pictures too; Chaplin was clearly experimenting to see what other emotions he could draw out of his audience. And while this never aims to be another laugh a minute slapstick riot of the sort that Mack Sennett expected, it is funny in its way.

Both the last points are highlighted by the scene we see after Madeline leaves with the "fair haired boy" and the neatly dressed artist transforms into the tramp that we know in the park that we know. Sitting on a bench, he's passed by his friend with Madeline

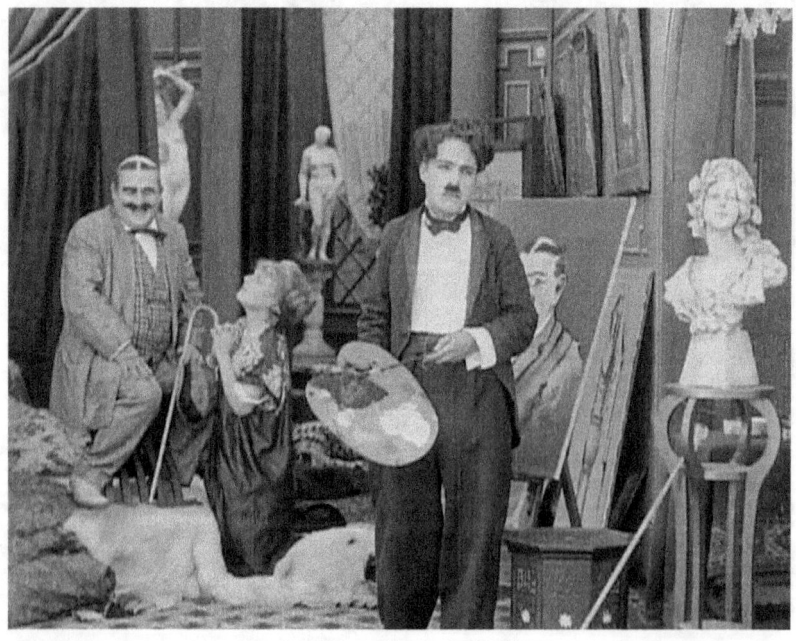

and five children in tow. He clearly thinks Charlie has it better.

And so we reach the title, at which point the parody reaches its peak. Already Chaplin has manipulated the poem for comedic effect and added extra scenes to enforce that take, but here he has a blast.

In the poem, the artist takes a piece of chalk "to sketch a face that well might buy the soul of any man" right there on the bar-room floor, but adding "another lock upon that shapely head, with a fearful shriek, he leaped and fell across the picture - dead!"

Needless to say that's not how it goes down in Chaplin's version. Finding it difficult to even reach the floor, the staggering drunk draws a face so stunningly generic that his fellow drinkers kick him out of the bar, generating at least an approximation of the riotous finalés that Sennett tended to expect at his studio. Of course, he gets back in to finish up his picture and collapse dead upon it, but Chaplin adds a further word to the last line. He's not dead, he's just dead drunk. He was always a particularly acrobatic drunk and he collapses impressively here over his childlike work.

That's about it for Chaplin's picture, certainly a more interesting entry in his Keystone filmography than an entertaining one, if one that deserves a better reputation than it's garnered.

There is a further episode in the poem's history though that has outlasted Chaplin's parody, even if the story behind it is, as always, told in many different ways. An illustrator for the *Denver Post* by the name of Herndon Davis really did paint a face on the bar-room floor of the Teller House in Central City, CO, in 1936, which promptly became a tourist attraction that in turn inspired a chamber opera by Henry Mollicone.

Some versions suggest that he did so to provide a punchline to an itinerant actor's frequent recitation of the poem there, an added joke being that it was the face of his own wife, Juanita, ironic for she was a prohibitionist. Others suggest that it was an attempt to leave something of him behind after a heated argument there with a local lady with much influence, before he left Colorado. Whatever the truth, it's sad that more see Davis's painting each year than Chaplin's film.

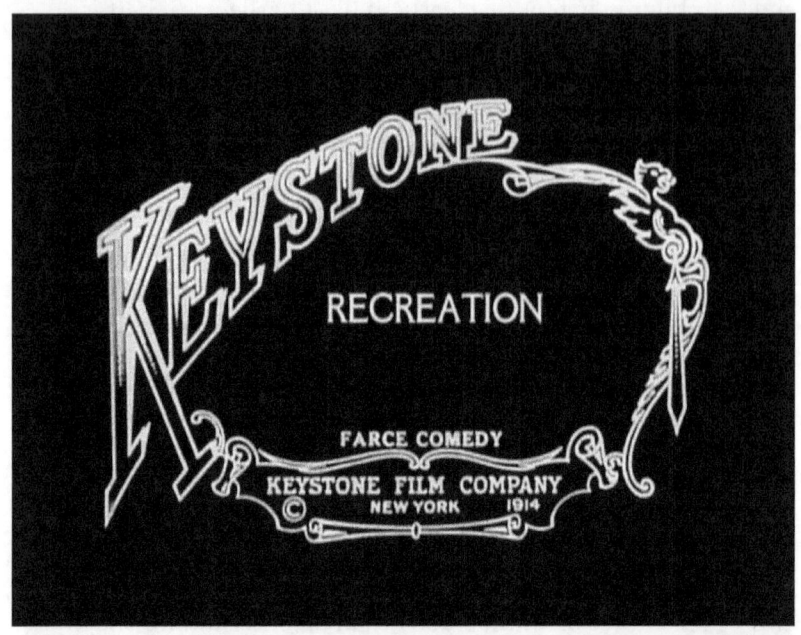

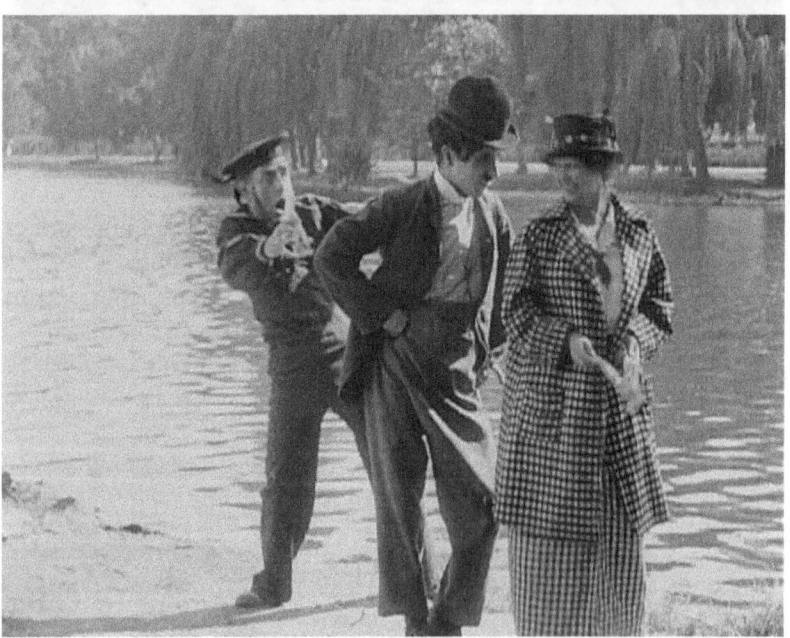

Recreation
13th August, 1914

Director: Charles Chaplin
Writer: Charles Chaplin
Stars: Charles Chaplin, Charles Bennett, Helen Carruthers, Edwin Frazee and Edward Nolan

If Chaplin was experimenting with new approaches to cinema in *The Face on the Barroom Floor*, he surely wasn't experimenting with anything new at all with *Recreation*. While Chaplin newbies may get a kick out of it, being a six minute distillation of everything they might imagine a silent slapstick short to be, those who have seen any of his earlier Keystone films will disregard it because, hey, it's a six minute distillation of everything he'd already been doing over and over up to this point.

Fans could describe it simply but effectively as yet another of his "park comedies" and other fans would know exactly what unfolds. When Chaplin famously suggested that, "All I need to make a comedy is a park, a policeman and a pretty girl", *Recreation* is the epitome of that comedy, merely with the minor additions of a sailor and a second policeman thrown in for good measure.

There's no doubt that it's the most predictable and familiar of Chaplin's Keystone films thus far with maybe only one single shot early in the film providing anything new, as Charlie considers suicide by drowning.

Advertising copy calls his character here a "down-and-out young man who finds a new zest in life in park flirtations conducted with inimitable vigour and humour, in which the police materially assist." That's something of an exaggeration, of course, as is the ensuing summary, "A short but uncommonly good one", but it's not far off the truth if you visualise that description.

It's the "down-and-out" bit that stands out, because Chaplin is initially not merely the Little Tramp here, he's the suicidal Little Tramp. Resting one leg on top of the guardrail of a bridge, he uses both hands to attempt to lift the other to match it, so he can topple over and plunge to his doom. In a neat bit of physical humour, he

193

inevitably ends up sprawled on the wrong side. He's about to take another shot when the inevitable pretty girl walks past and that's it for the real darkness in this film.

For the rest, we're firmly back in the familiar territory of routine slapstick, however much throwing bricks at people would be surely interpreted as a dark act rather than "routine" today.

I should add that there's another form of darkness here, literal darkness, because the known surviving copies of *Recreation* are, in the accurate words of Flicker Alley, "fragmentary, very damaged or of terrible quality picture." Restoration was performed from "the most complete element available, a 16mm dupe negative held in the Blackhawk Film Collection, Los Angeles, completed by the only surviving fragment of a nitrate positive print held by the B.F.I. National Archive in London."

They really aren't kidding about the poor quality, as I'm not even convinced that we're seeing the entire frame. That initial scene on the bridge, and those ensuing with Charlie and the pretty girl he plans to hit on, unfold with the tops of their heads chopped off by the top of the picture. This continues to be the case for a little while

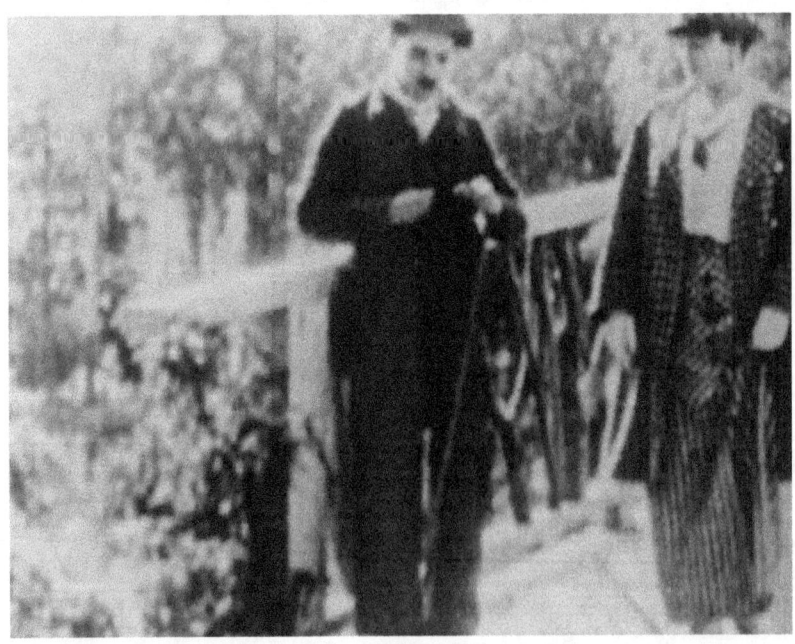

whenever anyone stands up, so we begin to feel that we only see things properly when they're sitting down. Somehow that seems much more annoying than the washed out picture quality in which faces are reduced to vague blurs of white.

Of all the films Chaplin made at Keystone to suffer this particular fate, this one is perhaps the safest, as even audiences of the time clearly knew how generic it was. A few months after the picture's release, in January 1915, the British trade paper, *Bioscope*, suggested that, "This quaint actor is here seen in one of his most typical parts." More tellingly, the very same review appropriately described the location of Westlake Park, renamed in 1942 to MacArthur Park, the one later commemorated famously in song by Jimmy Webb, as "that very beautiful park, which seems to be most frequented by Keystone comedians".

With the suicide flouted, not a single surprising moment can be found. The pretty girl is with a sailor, who's passed out on a park bench, so she moves to another where Charlie hits on her. When the sailor wakes, the two men have at it, from the initial standard slap, slap, duck, girl gets slapped by mistake routine to good old fashioned brick throwing time. When both men have been hit by enough bricks, a couple of Keystone Kops appear out of nowhere to get hit by bricks too.

The only surprising aspect, if you can call it that, is how quickly this all happens. Usually Chaplin had one whole reel to let this sort of thing take its course, but here he only had half that. *Recreation* ran 462 feet, which made it a "split reel", six minutes of slapstick comedy distributed to theatres on the same reel of film as another picture, a documentary short of similar length entitled *The Yosemite*, naturally about the national park, which sounds just as generic in its own way.

Given that the similarly generic title of this film would appear to have precisely nothing to do with the plot, which was quite clearly improvised during a one day shoot, I wonder what it really aims to describe.

Is it subversively suggesting that every male Keystone character dreams of nothing more than chatting up a pretty girl, stealing her away from her boyfriend, hurling bricks at him, escaping from the resulting policemen and booting them into a lake? Can we imagine idle chat round the office water cooler on a quiet Friday afternoon unfolding in this manner: "What are you planning for the weekend, Charlie?" "Oh, just a little recreation..."

Or, as I'd suggest is far more likely, is it suggesting that Chaplin and his cast of lesser Keystone names were themselves indulging in a little recreation shooting something so basic so quickly? I'd think that the following Friday night conversation in a bar outside the Keystone studio would be more realistic: "What are you planning for the weekend, Charlie?" "Oh, just a little recreation. How would you like to help shoot a park comedy on our day off tomorrow and see how quickly we can get the job done?"

When the picture quality finally kicks in, five minutes into the six, presumably from the B.F.I. print, we're reminded just how much better Chaplin's Keystone pictures have played when not presented in the washed out picture quality that we remember from so many cheap public domain DVDs. It's a strange feeling to witness this change happen while we're actually watching one of these movies, but the sudden shift in quality does bring firmly back to mind that this may well seem far better if seen as it was intended.

I believe that *Recreation* is a capable film that ably demonstrates Chaplin's mastery of the simple gags that constitute the building blocks of Keystone comedy, both as an actor and a director. While it's certainly an inconsequential and a redundant one to us today, given that we're able to watch all these gags time and time again in the films that came before this one, it may have been important to Chaplin at this point in his directorial career to knock out one of these just to prove to himself how easily he could do so.

If it was just an experiment to show how confident he was with the basics, it would seem appropriate that it was a one day location shoot with no other major Keystone names.

The girl is Helen Carruthers, whose brief career from 1914 to 1915 was dominated by Chaplin pictures at Keystone. She appeared in thirteen of them, only eight short of the total number in her entire filmography.

Her sailor boyfriend is Charles Bennett, who beat Chaplin to the big screen by two years and went on to a number of major features, like *The Adventures of Robin Hood*, *Citizen Kane* and *Mrs. Miniver*, before his death in 1943, but only in bit parts. Even back in 1914, he was a lot more memorable playing George Ham, the cheap actor who looked rather like a romantic poet in *The Property Man* than in the overeager shot he gives his role here.

That leaves only Edwin Frazee and Edward Nolan as the pair of Keystone Kops, the short one and the tall one respectively. Both were actors with short careers: Frazee shot 22 films in two years and Nolan only twelve, along with a single feature later on in 1920. Nine of Frazee's and eight of Nolan's were with Chaplin.

And that's about it. Being so relentlessly generic, there's very little of interest to add about *Recreation*, a film that could almost be entirely restored by copying and pasting scenes from other Chaplin Keystones together. With this picture quality, nobody would likely notice the difference, anyway.

Is it worth mentioning that Chaplin's initial pratfall may well have influenced Buster Keaton, who performed the same move so often in his career, which wouldn't begin for another three years? Is it noteworthy that there are two policemen in this film, rather than just one, and that they even have a brief tussle of their own before teaming up to hone in on the real throwers of bricks? Could it be

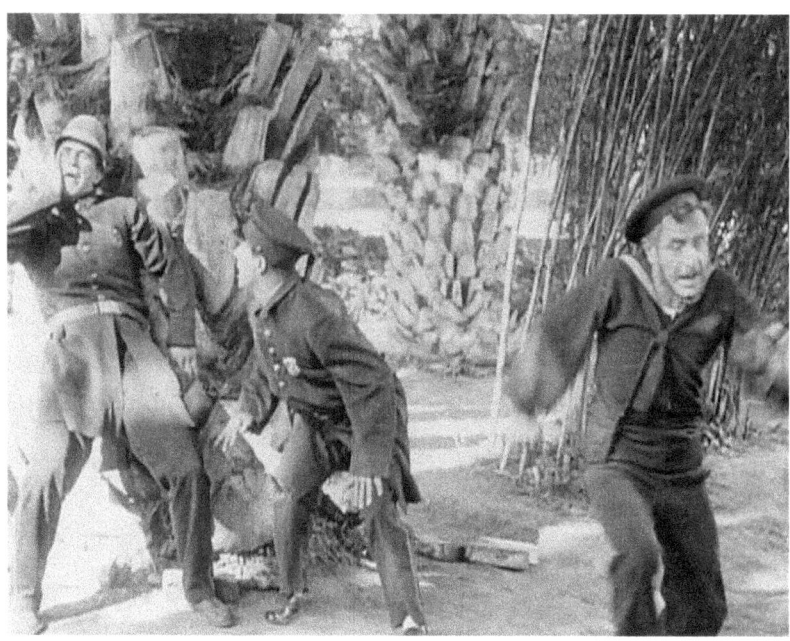

important that when the short ends, as perhaps every one of these "park comedies" ended, with characters getting pushed, pulled and kicked into the inevitable lake, the final intertitle rolls with every single character in the picture in the water?

I'd argue that only the first instance has any validity. This really is no great historical piece, it's just a solid example of the Keystone archetype conjured up in a single day.

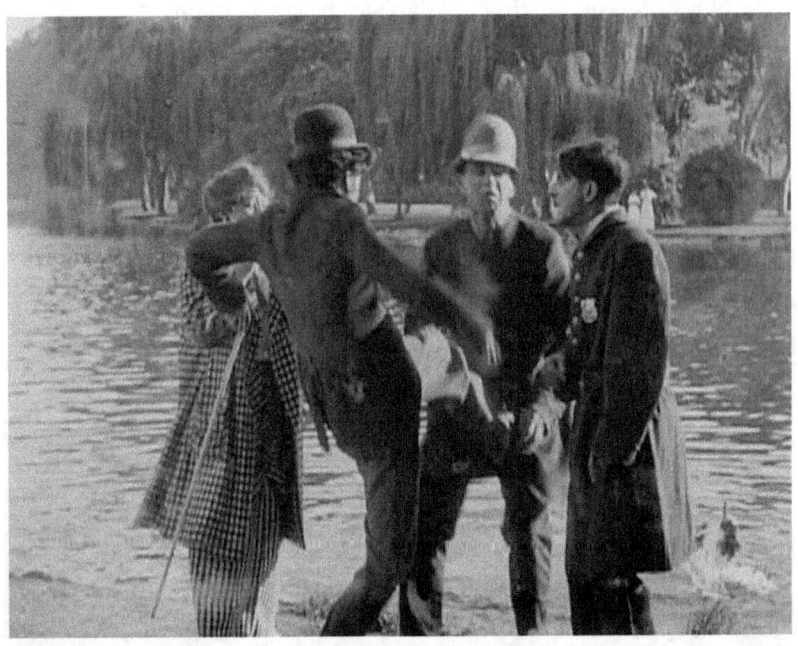

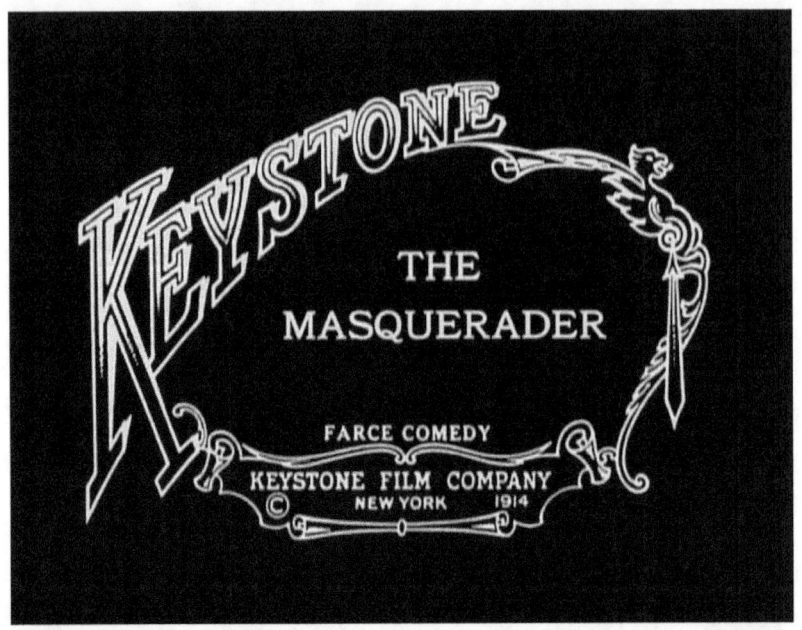

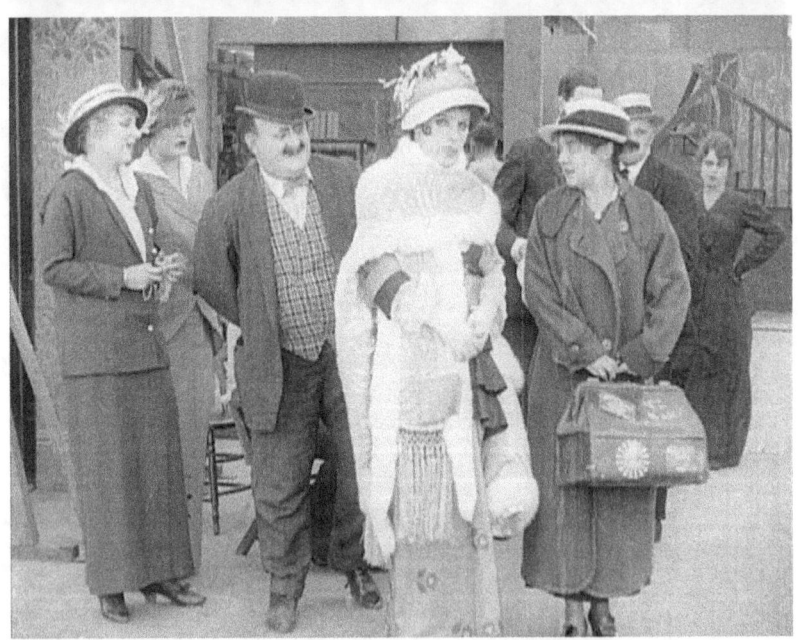

The Masquerader
27th August, 1914

Director: Charles Chaplin
Writer: Charles Chaplin
Stars: Charles Chaplin, Roscoe Arbuckle and Charles Murray

Without any doubt the most sophisticated of the shorts he had directed thus far, *The Masquerader* demonstrates that Chaplin was developing his skills quickly and he was more than ready for this meta story that reminds of a few earlier films but sets its sights firmly on the bigger and better films of the future.

Like his previous picture, *Recreation*, it plays with the traditional Keystone slapstick, but unlike that short where there was little else on show, those elements are firmly restricted to the background here. Like *A Film Johnnie*, the first of Chaplin's pictures to stand up on its own merits rather than as another historic first in his career, it uses Keystone Studios itself as a backdrop. However, it goes much further than merely introducing the Little Tramp to the studio as an outsider to cause chaos; it tasks Chaplin with playing a studio employee, effectively himself, who in turn plays the Little Tramp. Fired for being too distracted by the ladies to do his job, he returns as one for the second time in 1914 after his previous turn in drag in *A Busy Day*.

What impressed me most was the way in which Chaplin refused to restrict the comedy that unfolds to the fictional characters. Sure, initially he paints the "real people" seriously, as they prepare for a day's shoot, but their change into the characters you might expect to see in a Keystone film doesn't only happen with the application of make-up.

When Chaplin is late for work and so gets hauled away from the ladies by his ear, the act is something we might expect of the Little Tramp but he hasn't actually become the character yet. As he does so, on the other side of a dressing room table to Roscoe Arbuckle, the slapstick they indulge in is exactly what we might expect of their characters, but they're still themselves when they begin.

This is a melding of the real actors with the characters they play and it's neatly subversive, notably deeper than anything that he'd done previously and far beyond what anyone else was doing at the time. *Recreation*, as capably built as it was, suddenly feels like an antique from a different era, even though it was made only a single week earlier.

Of course, while Chaplin does initially portray an actor similar to himself, as do Arbuckle and Chester Conklin and others, not all of these people are that close to their real selves. Charles Murray, for instance, plays the director driven to fire Chaplin and he did briefly wear that hat in real life, but not quite yet. He didn't get to sit in the director's chair for real until December, when he quickly churned out three short films at Keystone before giving up that role for six years.

Perhaps, what happens to his character in this picture aside, he found that he enjoyed the idea and had a chat with Mack Sennett to make it happen for real. Fortunately the shorts he did direct don't appear to be anywhere near as outrageous as the fictional one he attempts to shoot here, with its villain outrageously threatening a sleeping baby with a knife. Keystone comedies did find their way

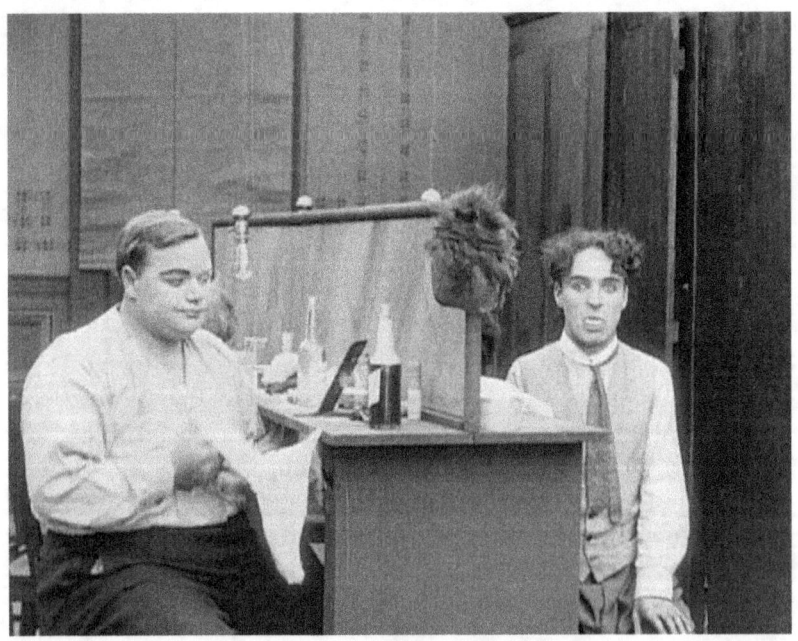

into notably dark territory on occasion, but this would seem to be one we can be thankful never made it from fictional plot device to real picture.

It's rendered even more outrageous by the fact that this is where Charlie fails to notice his cue because he's too distracted by the kisses of ladies backstage, leaving the villain frozen with his knife aloft and the baby blissfully unaware of the grisly fate hovering above it like the sword of Damocles. Fed up with waiting for Charlie to rush in and save the child, the director throws it at him instead, another dark moment in a light film.

Highlighting how the actors at Keystone were interchangeable on a moment's notice, his very next action is to substitute him with Chester Conklin. "He's rotten," pronounces the director. "You play the part." Of course Chaplin, who reminded of his regular character even before he put on the tramp's outfit, sabotages his replacement and treats us to another round of meta slapstick.

Of course, it's no surprise that Chaplin would be drawn to this sort of multi-layered portrayal, given that he came to Keystone's attentions through his work in Fred Karno's stage sketch, *Mumming Birds*, with its play within a play, but this is a much more modern take on the concept.

In fact, after kicking his director through a stage window and playing a number of tricks on him that we'll assume he borrowed from his alter ego, the Little Tramp, Chaplin is promptly fired and thrown bodily out of the studio in scenes that are reminiscent of the end of *Blazing Saddles*, their fight continuing on throughout a completely unrelated set.

While that film was notably ahead of its time in 1974, it may well have borrowed from this one made six decades earlier, as well as from the finalé of *The Knockout*, which I've already covered in this book. Film Historians really aren't kidding when they emphasise the importance Chaplin had to and the influence he had on screen comedy!

Of course, if his multi-level meta antics are ahead of their time, where he goes next is very much rooted in the past. Of course, male actors had been playing female characters on stage for centuries, but they'd also been doing it on film since its earliest days. Often they were quite obvious about it, but I can imagine great swathes of the audience in 1914 not realising that the leading lady who shows up after Chaplin's departure is Chaplin himself returning in drag.

And so, after playing an actor based on himself and then the character that he usually plays, Chaplin now takes on the role of a female actor to find his way back into the very studio that just fired him. He's overdressed, naturally, with a big ruff and an extravagant hat, but he's very believable, looking rather like a more feminine version of Liza Minnelli.

While his more transparent turn as a woman in *A Busy Day* was notably shrewish, violent even in the tradition of Mrs. Punch, his return to drag here is far more coy and coquettish. No wonder his director's hands start roaming and he throws all the actors out of the dressing room so the new leading lady can have some room, before chasing her around a table with amorous intent.

If, at this point, 1914 audiences hadn't seen through the ruse, they would have been shocked to discover this lady ripping off her wig in what looks like rather painful fashion. If this scene is anything to go by, female impersonators a hundred years ago must have had a streak of masochism.

And so returns the Little Tramp for a second run at the studio, albeit an inevitably brief one because even he can't have imagined he'd have been rehired after his ruse is exposed. Instead this odd discovery merely sets up the more traditional aspects of the film, prompting the inevitable chase finalé, which arrives complete with a quick bout of brick throwing and a rapid fire slapfest that made me burn up calories merely watching it.

It should be emphasised that it's done well, however traditional it all is and however inferior these last few scenes are when compared to the majority of the film. There's a lot of slapstick humour dotted throughout this short but it's done slowly, deliberately and in the holy name of character, something that Keystone was beginning to realise involved more than just a new facial hair design. The early scene with Chaplin trying to steal Arbuckle's drink but falling short in every way is cleverly done and can't fail to raise a laugh. Yet the more frenetic action at the end of the picture is so relentlessly generic and throwaway that it's not worth mentioning in the same breath except to say that it pales in comparison.

I wonder if Chaplin was wondering how much he could get away with, how far he could take this concept and how forward looking he could become without jeopardising his newly found status as the writer and director of his own pictures. If he finished up with some generic slapstick and a chase, nobody would say a word against it, right? It's the Keystone way, so he must have been following the guidelines.

I'd argue that it may have been even more important to Chaplin that this particular film be received well, because it had a higher profile cast than Chaplin had been trusted with thus far. Sure, *Laughing Gas* starred Mack Swain and Slim Summerville, but those films in between were with lesser known actors new to the studio. This one, however, features names such as Chester Conklin, Minta Durfee and Roscoe Arbuckle, who were all recognisable faces at Keystone before Chaplin was ever hired. I believe that's even Mabel Normand at the very beginning too, playing herself in a few frames in the "pleasure before business" scene before things get going.

It appears to have been well received, but with most praise given to Chaplin's "really remarkable female impersonation", as *Bioscope* described it. Perhaps its script was so far ahead of its time that it

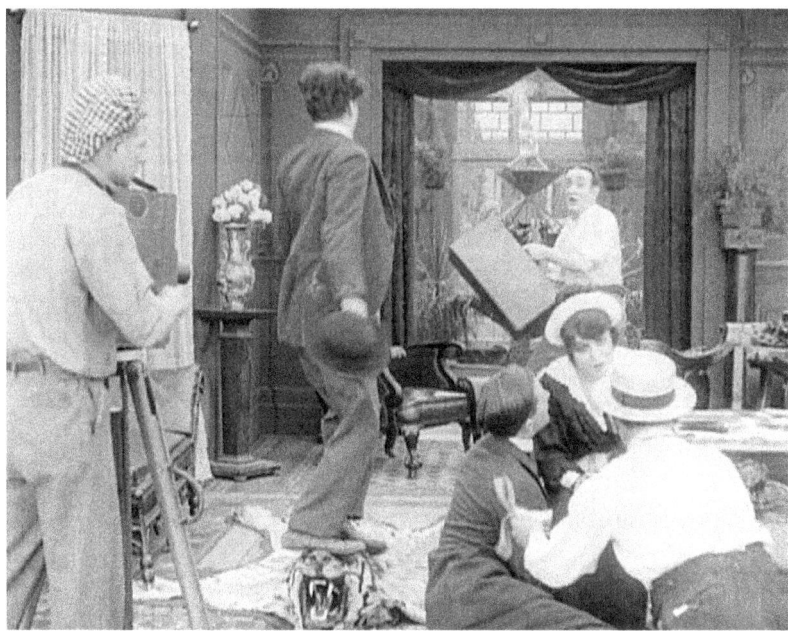

didn't get proper recognition in 1914.

Of course, with the magical power of hindsight, we don't only recognise how innovative Chaplin's writing was here, we also bear witness to the many little ragged edges that demonstrate just how far he still had to go before the undying classics that only we know would come later. When watching each film from 1914 at the speed they were released, this picture feels like yet another step forward, underlining the fact that this new screen comedian was someone to watch, but there would be a lot more steps before pictures like *The Kid* or *City Lights* were remotely possible.

The pacing is especially notable here, as the picture is neither too fast to feel rushed, at least until the finalé, nor too slow to drag. It's easy to imagine Chaplin feeling that he mastered the basics with *Recreation* and was quite ready for something much more ambitious in *The Masquerader*. It's far from perfect but it's his best and most sophisticated film up to this point.

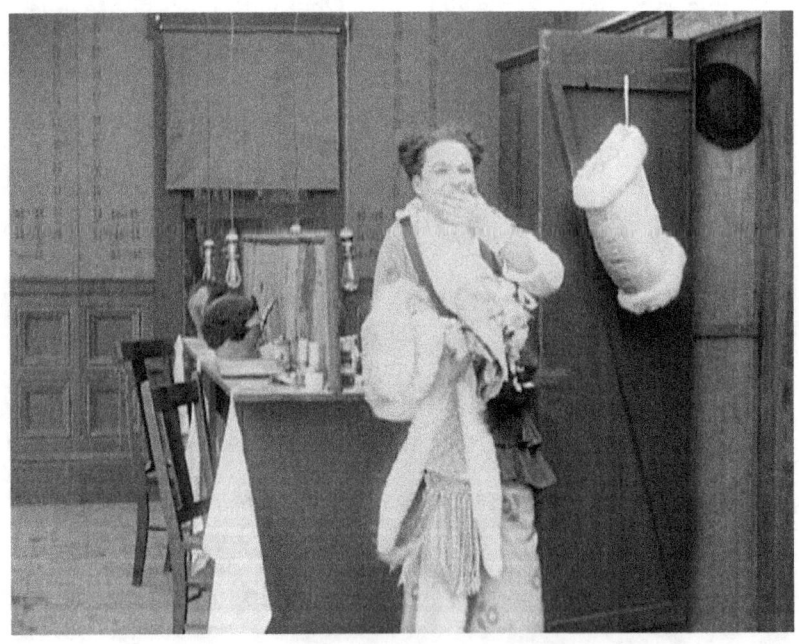

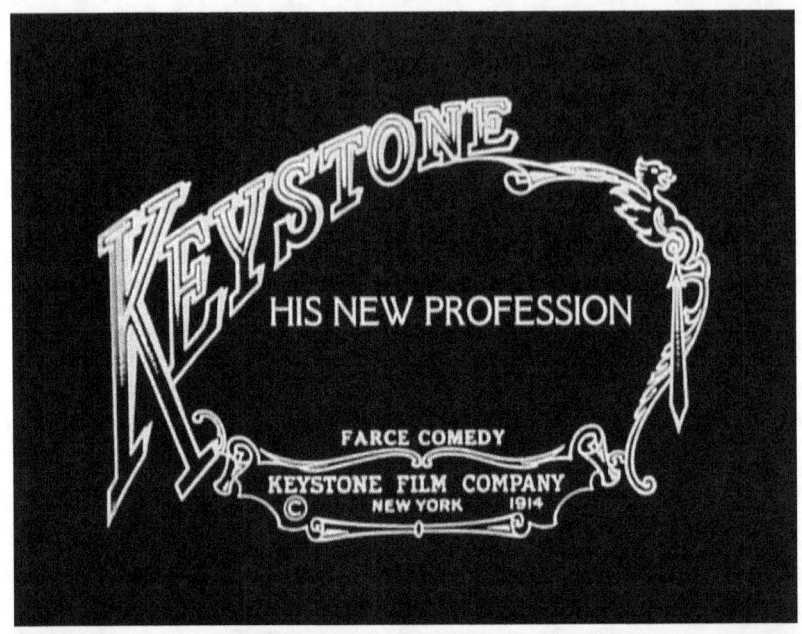

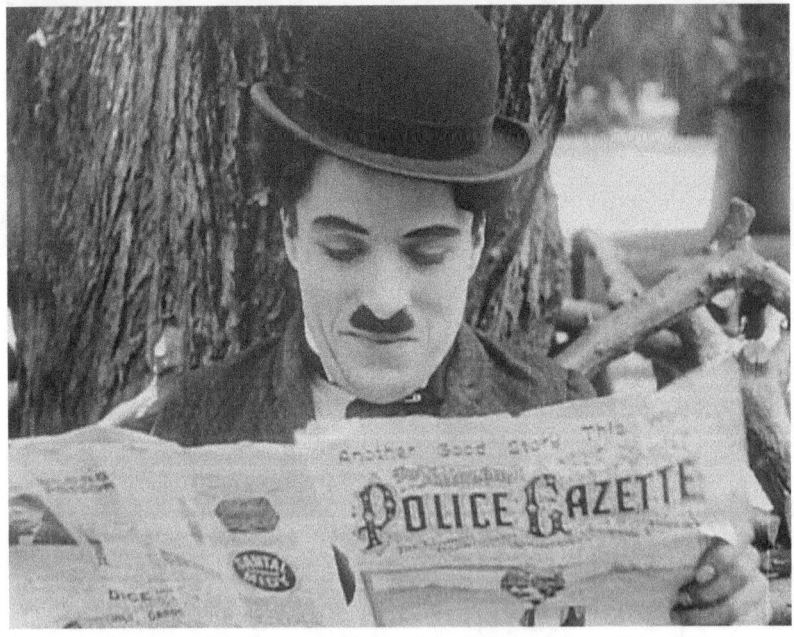

His New Profession
31st August, 1914

Director: Charles Chaplin
Writer: Charles Chaplin
Stars: Charles Chaplin, Jess Dandy and Charles Parrott

The Masquerader, Chaplin's most ambitious film thus far, allowed him to tell a few stories in one through meta manipulation. He played both his regular character and his regular character in drag, but he also got to play a fictional version of himself becoming both to mix it all up.

This isn't remotely as ambitious, not only because Chaplin just plays Charlie, the cheeky opportunistic layabout, but it does stretch the usual Keystone locations by bouncing us frantically back and forth between them: we start in the park, end up at the pier and spend time in the bar in between. We know all these locations well from other Keystone comedies and, frankly we know much of what happens in them too, but instead of taking those Lego brick gags, building them up into something big and then moving it all to a new location, he builds bits of it in different locations and keeps us shifting between them until they're all firmly connected together. The characters here cover a lot of ground, rushing onto the screen and off it again, ensuring that our eyeballs get a workout too.

Charlie is the focus from moment one in a story that ably builds his character. This little tramp isn't a bad man and he doesn't seek to do bad things; in fact, he doesn't seek to do anything at all, as appropriate reissue titles such as *The Good for Nothing* and *Helping Himself* ably highlight. However, he does keep his eyes open and if something just happens to fall into his metaphorical lap, there's no doubt that he'll take full advantage of it, however unethical or inappropriate it might happen to be.

Chaplin's story is written very much to dangle things his way and for him to benefit from them, all done for comedic effect. The most obvious example here is what sets up the whole film, as a young man wants to wander off with his girlfriend but is stuck with his uncle, who's confined to a bathchair with an apparent broken leg. If only he could find someone to babysit him for an hour or two! Enter Charlie, who's sitting by a different tree in the park reading the *Police Gazette*. He takes the job, but hardly for altruistic reasons; the first thing he does is take him to the Pier Bar and try to cadge a dime.

Of course, Chaplin doesn't skimp on the little opportunities for gags and there's a glaring target for them in plain view: the invalid uncle's broken leg. While the first painful moment comes when the bathchair is wheeled onto Charlie's foot, it's the uncle, played by Jess Dandy, who comes in for the lion's share of pain. That broken leg is sat on, bumped into and tripped over, bashed by no end of props and even hooked by Charlie's cane to turn him around.

There are those who call out certain moments in Chaplin's early films as cruel, such as the notable abuse of his elderly assistant in *The Property Man*, and I'm not going to argue too hard that they're wrong, but inflicting pain was one of the foundations of humour in the silent era and there's just no way that we can escape that. Most of the gags in this film are constructed out of someone's pain, but I didn't find them particularly cruel. Cruelty to me in Chaplin's early

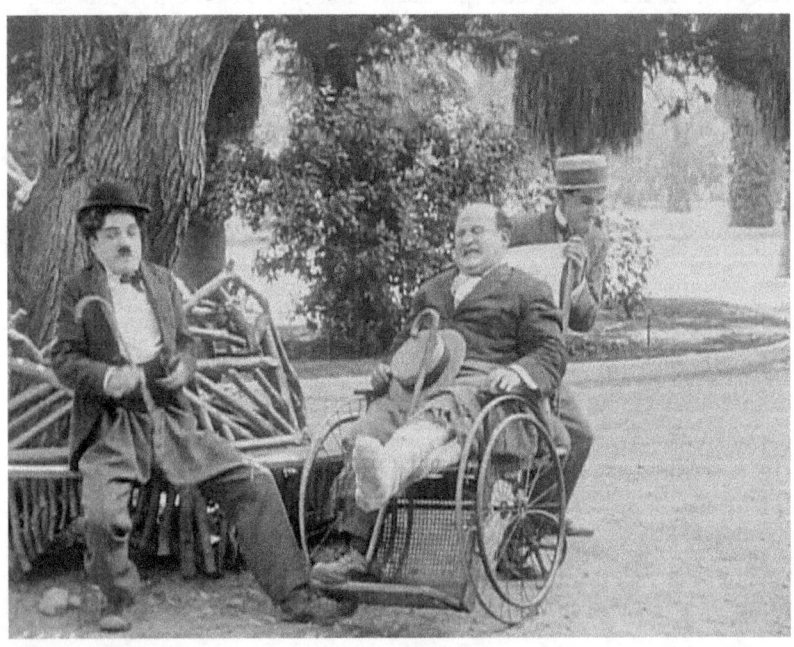

films is epitomised not in *The Property Man* but in the deliberate acts wrought upon Mabel Normand in *Mabel's Busy Day*.

It's also worth mentioning that, while Jess Dandy's uncle clearly suffers the most in *His New Profession*, Chaplin reserves a number of pratfalls for himself. The most notable arrives as he's struggling to lift the bathchair over a kerb because wheelchair ramps didn't exist in 1914, only to sit down in a mess of broken eggs, which had been dropped on the sidewalk by a young lady earlier in the picture. We laugh as much at the pain and inconvenience inflicted on Charlie as we do at that inflicted on his charge, so, if this is cruelty, at least it's equal opportunity cruelty.

The main difference is in the ability to react. The uncle is stuck in his bathchair throughout the picture, so doesn't have the freedom to, say, buttscoot on the grass to clean egg off his pants, as Charlie does twice here. He just sits back to endure whatever the script has in store for him, which is quite a lot, while Charlie can and does give as good as he gets. In fact, the uncle is so passive a target that he remains a prop even after he nods off.

It's also worth mentioning that the most overt cruelty in this film actually doesn't revolve around pain. After the uncle won't give him a dime on account to spend at the bar, Charlie waits for him to fall asleep and wheels him over to the pier. He parks him right next to a one-armed man, who's also dozing, a one-armed man behind a tin cup and a sign that reads, "Help a cripple". Needless to say, Charlie seizes the opportunity, steals both sign and cup for his charge and uses the first coin to finance his bar trip.

To be fair, we do eventually discover that this particular cripple is not a cripple at all, merely a con man, but Charlie doesn't know that. He deliberately steals what appears to be an invalid's only source of income, just so he that can get drunk, and yet he's the hero of the story! I might suggest that morality was a very different creature a full century ago, but I'm sure that the lowest common denominator comedians today would happily recreate the sort of wheelchair antics Chaplin sets up here, merely with bigger and more outrageous payoffs. Shows like *Jackass* owe plenty to slapstick cruelty.

And talking of *Jackass*, I wonder what safeguards were in place back in 1914 when Charlie kicks the uncle's bathchair away from him and he rolls on down the pier towards the sea. Getting knocked off a pier into the ocean was no rare fate in Keystone comedies, as Charlie found out in *A Busy Day*. I should put your consciences at ease by pointing out that the gentleman who does end up in the ocean here was not in a wheelchair at the time, but Dandy does come close on not one but two separate occasions and the various shenanigans that go down during the finalé can't have been the safest stunts that Keystone actors had ever performed.

Even less outrageous activities, like the manhandling that Charlie gives his employer's girlfriend after she puts her hand on his knee, looks like it could well have been painful. And I'm still not sure where that scene even came from. Perhaps Chaplin, ever the ladies' man, wanted to make sure he got to play with at least one of them in this picture, even if it made precisely no sense whatsoever in the grand scheme of things.

I have no idea who the actress is, but she epitomises how difficult it sometimes is to keep track of actors in films which didn't have credits. IMDb lists her as Peggy Page, who debuted here and then appeared in the next four Chaplin movies. Wikipedia doesn't have a credit for "Nephew's Girlfriend", so may suggest Helen Carruthers as "Woman" instead. The B.F.I. adds Gene Marsh to the possibility list, viably as IMDb has her first seven films listed as being Chaplin shorts. Perhaps that should be eight. Then again, the B.F.I. also lists Minta Durfee as "Woman" and I didn't see her anywhere in the film.

Other actors are clearer to identify, as that's certainly Roscoe Arbuckle who's briefly visible as the bartender of the Pier Bar, for instance. Cecile Arnold is the young lady who dropped the eggs, appearing in yet another Chaplin short. Her first five confirmed roles were in Chaplin films, beginning with *The Property Man*, and she'd go on to appear in six more. It isn't escaping me that so many young ladies had brief careers at Keystone that were dominated by Chaplin shorts.

The most notable supporting actor here, however, is male. It's Charles Parrott, a twenty year old actor who plays the young man who hires Charlie to look after his uncle. He was four years younger than Chaplin, but he started in film two years earlier, at the Christie Film Company in 1912, and moved to Keystone a year later, where his first IMDb credits show up. He'd appeared in Chaplin pictures before, though predominantly as an extra. This was his sixth short with Chaplin and he's easily at his most obvious here, running over Charlie's foot with the bathchair and popping up behind a sign to surprise his girlfriend.

It's easy to see the promise that's inherent in his work and so it shouldn't be too much of a surprise to discover that Charles Parrott would eventually be known as the fourth great solo silent screen comedian, ranking only behind Chaplin, Keaton and Lloyd. If you don't recognise the name, it's because he didn't become known as Charles Parrott but Charley Chase, which screen name he adopted in 1923. By that point he had directed over a hundred films for Hal Roach, including some starring Chaplin impersonator Billy West, and he found some fame as a character variously named Jimmie, Jimmy or Jameson Jump.

This was yet another reminder to me about how time can blur achievement. Even as a child, I was aware of Charlie Chaplin, Buster Keaton and Harold Lloyd, but I viewed them all as contemporaries, some sort of community of great silent comedians, crafting their masterpieces an unfathomable distance in time away from me. Only

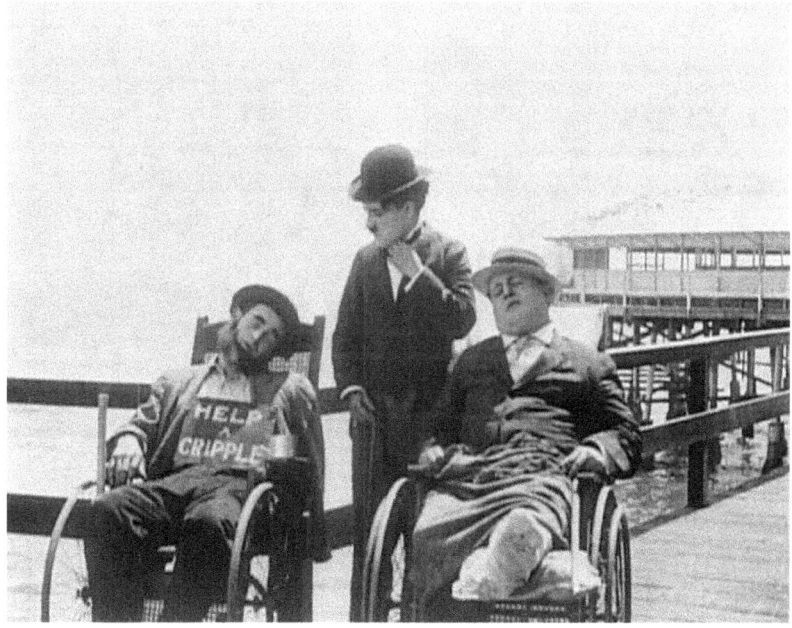

later did I realise that they weren't really contempories, that even within the silent era there was progression and legends were built on the prior work of other legends.

It was actually Harold Lloyd who debuted on screen first but at this point he was still stuck as an extra, playing roles like a hottentot in *The Patchwork Girl of Oz*. He wouldn't become at all prolific until he became Lonesome Luke, a Chaplin knock-off for Hal Roach in 1915. Buster Keaton didn't appear until 1917 and spent his first four years as Roscoe Arbuckle's sidekick. By the time he made his first solo film, Chaplin had become his own writer and director, become the first international star of the screen, moved to Mutual for $670,000 a year then to First National for a cool million dollars, built his own studio and, with three of the other biggest names in Hollywood, founded a distribution company, United Artists.

He wasn't the first screen comedian, of course, and he arrived at Keystone Studios in 1914, the home of many recognisable faces, to replace a major star, Ford Sterling. Roscoe Arbuckle was already there, making many pictures, as were Mabel Normand and many others, but Chaplin was the first to refuse to continue doing the

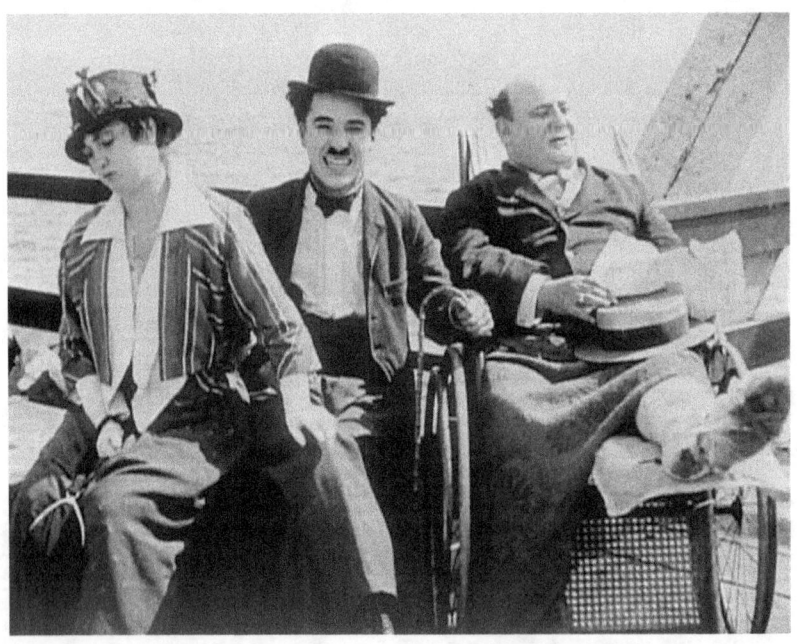

same ol' same ol' throughout his contract, let alone take on what someone else was finding success with. This project served well to open my eyes to the sheer scale of his achievement.

His New Profession is a long way from being a great short film, let alone the greatest comedy ever made, and there are a whole slew of raw edges in evidence, not aided by the restoration work apparent on the Flicker Alley box set not being as effective as on many of his earlier films. However, it does feel like the product of a different era entirely to *Making a Living* or *Kid Auto Races at Venice, Cal.* At this point in the project, I had to force myself to remember what those earlier films were like while watching the newer ones. To realise that *Making a Living*, fully 25 pictures away, was made a mere seven months earlier is jawdropping.

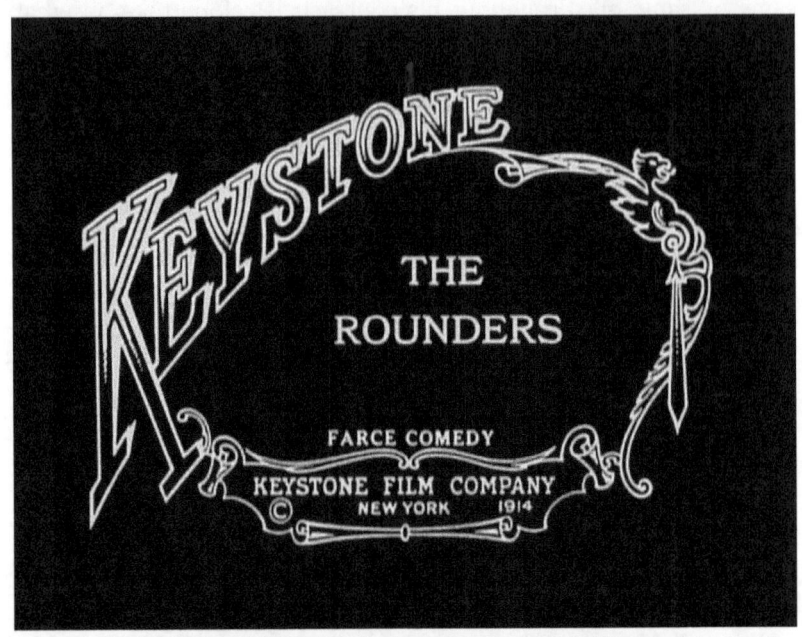

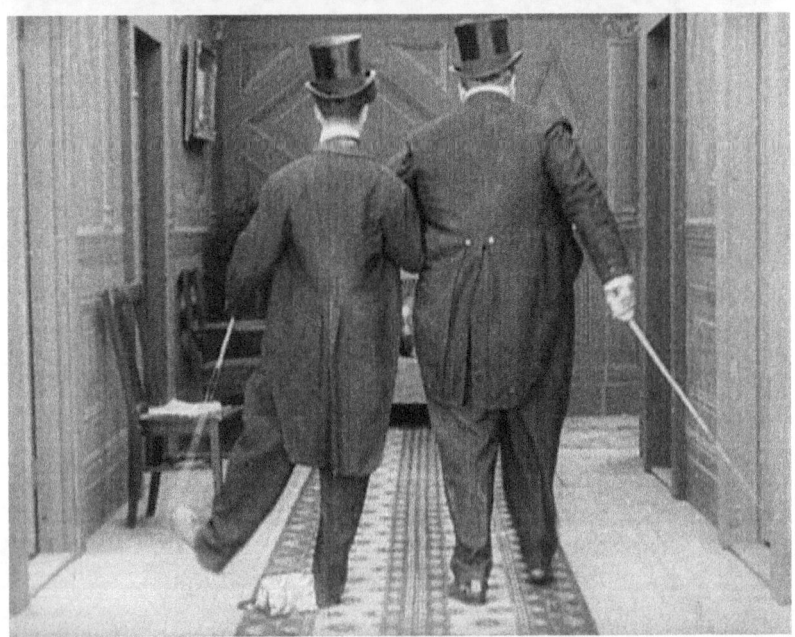

The Rounders
7th September, 1914

Director: Charles Chaplin
Writer: Charles Chaplin
Stars: Charles Chaplin, Roscoe Arbuckle, Phyllis Allen and Minta Durfee

The pre-Charley Chase appearance of Charles Parrott in *His New Profession* reminded me yet again how early Charlie Chaplin's work was when compared to the other great silent comedians. Adding to this, *The Rounders* highlights what could have been: a pioneering comedy double act, not only because the characters of Mr. Full and Mr. Fuller display some notable chemistry between Chaplin and Roscoe Arbuckle that could easily have been built upon in future films, but because there's little else here except that double act, the story threadbare but the laughter acute.

Arbuckle was established before Chaplin, of course, starting out five years earlier at the Selig Polyscope Company before switching to Keystone in 1913, where he established his regular character, the decidedly not politically correct Fatty. His double act with Mabel Normand, which ran from late 1914 into 1916, may have begun with his title role in *Mabel's New Hero* in 1913. Had Chaplin not left his first studio after a year, the history of silent comedy could have been written very differently, as this film ably highlights. Instead, Arbuckle teamed up with Buster Keaton in 1917.

There were many double acts in the slapstick age but none come quicker to mind today than Laurel and Hardy, a partnership which outlasted the silent era by decades, their final film together as late as the 1951 feature, *Atoll K*.

It's worth highlighting that Laurel and Hardy were both young men in their early twenties in 1914, Stan Jefferson still with Fred Karno's vaudeville troupe, the very one which Chaplin had left for Keystone, and Babe Hardy starting out on screen in split reelers for the Lubin Company in Florida. Their double act wouldn't officially debut for thirteen years in 1927's *Putting Pants on Philip*, though they did appear in a couple of earlier films together. The first of them,

The Lucky Dog, wouldn't arrive until 1921 and Stan Laurel's debut on screen wasn't until 1917's *Nuts in May*. When Arbuckle and Chaplin were pioneering the little and large double act in *The Rounders*, the latter's former understudy, Stanley Jefferson, seven years before taking his stage name of Stan Laurel, was doing impersonations of him on stage for Fred Karno.

Chaplin, of course, was too independent to be locked down to a mere partnership. He was the epitome of a solo artiste, even if he proved as early as his fifth film, *Between Showers*, that he could work well with a partner, albeit the actor he was replacing at Keystone, Ford Sterling. Within a couple of weeks these two would do more work together worthy of a double act in *Tango Tangles*, most notably a superb scene towards the end where they try to put on the same coat at the same time.

Arbuckle and Chaplin were both major names at this point for the Keystone studio and they had already shared the screen in six previous pictures, though none are real partnerships. The most time they shared together before this was either in *Tango Tangles*, in which they literally battle on the dancefloor for a pretty hat check girl, or *The Knockout*, a film starring Arbuckle as a man who ends up in a boxing match officiated over by Chaplin in one of his guest slots in pictures belonging to other Keystone stars. However, after this success, they'd never share the screen again.

Beyond the obvious potential for an ongoing double act that never happened, what leaps out here is the pacing. Chaplin's script may have had very little to say but it had a lot to say about how it should unfold. He introduces us to each of the four principal characters individually, giving them a firm opportunity to develop before they start colliding with the others, collisions which grow naturally.

Chaplin is Mr. Full, yet another opportunity for him to haul out his drunkard routine, as he's three sheets to the wind when he first staggers onto screen; the odd word in the title comes from an old slang term for drunkards, presumably those who make the rounds of bars. Jeffrey Vance describes this as "the best of Chaplin's drunk roles for Keystone" and I'm not going to argue with that, especially as he's notably better at it than Arbuckle, who would have sold his drunk routine more effectively if he wasn't tasked with trying to match an actor who was hired by Mack Sennett on the basis of his stage role as a drunk in Karno's *Mumming Birds.*

Chaplin's introduction is very reminiscent of that in his third film, *Mabel's Strange Predicament*, in which he stole the early scenes by stumbling around a hotel and getting in the way of everyone else in the picture. Here he's stumbling around a different hotel but its geography is exactly the same. In both pictures, he stumbles first into the lobby, where he interacts with a lady in a chair to his right and another in one on his left. Eventually he makes his way up the stairs at the back which lead to a hallway with a pair of rooms on each side.

We find our leads in the two rooms nearest to the camera. Here, Mr. and Mrs. Full have the room to our right, while Mr. Fuller and his wife occupy the one opposite. These characters are bounced between them, often quite literally, as the story progresses. In the earlier film, Mabel and her significant other had the room to our right, while the couple they get caught up with are on the other side of the hallway. Some things are apparently clearly defined in the cinematic comedy rulebook; even the carpet is identical.

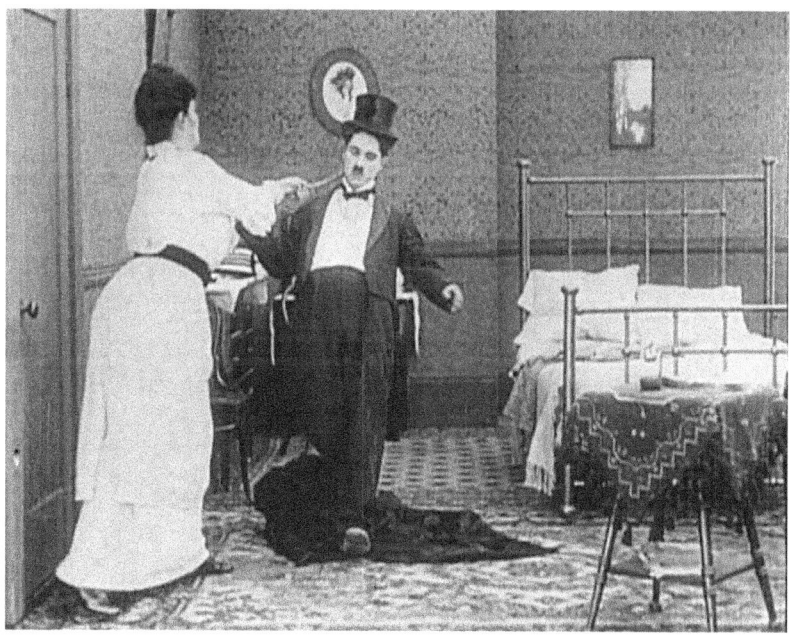

As Mr. Full, Chaplin is apparently doing much better for himself than he had for a number of shorts, even if he forgot to change his shoes along with the rest of his costume. Initially, we have no idea why he's so drunk, but we get one when we meet his wife, who's a formidable battleaxe in the form of Phyllis Allen, overbearing and violent. No wonder he has eyes for the fluff in the lobby!

It's telling that she uses his cane to pull him towards her in a similar way to how Charlie pulled his employer's girlfriend to him only a week earlier in *His New Profession*, albeit with a completely different intent. Charlie was merely getting fresh in that film; Mrs. Full is attempting to keep him upright so that she can upbraid him some more.

Once we have their relationship down, Mr. Fuller and his wife can make their entrances, introduced in a similar way that highlights both the similarities and differences. Fuller enters just like Full, only instead of ogling the girl, he sits on her. His wife is initially as weepy as Mrs. Full is violent, but only initially. When she gets going, she really gets going.

If this setup is utterly reminiscent of *Mabel's Strange Predicament*,

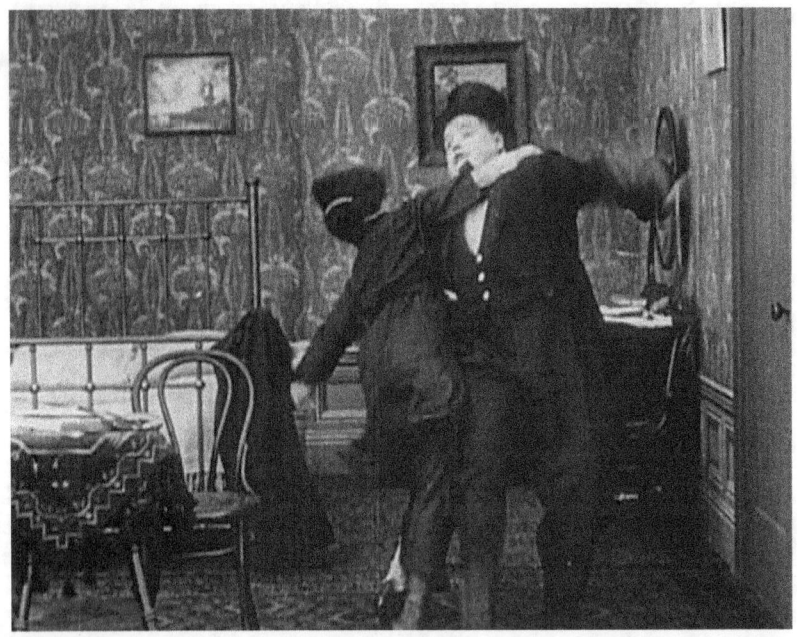

fortunately the ensuing chaos is not. The earlier film had a more substantial plot, but it was a imbecilic one, better suited to the pantomime stage with its hide and seek shenanigans. This doesn't go far beyond two drunks dealing with their upset wives, in a way that brings them together, when they realise that they're masonic buddies or some such and escape their collective wrath of their wives arm in arm for a nearby café, but that's an improvement.

The gags are improved too, Chaplin's in particular. One has him unable to get up from the floor because he's standing on his coat; another sees him hurled bodily onto the bed, where he discovers himself upside down as his feet have caught on the headboard. Arbuckle does well in the scene with his wife too, though perhaps partly because she really was his wife. Minta Durfee and Roscoe Arbuckle made a strange couple, but they wed in 1908 and stayed married until 1925, though they were estranged before his legal turmoil in 1921.

The best and worst moments of the film unfold at Smith's Café.

The latter is clearly the decision to have Billy Gilbert play the doorman in blackface, something that admittedly wasn't offensive at the time but is still completely unnecessary to the picture as a whole, which makes it all the more offensive in hindsight.

The former arrives when we find ourselves trying to figure out which of the two leads we're supposed to be watching. After Mr. Fuller attempts to lift an almost paralytic Mr. Full off the floor using not one but two canes, their action splits in two. Arbuckle is trying to disentangle his jacket from his hat, drinking tabasco sauce or something similar and using the the champagne bucket as a footstool. Meanwhile, Chaplin is at the next table causing problems for Jess Dandy's unnamed diner. Only when both of them end up using their respective tablecloths as blankets and collapsing onto the floor into drunken sleep does the action bring them back together again, quite literally and with a thump.

This would have been a good ending, especially as the slower, more methodical pace makes it seem like we've already reached the end of a reel, but there's the traditional Keystone chase to come, another one that takes us into Echo Park where characters end up as always in the Echo Park Lake, but with a notable change: this time we see a growing crowd of onlookers on the other side of the lake as the action moves on.

They're too far away for us to see any detail, but California locals had been apparent in a number of the pictures Chaplin made at Keystone which were shot in public spaces and how those everyday folk interacted with them changed over time. Initially they tended to be disinterested, even annoyed, by the distraction Chaplin was at the beginning of *Kid Auto Races at Venice, Cal.*, but they moved to enjoyment by the end of that film, then on to casual acceptance in *Tango Tangles*, grinning awareness in *Mabel's Busy Day* and now on to standard tourist activity in *The Rounders*. Such was Chaplin's rise in fame during 1914.

As always, there are problems with the film, though it is another strong step forward in terms of pacing and structure, as well as the manipulation of more emotions than tended to be found in the comedies of this era.

Rounders are dissolute drunks, debauchers, but Mr. Full and Mr. Fuller aren't as obnoxious as some of the drunkards Chaplin had played already at Keystone. These particular rounders have gained our sympathy by the point they swap their secret handshakes and

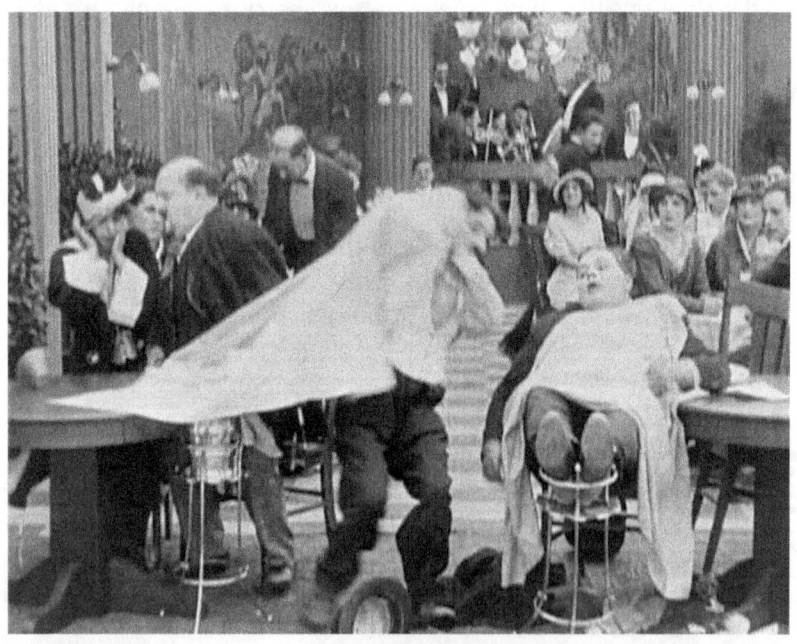

we're with them all the way to the end of the picture, but we didn't need Arbuckle's attempt to strangle his wife in order to stop her beating him up. Phyllis Allen is overly violent to her husband as well, throwing Chaplin across the room with a vengeance. At least her performance is far more consistent than that of Minta Durfee, who pantomimes a great deal too much, the old school overdone silent acting she throws out in her solo scenes reminding at once of how much of that we got early in Chaplin's 1914 pictures and how much it gradually decreased. Allen and Durfee do rage well at each other though.

Chaplin is the star here, of course, as writer, director and lead actor, but he plays very well with Arbuckle, who brought a new level to his co-star's regular routine as a drunk, one of my favourite moments in this film being when Mr. Full trips on the welcome mat outside the hotel and Mr. Fuller keeps on going, literally dragging his colleague along behind him as they're arm in arm.

Arbuckle was a big man, so prompting the nickname he never appreciated that became the name of his regular character, but he was often able to use that attribute to his advantage. He's not loose enough to be as believably drunk as Chaplin and he's too obviously aware of his surroundings when he's bouncing people off his belly, but the pair of them are great on screen together.

Arbuckle later praised Chaplin and his work, saying that, "I have always regretted not having been his partner in a longer film than these one-reelers we made so rapidly." He's not alone. Lack of story aside, I got a real kick out of this one and wish they'd have been a double act for longer.

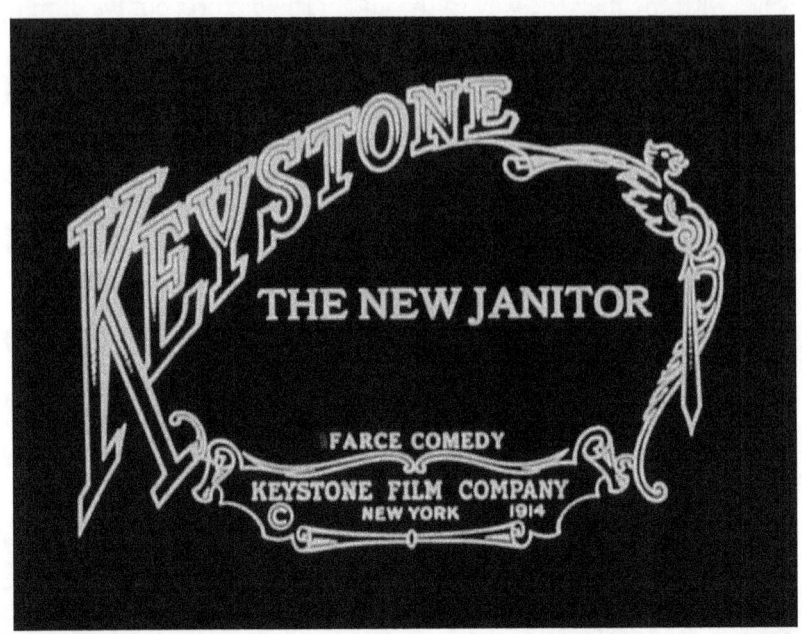

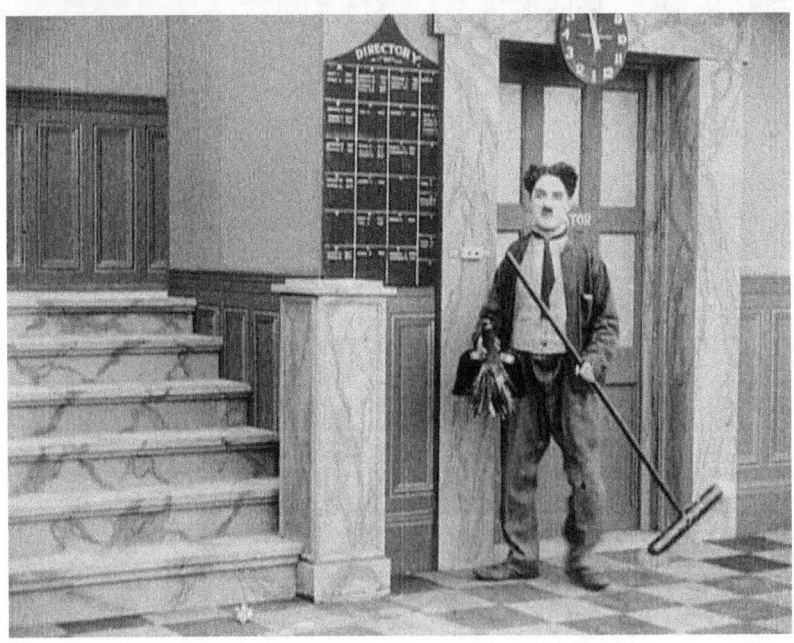

The New Janitor
24th September, 1914

Director: Charles Chaplin
Writer: Charles Chaplin
Star: Charles Chaplin, Jess Dandy, Jack Dillon and Peggy Page

From the distance of a century, we can mostly only guess at what was going through Chaplin's mind during his last few months at Keystone, but we do know some things for sure and others would appear to be safe guesses.

For a start, he was certainly already both an ambitious man and a perfectionist, attributes which led his drive to direct his own films. At this point, he had no less than 27 pictures already behind him that had generally done better than regular Keystone product. He had also been his only director for a couple of months and was enjoying the learning process. Each new short during this period seems to highlight how he nailed down a new technique, to build on with the next. *The Masquerader*, three pictures earlier, was by far the most ambitious film he'd made, allowing him to tell more than one story. With *His New Profession*, he told his story in more than one location, bouncing around between them rapidly. *The Rounders* was an experiment in pacing and *The New Janitor* combines all those techniques to great effect within the best sets he'd worked on yet.

So Chaplin was moving relentlessly forward, to the degree that this doesn't even feel like either a Keystone film or one from 1914. He must have been acutely aware that he was closing in on the end of his year's contract at the studio too and, as he confirms in his autobiography, he "knew the ephemera of it".

In other words, even as his pictures got better, grander and more consistent, he wasn't counting on any lasting fame, so he asked Mack Sennett, for a raise to a thousand dollars per week, which his boss pointed out was more than he earned himself as the owner of the studio. Chaplin politely replied that "the public doesn't line up outside the box-office when your name appears as they do for mine."

Of course, he didn't get the raise, but Essanay soon offered him more: $1,250 per week, along with a signing bonus of $10,000, so naturally he jumped ship. This discussion with Sennett appears to have been at some point in August, meaning that while he was making The New Janitor late in that month, he already knew that he was leaving the studio, even if he didn't know where he was going.

My interpretation of his late 1914 work is that he was learning all he could in preparation for his move to a new studio, whichever it would be. He slowed down to a less frantic and more consistent pace than he had kept throughout the year; both June and August had seen five new Chaplin pictures in theatres, with only one in July, but from this point forward it was two shorts each month, with only one extra in October. Generally speaking, he took longer to make them too, presumably because he could, with a gap between each of them. He still kept a busy schedule, but he was averaging a new picture every two weeks rather than every one, and he wasn't overlapping productions any more. It seems obvious that he wasn't merely experimenting with the cinematic toolbox, he was firmly learning how to produce a picture in a sustainable, professional manner. This progression usually takes new fish years to achieve, but it's somehow appropriate that the madcap factory that was Keystone gave Chaplin the opportunity to do it in only one.

While he devotes little space in his autobiography to his time at Keystone, merely a lone chapter, he does take time to explain something he learned specifically while shooting The New Janitor. As the character of the title, he finds himself at one point fired by the president of the company for which he works, hardly a surprising act given that he's just dumped a bucket of soapy water on him from a dozen floors up in the company skyscraper.

"In pleading with him to take pity on me and let me retain my job," he explained, "I started to pantomime appealingly that I had a large family of little children. Although I was enacting mock sentiment, Dorothy Davenport, an old actress, was on the sidelines watching the scene, and during rehearsal I looked up and to my surprise found her in tears. 'I know it's supposed to be funny,' she said, 'but you just make me weep.' She confirmed something I already felt: I had the ability to evoke tears as well as laughter." This pantomiming didn't make it into the resulting film, but the feeling certainly did.

What struck me immediately with *The New Janitor* was the sets, which are much roomier and far more ambitious than I'm used to seeing in Chaplin's Keystone shorts. We start out in the company lobby, with a chequered floor, marble stairs and apparently working lift. The elevator boy, Al St. John, is cheeky enough to avoid letting him in, so he walks the twelve flights up to the top floor, which could be the very same set from a slightly different angle, but with the stairs changed. He quickly moves down the corridor outside the executives' offices, with panelled walls and a window to the outside world, then enters one of those offices, with another window and a wall covered with the little drawers that hold cards. Another blink and we're in the president's office, with its prominent safe and a third window. That's five locations in less than two minutes, with different floors, walls and props. That might not seem like much to us today, but some of Chaplin's early pictures never left a single square room.

Of course, these are still clearly sets, the work of the Keystone carpenters commendable but not strong enough for us to buy that we're in a real skyscraper, at least until Charlie almost falls out of

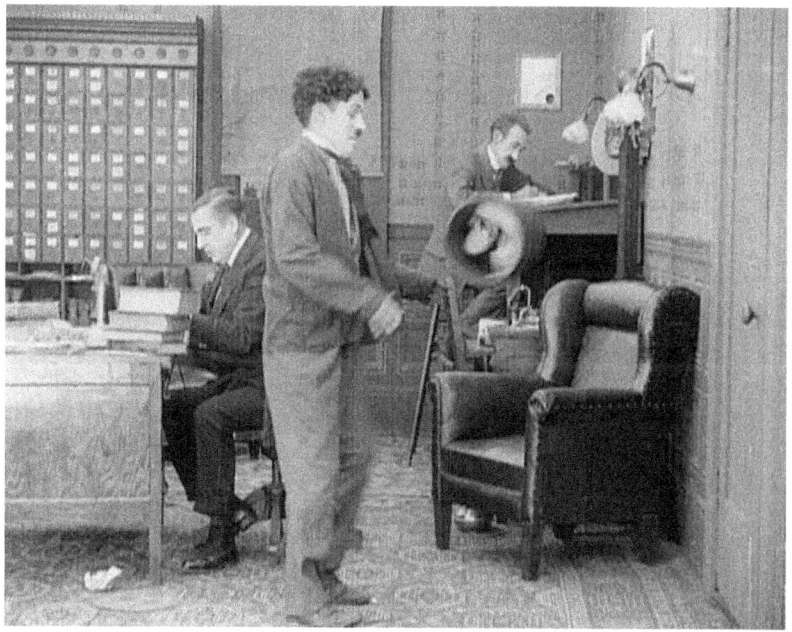

the one real window, the one in the president's office. The others are painted, as are the drawers, the panelling and the marbling on the staircases, but it took more work to put it all together, both mentally and physically, than Keystone usually took.

The shots of the outside of the building are real, with Chaplin really hanging out of that window; Jeffrey Vance identified it as the Marsh Strong Building at 9th & Main in Los Angeles, built only a year earlier. John Bengtson, "the great detective of silent film locations", highlights how close this building is to other locations Chaplin used in other Keystone pictures, such as *His Musical Career*, only four films away. This scene is what Vance calls a "high and dizzy" scene, a couple of years before Harold Lloyd, among others, would make them popular in pictures that were as thrilling as they were comedic.

Once the sets are established, what leaps out are the characters and how they all have a purpose within the script.

It's long been suggested that Keystone films didn't have scripts at all, just starting points from which to improvise a succession of gags, but that belief was firmly debunked by Simon Louvish's book,

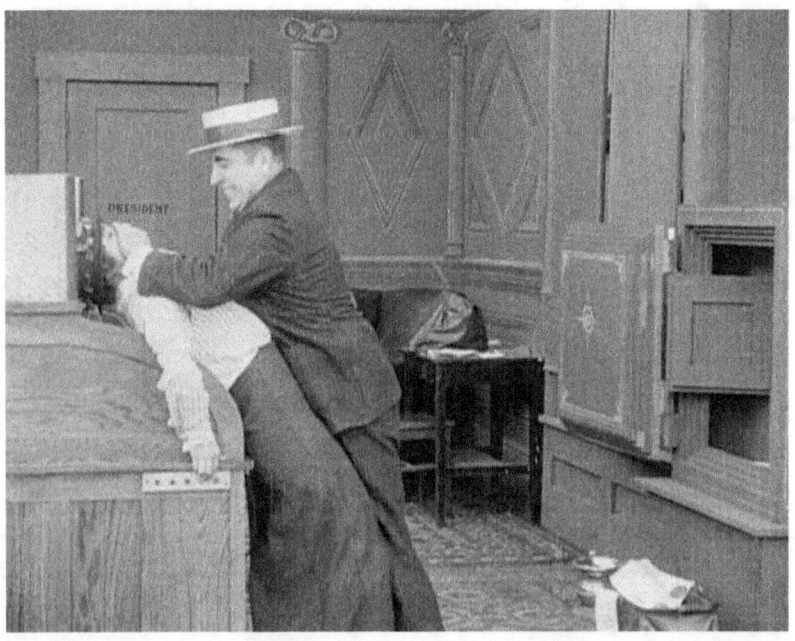

Keystone: The Life and Clowns of Mack Sennett, as he reprints a number of Sennett's scenarios. They're hardly traditional scripts with stage directions and dialogue, but they do show how much thought often went into the progression of the stories. I raise this here because I can't remember any other picture at Keystone that screamed so loudly that it had a firmly defined script. Each of the characters is defined, with their own motivations and their own story arcs. Novelist Gini Koch once told me that any writer should be able to imagine their story from the perspective of any of its characters and it's clear that Chaplin set his script up with that sort of idea in mind. He's the lead, but everyone else has their place too and we can easily extrapolate the story from their perspectives.

And there are a few such characters, even if we discount St. John's elevator boy, whose part is restricted to forcing Chaplin to use the stairs. There's a villain, one of the company's managers who might work in the office opposite the president's but still owes a lot of money to a bookie. His story arc is established quickly, as the debt is being called in and he only has a day to raise the funds or he'll be exposed; with a safe as close nearby as the other side of the hallway, it's clear what his direction will be. The president gets to show two sides too, initially a negative one as Charlie accidentally drenches him with the water he's using to wash his windows, but a positive one later on when Charlie comes good during the bigger holdup scene. Stuck in between is the president's secretary, whose honesty turns out to be Charlie's salvation, albeit not because he absentmindedly dusts her backside after the safe. This particular story couldn't exist without all four characters, but she's the glue that keeps them and their scenes tied together.

Of course, as tends to be the case with the ladies in Keystone pictures, her identity is unclear. IMDb says it's Peggy Page, who Charlie manhandled in *His New Profession*, and the two actresses do look a lot alike. Wikipedia suggests that it's Helen Carruthers, as it did in *His New Profession*, perhaps because she appeared in so many of Chaplin's Keystone shorts. The B.F.I. claims that Minta Durfee played the part, but it's clearly not her so we can discount that suggestion. Whoever it is, she does her job capably, showing some elegance and charm before being choked out by the villain, even though she's a second rank player at Keystone like most of the rest of the cast.

We know that her boss and Charlie's is Jess Dandy, who appeared in most of Chaplin's pictures at this point, while the massively experienced Jack Dillon is the thieving manager. He started out in film as early as 1908 and had over a hundred films to his name by this point, albeit with few left to go. So many of these silent actors didn't even get to fail to make the transition to sound.

While *The New Janitor* can hardly be said to be a sophisticated piece of work today, it certainly was at this particular point in Chaplin's career.

It's less funny than many of his prior films, mostly because the gags refuse to stand in the way of the story and exist to serve it instead. There are some neat ones, such as when Chaplin holds the would be thief at gunpoint by pointing the gun through his own legs while he's bent over double, or when he clambers over his broom when entering the president's office because he apparently can't turn it around; the moments where he nearly falls out of the window are notable too.

However, it's much more consistent than his pictures had been

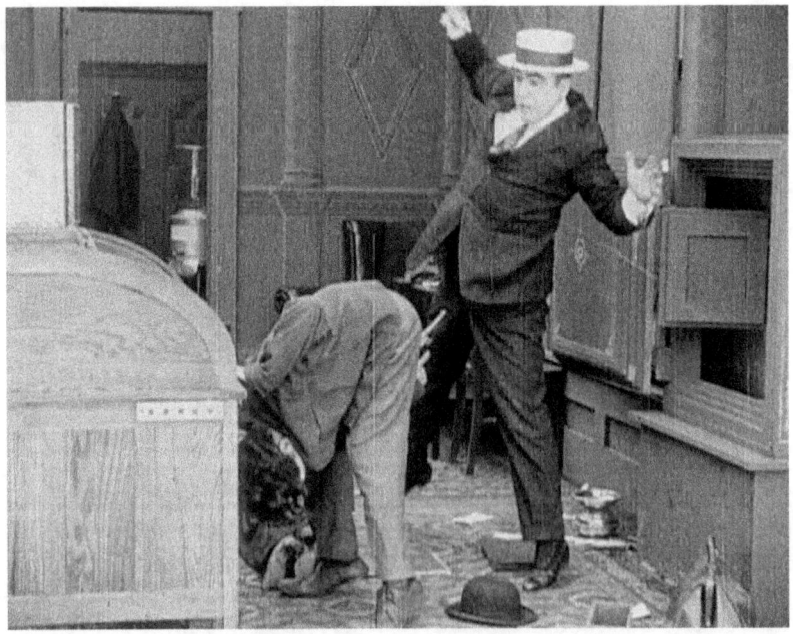

up until that moment, lavishly outfitted (at least for Keystone) and thoughtfully constructed. It serves as yet another step forward for Chaplin, in what feels like his cleanest and most progressive picture thus far with one of his more likeable parts. While historically important, it's often difficult to enjoy Chaplin's more primitive pictures, but this one is an easy one to like.

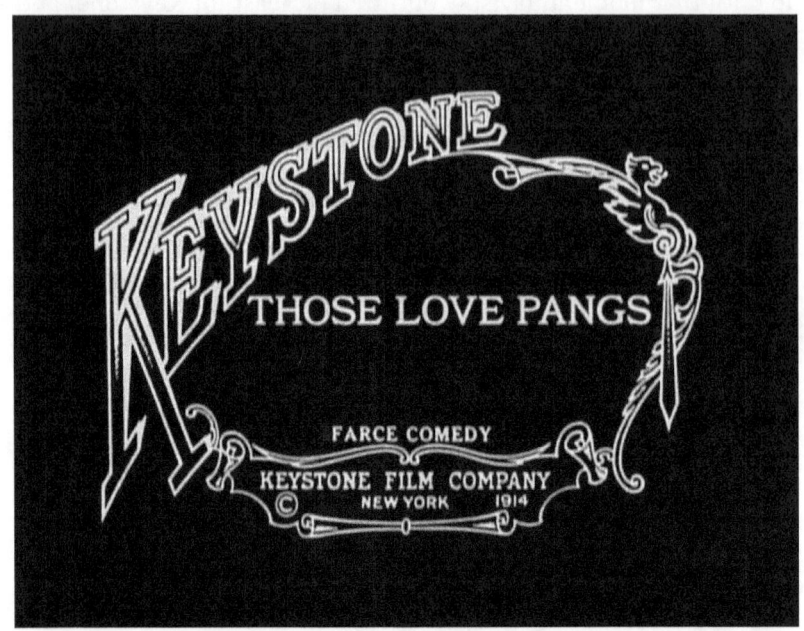

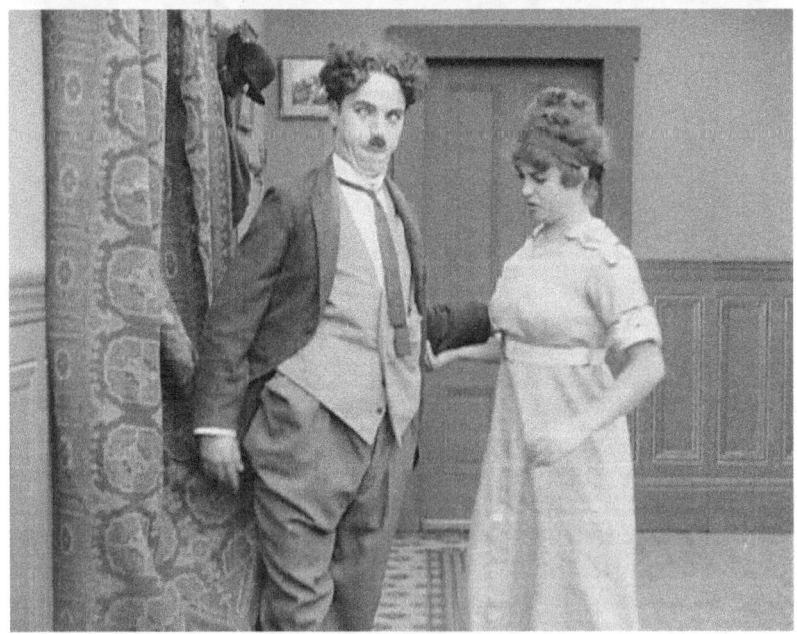

Those Love Pangs
10th October, 1914

Director: Charles Chaplin
Writer: Charles Chaplin
Stars: Charles Chaplin and Chester Conklin

After highlighting that Chaplin's famous (or perhaps infamous) perfectionism was starting to show in the way he was mastering individual aspects of filmmaking in his previous four films, I should point out immediately that very little of the sort appears to be evident in *Those Love Pangs*, clearly a lesser entry in Chaplin's late Keystone period. I should also add that there's a good reason for this.

Jeffrey Vance cites studio boss Mack Sennett as explaining the changes that took place during development. Apparently Chaplin started out on this one reel picture with the simple idea of Charlie and Chester Conklin as rivals for the amorous attentions of their landlady. You can easily imagine some of where that idea would be likely to take them, but it quickly went a great deal further, so far that it expanded into a two reel comedy, *Dough and Dynamite*, often regarded as the best of Chaplin's Keystone pictures. With all that development diverted, *Those Love Pangs* became little more than an afterthought, devoid of much of the care and attention audiences were getting used to from Chaplin at the time.

That's not to say that he didn't work on the little details, because there are still some magnificent points that fit into the progression we've been seeing. However the big picture is notably weak, rather unsure as to what it wants to be.

The best part is the beginning, which is closest to the original goal of the short. With their landlady outside their door, each of the boys position themselves to be the one who will greet her. Charlie's first in line, but Chester outmanouevres him by suggesting that there's a woman under the table. When Charlie's curiosity, not to mention his gullibility, gets the better of him, Chester nips out to grasp the landlady's hand.

Charlie's response is violence, as it so often was in the Keystone shorts, but it's a calm and thoughtful sort of violence for a change. He picks up a fork from the table, tests it, thinks about it, lines himself up and jabs Chester hard in the backside with it, spoiling his moment. He even puts it to his mouth afterwards to pretend that it's a makeshift mouthharp. It's very thoughtfully done.

Of course, if Chester has his moment to shine with the landlady, Charlie's surely going to get one too and that moment is even more thoughtfully done. Of course, Chester picks up the fork and gets ready to reprise the gag, but Charlie's no fool. Realising that he's in precisely the wrong spot, he carefully switches places with the girl. Then he realises that he's inadvertently set her up, so tries to manoeuvre them both into positions of safety. Of course, this fails catastrophically; the landlady rejects his advances and pushes him backwards at just the right time for the fork to hit its originally intended target.

Chaplin is superb here, pantomiming for sure, but with much more subtlety than was usual at Keystone. Conklin isn't bad either and the pair of them do work well together, albeit not so well as Chaplin did with Roscoe Arbuckle in *The Rounders*. What's most notable about the rest of the film isn't so much where they go and what they do but who they meet while they're doing it. One scene in and the landlady is apparently forgotten.

Charlie's all set for the bar, cunningly conning his rival out of a coin, but he's promptly distracted by a slim brunette who waltzes past and looks enticingly at him. She's Vivian Edwards, in her sixth film, five of which were Chaplin pictures. This is the most audiences had got to see of her thus far and she's suitably delightful, as promised by her role as one of the Goo Goo sisters in *The Property Man*.

Her fellow sister in that film, Cecile Arnold, promptly shows up here too, as a similarly delightful blonde who looks more than enticingly at Chester; she actively calls him over, by name too if I'm not very much mistaken. I'm no lip reader but it's so clear that I don't think I need to be.

The difference, of course, is that Charlie is promptly run off by a tall man who shows up to steal the brunette's affections instead, while the blonde is all over Chester, so flagrantly that Charlie throws his hands up in disbelief at his rival's astounding success, then prepares to leap into the lake to literally drown his sorrows.

What's notable isn't who's playing the girls, as both had become regulars at this point in Chaplin's films. Had Arnold shown up in *The Rounders*, it would have meant that she'd been in as many as Edwards and in all the same ones too; presumably they came as a double act. What's notable is what they are, which has generated something of a debate amongst silent film aficionados.

In a silent film, with few intertitles, we can't know for sure, but the suggestion is that they're a pair of prostitutes. Perhaps only one of them is, perhaps the other, perhaps both. Who knows? Well, beyond the suggestion that two such elegant ladies might possibly be interested in a couple of gentlemen who look like Charlie and Chester, who's in an outfit that somewhat mirrors Charlie's in that it clearly doesn't fit properly and in many similar ways, the blonde sticks her boot up on a bench that Charlie's sitting on, pulls a wad of cash out of it, counts it carefully and puts it into Chester's pocket. Are we to believe that she's paying him?

No, surely we're to believe that she's a lot more to Chester than merely a blonde in a park. If she knows his name, lavishes him with

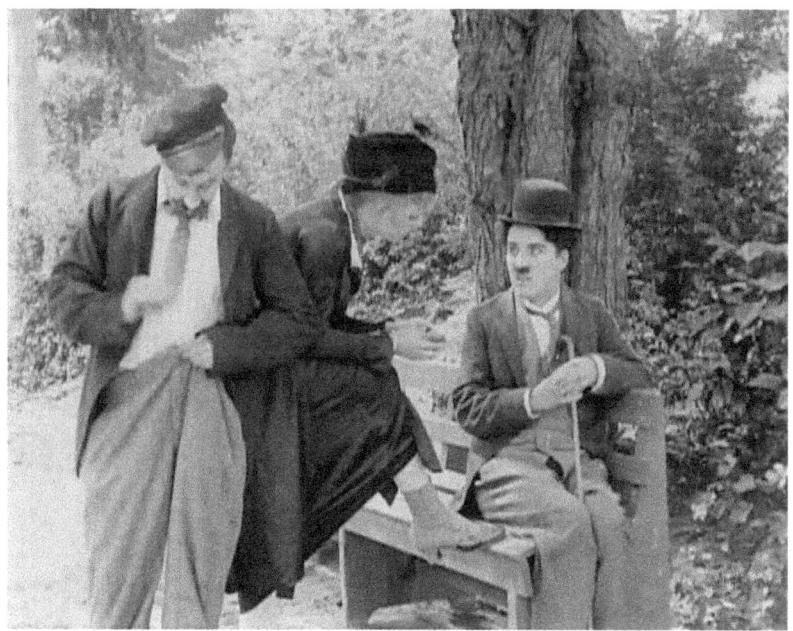

kisses and gives him a large chunk of cash to boot, Occam's razor suggests that he's her pimp. There are other possibilities, of course, but that's by far the most obvious.

Maybe he's really her boyfriend and he'd loaned her some cash, but then what's he doing chasing the landlady, what's she doing hanging out in the park on her lonesome and why does she have the cash secreted in her boot? Maybe she is only a random girl in the park whom Chester cleverly enlists into an elaborate scheme to pull a fast one on Charlie. Maybe there really is no accounting for taste and we shouldn't get so caught up in how to interpret an innocent situation.

No, I don't buy that either, especially as the girls are clearly with whoever has money at any time, even Charlie after they drift away to the nickelodeon and suddenly find him very agreeable company in the front row. They're prostitutes and at that point he has the cash to pay them.

While the quality of the material generally deteriorates as the picture runs on, there are other moments that are worthy of note. Chaplin is still finding new and innovative uses for his cane, for a

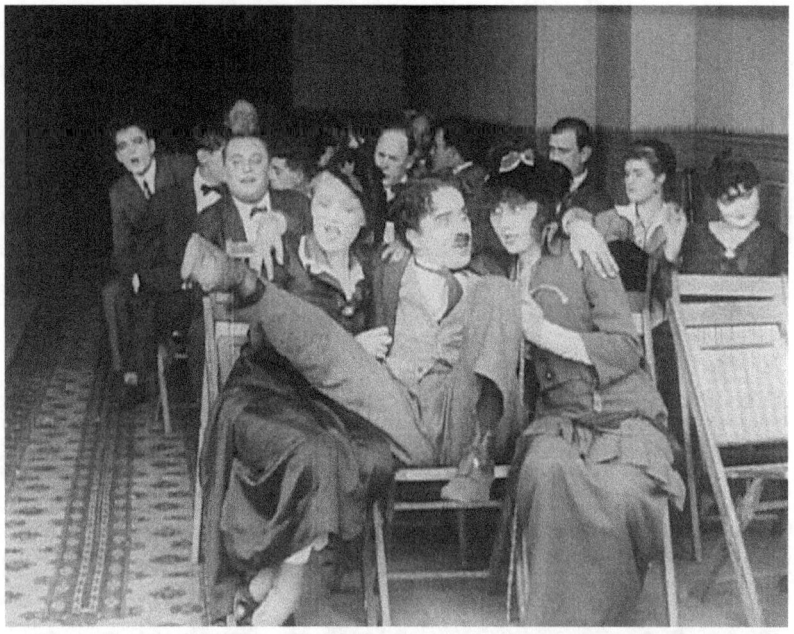

start. He reprises its use as the means to pull someone towards him that he did so notably in *His New Profession*, here dragging Chester along behind him as they leave the house and down its front steps. Later he does exactly the same thing to the tall man who hooked his brunette; he hooks him in return, right into the lake. Later still, he uses it repetitively on Chester, pulling him in to bounce him off his belly in a strange sort of fighting style that he might have learned from Arbuckle. A little more subtly, he also finds two uses for the other end: to clean his nails and pick his teeth. I'm less sure about another lauded moment, but I did find some charm in the way Charlie talks with his feet in the theatre because his hands are occupied around the girls' shoulders. The idea of using an upside down Chester as a temporary seat was more fun to me.

What all this means is that the details are often praiseworthy, even if the picture itself fails to maintain even a modicum of consistency.

It starts out like the many hotel pictures, hints at becoming a bar picture (one of the reissue titles was *The Rival Mashers*), becomes instead a park picture and ends up as a movie theatre picture. Rather than building a frenetic pace by bouncing us between these settings, as Chaplin did in *His New Profession*, he merely shifts the action gradually from one to the next without any of them seeming to benefit. Most of it takes place in the park, where we're reminded of Chaplin's famous quote to Sennett that, "All I need to make a comedy is a park, a policeman and a pretty girl." Here he had all three and a delightful pair of the latter to boot. The time spent at the nickelodeon is especially sparse, with the inevitable eventual chaos restricted to a few gags and a few seconds before Charlie finds himself thrown through the screen. He'd already made better films in each of these settings and some that used all of them.

Shooting was quick, taking only four days compared to the nine for *The New Janitor* before it and eight for *Gentlemen of Nerve* after it. *The Rounders* only took four days too, but it doesn't show its seams the way this one does. Sure, there was a crowd of people watching from the opposite side of the lake during the finalé of that picture, but there's little that Keystone could do about that in a public park. Here, there are at least two goofs that could have been fixed. The first is the number of obvious onlookers reflected in the door of the bar from whose delights Charlie is distracted by Vivian Edwards. My better half noticed the second a little later in the park, when Charlie first sits down on a bench; someone peeks over the bush behind him, only to vanish quickly, presumably when he realises that he's just interrupted a live shot and that was never edited out or the scene reshot.

Surely the main flaw here lies in how quickly the film was put together. Chaplin simply had to finish things up, so he could make *Gentlemen of Nerve* before shifting straight into *Dough and Dynamite*, which the original idea of this film became.

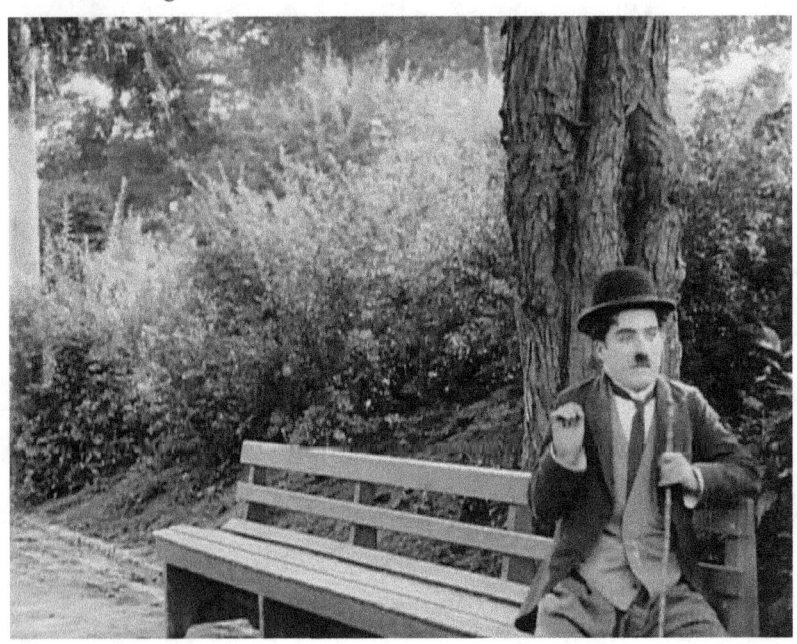

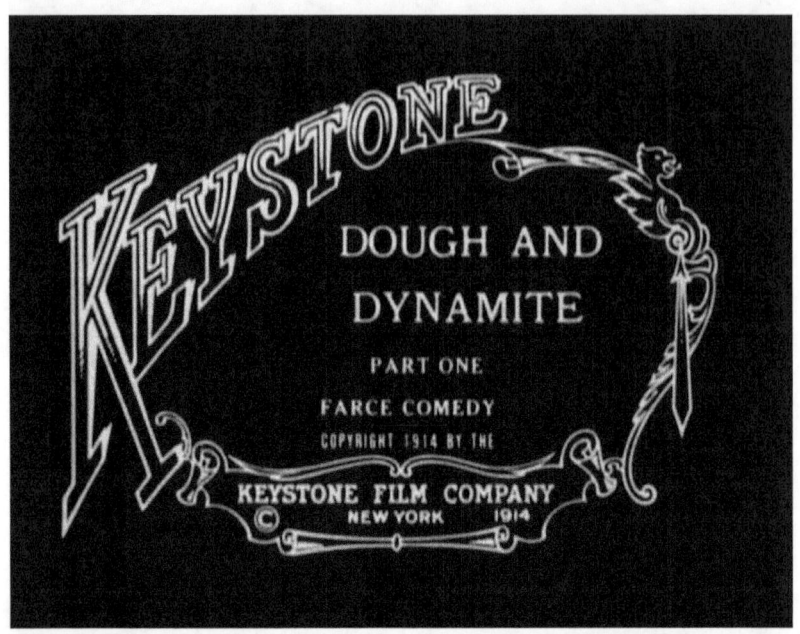

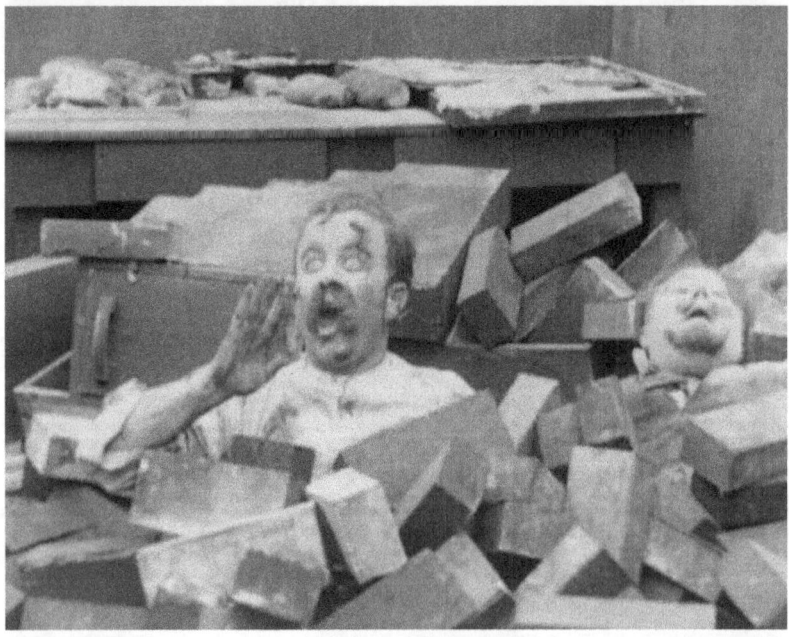

Dough and Dynamite
26th October, 1914

Director: Charles Chaplin
Writers: Charles Chaplin and Mack Sennett
Stars: Charles Chaplin and Chester Conklin

If *Those Love Pangs* was a lesser picture in Chaplin's filmography, there's good reason; all the best material had been left out, marked instead for this film.

That picture had aimed at setting Charlie and Chester Conklin up as screen rivals for the attentions of their landlady, without any real idea of how that was going to unfold. Chaplin developed the idea of them working at a bakery and that soon grew into such promising material that it was shifted out to be a separate picture, this one. *Those Love Pangs* was therefore developed once again, was shot quickly in only four days and ended up feeling much like an afterthought, albeit one that benefitted from Chaplin's continued growth as a filmmaker; he endowed it with enough interesting detail that it doesn't feel unworthy of attention. However, it's immediately obvious that *Dough and Dynamite* overshadows it completely, as Jeffrey Vance ably highlights: "In the early silent-film era," he explains, "*Dough and Dynamite* was generally regarded as one of the greatest of all Hollywood comedies."

He also calls it "perhaps the most important comedy Chaplin made in his early ascent to screen stardom and the most profitable of all the Keystone two-reel comedies." These are powerful but deceptively simple words that deserve to be expanded.

Most of Chaplin's Keystone pictures were one-reelers, which describes both their length and their importance. A reel is a single magazine containing one thousand feet of film. In the sound era, reels were projected at 24 frames per second, which meant that one reel amounted to eleven minutes or so of material. Back in the days of the silents, projection was slower, varying between 16 and 22 frames per second, so that reel played for longer, as much as fourteen or fifteen minutes. Two-reelers took up twice as much film and twice as much running time, so were generally reserved for more important pictures. While Chaplin had acted in a few two-reelers, he had only previously made one as a director, *The Property Man*. Both *Those Love Pangs* and *Dough and Dynamite* were initially slated for one reel only.

In his autobiography, Chaplin explains that he went notably overbudget, not a good sign for a director today and not a good sign back in 1914 either. Mack Sennett expected each Keystone picture to cost under a thousand dollars, but *Dough and Dynamite* bloated up to eighteen hundred, losing Chaplin his $25 bonus for bringing it in under budget. That sort of thing might have cost him more, such as the creative freedom he had to continue writing and directing his own pictures, but the result was recognised by an unprecedented success at the box office.

To quote Chaplin's own words: "The only way they could retrieve themselves, said Sennett, would be to put it out as a two-reeler, which they did, and it grossed more than one hundred and thirty thousand dollars the first year." With the picture making that much money, no wonder Chaplin remained in charge of his own films. However, Sennett fought the idea that spending more opened up the possibility of earning more, one prominent reason why Chaplin was already seeking a new employer, even as he was bringing his brother, Sydney, to Keystone.

If he was spending more money than his boss wanted, Chaplin was at least becoming more efficient as a filmmaker. Shooting of *The Property Man* ran over seventeen days, not counting any taken off, but *Dough and Dynamite* took only fourteen, beginning on 29th August and ending on 11th September, an unfortunate coincidence for a film whose conclusion includes a successful terrorist attack. Chaplin's autobiography cites nine of those days as being shooting days, but there's so much crammed into the picture, which runs almost half an hour, that it's amazing to think of how quickly the complex choreography must have been mastered.

It's that interplay between characters that leaps out the most in this picture, not only in how well it's done but in how much of it there is and how constantly and consistently it continues. While the action certainly escalates, as we might expect, to that explosive finalé, it feels much more natural in its progression than usual and it's paced magnificently. We breathe easily throughout, even as we're presented with a constant barrage of slapstick.

Charlie is a waiter again, but this time at a bakery with its own restaurant, and he's about as effective at it as usual. He starts out merely collecting plates from tables but he's so absent-minded that he collects one that's only just been delivered, scraping leftovers from other plates onto it before the customer is able to take a bite. Within forty very busy seconds, he's reprimanded by the customer, apologises for his actions, returns his food, retrieves the leftovers with his fingers and drops some in the man's lap, samples what's left and wipes his fingers on both his own trousers and the customer's jacket.

This scene highlights just how much is going on in this picture. While it's a cliché for critics to suggest that viewers shouldn't blink or they'll miss something, it's a fundamental truth in *Dough and Dynamite*, as the detail continues to be this dense throughout and it rarely lets up. In fact, there's a great deal of prestaging going on here: often what seem like throwaway mistakes turn out to be carefully setting up later moments, but more of that later.

Of course the sense of hygiene is terrible: Gordon Ramsey would

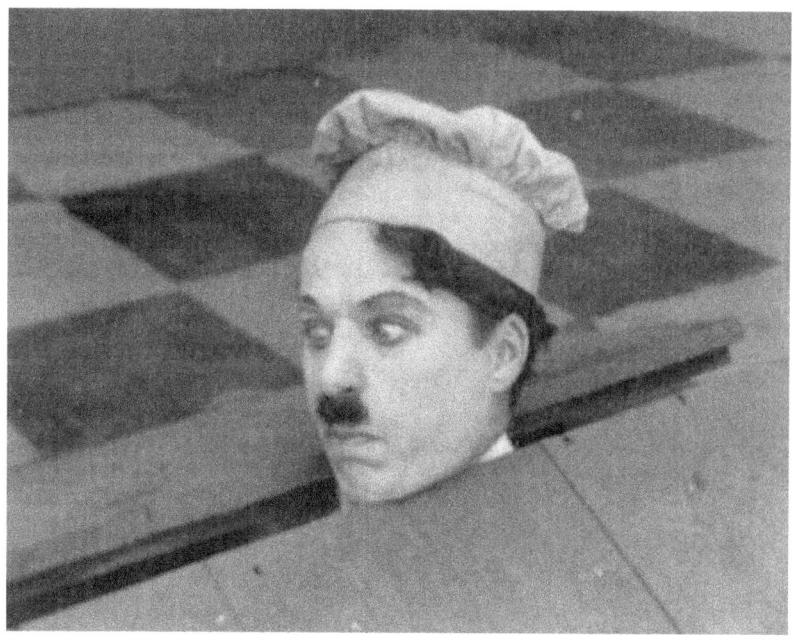

be utterly horrified and we haven't even found our way down to the kitchen yet. That's downstairs, through a trapdoor set in the floor of the main dining area, opposite the door to the kitchen. There's no way that that could go horribly wrong, huh?

Well, at this point, the place seems to be running very smoothly, Charlie being the only spanner in the works or fly in the ointment, driven both by an abiding laziness and an eye for the ladies. He promptly leaves that customer with a collection of plates because a lovely young creature has just wandered up to the front, its counter display neatly labelled "Assorted French Tarts". This allows him to both imitate her enticing sway and play havoc with a plate of pastries, one naturally flying through the air with the greatest of ease onto the face of the very same beleaguered customer Charlie had already caused so much trouble for. We're only two scenes in and both props and people (not that there's much difference) are already being re-used and built upon.

It's not surprising to see why audiences adored this picture. The slapstick arrives quickly and, while it's hardly high brow stuff, it's impeccably timed and carefully choreographed and it continues on

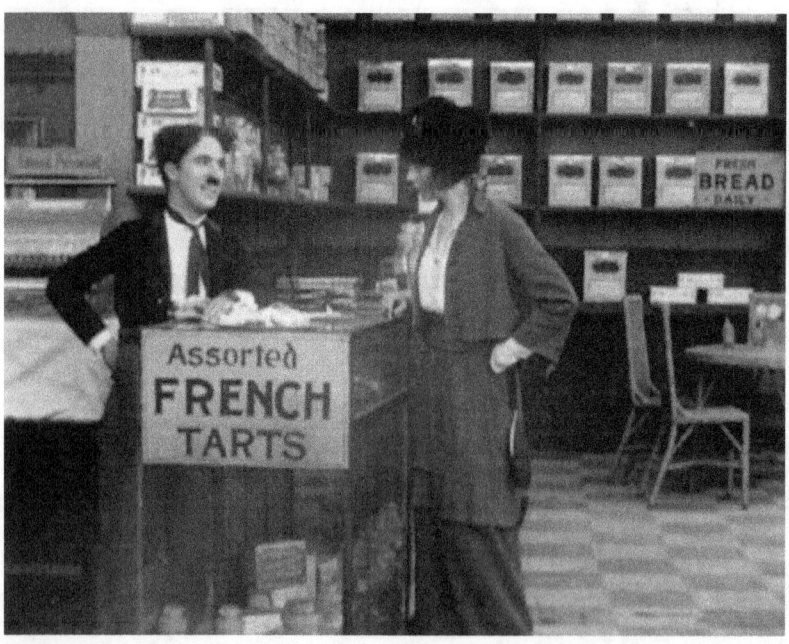

unabated. Even though many of these moves, especially those that exist within fights, are routine ones that we've seen many times before (and not only in Chaplin's films either), they're put to use magnificently and, if the film could be regarded as a piece of music, they serve ably as its beats.

There's a real rhythm here that goes far beyond anything that was achieved in any of the earlier Chaplin shorts and it persists for much longer. Where most Keystone films begin with an idea that spawns action and then escalates rapidly into a frantic chase scene, Chaplin had already been aiming at a different approach for some time and here finally mastered his counter. This feels more like a dance, in which the tempo is just as important as the choreography and the payoff at the end is grown as much through the expansion of participants and scope than the actual moves they make.

Chaplin's growing sophistication is highlighted not only through the number of people who actually have something to do here but through how he introduces them. Keystone pictures were never known for their subtlety, so characters tended to have one function and they showed up just in time to perform it before scooting off again once it's done. In this picture, many have a whole bunch of scenes in which they do very little except act naturally until the moment they're called upon to shine.

The story even has a grand sweep that actually makes sense within the logic of the film, even if it doesn't make a lot of sense outside of it. The idea of Charlie and his partner in crime, played by Chester Conklin, being elevated from mere waiters to replace the entire staff of bakers, was apparently prompted by industrial action really sweeping Los Angeles at the time, but I'm at the same loss as Jeffrey Vance to see how striking bakers might better find their demands met by blowing up the places at which they work. Chaplin was outspoken politically but this doesn't feel like social comment.

Instead it feels like simplification. This unnamed bakery is run by Fritz Schade and his wife Norma Nichols. Chaplin and Conklin are their waiters, while Cecile Arnold and perhaps Peggy Page are the waitresses. Jess Dandy, appearing in drag, is the stunningly homely cook, reminding very much of the female characters comedian Les Dawson would play many decades later. All these are portrayed in a neutral light, as neither good nor bad; that extends to each of the customers, played by Vivian Edwards, Phyllis Allen and Charles Parrott.

The bakers, who are led by Glen Cavender and also include Slim Summerville and possibly Edgar Kennedy, among others, are the ones with emotional bias. They "want less work and more pay", as one intertitle highlights, and though there's nothing to suggest whether their demands might be fair or not, it's abundantly clear that their subsequent actions aren't. They storm out, gesticulating wildly, then buy a loaf of bread, stuff it with dynamite and have a little girl return it to the bakery for them. Oh yes, they're villains.

With that framework outlined, you might imagine the rest of the picture yourselves. However, your imagination might fall short for a change, as this one's a marvel, the scenario written by Chaplin but apparently in collaboration with Sennett, who didn't have any of the subtlety that's on show here.

The choreography, tempo and attention to detail must all belong to Chaplin; I can't see what Sennett might have contributed, unless it was gags. There are some strong setpieces, like one where Charlie parades up and down in front of Schade with a tray of loaves on his head. We're impressed by his achievement but still believe that he slips up and drops one until we realise that it's all a setup; he leans over to retrieve it and promptly loses the rest. Another has Charlie effectively handcuffing himself behind his back with dough, having to climb through his arms to escape. There are setpieces in many of Chaplin's early pictures though; more of them, however well done, aren't groundbreaking. What I found new here were the more subtle things in the background.

Some tied to the reuse of props. Another apparently throwaway moment that I initially thought was a mistake arrived when a baker attempts to transfer dough from a vat to a table to knead but lets most of it fall on the floor instead. It's ignored for a while, as if it never happened, but later it comes into focus when Chester slips on it and then again when Charlie picks it up and throws it back into the vat, highlighting the ineptitude of the waiters and their horrible approach to industrial hygiene.

Other subtleties tie to gradual discovery too, but by us catching up to them rather than the plot. One of my favourite moments in the film arrived after Charlie finishes cleaning up the kitchen and sits down on a large sack of flour. Only at that point did I realise that Chester Conklin had been in the scene all along, still pinned underneath the sack after Charlie had dropped it down the stairs onto him a little earlier in the film. To me, this highlighted just how much Chaplin was becoming totally aware of everything going on in his films, so that he could best use those details to this sort of strong effect.

Another aspect to leap out at me in *Dough and Dynamite* is the democratic manner in which abuse is dished out. While we know the Little Tramp today as a sympathetic creature, he could be and often was actively obnoxious in some of his earlier pictures. Critics have called out a number of instances where he heaps violent abuse on characters in completely one-sided acts that are often difficult or impossible to justify. Here, nobody escapes!

Chaplin is on the receiving end just as much as he dishes it out to others, as is Conklin. The waitresses may escape more than most but they get theirs too, as does the boss, the cook and even the customers, some of whom also get a few notable shots in of their own. Of course, the terrorist bakers receive plenty, just as they

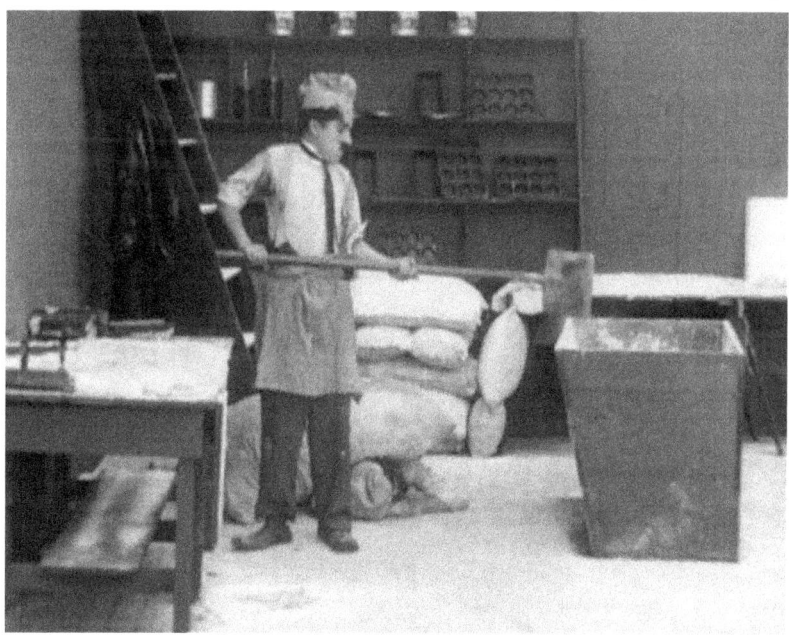

deliver plenty, including that explosive grand finalé.

I could easily imagine Sennett dishing some out to Chaplin too, off screen for notably failing to keep within budget, but Chaplin, who certainly delivered here his best film thus far, clearly had the final word: a hundred and thirty thousand of them.

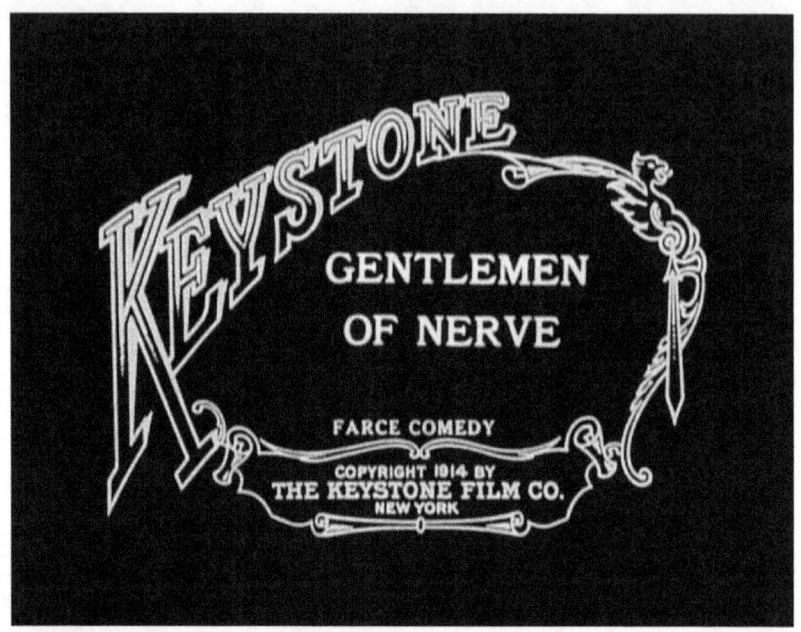

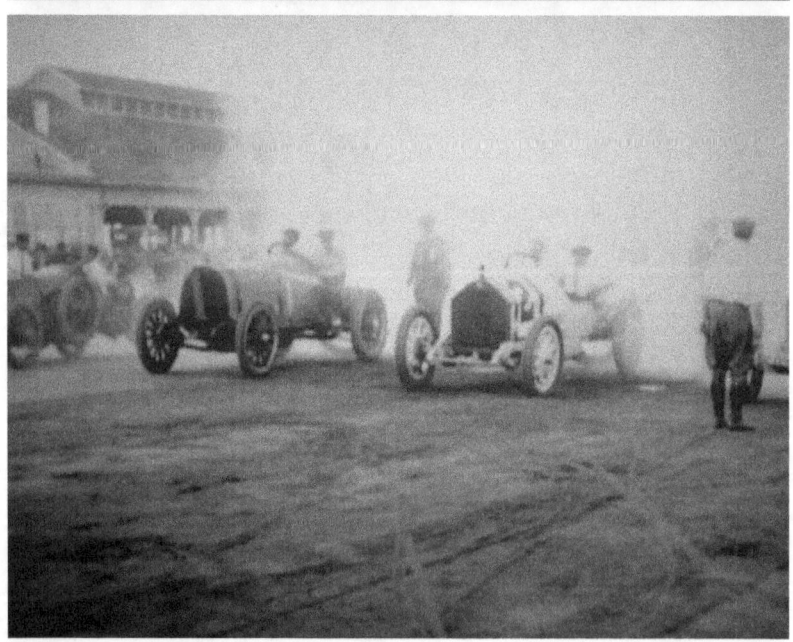

Gentlemen of Nerve
29th October, 1914

Director: Charles Chaplin
Writer: Charles Chaplin
Stars: Charles Chaplin, Mabel Normand, Chester Conklin and Mack Swain

The grand sweep of Chaplin's Keystone pictures, especially those during the second half of 1914 which he wrote and directed himself with the benefit of substantial creative control, is clearly all about his growth as a filmmaker.

Most of these self-directed films highlight his newfound mastery of something and a new experiment to attempt to solve something else. Given that his previous film, *Dough and Dynamite*, was a peach of a picture, surely his best yet, it's somewhat frustrating to realise that this one absolutely and emphatically isn't.

I have no doubt that the title of *Gentlemen of Nerve* is supposed to have at least three meanings, but I'm also seeing a fourth, which is the sheer nerve of the gentlemen at Keystone, including Chaplin himself, who shot this overly generic revisit to a number of his earlier films and released it three days after what became his most successful Keystone picture and arguably his best too. A quarter of the way into this film, my better half asked me, "Didn't we see this one already?" and I knew exactly what she meant.

The first deliberate meaning of the title refers to the real drivers racing their real automobiles at the Ascot Park Speedway in Los Angeles on Sunday, 20th September, 1914.

This is the very same venue which served as the background for *Mabel's Busy Day*, four months earlier. As that was ostensibly a Mabel Normand film, with Chaplin attempting to steal it out from under her, while this is a Charlie Chaplin picture, with Normand trying to steal it from him, it could easily be regarded as a either riff on the earlier film or a thematic sequel.

I found *Mabel's Busy Day* not only the worst of Chaplin's pictures for Keystone but the one in which he was at his most obnoxious and least sympathetic; he returns to that here somewhat but not to the same degree. Fortunately, Mabel, an annoying character in that film too for her constant "woe is me" attitude and her unbelievable copout at the end, is an absolute joy here and surely the cause of some of the best moments to be found anywhere in the picture.

The second meaning isn't obvious on screen, but refers to Bert Dingley and Ed Swanson, for whom this event was a benefit, as they'd been recently injured racing in Tacoma. Dingley was a major name, known at the time as the first American Championship Car Racing champion, having won the championship in 1909. Racing was a dangerous sport and injuries and even death were routine occurrences. In 1929, for instance, after a full decade and a half of advancement from the vehicles seen here, the Indianapolis 500 was filmed for *Speedway*, a William Haines feature; a driver died during that race, possibly in one of the many on screen crashes, and the winner died almost three weeks later in another race.

This benefit was therefore not just a race but a complete event, with a number of what were termed as "freak races" "including a foot-auto-horse and bicycle race, quart of gas race, dress up race, quarter-mile slow race in high gear, exhibition mile, tug of war between motor trucks, and junior race." Attendees paid fifty cents per ticket, even members of the press, so the 5,000 who showed up raised $2,500 for the injured men.

Of course, the third and last deliberate meaning of the title refers to Charlie Chaplin and Mack Swain, as they attempt to find their way into the event without paying, just as Charlie managed to do in the earlier picture.

Everywhere I look seems to identify the two as friends, but they don't appear to be; they're merely both trying to do the same thing at the same time. There is some humour in their interaction, but mostly it was the bystanders who engrossed me. *Gentlemen of Nerve* was the fourth Chaplin picture at Keystone to be shot on location during real auto races and it's been fascinating to watch how the regular audience interacted with what he did and how that changed over time. During *Kid Auto Races at Venice, Cal.*, shot in January, nobody had a clue who he was as he didn't appear on screen until February and so they watched the races instead, at least for a while. By the end of May, when *Mabel's Busy Day* was shot, they knew exactly who he was and they watched him instead. Here, in October, they're lining up to see what he has in store and he plays that up.

Mack Swain was a talented comedian, as we've seen in many of Chaplin's Keystone shorts, but he's more of a lumbering ox here without anything much to warrant his presence. It's telling that his best scene by far is the one where he tries to get into the races through the gap made by a missing board in a wall. He gets stuck, naturally, and nothing seems to help, not even the time-honoured Keystone boot to the rear, which Charlie attempts a number of times before handing over the reins to the cop who shows up to try to pull him back.

The best bit about the scene is Charlie clearly getting fed up with the wait and crawling through Swain's legs instead. The next best is how the folk in the makeshift bar on the other side of the wall act once he shows up. One lady passes him a seltzer bottle, which he puts to good use, though its spray mysteriously attains the magical power of a fire hose when it goes through the gap in the wall to hit the cop on the outside in the face. In other words, none of the best bits are Swain's and yet this is his best scene in the picture.

For such a throwaway short film, the cast is a strong one. Before

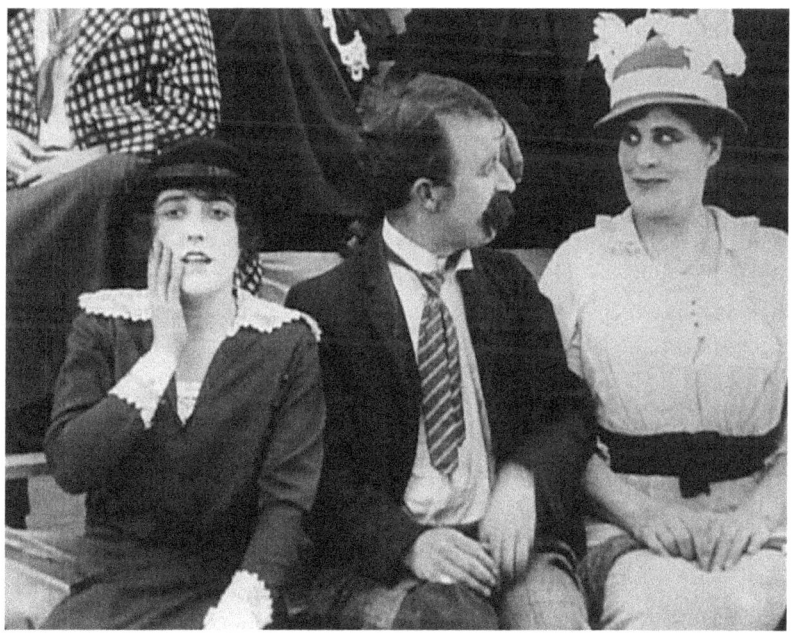

Chaplin shows up to start shenanigans at the gate, we've watched Mabel Normand and her beau for this picture, Chester Conklin, pay their way in and sit down to watch the fun. Unfortunately, they sit right next to Phyllis Allen, who flirts up a storm with Chester and pisses Mabel off no end.

Of course, with Mabel on his arm, we really have no idea why Conklin is interested in this flirtatious woman; Conklin was born in 1886, so Normand, believably a former postcard model and bathing beauty, was six years his junior, while Allen, a bulky battleaxe, was a full quarter of a century older. None of it makes any sense, but it is at least mildly amusing until Normand elevates it by orchestrating her revenge with a neat stamp to her competitor's foot. She goes on to elevate the picture in this sort of way a couple more times too, the other times opposite Chaplin rather than Allen. That she steals both of those scenes from him highlights her talent well.

Mostly though, I found that I wasn't watching the cast, I was watching the audience. Swain is only ever used for his bulk while Conklin is given ridiculous scenes to set up Normand who, as good as she is here, isn't given a lot to do. Chaplin is the focus, of course, at least once he actually shows up, which is a surprising amount of time into the picture, but even when he's shining, he's generally shining in front of a host of folk who can't wait to see what he's going to do.

Beyond being the next step in the progression of how audiences saw Chaplin's star rising, there are two further reasons why this is interesting. One is that Keystone weren't just here to shoot a film, they were here to be part of the event too and it's clear that Chaplin was playing to the crowd. The other is that there are ringers dotted amongst it, so that he can interact with them. Who they are, I have no idea, but it was fun trying to figure out which of them were Keystone actors and which mere members of the regular audience. There's a great interactive scene where Charlie antagonises some of them that would play even better if we didn't know the history.

There are other strong moments too. One minor but enjoyable one involves Charlie and Mabel, who has ditched the unattentive Chester for the overly attentive Charlie, and an amazing vehicle, identified by a sign as being the Franklin Wind Machine. It's a large automobile with a huge propellor on the front; as Charlie leans on the latter, it knocks off his hat, and when it's started up, both he and Mabel are literally blown away. In an earlier scene, before Mabel finds her way to Charlie, he sits down by another girl who has a drink with a straw; he cleverly sneaks enough of it while she isn't looking that she eventually just gives it to him. I particularly liked the scene where Conklin's character kisses Allen's and she goes ballistic, but that's as much for the reaction of the crowd around them as it is for the characters. These various moments help to keep the picture a lot more interesting than *Mabel's Busy Day* and perhaps the best of them is left for last, as Charlie aims to kiss Mabel, only for her to rebuff him in a great scene-stealing moment.

Sadly, these moments are peppered through a notably weaker script than usual. It's a racing film without any real racing, though there is one beautifully atmospheric shot of cars lined up for a tyre change race, mostly obscured by smoke. While Chaplin is more sympathetic here than in *Mabel's Busy Day*, he's still firmly back in obnoxious mode and there are a couple of notably violent moments that feel more like the first half of his year at the studio than the

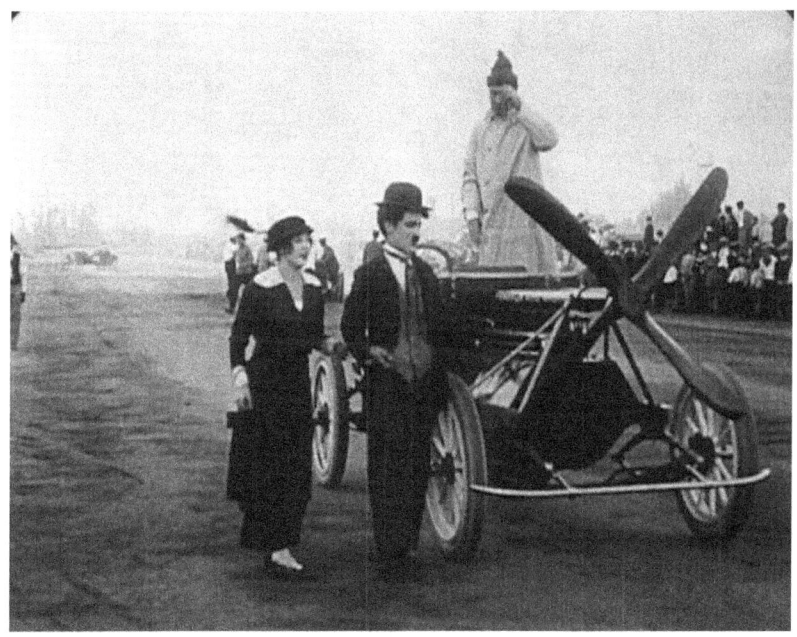

second: in one he bites Conklin's nose, like Ford Sterling might have done, and in the other pokes a lit cigarette onto Swain's. Who nose why those were deemed appropriate at this point in time, when his general direction was firmly away from that sort of thing!

The editing is notably rough too, more like a workprint than a polished film. Mostly, the whole thing is one long string of déjà vu as it's all reminiscent of, if not replicated outright from, a host of earlier Chaplin films. We might be able to bend a little, this being part of a charity event, though I don't know the financial details, but we can't fully forgive the relentless familiarity of it all.

Incidentally, Chaplin's character name in this film is Mr Wow-Wow, which doesn't seem to have any connection to the piece at all. Instead it was sourced from the Fred Karno sketch, *The Wow Wows*, one which the impresario had written specifically for an American audience and chosen for his company (which at the time included not only Chaplin but also Stanley Jefferson, later to become Stan Laurel) to play when they toured the United States in 1910, though they had all advised him against it.

A skit on secret societies like the freemasons, it played fairly well

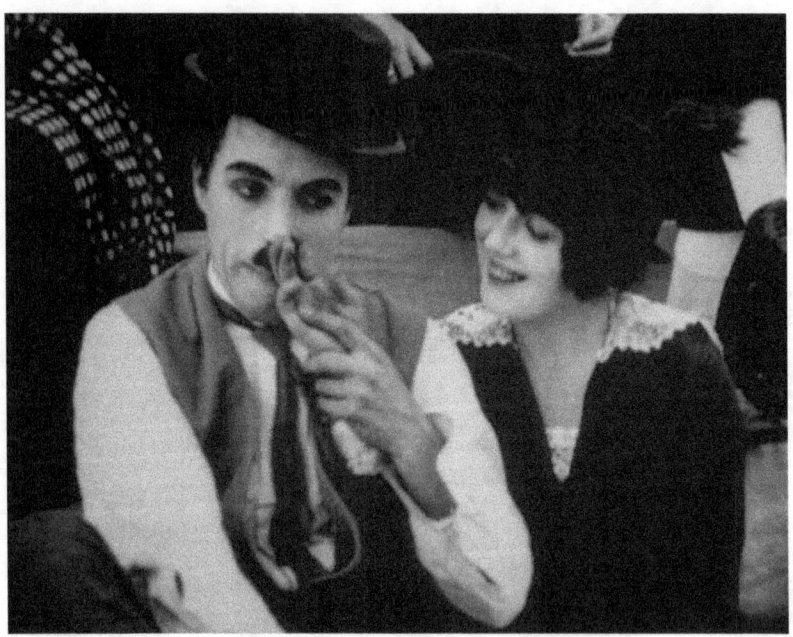

but failed to engage with audiences and Karno found much greater success after he replaced *The Wow Wows* with *Mumming Birds*, then retitled *A Night in an English Music Hall*, which was a tour de force for Chaplin, the very reason Mack Sennett sought him out for Keystone and from which he liberally borrowed for a number of films for the studio, most especially *The Knockout*. He didn't do the same with *The Wow Wows* but, from his choice of character name here, it must have resonated with him at least a little.

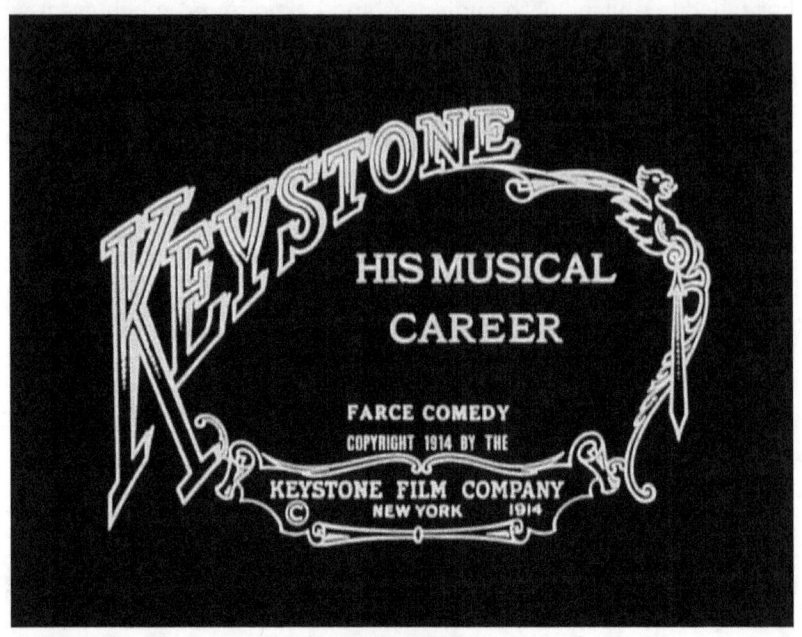

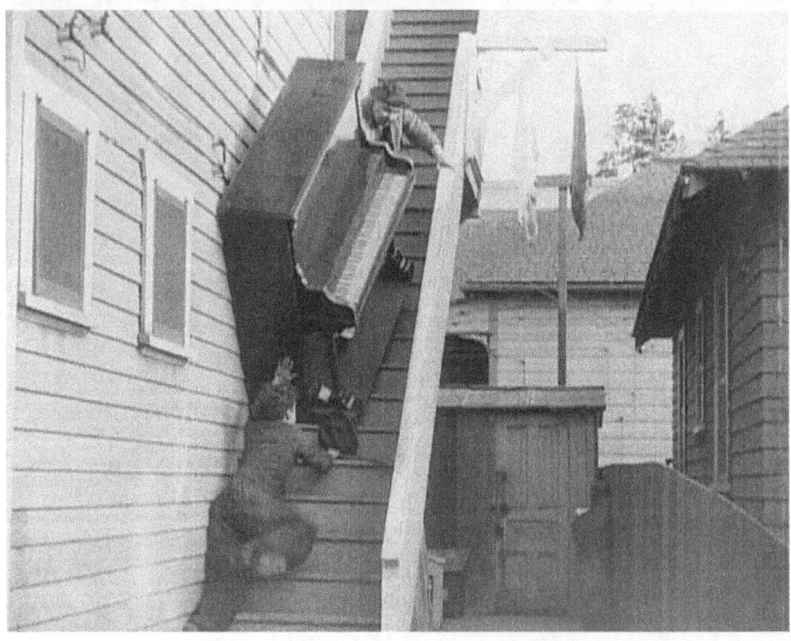

His Musical Career
7th November, 1914

Director: Charles Chaplin
Writer: Charles Chaplin
Stars: Charles Chaplin and Mack Swain

His Musical Career isn't a bad picture but it's far more notable for what it inspired than for what it is. Most obviously it's one clear inspiration for the Laurel and Hardy comedy, *The Music Box*, which won the debut Academy Award for Live Action Short Film (Comedy) in 1932, eighteen years after this film was released.

Technically, *The Music Box* was a vague remake of their 1927 short film, *Hats Off*, which is sadly now lost; in that picture, Stan and Ollie hauled a washing machine up a long flight of steps in the Silver Lake district of Los Angeles, but they reverted in the later short to the piano that Chaplin introduces as a prop here. They did retain the same stairs though, which are today unsurprisingly a tourist attraction and which had been already used by Billy Bevan in *Ice Cold Cocos* in 1926, as well as Charley Chase for *Isn't Life Terrible?* one year earlier. *His Musical Career* isn't another one, but the stairs that Chaplin and Mack Swain climb here with their piano appear longer, narrower and steeper.

Many connections exist between *His Musical Career* and *The Music Box*, even if we bypass *Hats Off* as an intermediary step. Chaplin and Laurel knew each other well, of course, having both worked for Fred Karno in England and travelled to the States with him in 1910, when the latter was still Stan Jefferson, the former's understudy. *The Music Box* was also made at Hal Roach Studios, where it was directed by James Parrott, the brother of one of the studio's biggest stars, Charley Chase. The latter, under his birth name of Charles Parrott, which he continued to use as a director, started out as an actor at Keystone Studios in 1914, as did Chaplin, and the two appeared in many of the same films. In fact, his first three confirmed roles were in Chaplin shorts, *Mabel at the Wheel*, *The Knockout* and *Mabel's Busy Day*, which were Chaplin's 11th, 18th and 19th films respectively, giving the latter a little head start. What's more, Parrott was in this picture too, briefly as the manager of the music store which hires Swain and Chaplin to take care of their deliveries.

The most obvious connection though is the gag that involves one large man and one small man hauling a piano up a long and narrow flight of stairs. However, *The Music Box* treats this as the core of its story and tasks its leads with handling just one piano over three reels of film; here, Swain and Chaplin handle a pair of them in only one reel, with this being only one gag to play with. In fact, while it's played well, it may not even be the best gag in the film, that honour going to the one that immediately follows it, as Charlie staggers around the apartment of Mr. Poor with the whole weight of the piano on his back while the three other people in the room dilly dally about deciding where he should put it down.

So, while Laurel and Hardy's Oscar winning short isn't a remake of this film, it's still clearly inspired by it. It's also a much better picture, not only because it had three reels and a lot more money and time to play with. Chaplin had one more single reeler left after this one at Keystone but, after *Dough and Dynamite*, his mind was clearly on longer material.

We open in relatively lackluster fashion, with Chaplin getting a job working for Mack Swain, both of them presumably using their regular personae of Charlie and Ambrose, even though they have been sometimes credited as Tom and Mike. The main gag here is a routine prank which Charlie plays on Ambrose by switching two identical tins of liquid so that he takes a swig of the piano varnish instead of the water. It's hardly high art and it's followed only by Charlie taking a nap on the keyboard and falling off.

What's most important here is how Chaplin strips off his shirt to emphasise the size difference between him and his co-star. He was a mere 5' 5" tall, while Swain was 6' 2" and much larger in every direction. With this setup, the contrast is even more obvious than it was between the 5' 8" Laurel and the 6' 1" Hardy. Chaplin flexes his muscles, which only serves to show how scrawny he was compared to Swain, so, naturally, it's Charlie stuck underneath the piano on its way up those stairs and once it makes it to the top.

There's another contrast in play, a simple but effective one. Mr. Rich buys a piano from the store and Mr. Poor is unable to keep up the payments on the one he already has, their names being as representative of their financial status as you might expect. That's fair enough for 1914, especially as they both live on Prospect St., but it doesn't raise the laugh that accompanied the inspired names in *The Rounders*, a mere two months earlier, of Chaplin as Mr. Full and Roscoe Arbuckle as Mr. Fuller. Mr. Rich's place is number 999 and Mr. Poor is at 666; the two unsurprisingly get mixed up, albeit by the store manager rather than Ambrose and Charlie, as is usually claimed, given that we clearly see the house number at Mr. Rich's.

Character names aside, these early scenes are notable less for Chaplin, Swain or Parrott and more for Frank Hayes, another actor hired by Keystone in 1914, albeit not in a remotely positive way. His flamboyant overacting, in which he doesn't act so as much as he dances with the air, ably highlights why his career trajectory didn't match Swain's, let alone Chaplin's and Parrott's.

And so to business. The first hints at the real Chaplin arrive when they move the piano outside, where we discover a real storefront belonging to the Wiley B. Allen Co. on South Broadway in Los Angeles, only a few blocks away from the Marsh Strong building,

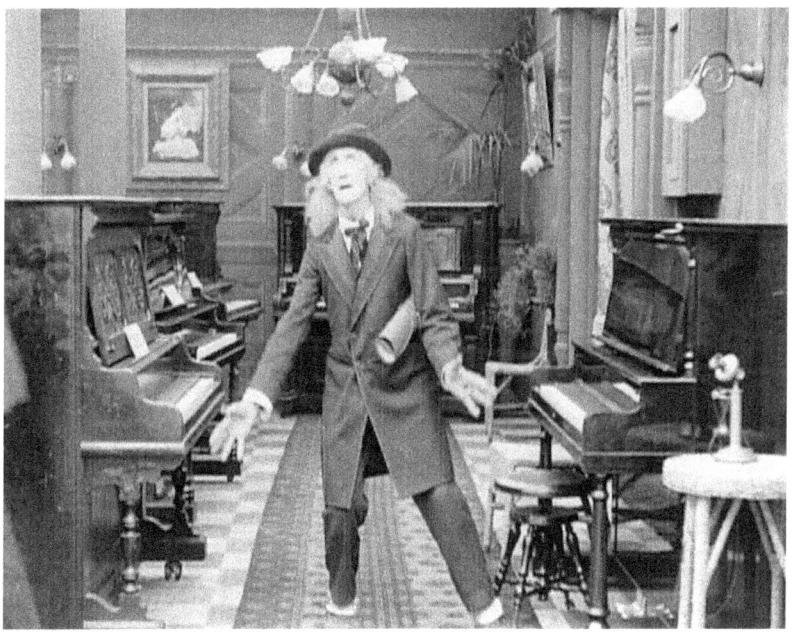

out of which Chaplin had hung precariously four pictures earlier in *The New Janitor*. In fact, as John Bengtson, "the great detective of silent film locations" notes, we're able to see that very building in this very scene, while Swain and Chaplin load the piano onto their mule-drawn cart outside the store.

There's a great moment here as Ambrose pulls the piano off the shop floor and Charlie slides along behind it; another one follows immediately as Ambrose stops and Charlie discovers that he can't move it himself, whatever amount of effort he puts into the task. Unfortunately, this scene is let down with a return to the infamous one in *The Property Man* when Charlie's aged assistant gets stuck under a heavy trunk. In this film, it's Swain under a piano, but there are less shenanigans and even less to be offended by.

In the restored print made available by Flicker Alley in the *Chaplin at Keystone* box set, it's easy to see an abundance of members of the public reflected in the shop window. Presumably they're merely passers by eager to see the filming in progress and we can see how they were moved back for the next shot in which the dynamic duo load the piano onto a rickety looking cart. We can also

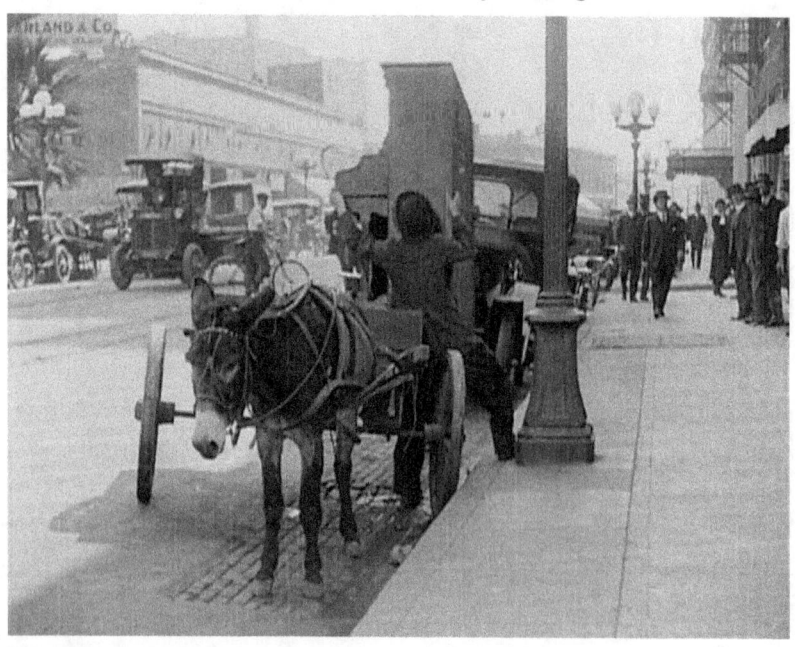

see the shadows of whoever tilts the cart after it crawls to a stop, given that the drivers have fallen asleep and the mule can't be bothered any more. Up goes the mule into the air a couple of times before they move on.

This makes for a memorable shot, if not one that could perhaps be accomplished today with animal safety laws that were notably absent back in the silent era. And so, we finally reach 666 Prospect St., with over half the picture already behind us, for the supposedly dangerous looking scene where Ambrose and Charlie haul the piano up those steep and narrow stairs. It would seem more dangerous if only the piano wasn't clearly a light and hollow shell.

It's still pretty effective though, with Swain leading the way and Chaplin following on behind, ambitiously attempting at one point to hold the piano above him through the use of only his bamboo cane. Of course it doesn't work and down comes the piano, but they do make it on the second try, which, as we discover later with Laurel and Hardy, lets the instrument off far too easily. Rather than build this particular gag, Chaplin sees it as done and he promptly moves on to the next one, which memorably has Charlie flounder around with the piano on his shoulders, fervently wishing that someone would decide where he should put it down.

I liked the delays here and Chaplin makes the most of them, staggering around, wiping his brow, almost doing the splits. It's impressive physical humour, however light the piano shaped prop really was. I liked how he couldn't stand up straight afterwards too, requiring Swain to tip him over onto his head and push him back into shape with his big boot. So much for the flight of stairs.

The entire section at 666 Prospect St. took less than four minutes to unfold, pretty impressive given that it took Laurel and Hardy three reels to do the equivalent, but that leaves even less time for the dynamic duo down the road at 999. At least here we don't have to put up with Frank Hayes gurning up a storm as if he was being paid by the facial expression; instead we get the lovely Cecile Arnold wondering why they seem to be taking a piano away instead of delivering one.

There's a little fun with the rich and expensive knicknacks and furnishings in a set as lavishly decorated as Mr. Poor's wasn't and they do get to violently push over an employee and even disrespect

Mr. Rich himself, but mostly this seems rather like an afterthought because the film was a one reeler and time was running out. The very last scene, in which the piano and its handlers descend a hill and end up in a lake, could have been a reel all on its own but has to settle for a few seconds instead because that's all there is left.

I wonder why Chaplin felt he should cram all this material into one single reel of film. He was experienced in one reelers by this point, having acted in a bunch, then written and directed a bunch more, but he had at least a few two reelers behind him as well, so he knew how much could comfortably fit in each format. It's always possible that it was supposed to be a two reeler but became one, but I doubt it; it's much more likely that Chaplin was still learning what worked and what didn't.

Perhaps this was an experiment to see how much he could viably fit into a reel and the end result was his discovery that this was too much, with many scenes truncated far beyond viability. By the end of the film, it's not difficult to blink and miss a gag, if not an entire scene. Could that be deliberate choice on Chaplin's part to escalate, especially as the pace notably speeds up in a relatively consistent

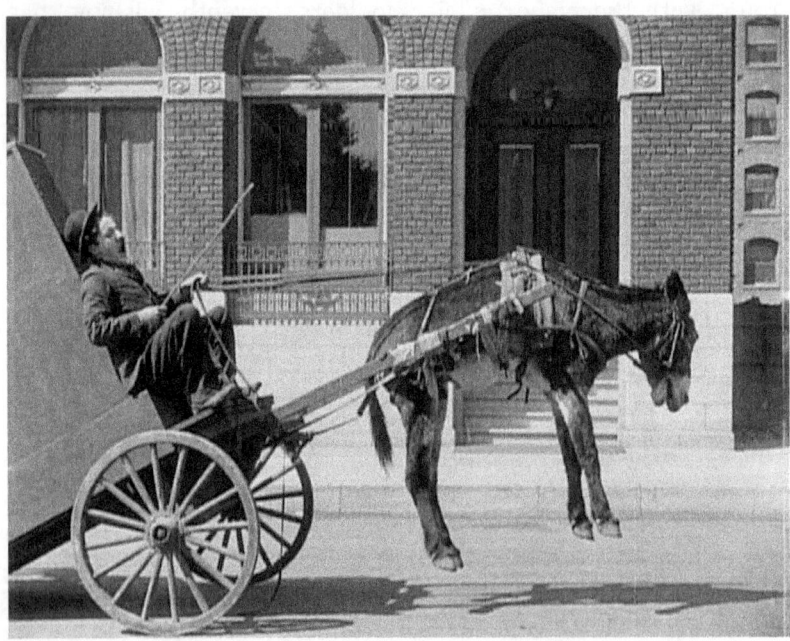

fashion throughout? Again I doubt it, even if he was avoiding the traditional Keystone chase finalés. Whatever this is, it's too much and not enough all at once, capable but hardly essential.

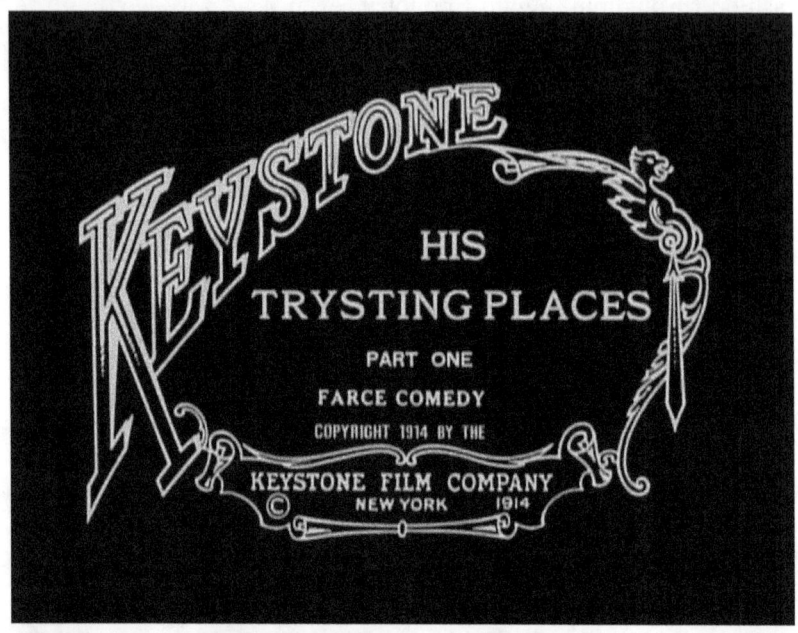

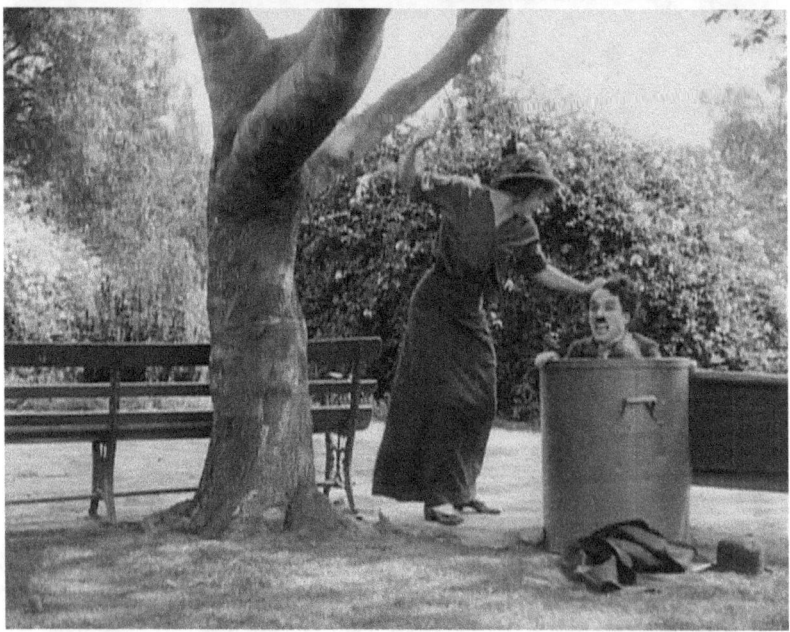

His Trysting Place
9th November, 1914

Director: Charles Chaplin
Writer: Charles Chaplin
Stars: Charles Chaplin, Mabel Normand, Mack Swain and Phyllis Allen

If *His Musical Career* often felt like a two reel comedy crammed into a single reel, often with the funniest bits skipped over too quickly or left out entirely, *His Trysting Place* feels far more like a coherent story which unfolds at a more appropriate pace. Clearly it isn't up to the levels of *Dough and Dynamite*, but it is still a success and it ably shows how Chaplin was enjoying the opportunities that he found for character and story by simply doubling the length of his pictures.

If anything, this one could have easily been expanded to a third reel, as he set up four characters but wasn't entirely consistent in how well he explored them. Also, the introduction of a baby to the mix, for the first time in the context of Charlie being a father, adds a whole new dynamic that he found he wasn't able to explore. The baby is less of a character here and more of a prop, which ironically emphasises how he wasn't ready for this sort of thing; *The Kid* was seven long years away. It's obvious that the baby should either have been excised entirely or built up to a more substantial role.

Little Peter is introduced right at the beginning, a chunky little kid who cries quite a bit. Then again, that's hardly surprising given that he's suddenly found himself in a Keystone picture with Charlie and Mabel as his screen parents.

The astounding scene that sets the film in motion unfolds in their cramped kitchen as they cook dinner. Charlie, distracted by a newspaper, is tasked with supervising the open range with its powerful fire blazing under the saucepan. Mabel, right next to him, is preparing food on the table with the baby in her arms. Gags almost write themselves and Charlie runs through a whole bunch of them. He sits in the fire, leans his elbow and hand on it, puts his feet up on it, you name it. In 1914, it was good riffing on a prop but, a hundred years later, all we can fearfully wonder is how close that baby is going to get to that fire, especially given what Mack Sennett said in his ghostwritten autobiography, *King of Comedy*, that Chaplin "preceded W. C. Fields by many years with scenes in which he got laughs by being mean to a baby."

Jeffrey Vance highlights the major difference between Charlie as a father in this and in later films with reference to his "frequently cruel screen characterization". Without doubt, he's a long way from being a model father here, hauling his baby around by the scruff, then giving him a real gun to play with while he relaxes with the paper in the kid's crib. I wonder how much of it is really cruelty, though, and how much a combination of laziness, distraction and incompetence, not to mention the yawning abyss of a hundred years between then and now.

Today, this couldn't be shot without CGI for safety reasons, but back in 1914 I doubt anyone thought twice about it. As I reviewed this film on its centennial, my youngest two grandchildren were under a year old today but, when the picture was shot in 1914, my own grandfather was only five years old. It's sometimes difficult to

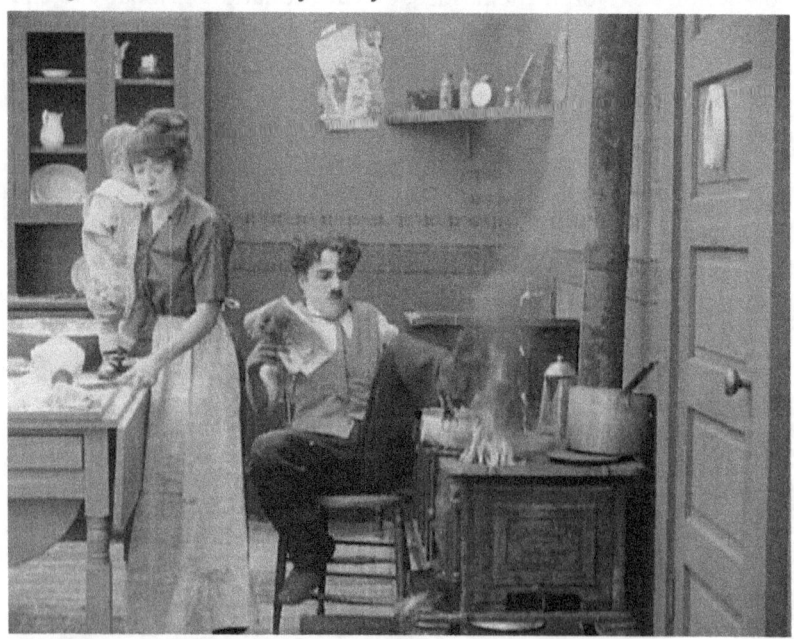

imagine how much has changed in a mere century, but this fabulous medium of film helps us to see it in scenes like these. It wouldn't surprise me if kids in another hundred years would be as surprised by the presence of a newspaper as by an open range. Perspective is everything.

Charlie and Mabel are one of two couples in play. They're hardly living in poverty, especially if we look at future Chaplin pictures for comparison; they have a decent home with a well dressed child and numerous comforts to hand. Charlie's trousers seem to fit better than usual, even if his coat is still notably too tight. However, they're not living in the lap of luxury, which is far more apparent in the other couple they run into here, Ambrose and his unnamed wife, played respectively by Mack Swain and Phyllis Allen. They live in what seems to be a swanky hotel and it's as Ambrose leaves for a walk that the situation comedy that drives *His Trysting Place* starts to fall into place.

Clarice is a young lady working in the lobby, presumably some sort of secretary, who knows Ambrose and asks him to post a note for her. Naturally, it's a smoking gun letter, a "meet me in the park this afternoon at our little trysting place" love note, addressed only to "my darling". It's a great foundation stone from which to build a slapstick comedy and it's put to good use.

Firstly, of course, the filmmakers have to get it into the wrong hands, which happens at a restaurant. Charlie heads out to buy something for the baby (and thus perhaps impress his wife who's clearly fed up with him) and he ends up at the same restaurant as Ambrose, the pair ending up seated next to each other over bowls of soup. Charlie hasn't endeared himself to the establishment as, after hanging up his coat, he steals from a customer's plate and then dries his hands on the man's long beard, but it'll soon get worse. Ambrose, it seems, is unable to slurp quietly, so the meal, itself cleverly choreographed, promptly turns violent and becomes a fast paced fight with all the expected Keystone moves delivered rapidly, right down to the patented Keystone pie that Charlie hurls at a departing Ambrose, only to catch a well dressed passerby right in the face instead. Of course, in this kerfuffle, Ambrose escapes with Charlie's coat and Charlie ends up with Ambrose's and we're in business just as the first reel gives way to the second.

Perhaps the best aspect of the film is its pacing, which devotes its entire first half to setup and its second to the increasingly fraught misinterpretations which drive the comedy.

The scripts reproduced by Simon Louvish in *Keystone: The Life and Clowns of Mack Sennett* put paid to the long standing belief that Keystone pictures were almost entirely improvisations leading up to chase finalés, but they were still generally episodic in nature and without much real structure. Chaplin's scripts were already clearly moving beyond Sennett's, most obviously with his two reelers, and this is a great example. It introduces characters and sets up the gags to come, pivots halfway to allow those gags to play out, then escalates all the way to the finalé, with one extra gag held in check until the very end. It's not *Dough and Dynamite*, but it's yet another example of how Chaplin was slowly but surely mastering his art. While there are flaws to be found in the structure, there is little to argue about with the pacing.

Those flaws mostly tie to the disparity between the characters. Thus far, it's been predominantly Charlie and Ambrose, with a little attention given to Mabel and some distraction with their baby, little Peter. Ambrose's wife is almost unseen in the first half, only on screen to bid him farewell as he wandered off for his stroll. All that changes in the second half, with the ladies given just as much time as their husbands, even if one never does get a name.

Mabel, a subservient character in the first half, begins this shift as Charlie arrives home and she wonders what he brought for the baby. Of course, she finds Clarice's note instead and immediately takes charge, letting him have it to the degree of breaking her ironing board over his head, until he flees home and makes for the park. Meanwhile, already in the park, Ambrose is getting plenty of attention too, from his wife, who cuddles him on her ample bosom. I've never been a big fan of Mack Swain's goggling eyes but they're highly appropriate here, as is his widow's peak which becomes more of a proto-devilock.

It's no chore to guess how everyone's going to meet up. Charlie actually sits down on Ambrose's wife, before he starts to unload his troubles on her instead. "My wife's gone foolish," he begins, while setting the stage for Mabel's imminent arrival; she's hot on his heels, having paused only to leave their baby with a Keystone Kop.

Mabel Normand has a fair shot of stealing this part of the film, but Chaplin holds his own with the aid of a dustbin put to glorious use as a prop. To give him credit as a screenwriter, while he gives himself and his side of the story great moments, he doesn't forget that Ambrose and his wife are the other half of that story and he gives them great moments too. I don't believe that Phyllis Allen ever underacted, even by the standards of 1914, but she does faint well when she discovers the baby bottle in her husband's coat and assumes that he has a child that he's hidden from her. That husband gets a few moments of his own too, in both halves of the action, before they all catch the error and start to put things to rights.

There's a lot to like here, in a two reeler that is somehow full and yet unhurried at the same time. Chaplin does a lot with *His Trysting Place* but he lets it unfold naturally, his gags playing out well and the regular Keystone actors easily up to the task.

The lesser side of the picture comes through how the baby is so ruthlessly used as a prop rather than a character, something that Chaplin would soon switch around, and how its time was stolen

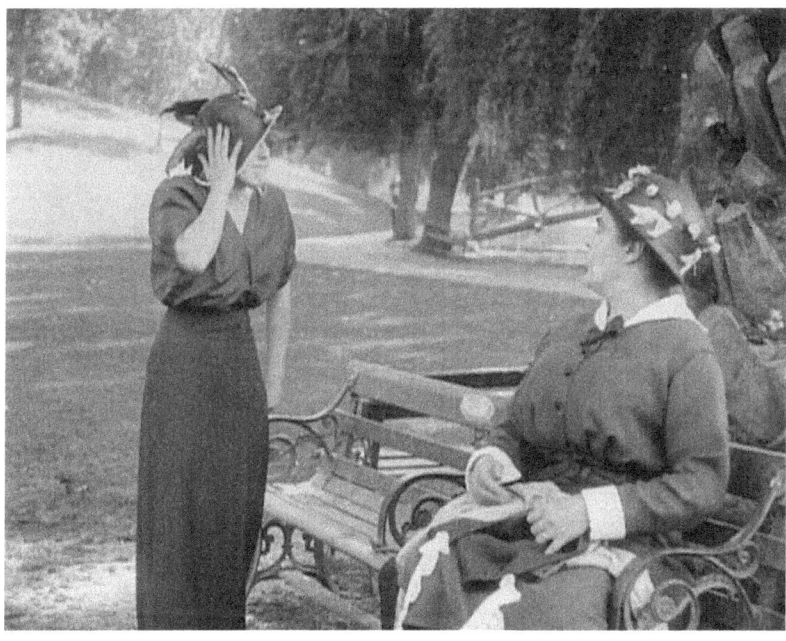

from Ambrose's wife, who deserved as much build up as the other leads. It's easy to imagine her unable to have children, for instance, thus explaining her babying of her husband and her fainting dead away after finding the baby bottle in Ambrose's coat, but it's never called out because she doesn't even have a name in this picture, let alone a background.

Glen Cavender has less to do here than perhaps any Keystone Kop ever did, mostly there as a suggestion that's never put to real use. It could easily be argued that Nick Cogley had more to do as the bearded customer at the restaurant, who vanished to vacate a seat for Charlie.

The British Film Institute's resource pages on Chaplin carry a variety of dates for his films, including when they were shot, when the negatives were sent from Los Angeles and received in New York and when they were first released to theatre audiences. If they're to be trusted, this was the first of Chaplin's films to be shown out of order.

It wasn't uncommon for some to overlap, especially the one day shoots that enabled *Kid Auto Races at Venice, Cal.* to reach audiences

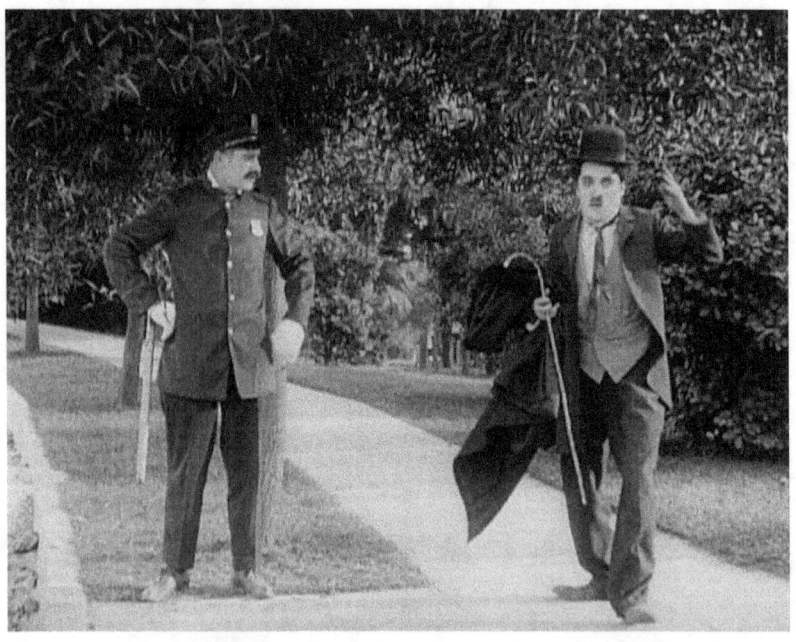

before *Mabel's Strange Predicament*, for example, but this marked the first time that one picture, completely shot before another, would be exhibited after it.

His Trysting Place was shot before *His Musical Career*, concurrent with the post-production of *Gentlemen of Nerve*. That picture was in production between 20th and 27th September, although the race at which it was shot took place on day one, while this is listed from the 19th to 26th. I have no idea why this picture was effectively sat on in New York for over a month but it was certainly worth the wait, better than Chaplin's previous two films combined.

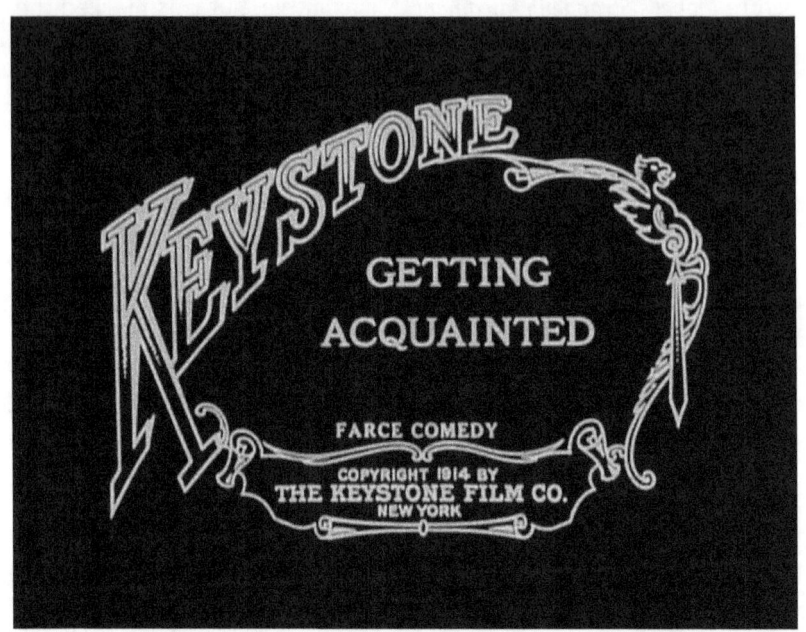

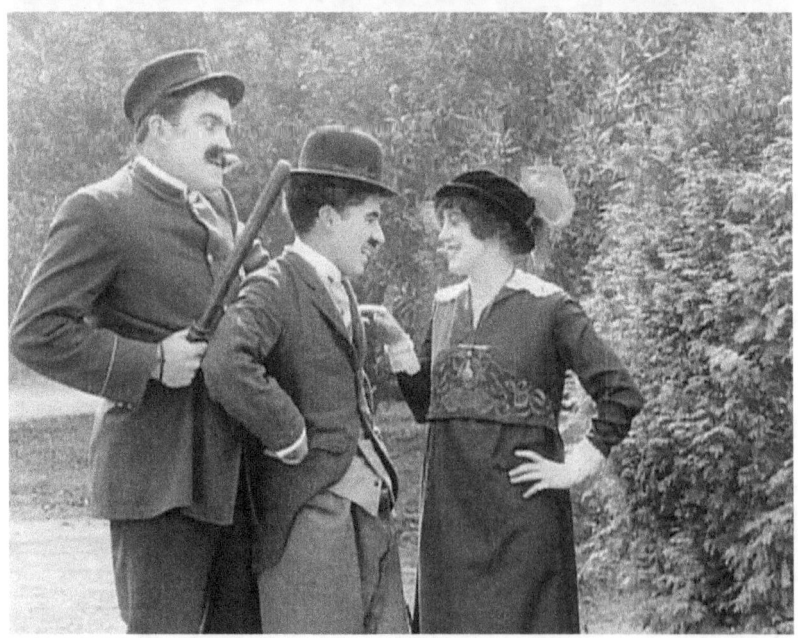

Getting Acquainted
5th December, 1914

Director: Charles Chaplin
Writer: Charles Chaplin
Stars: Charles Chaplin, Mabel Normand, Mack Swain and Phyllis Allen

There's a particular irony in the title of this picture, as Chaplin's 34th of 1914 alone features many of the same faces as many of the 33 that predate it. Working through them on their centennials, mimicking the hypothetical experience of an admittedly dedicated audience member of the era, has made this set of films feel rather like a television sketch show, where we fully expect the core cast to play a different role each week (or even each skit), regardless of gender, race or age. Thus audiences had been getting acquainted with the players of *Getting Acquainted* long before it was made and they'd surely got very used to their respective traits by this point.

There's nothing surprising about any of these characters, played by Charlie Chaplin, Mabel Normand, Mack Swain and Phyllis Allen, as they had played similar ones in similar pictures over the prior year. What's new here is really only the odd introduction of a Turk, apparently out of the blue, and the removal of many of the usual slapstick props and moves that Keystone was known for, as Chaplin finessed his material.

The template for this one seems to be *Gentlemen of Nerve*, three films earlier in Chaplin's career and itself highly derivative of still earlier pictures. That one saw Chaplin and Swain at a racetrack, where Charlie picked up Mabel because her beau, played by Chester Conklin, was trying it on with Phyllis Allen instead. Mack Swain was in that picture too, but mostly just to get stuck in a wall, rather than to get embroiled in the tangled web of changing relationships. Here, he gets to join in, because Ambrose and Mabel are an item in this picture, while Charlie is with Allen's character, as unnamed as always.

This time out the action unfolds in a park, but to emphasise the influence of the racing film, Joe Bordeaux promptly drives up in a glorious automobile (the simpler word, "car", just doesn't cut it) which putters out in front of Ambrose and Mabel. Ambrose lends a hand in cranking it back into motion, thus leaving Mabel open to Charlie's unwanted attentions which, in turn, leave Ambrose able to try it on with Phyllis Allen and the dance of the flirts is in play.

In fact, the working title of the film was *The Flirts* and it makes a lot more sense than *Getting Acquainted* for the majority of the film's running time, at least until the combination of a bundle of complex connections within such a small cast of characters means that the pairings change. We usually see what we saw in *Gentlemen of Nerve*, when Mabel showed up with Chester Conklin but left with Charlie, but here the connections aren't defined by relationship, rather by commonality.

As Charlie and Ambrose begin to weave their respective ways in and out of scenes with increasing rapidity, Mabel ends up on the same bench around the same tree as Phyllis Allen and, as ladies who have new stories must, they naturally share them, so building a connection. Meanwhile, their respective husbands end up in the same place too but, rather than a neat bench, it's the shelter a bush

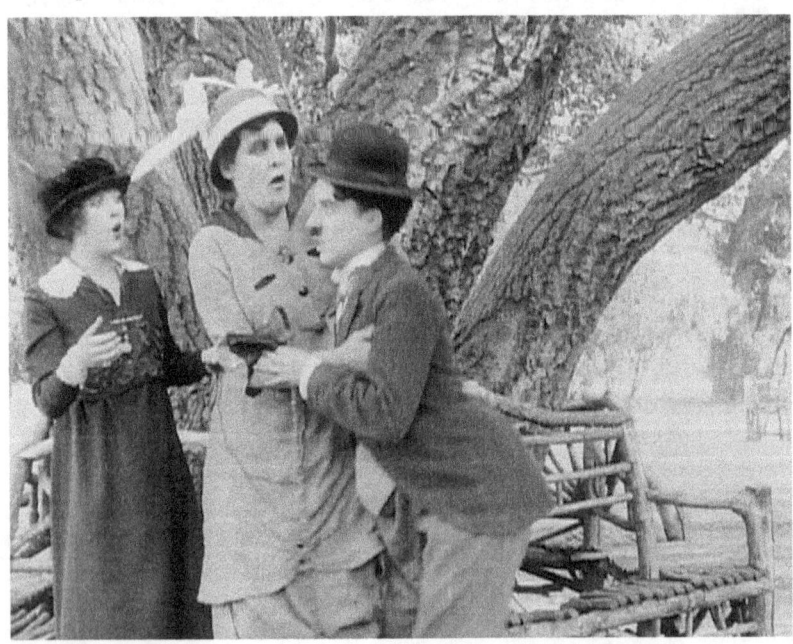

offers them from the inevitable Keystone Kop that appeals. Both men are hauled off by their wives in the end, but the ladies have connected and so have the gentlemen.

What this leaves us with is something that feels far more British than anything Chaplin had done, even if we include the potential Mr. Punch influence of *A Busy Day*. The structure reminds of the sophisticated English drawing room farces which would become the rage on stage, just translated into the setting of an early American film comedy. It's light years away from a Noël Coward play, as none of the characters are remotely sophisticated, but the format fits and the tone is a lot closer than usual because they don't indulge in any of the usual Keystone slapstick.

While there is a Keystone Kop on hand, played this time out by Edgar Kennedy, and while he is kept incessantly flustered, there are no pies or bricks hurled, no asses kicked and none of the wrong people slapped. Even more notably, this Keystone park comedy does not, I repeat not, end with at least one key member of the cast dumped unceremoniously into the lake. That's a little jarring, as we've been reinforced to expect it, over and over again, making this

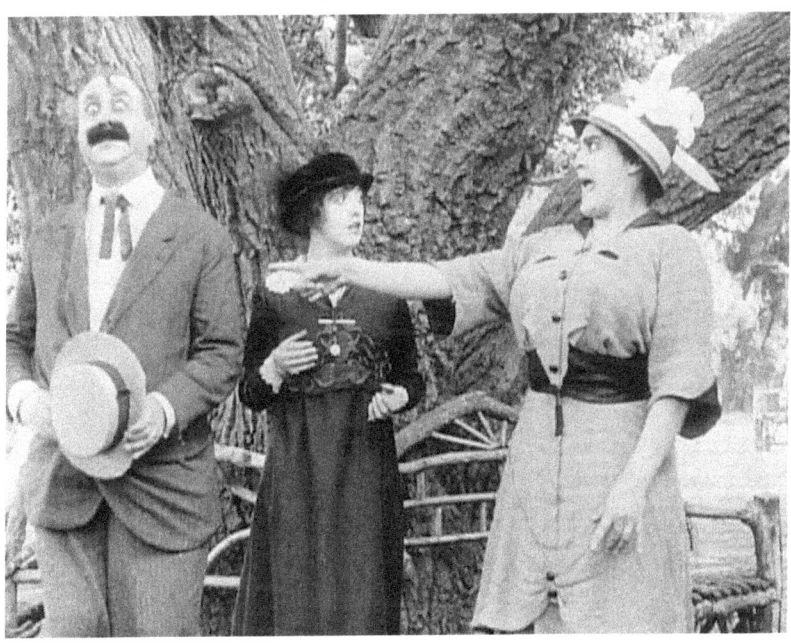

feel somewhat like a familiar joke whose punchline has suddenly been changed.

The point of course is that the comedy in *Getting Acquainted* isn't based on physicality, it's based on the characters and their varied interactions, which here include "a passing Turk", an exotic stage stereotype who arrives complete with fez and dagger.

The very first scene is a perfect example as, to the standard Keystone way of thinking, absolutely nothing happens but, to Chaplin's mindset, it sets the stage perfectly.

Charlie and Phyllis are a couple, but clearly not a happy one, as Chaplin's face suggests. She trumpets and complains and blows her nose, while he merely reacts to her. What's more, he looks directly at us through the fourth wall as he does so, in an attempt to involve us in the conversation. In just over thirty seconds, his eyes switch back and forth between his wife and we, the viewers, over twenty times, as if to ask, "You see what my world is like?" Without a single intertitle, the two of them provide us with their entire relationship. By comparison, Mabel and Ambrose look happier together, but he clearly doesn't listen to her in the slightest.

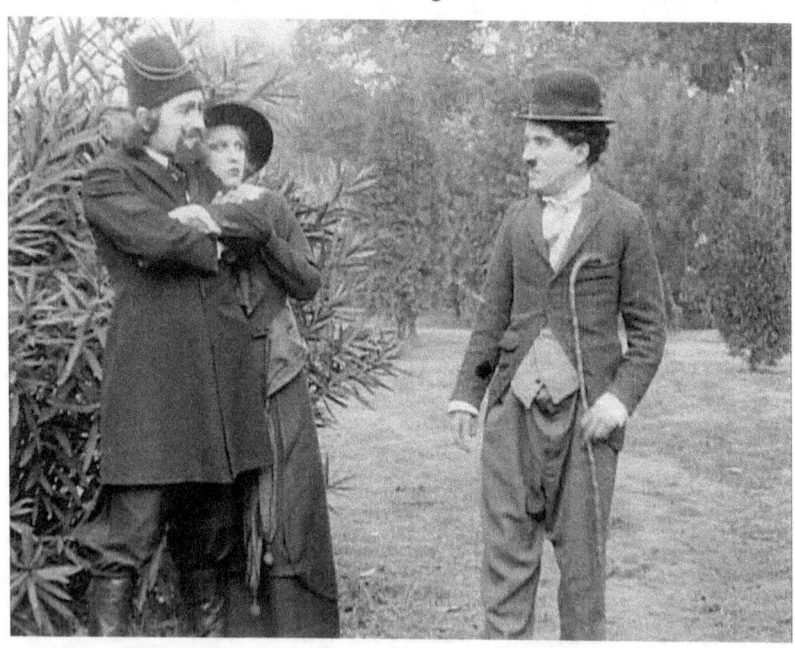

Of course, from these first two scenes, we fully expect that Phyllis is going to go to sleep and Ambrose is going to drift away, leaving Charlie and Mabel free to connect yet again, but Chaplin didn't want to keep things so obvious. Sure, Phyllis goes to sleep and Ambrose works on the automobile, but Cecile Arnold is the first distraction for Charlie. She's so blatant that, after Charlie shimmies away from his sleeping wife, she bends over right in front of him. However, naturally following her, he finds his way blocked by a fearsome Turk.

Why we have a Turk in this movie, I have no idea, but he appears out of the bushes as a defender of the lady's virtue, with his arms crossed, his stare wicked and his dagger very quickly forthcoming. Charlie is quick to take the back foot but the Turk promptly stabs him, almost in slow motion, in the nether regions and the chase is apparently firmly on. From here on out, it's merely a question of how intricate that chase will get, as it gradually involves Charlie, Ambrose, the Turk, the Keystone Kop and a variety of ladies.

If this sounds like Chaplin was moving forward yet again, you'd be right. Keystone comedies didn't tend to have too much structure beyond the general format of slapstick shenanigans leading to a chase, but this is a complex creature with intricacies put together more cleverly than anything Chaplin had done thus far.

If anything, the minimalist setting aids this magnificently. *Dough and Dynamite* had a lot going on too, but its action was staged in an environment that helped build the story, with bakers pitted against their boss, waiters against customers and all them caught up in a whole set of escalations to reach the literally explosive finalé. In this picture, there are people and a park and that's it. None of the luxuries of the earlier exist here. There are names in the intertitles, but we aren't given professions. There are no sets and no props, just the park itself and anything the characters brought with them, like Charlie's cane and the Turk's dagger. Everything has to be conjured out of thin air and, as Chaplin ably demonstrates, that's all he needs.

Emotionally, we don't really feel for the beleaguered women, for various reasons. Phyllis, yet again, is the battle axe that she usually played and it's always fun to watch her bubble burst. Mabel is more sympathetic, of course, but we can't fail to appreciate her part in the extravagant set up Charlie employs to get her lips close to his, involving removing a stray hair from her shoulder and balancing it on his nose until she's near enough to grab. She's also both able and willing to slap him when he goes too far, which he does more frequently than usual, even using his cane to pull up her skirts.

If anything, we feel more for the Keystone Kop, whom Kennedy unfortunately overplays with silent era gusto, literally leaping into action, because he just can't keep track of who he's supposed to chase. With two ladies suffering from the unwanted attentions of men (hardly gentlemen), he has two to pursue and the fiery Turk makes three. It's a hard life being a Keystone Kop, that's for sure! The ladies do find some confusion of their own too, of course, as the dance progresses.

And this really is a dance, as much as anything else. While silent era movies were clearly not written for dialogue, they often did revolve around intertitles, the equivalents of the day, to varying degrees. That's true for many Chaplin films too, where an intertitle would set a scene of improvisation in motion, but it's not true here. This picture was clearly written entirely around the choreography, which is pretty astounding given that, according to Jeffrey Vance, *Getting Acquainted* was shot in a single day. The B.F.I. details four days, a long weekend from Friday to Monday, with the negative being shipped to New York the next Sunday.

It has to be said that the Keystone crew had spent so much time in Westlake Park during 1914 that it must have been viable to choreograph the whole picture from memory. It's understandable that we might see the park as Keystone property, but it wasn't, and the glimpses of what we might believe to be extras or the dogs of extras are probably just other patrons of the park straying into shot because someone dropped the ball in security.

If the obvious standout here is the choreography, following rapidly behind is the editing. Just as the way this comedy of errors proceeds like a dance, so does its editing, which is as fast paced as anything that I've seen from 1914, especially during the second, frenetic, act. The introductory scenes are just as long as usual, as are the final scenes to wrap things up, but in between them the cuts come thick and fast, to keep all the characters in play and to telegraph where they're going next.

As these cameras don't move, it might seem like a foreshadowing of what Russ Meyer would later become infamous for, but there's little to suggest specific motion here, merely that there's a lot of it happening. Certainly, it's far ahead of the editing at the beginning of Chaplin's year at Keystone, where it was notable only in how unnotable it was.

Chaplin's mastery of the medium clearly wasn't just restricted to being in front of the camera. This highlights yet another aspect that he was starting to understand and nail down for future work.

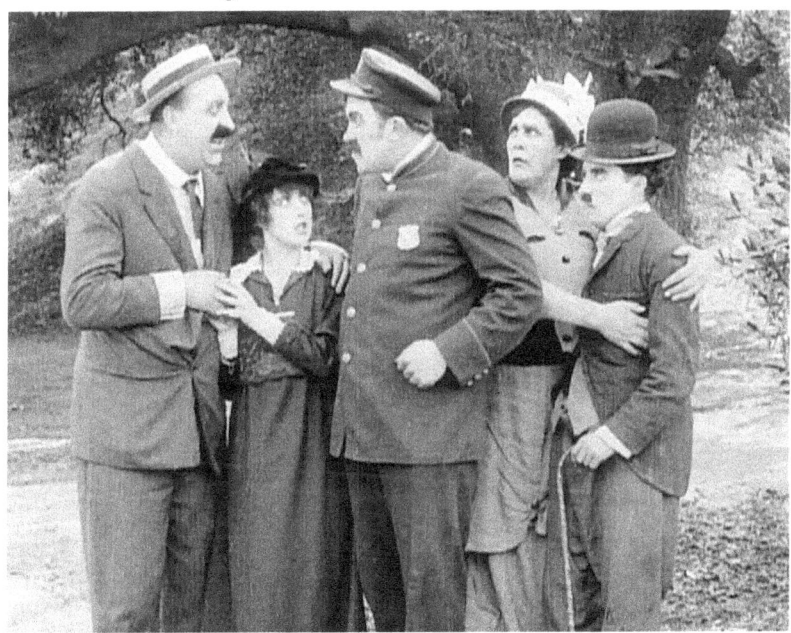

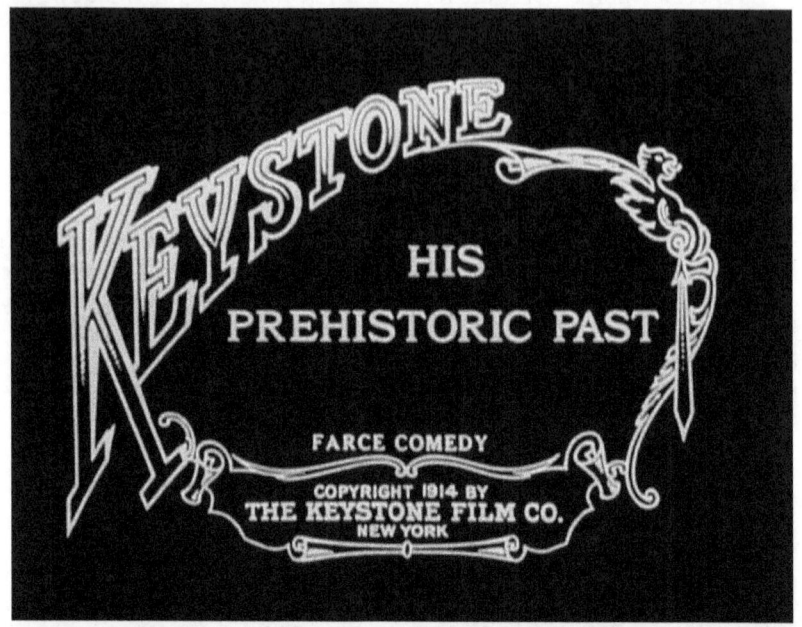

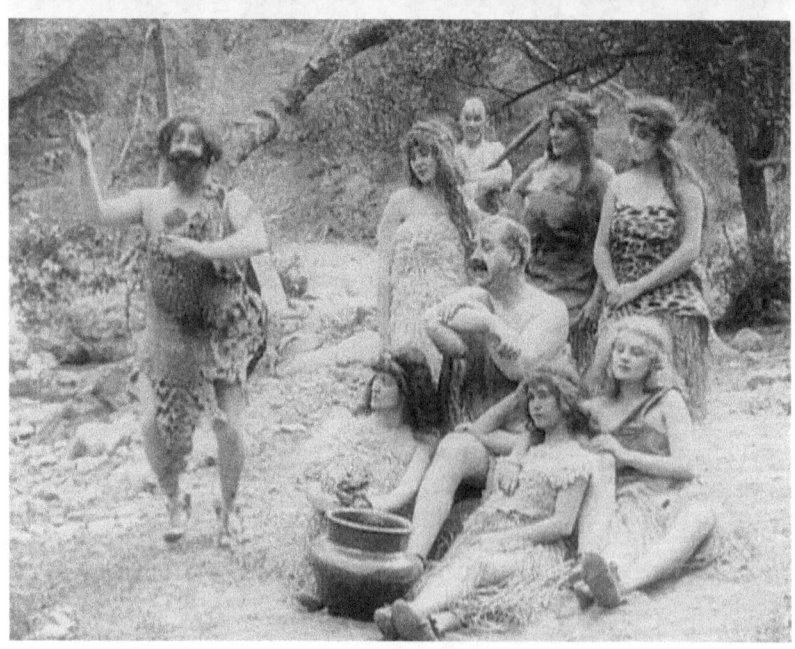

His Prehistoric Past
7th December, 1914

Director: Charles Chaplin
Writer: Charles Chaplin
Stars: Charles Chaplin, Mack Swain, Gene Marsh and Fritz Schade

His Prehistoric Past sits uncomfortably at the end of Chaplin's year at Keystone Studios, his final short film to reach theatre screens. It wasn't the last one that he shot, as it was in the mail to New York two full weeks before *Getting Acquainted* was begun, but that picture was released two days before this. Neither was it the final chance for audiences to see Chaplin's name in a Keystone title, as *Tillie's Punctured Romance*, the feature for which he'd shot a number of scenes in support midway through the year, was still going through post-production and wouldn't reach any theatre screens until 21st December.

However it's more of an ending to me, because it feels rather like an afterthought. At first glance, it's merely weak, albeit in an oddly interesting way, as a period piece set as far back as the stone age, with the Little Tramp in a loincloth but comically retaining his hat and cane. The catch is that it's less funny than anything else that had carried his name for months, and it runs on for two reels with less material on show than he'd often used to fill one.

It's difficult to look at it as anything other than a contractual obligation, that he knew he was leaving the studio and couldn't be bothered to put as much effort into this last picture as he was into the negotiations with competing studios about where he would move to next and for how much money.

While he does claim in his autobiography that "it was a wrench leaving Keystone", it certainly wasn't a slow one. "I finished cutting my film on Saturday night," he explains, presumably talking about *Getting Acquainted* rather than *His Prehistoric Past*, "and left with Mr. Anderson the following Monday for San Francisco."

That's Bronco Billy of the Essanay Company, at which he would spend the next year and a half at the salary of $1,250 a week, on top of a $10,000 signing bonus. Mack Sennett had baulked at $1,000 a week, saying that it was more than he earned as the head of the studio, but midway through 1916, Chaplin moved again, this time to the Mutual Film Corporation, for $150,000 and a salary of $10,000 a week. *His Prehistoric Past* was surely quickly forgotten.

However, on analysis, there's a little more going on in it than initially meets the eye. For a start, it's not a new concept that Chaplin had conjured up out of thin air; the whole piece is a parody of a two year old D. W. Griffith picture called *Man's Genesis*, which appears to be a rather serious fable told by a grandfather to his little ones, but it carries an unwieldy subtitle, *A Psychological Comedy Founded on Darwin's Theory of the Genesis of Man*, just in case.

In *Man's Genesis*, which still exists today, a young cavegirl called Lilywhite, with a straw outfit that makes her look like Rapunzel, is eagerly sought after by both Weakhands and Bruteforce. She wants the former but, of course, she gets the latter instead, because the characters are appropriately named. However, while Bruteforce has brawn, Weakhands has a brain. Back in his cave, he puts a doughnut on a stick and thus manages to create a club, with which he wins the day. It's effectively the "Dawn of Man" sequence from *2001: A Space Odyssey*, phrased as a fable to demonstrate how brain always beats brawn, even if it happens to be with a club.

As a serious piece of art, *Man's Genesis* is rather comedic, which may explain the subtitle, but it certainly explains why Chaplin felt it ripe for parody. Instead of an old man sitting down to stop his grandchildren squabbling, we get the Little Tramp curling up on a park bench and promptly dreaming of the stone age, in the form of "the kink of 'Wakiki Beach' surrounded by his favorites".

The "kink" is Mack Swain, wearing a great deal less than usual but still retaining his full Ambrose moustache; the reason for the apparent typo in "king" is that he has a sexy sextet of cavegirls seated around him. Other sources identify him as King Low-Brow, which might explain why he's watching Cleo the bearded medicine man attempt some sort of prehistoric ballet rather than putting those "favorites" to good use. The blonde is Cecile Arnold, but her sisters in skins don't seem familiar, even if the B.F.I. lists one as Vivian Edwards. His favourite "favorite" is Gene Marsh, whether that means his favourite water maiden or his favourite wife, but Weakchin soon hones in on her anyway.

No guesses as to who Weakchin is, but he gets a memorable enough entry for Chaplin to remember it in his autobiography. They do say the clothes make the man and he's a fetching sight in his bearskin, with the usual bowler hat and bamboo cane retained for laughs, however anachronistic they clearly are. He has a pipe too, which he fills with hairs which he plucks from the bearskin and lights with a rock that he strikes on his leg instead of a match.

Leapfrogging the majority of the plot of *Man's Genesis*, he also arrives complete with a spiked club in hand. Gene Marsh isn't as ethereal a girl as her namesake, Mae Marsh, was in *Man's Genesis*, but the outfit is far too close to be accidental. She cosies up with Weakchin, but the battle is soon commenced when Cleo spies them together and shoots the newcomer in the back end with an arrow. For a while, it's a painful experience for us as much as them, with Weakchin, Cleo and Low-Brow improvising a set of gags around a huge boulder, as if they had invented the first pantomime, but it does, thank goodness, get a little better.

Many of the laughs come from attempts to apply modern day concepts to the stone age like they're in a town called Bedrock and

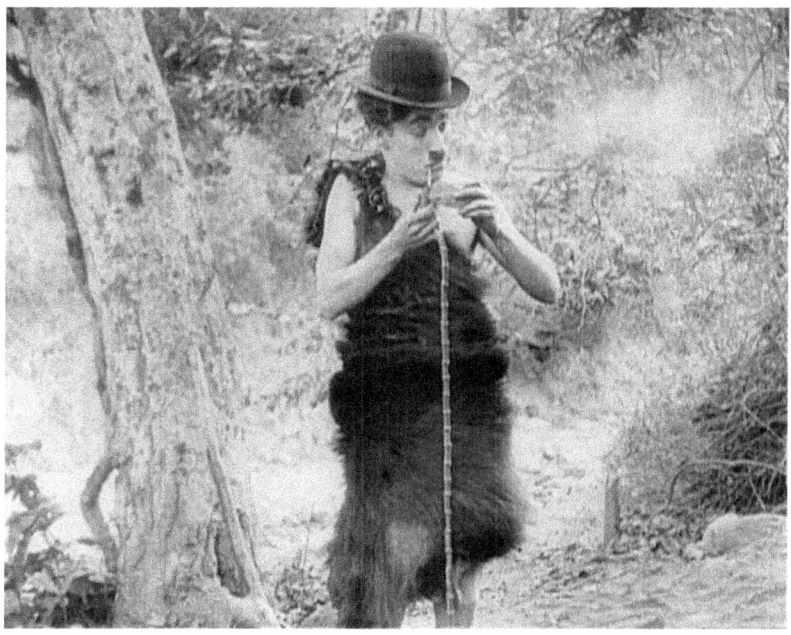

they're a modern stone age family. This is *Meet the Keystones*, right? I did get a mild chuckle out of swapping cards or mixing cocktails, but the king's cave is quite obviously a bundle of tarps and never rings remotely true.

Of course, Weakchin soon finds himself alone on the beach with the bevy of beauties because this is a Chaplin picture, after all, and when another suitor attempts to steal them away, he has his club ready to steal them back. Showing a little restraint, he hones back in on Gene Marsh, who is clearly uncomfortable, not so much to be stolen away by Chaplin but because her outfit apparently has a strong habit of falling off. As they frolic in the ocean, she spends a conspicuous amount of time trying to keep it on and, at one point, apparently loses that battle. There definitely appears to be some sort of wardrobe malfunction going on as they try to clamber back out of the water, suggesting that body parts are on display that shouldn't be.

What leaps out here most is that *His Prehistoric Past* is a lot slower than it has any reason to be. It makes little sense to see something like *His Musical Career* crammed into a single reel, while this picture

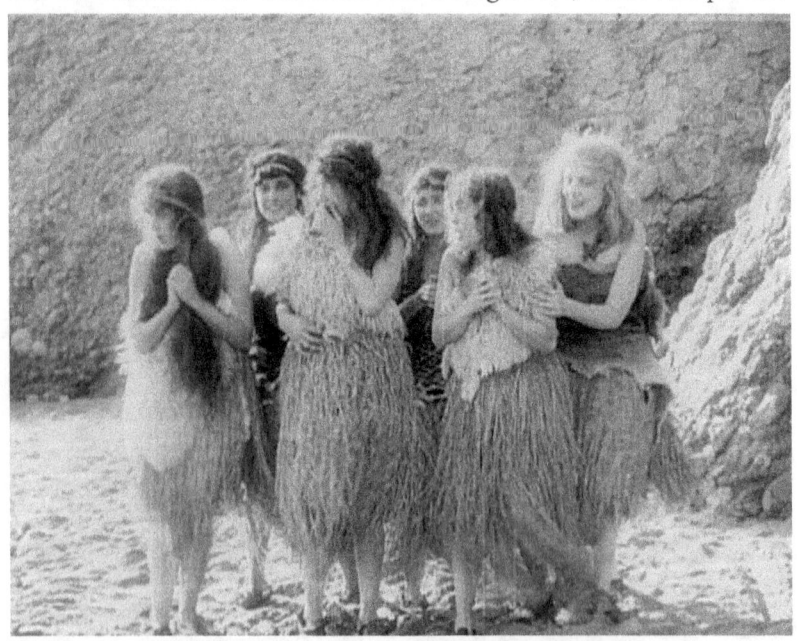

benefits from a second for no reason at all.

There are moments of note, not only Weakchin's entrance but Gene Marsh's come hither looks on the road and Mack Swain literally getting kicked off a cliff, but they're few and far between. Instead we have to settle for Fritz Schade's ballet dancing, Al St. John being used as a footstool and that cringeworthy chase round the boulder. Mostly we're stuck with a lack of imagination, a lack of energy and a lack of sophistication.

Chaplin had been learning so much at Keystone, from the very beginning but especially during the second half of 1914 when he had more creative control, and watching each of these pictures on their centennials has ably highlighted just how much, not just in acting, but in his use of character, emotion, pacing, composition, editing, choreography, you name it. Almost none of that is on show here.

And, of course, the most obvious reason is that this perfectionist really didn't care any more. He was about to take his talent and his newfound knowledge of the cinematic arts to Essanay Studios, not only for the increased salary but to serve as the next step in his growth. It's so easy to dismiss this as a half-assed last effort to finish up and get gone, but there's one massive reason why I can't buy it.

That's because, when we get to the very end of the film, when Weakchin has occupied the kink's cave with his favourite girl, when King Low-Brow shows back up and drops a large rock on his head, when we leap back into the present day to see that transform into a Keystone Kop's truncheon waking up the Little Tramp from his slumber, we simply can't ignore the final scene. That's not just any Keystone Kop smiling at Charlie, that's Chaplin's half-brother Syd, four years his elder, who had finally joined him in Hollywood and the movie business. It was Syd who had introduced Charlie to Fred Karno in 1908 and now Charlie was returning the favour, six years on, by introducing him to Mack Sennett.

Oddly, Syd's contract was earning him $200 a week, $25 more than his now very well established brother was getting, but Chaplin had a good idea what he was worth and his salary was about to leap forward. He held no grudges and even offered Syd a partnership in their own production company, but the latter felt that it was a risky proposition, especially as he was now earning more money than he had ever earned in his life before.

So Syd held back at Keystone for another year, where he made a number of films including *A Submarine Pirate* which, after *Tillie's Punctured Romance*, would become the highest earning picture that the studio ever made. After leaving Keystone, Syd would become Charlie's manager, securing him contract after contract that broke records, and they would work together for years.

Given how close they already were and would remain, I just can't help but see this final scene as a very deliberate setup: Charlie's last moment in a Keystone short but Syd's first in a Chaplin picture, a real passing of the torch scene. It's a good moment, but it really deserved to be in a much better picture.

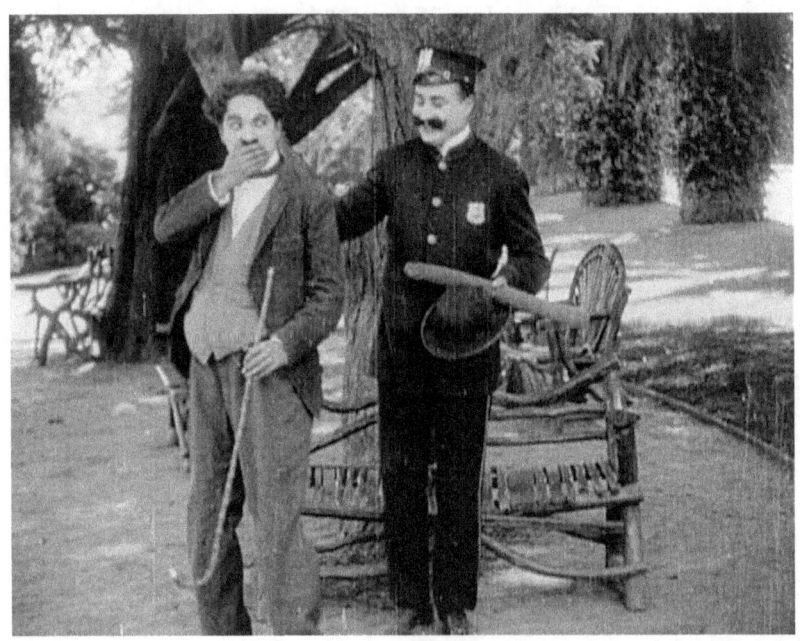

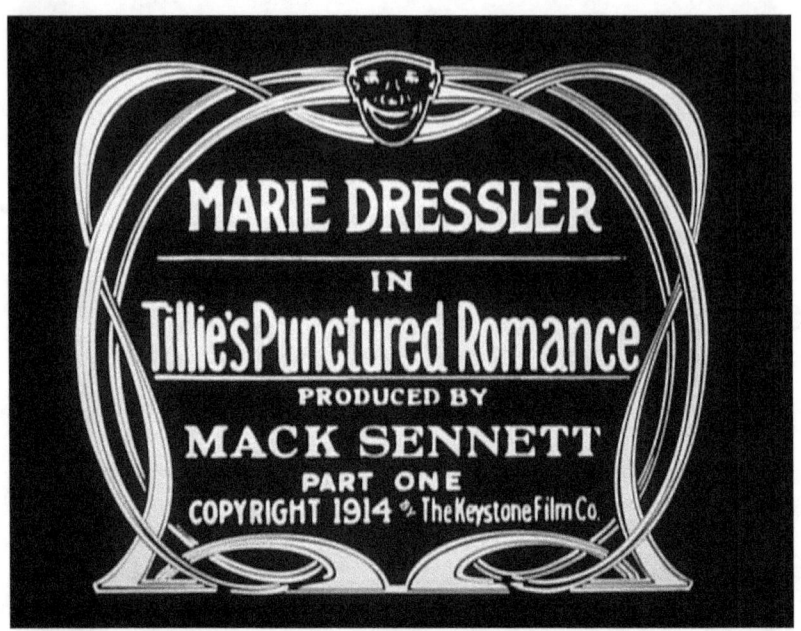

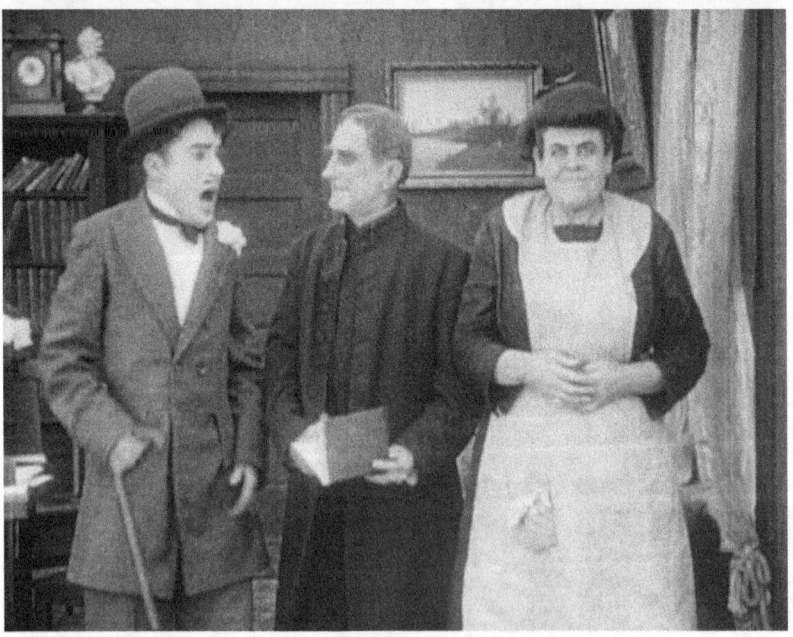

Tillie's Punctured Romance
21st December, 1914

Director: Mack Sennett
Writers: Mack Sennett, Craig Hutchinson and Hampton Del Ruth, from the musical play, *Tillie's Nightmare*, by A. Baldwin Sloane and Edgar Smith
Stars: Marie Dressler, Charles Chaplin, Mabel Normand, Mack Swain and Charles Bennett

It's strangely appropriate that the very last Chaplin picture at Keystone to be released to theatres turned out to be the one and only feature that he shot there, *Tillie's Punctured Romance*.

While it's far from his most memorable work for the studio and it was far from the last thing he shot there, it was a notable milestone in cinema and it works well as a broad dividing line between the two halves of his Keystone career, the first half in which he learned his trade acting for other directors and the second in which he finessed his skills while he directed himself.

Shooting began on Tuesday, 14th April, three days after Sennett had shot Chaplin in a one day film, the aptly titled *A Busy Day*. Before that, Chaplin had made fourteen pictures for six different directors, sitting in the director's chair himself for only one and a bit. By the time shooting wrapped on Tuesday, 9th June, he had made five more, all of them (or at least four, depending who you trust) directed by Sennett. However, the remaining fifteen he would go on to make were all under his own direction; this was the final acting job he did for another director at Keystone.

The milestone isn't merely that this was Chaplin's debut feature, not to be followed until *The Kid* in 1921, or that it was the first feature shot at Keystone Studios; it's generally regarded as the first feature length comedy ever made (though some film historians cite *Battle of Gettysgoat* instead, released in the same year by the Lubin Manufacturing Company).

Features themselves weren't new, but they had never before been comedies. The first dramatic feature, the Australian film, *The Story of the Kelly Gang*, predates this by eight years. France, for once not the pioneer, followed in 1909 with an adaptation of *Les Misérables*; and Italy and Russia produced their debut features in 1911. The U.S. didn't catch up until 1912, a year in which it produced at least four features.

Incidentally, 1912 was the same year in which Mack Sennett left Biograph to found Keystone, one of fifteen production companies at the time in what would become known, a year later, as Hollywood. 1913 marked a notable year of expansion, with theatres replacing nickelodeons and the middle class finally starting to accept motion pictures as respectable entertainment. In only half a decade, the United States went from producing four features a year to over six hundred.

It's no surprise that early efforts were notably rough around the edges and the first American feature to be widely acclaimed as a masterpiece wouldn't arrive until 1915, that being *The Birth of a Nation*, directed by Sennett's former boss at Biograph, D. W. Griffith. It's no great challenge to find the flaws in *Tillie's Punctured Romance*, even if it was adapted from the stage, *Tillie's Nightmare*, written by A. Baldwin Sloane and Edgar Smith and first staged in 1910, being an established success.

The lead actress whom Sennett hired, Marie Dressler, was clearly the best choice, given that she had originated the role on Broadway and toured with it for three years. This was her first movie, though she was already 45 years old and had been a Broadway success since 1892, so to support Dressler, Sennett cast most of the recognisable faces in his company, led by Chaplin and Mabel Normand. Only a few, such as Roscoe Arbuckle, are notable for their absence.

So, Sennett had a successful play, its successful leading lady and a successful supporting cast. What could go wrong?

Well, the most apparent problem is that nobody had done this before. Sennett knew well that what might work on stage wouldn't necessarily work on screen, but he had no real conception of what would keep his audience laughing for the then unimaginable length of 85 minutes.

While he succeeded in keeping the script moving, the pacing is utterly broken, mostly because the concept of time is non-existent. We literally have no idea how much time has passed at any point, a need that seems obvious in hindsight given that there are two separate stories unfolding for half the movie and we're constantly waiting for them to collide. This problem is why the pace is off and why there's neither suspense nor surprise to be found. My better half, watching this for the first time with no foreknowledge of events, found it child's play to explain what would happen later in the current act and to what that would subsequently lead in the next. It really is a predictable affair, painted in broad strokes and constantly telegraphed. Anything positive to say on those fronts is wrapped up in the word "first".

So let's take a look at what this first comedy feature had to offer. It's all about Tillie, as you might expect from the title, even though Chaplin's star rose long before Dressler's on the silver screen and so reissues tended to shift his name above the title and hers below it. She's a country girl who works the family farm and she's outside with her hoe when Chaplin arrives, throwing a brick for her dog to fetch and hitting him instead.

We see him from behind first but his outline is instantly recognisable, even though he's not the Little Tramp this time out. He does have tears in his jacket and a familiar bamboo cane to twirl,

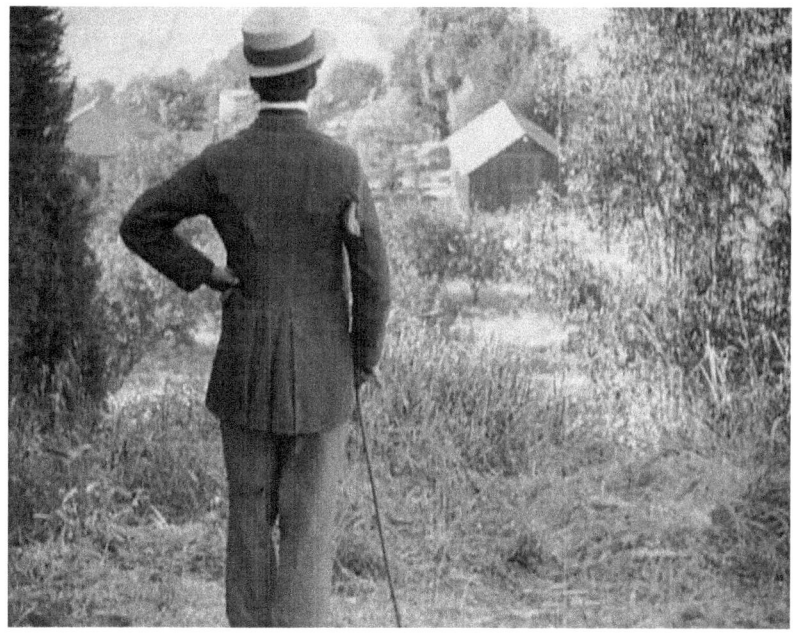

but he's a lot more dapper than usual, with a pork pie hat, a tie and a sash. His jacket fits for a change and there's a suave moustache rather than his usual toothbrush. His hair makes a statement too, as if to highlight that this is the Little Tramp playing the Latin Lover. Naturally, Tillie is quickly smitten and she gets all girlish after she literally carries him inside to recover from the brick.

Thus far, we've learned that Dressler is more than able to work the slapstick routines that Sennett wanted. We also realise that he's inordinately fond of having characters kick each other in the ass, a frequent move in Chaplin's early Keystone pictures but one which gradually vanished after he gained some creative control. It appears so often in this one that it's almost like the film's heartbeat.

Chaplin's character, an unnamed City Stranger, learns from a casual kitchen transaction that Tillie's father is rolling in dough. He knows its location too, because it's poorly hidden. So he escalates his flirtation, eventually upbraiding Tillie's father for kicking her ass and becoming firm and devilish with her, almost stalking her as he suggests an elopement, to be paid for with her father's money, of course.

Tillie has enough sense to hold on to the cash, but little enough that she goes along with the stranger's plans. Yes, this good country soul is robbing her dad to elope with a stranger she met an hour earlier. Credulity is certainly stretched

That's the end of the first of the six acts which are layered on top of each other to comprise this feature. I wonder if the title cards that announce each of them were a means for the audience to keep track of how long they had to wait until it was over.

Act two begins with the couple in town, Tillie floundering around in traffic, and the third wheel about to make her appearance. This is Mabel, looking a lot more dreamy in an Oriental outfit with a huge ruff than Tillie does in her outrageously awful dress and still more horrendous hat, complete with, get this, an actual duck standing up between its flowers.

Mabel is Charlie's girl, or at least she was, so she's a little taken aback to see her man back in town with another. This escalates in a bar, where Dressler hams up her first drink with abandon. Charlie ends up with the cash, so does a runner with Mabel, leaving Tillie to become a drunken pauper, ejected with prejudice for being unable to pay her tab. A mere few minutes later she's in the Keystone Kop station, biting the booking officer's finger, while Charlie and Mabel purchase clothes in a posh store.

You can be sure that we're going to get a heck of a lot more to the "punctured romance" of the title than the two halves of Charlie's con. It all happens through him getting back together with Tillie whenever it seems fortuitous for him to do so, and then doing another vanishing act whenever it stops being fortuitous.

The discovery that her uncle is a millionaire sparks only a first return to her, but Charlie bounces back and forth between Tillie's money and Mabel's looks so often that we do wonder why either of them would put up with him. Eventually, of course, they don't, and how the three of them end up is far from surprising.

What's surprising is that it's Mabel who gets to grow with the story; Charlie is exactly the same person at the end that he is at the beginning and Tillie doesn't find any real change either, even though most of the things that happen in this movie happen to her. Mabel's character grows both through a gradual realisation what Charlie is and through a clever parallel in a movie, entitled *A Thief's*

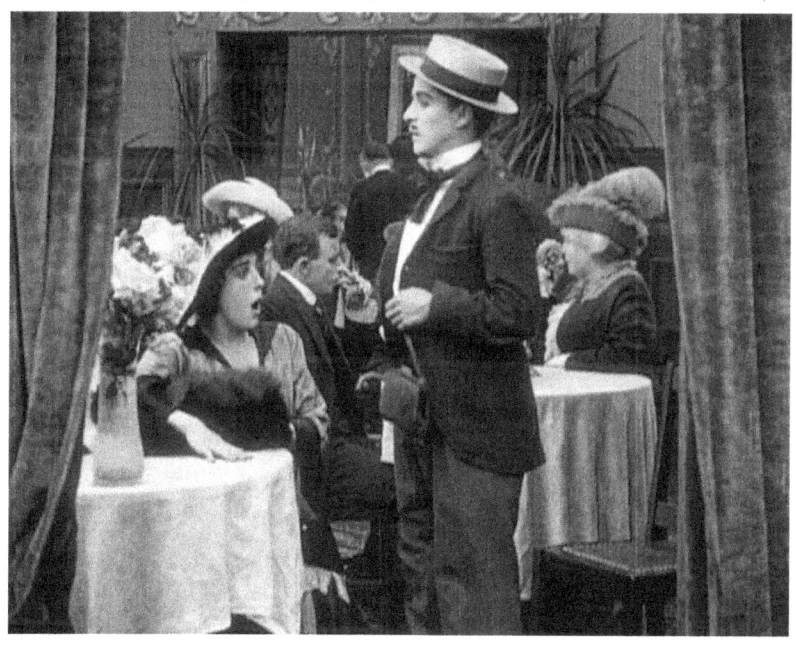

Fate, which Charlie takes her to see, inadvertently sitting next to a cop in the process.

So, while the feature itself is generally clumsy, predictable and unimaginative, there are moments where the combination of actors and situation generate some magic. Charlie's amorality, Mabel's growing guilt and the increasingly suspicious glances from the future Charley Chase as the cop sitting next to her are one of my favourites. The brief flirtation between Tillie and Charlie is another, with Dressler acting rather giddy and coquettish, no mean feat for someone of her considerable size; she throws flowers at him, while he throws a brick at her.

Tillie's drunken scenes all raise a laugh, even though Dressler overplays them throughout; she's fun in jail and she's even more fun dancing a jig over crossed swords at her uncle's mansion. Mabel is given drunk scenes too, which also work well, but they're later in the film during the rapid fire finalé, where the technical side of the picture finally decides to earn some praise through some capable editing. It's hardly an impressive picture otherwise from any of the many technical angles, though it could have been a lot worse.

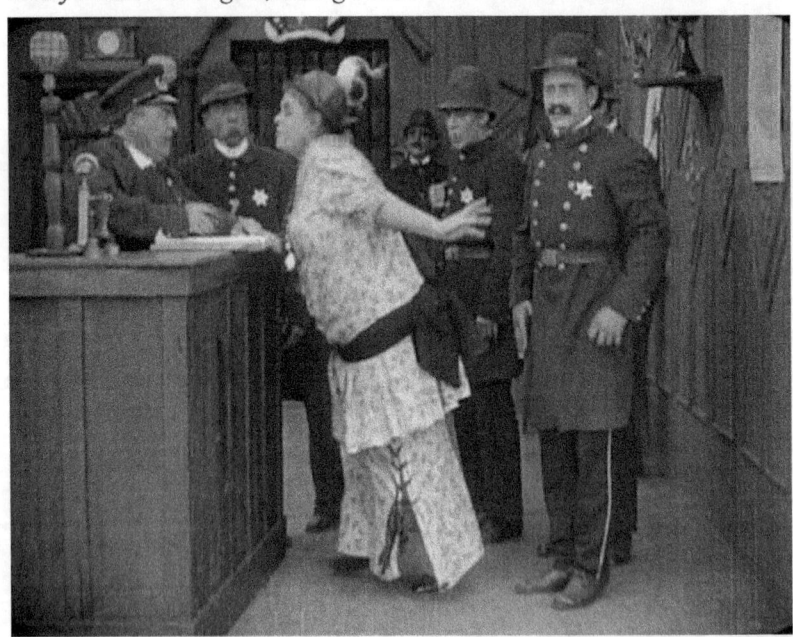

Most of the problems are understandable for the first comedy feature ever made. Everyone involved with this picture, whether in front of or behind the camera, was used to making short films, one reelers or two reelers but never a six reeler, and it's very obvious that they treated it like six individual short films that they could later lump together into one feature. They had no idea how to scale, so the aspects that annoy the most over a six reel length could have been easily shrugged off in a single reel.

For instance, there's a stretch of road that appears more often than many of the name actors, as it's right outside every location. It's in front of the bar Tillie gets drunk in, outside Tillie's uncle's mansion, outside Heywood's clothes store, even outside the theatre playing *A Thief's Fate*, you name it. What's more, it's always shot from the same position. It's not the location, it's the repetition. A different sort of repetition is annoying too, because this picture checks off all the usual Keystone locations: a park, a bar, a pier. Often this feels like *Keystone's Greatest Hits*, especially when taking a look after watching Chaplin's 35 other 1914 films.

Critics haven't been too kind to *Tillie's Punctured Romance*, which tends to be remembered for nothing more than being a milestone. They might grant a little leeway here and there for a century old picture, but not much.

Of course, Marie Dressler would go on to much greater success on screen but not until she'd left it in 1918 and returned to it again in 1927. While she showed here that she was capable of performing slapstick on a debut outing just as well as the various veterans who supported her, it was sound comedy that led her to win an Oscar in 1930-31, for *Min and Bill*, and become the biggest star in Hollywood in both 1932 and 1933. She died in 1934 at her peak.

In my opinion she's unfairly slighted for this picture. Certainly she overacts throughout, unlike the far more realistic style she'd use in the early thirties, but this style fit the material and she did it well, enough to return to the role for two sequels, the dubiously titled *Tillie's Tomato Surprise* in 1915 and 1917's *Tillie Wakes Up*. A more grounded portrayal might have dated better but may have felt out of place at the time.

Mabel Normand has been remembered more positively for this film than Dressler, but her sympathetic performance is grounded in a character written with sympathy. Tillie's too much of a fool, a bouncing village idiot, for us to really feel for her when she ends up in the mess we always knew she would end up in. Mabel may be a fool too, but she comes to realise it and, once she's at that point, she does something about it, thus garnering some real sympathy, especially at the end. We feel for her when we don't feel for Tillie and we cheer for her when we don't cheer for Tillie.

Bizarrely, what Normand does in this film to gain our sympathy is precisely what she doesn't do to gain our sympathy in *Mabel's Busy Day*, made right in the middle of the shooting schedule for this feature. Here she grows her character so she can draw us over to her side through use of well phrased subtleties; in the short film, she merely plays the "woe is me" card throughout and we can't feel for her in the slightest. This is a much better opportunity to see her really act.

But, of course, we're not watching because this is either a Marie Dressler picture or a Mabel Normand picture. Most people watching *Tillie's Punctured Romance* today are watching because it's a Charlie Chaplin picture, his first feature, made as he was starting to be really noticed and released as his star was seriously rising.

He didn't think much of this film. "It was pleasant working with Marie," he remembered in his autobiography, "but I did not think the picture had much merit." He was right, of course, but it didn't matter. While his character has little depth, certainly none of the complexity that the Little Tramp would find in later years, he does play him more as a crook than a villain. It would h11ave been simple for him to reprise the stereotypical silent movie villain that he played in his very first film at Keystone, *Making a Living*, but he'd already moved far beyond such banalities. By the time this feature was released, he'd moved on again, his work in a recent short like *Getting Acquainted* far more clever in every way.

But in contemporary reviews, Chaplin was still singled out for praise, the big success of the film, ending his Keystone career on a high note with the future wide open.

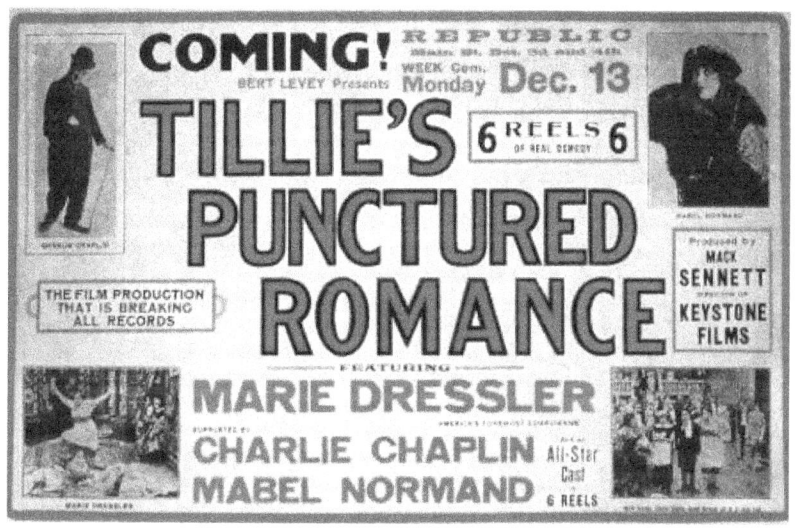

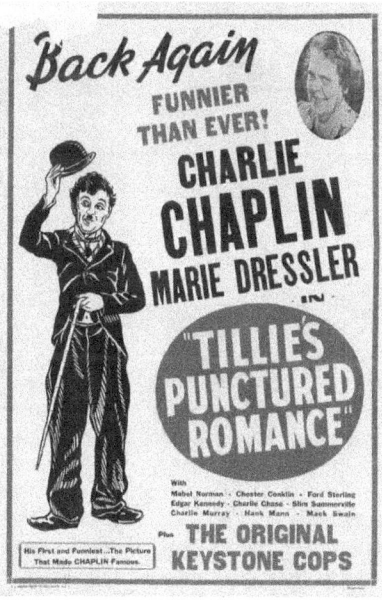

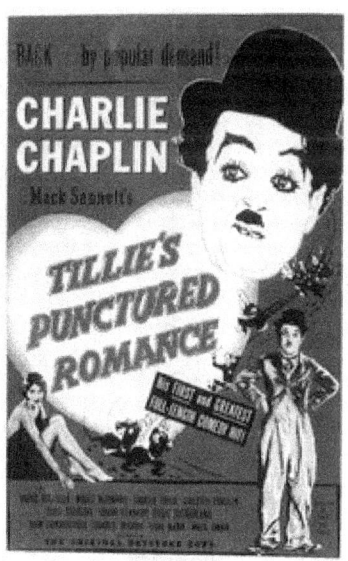

Chronology

This table details when each film was shot, shipped to New York and first exhibited in theatres. Gaps mean that dates are unknown.

This highlights just how quickly Keystone Studios made films and how Chaplin was able to appear in 36 of them in 1914 alone.

Title	Shot	Shipped	Released
Making a Living	17th December - 9th January	14th January	2nd February
Kid Auto Races at Venice, Cal.	10th January	17th January	7th February
Mabel's Strange Predicament	6th - 12th January	20th January	9th February
A Thief Catcher	?	29th January	19th February
Between Showers	27th - 31st January	7th February	28th February
A Film Johnnie	1st - 6th February	11th February	2nd March
Tango Tangles	4th - 10th February	17th February	9th March
His Favorite Pastime	11th - 17th February	19th February	16th March
Cruel, Cruel Love	21st - 27th February	5th March	26th March
The Star Boarder	2nd - 9th March	19th March	4th April
Mabel at the Wheel	26 February - 16 March	31st March	18th April
Twenty Minutes of Love	19 - 24 March	11th April	20th April
Caught in a Cabaret	27 March - 2nd April	18th April	27th April
Caught in the Rain	7th - 13th April	18th April	4th May
A Busy Day	11th April	16th May	7th May
The Fatal Mallet	10th - 12th May	22nd May	1st June
Her Friend the Bandit	11th - 18th May	29th May	4th June
The Knockout	11th - 18th May	30th May	11th June
Mabel's Busy Day	17th - 26th May	6th June	13th June
Mabel's Married Life	30th May - 2nd June	26th June	20th June
Laughing Gas	15th - 22nd June	20th July	9th July
The Property Man	25th June - 11th July	20th July	1st August
The Face on the Barroom Floor	13th - 20nd July	21st July	10th August
Recreation	?	12th August	13th August
The Masquerader	25th July - 1st August	12th August	27th August
His New Profession	3rd - 8th August	14th August	31st August
The Rounders	12th - 15th August	21st August	7th September
The New Januaryitor	18th - 26th August	3rd September	24th September
Those Love Pangs	14th - 17th September	19th September	10th October
Dough and Dynamite	29th August - 11th September	18th September	26th October
Gentlemen of Nerve	20th - 27th September	7th October	29th October
His Musical Career	1st - 10th October	17th October	7th November
His Trysting Place	19th - 26th September	1st October	9th November
Getting Acquainted	13th - 16th November	22nd November	5th December
His Prehistoric Past	14th - 27th October	31st October	7th December
Tillie's Punctured Romance	14th April - 9th June	4th December	21st December

Bibliography

In addition to expected sources like IMDb and Wikipedia, the British Film Institute's online Charlie Chaplin archives were useful, as were these books, articles and websites:

Horseless Age: The Automobile Trade Magazine, Volume 34 (2011)
Uno Asplund - *Chaplin's Films* (1976)
Charlie Chaplin - *My Autobiography* (1964)
Martin Gardner (ed.) - *Famous Poems from Bygone Days* (1995)
Simon Louvish - *Keystone: The Life and Clowns of Mack Sennett* (2003)
Gerald McDonald, Michael Conway & Mark Ricci - *The Complete Films of Charlie Chaplin* (1988)
James L. Neibaur - *Early Charlie Chaplin: The Artist as Apprentice at Keystone Studios*
David Robinson - *Chaplin: His Life and Art* (1985)
Jeffrey Vance - *Chaplin: Genius of the Cinema* (2003)

Bart Anderson - "Whose Face is It?" (2002)
Anon. (Associated Press) - "Long-lost Charlie Chaplin film, found in Michigan, to debut at Virginia festival" (2010)
Jeffrey Stanton - "Abbot Kinney Pier" (1998)
Brent Evan Walker - "Charlie Chaplin in *A Thief Catcher*, and other rarities at Slapsticon" (2010)
"Edgar Kennedy, Film Actor, Dies", *The St Petersburg Times* (10th November, 1948)

Anonymous review in *Bioscope* (21st January, 1915)

Charlie Chaplin - Official Website
http://www.charliechaplin.com/

British Film Institute: Charlie Chaplin
http://chaplin.bfi.org.uk/

John Bengtson - *Rare Chaplin Scenes in Downtown Los Angeles*
http://silentlocations.wordpress.com/2011/06/14/rare-chaplin-scenes-in-downtown-los-angeles/

Notes on Images

To avoid filling up the book proper with notes on the images, here they all are in one place.

Making a Living
p14 - Edgar English (Charles Chaplin) cadges money from a stranger (the film's director, Henry Lehrman).
p17 - Chaplin and Lehrman with Virginia Kirtley and Alice Davenport.
p18 - Edgar English threatens newspaper employees.
p20 - Chaplin and Lehrman brawl in front of an oncoming tram.

Kid Auto Races at Venice, Cal.
p22 - This intertitle ably describes the entire picture.
p24 - Charlie (Charles Chaplin) wanders in front of the camera during the Junior Vanderbilt Cup on the boardwalk at Venice Beach.
p27 - A policeman (and especially the real crowd) watch Charlie. Note the loose dog on the track.
p28 - Presaging his character's future growth, Charlie makes faces at the camera.

Mabel's Strange Predicament
p30 - The title card of this French reissue highlights the change in stature of Mabel Normand and Charles Chaplin since the film's original release.
p32 - Mabel (Mabel Normand) is discovered hiding under the bed in the wrong hotel room.
p35 - A drunken Charlie woos Mabel in the corridor outside the hotel room out of which her dog has locked her.
p36 - Charlie whacks Harry McCoy with his bamboo cane in front of Sadie Lampe.

A Thief Catcher
p38 - Ford Sterling, the star who Chaplin replaced at Keystone Studios, stuck in the yeggmen's hideout as they toss a coin over which will kill him.
p41 - Sterling's rural sheriff capturing a photo of two yeggmen tossing the third of their number over a cliff.
p42 - Pointlessly, Sterling literally points out to us his literally hair-raising experience.
p44 - Chaplin as a Keystone Kop accosting the yeggmen (Edgar Kennedy and Mack Swain).

Between Showers

p46 - Mr. Snookie (Ford Sterling) and Emma Clifton contemplating a deep puddle, the reason why the film was made.

p48 - Chester Conklin wooing Sadie Lampe as Ford Sterling prepares to steal the policeman's umbrella.

p50 - Charlie accidentally whacks Sterling with a plank of wood in a standard slapstick manoeuvre.

p52 - Charlie enjoys the snook that he just cocked at a policeman.

A Film Johnnie

p54 - Behind the scenes at Keystone Studios. Note the good luck swastikas on the "good scene" board.

p57 - Charlie blows a kiss at his favourite, the Keystone Girl, on a movie poster outside a nickelodeon.

p58 - Charlie suddenly discovers himself standing next to the film star he adores. Is this Virginia Kirtley (see p17) or Peggy Pearce (see p73)? I'd suggest the latter.

p60 - Charlie, drenched by a fire hose aimed in his direction by the Keystone Girl, gives up on Hollywood.

Tango Tangles

p62 - Two unknown but presumably professional dancers take to the floor at the Venice Dance Hall on Abbot Kinney Pier in Santa Monica.

p64 - A drunken Charlie fails spectacularly to hand his hat to the hat check girl (Sadie Lampe).

p66 - Roscoe Arbuckle effortlessly tosses a dance hall patron over his head while Lampe cringes and Ford Sterling runs.

p68 - Chaplin and Sterling attempt to put on the very same coat at the very same time.

His Favorite Pastime

p70 - It would seem that Charlie's favourite pastime is drinking at his local bar.

p72 - Roscoe Arbuckle attempts to steal a drink from Charlie. but the Little Tramp is too quick for him.

p73 - Charlie meets Peggy Pearce on screen, the first woman in which he fell in love at Keystone Studios.

p75 - A drunken Charlie gets hit by a swinging door, which gets the better of him.

p76 - Charlie gives the restroom attendant (Billy Gilbert in blackface) a lit cigarette as a tip.

Cruel, Cruel Love
p78 - Lord Helpus (Chaplin) moonfaced over his fiancée (Minta Durfee).
p81 - Lord Helpus unwittingly caught in a compromising situation with his fiancée's maid (Eva Nelson).
p83 - Lord Helpus's butler (Edgar Kennedy) in stitches because his master has drunk water that he thinks is poison.
p84 - Lord Helpus imagines himself tormented in Hell in a neat double exposure shot.

The Star Boarder
p86 - Charlie is the star boarder at Minta Durfee's boarding house.
p88 - Edgar Kennedy in outrageous facial hair is the man of the house but under his wife's thumb.
p91 - The landlady's son (Gordon Griffith) sits back and enjoys all the inappropriate photos he's screening to guests his magic lantern show.
p92 - Those guests react in a rather different way!

Mabel at the Wheel
p94 - Mabel Normand substitutes for her boyfriend behind the wheel in an auto race.
p97 - Mabel's boyfriend (Harry McCoy) about to be waylaid by villains.
p98 - Chaplin and his moustachioed henchmen (Andy Anderson and Grover Ligon).
p100 - Mabel biting Chaplin's hand as he attempts to abduct her, perhaps with vigour given how he had accused her of incompetency

Twenty Minutes of Love
p102 - Charlie woos yet another girl (Eva Nelson) in yet another park.
p105 - Charlie interrupts Edgar Kennedy and Minta Durfee's make out session on a park bench.
p106 - Charlie picks the pocket of a pickpocket (Chester Conklin).
p108 - A well-timed duck means that Charlie hits the wrong target.

Caught in a Cabaret
p110 - Charlie surrounded by various patrons of the bar and café at which he works.
p112 - Charlie leaps into action to save Mabel from a threatening crook (William Hauber).
p114 - Charlie the waiter pretends to be the Prime Minster of Greenland so he can steal Mabel's hand from Harry McCoy.
p116 - Yet another well-timed duck and yet another wrong target hit by Charlie.

Caught in the Rain
p118 - Charlie caught in the rain in *Caught in the Rain*, stuck outside on a balcony.

p121 - Mack Swain as what is surely an early version of his regular character, Ambrose.

p122 - The stairs get the better of Charlie.

p124 - Charlie rarely has the luck with the ladies that he'd like.

A Busy Day
p126 - Mack Swain's wife (Chaplin in drag) reacts to the discovery of his sudden absence.

p128 - In scenes reminiscent of *Kid Auto Races at Venice, Cal.*, Charlie in drag wanders in between the cameras and a parade accompanying the expansion of the Los Angeles Harbor.

p131 - Charlie in drag quite literally breaks her umbrella over Mack Swain's head.

p132 - Finally fed up of his wife, Mack Swain pushes her off a pier into the Los Angeles Harbor in front of a large crowd of onlookers.

The Fatal Mallet
p134 - Charlie and Mack Sennett, his screen rival for the hand of Mabel.

p136 - Mack and Mabel, an item in real life, and future musical title.

p137 - Charlie and Mabel, not an item in real life though he did try.

p139 - Chaplin and Sennett prepare to throw bricks at Mack Swain but hopefully not Mabel.

p140 - In what must have been a meaningful moment for Mack Sennett, he and Mabel prepare to leave arm in arm while his rivals (Swain and Chaplin) look on from a lake.

Her Friend the Bandit
p142 - Ephemera like this advert in *Bioscope* is sadly all that we have left of *Her Friend the Bandit*.

The Knockout
p146 - Edgar Kennedy prepares to deliver a punch to Roscoe Arbuckle while referee Chaplin looks on from the canvas.

p149 - Arbuckle and his real life wife, Minta Durfee, is pressured by his real life nephew, Al St. John.

p151 - Charlie prepares for the fight between Arbuckle and Kennedy to begin, while the outrageously moustachioed Mack Swain waits in his box.

p152 - Somehow Arbuckle can both climb onto roofs and fire pistols while still wearing boxing gloves.

Mabel's Busy Day
p154 - Mabel prepares to sell a hot dog to a customer.
p156 - Mabel bribes Chester Conklin with food to let her into the Ascot Park Speedway.
p159 - Charlie saves Mabel from a thief only to rob her blind himself.
p160 - Does Charlie really feel bad for destroying Mabel's livelihood?

Mabel's Married Life
p162 - Mabel and Charlie, man and wife at last.
p165 - Charlie aims to kick Mack Swain in the ass for hitting on his wife.
p166 - Mabel gets ready to test out the boxing dummy she's just bought.
p168 - A drunken Charlie mistakes the boxing dummy for a burglar.

Laughing Gas
p170 - Dentist Fritz Schade administers laughing gas to Josef Swickard.
p172 - Charlie and his fellow dental assistant (Joseph Sutherland).
p175 - Charlie has accidentally ripped off the dress of Dr. Pain's wife (Alice Howell) and patient Mack Swain runs to the rescue.
p176 - Charlie gets fresh with a pretty patient (Helen Carruthers).

The Property Man
p178 - Charlie the property man.
p181 - The lazy Charlie has old Josef Swickard do all the heavy lifting.
p182 - A mostly appreciative audience, including studio boss Sennett, with Harry McCoy asleep on his shoulder.
p185 - Charlie drenches everyone in the show with a firehose.

The Face on the Barroom Floor
p186 - A drunken Charlie attempts to draw a face on the barroom floor in chalk.
p189 - Painter Charlie sees an urn in the curvacious rump of his lady love, Madeline (Cecile Arnold).
p190 - Alas! Madeline clearly prefers the "fair haired boy" (Jess Dandy).

Recreation
p192 - A sailor (Charles Bennett) discovers Charlie hitting on his girl (Helen Carruthers).
p194 - The poor picture quality of much of this film hides the "pretty girl" whose serendipitous arrival washes suicide from Charlie's mind.
p197 - The sailor escapes from a pair of policemen (Edwin Frazee and Edward Nolan).
p198 - Everyone ends up in the lake in this picture!

The Masquerader
p200 - Charlie is back in drag again as the masquerader of the title.
p202 - Charlie shares a dressing room with Roscoe Arbuckle.
p205 - Charlie escapes from his set through another one.
p206 - Charlie giggles as he prepares to reveal that the lady hired in his place is really him.

His New Profession
p208 - Charlie reads the *Police Gazette*.
p210 - Charles Parrott (not yet Charley Chase) parks uncle Jess Dandy's wheelchair on Charlie's foot.
p213 - Having parked his charge next to a sleeping cripple, Charlie prepares to steal his take.
p214 - Charlie enjoys the unintended attention his employer's girlfriend (Peggy Page) gives him.

The Rounders
p216 - Mr. Full and Mr. Fuller (Chaplin and Roscoe Arbuckle) prepare to step out on the town.
p219 - Mrs. Full (Phyllis Allen) catches her drunken husband with the same bamboo cane hook he'd used on so many pretty girls during 1914.
p220 - Mrs. Fuller (Minta Durfee) clotheslines her obnoxious husband (both on screen and in real life).
p222 - Mr. Full and Mr. Fuller cause chaos at Smith's Café.

The New Janitor
p224 - Charlie as the new janitor of the Marsh Strong Building.
p227 - Charlie's duties include taking care of everyone.
p229 - A thieving manager (Jack Dillon) attacks the only witness to his crime (Peggy Page).
p230 - Charlie holds a gun on the villain from an unusual position.

Those Love Pangs
p232 - Charlie attempts to woo his landlady (Peggy Page) after hiding his rival for her affections, Chester Conklin, behind the curtain.
p235 - Charlie looks on in amazement as Cecile Arnold counts money retrieved from her boot to give to Chester Conklin.
p236 - Charlie clearly enjoys the company of Cecile Arnold and Vivian Edwards.
p238 - Shooting quickly in public parks means occasional goofs get missed, such as the onlooker in the top right of this shot.

Dough and Dynamite
p240 - Chester Conklin is buried in bricks after striking bakers blow up their workplace in protest.
p243 - Charlie gets stuck in the trapdoor to the bakery.
p244 - The jokes write themselves and Charlie is happy to play along.
p246 - Charlie cleans up in the bakery with Chester Conklin unconscious under the sack of flour behind him.

Gentlemen of Nerve
p250 - Real drivers prepare to race on the Ascot Park Speedway.
p253 - Phyllis Allen flirts with Chester Conklin, who's supposed to be with Mabel Normand.
p255 - Charlie and Mabel check out the Franklin Wind Machine.
p256 - Mabel successfully steals another scene from Charlie by tweaking his nose.

His Musical Career
p258 - Charlie and Mack Swain attempt to deliver a piano up a steep flight of stairs.
p261 - Mr. Poor (Josef Swickard) laments the imminent loss of his piano.
p263 - Charlie and Mack Swain load Mr. Rich's piano onto their mule-drawn cart. The building in the distance just to the left of the piano is the Marsh Strong building, out of which Charlie had hung in *Those Love Pangs*.
p264 - An airborne mule in the early days before animal safety laws.

His Trysting Place
p266 - Mabel attacks Charlie because of a misunderstanding.
p268 - Charlie knocks a pan of boiling water off an open range into the path of Mabel and their baby.
p271 - Mabel looks daggers at Phyllis Allen.
p272 - For once, the trouble Charlie's in isn't of his own doing.

Getting Acquainted
p274 - Policeman Edgar Kennedy aims to protect Mabel from Charlie.
p276 - Phyllis Allen introduces Charlie, her husband, to Mabel, the lady with whom he's been flirting.
p277 - In turn, Mabel introduces Mack Swain, *her* husband, to Allen, with whom *he's* been flirting.
p278 - A "passing Turk" (Glen Cavender) protects Cecile Arnold from a roving Charlie.
p281 - A frustrated Kennedy finally discovers the truth about everyone getting acquainted.

His Prehistoric Past
p282 - The "kink of Waikiki Beach" (Mack Swain) sits with his harem.
p285 - Weakchin (Chaplin) lights his pipe with a rock.
p286 - Surely a prehistoric version of Mack Sennett's bathing beauties!
p288 - Back in the present, the Little Tramp is woken up by Chaplin's real life brother, Syd.

Tillie's Punctured Romance
p290 - Tillie (Marie Dressler) weds an unnamed City Stranger.
p293 - The City Stranger already has an unmistakeable silhouette.
p295 - The City Stranger and the third wheel, Mabel Normand.
p296 - A drunken Tillie dances in front of the Keystone Kops.
p299 - Over a short period of time, *Tillie's Punctured Romance* went from being a Marie Dressler movie to a Charlie Chaplin movie.

About Hal C. F. Astell

While he still has a day job, Hal C. F. Astell is a teacher by blood and a writer by inclination, which gradually transformed him into a movie reviewer. He mostly reviews films at his own site, Apocalypse Later, but he also reviews books at the Nameless Zine and provides film festival coverage for Nerdvana, among others.

He owns and runs the Apocalypse Later International Fantastic Film Festival, as well as mini-film festivals at Arizona and California conventions including Phoenix Comicon, San Diego Comic-Fest, Wild Wild West Con, Phoenix FearCon, Gaslight Gathering et al, screening award-winning international sci-fi, horror or steampunk.

Born and raised in the rain of England, he's still learning about the word "heat" after a decade in Phoenix, where he lives with Dee, his better half, in a house full of assorted critters and oddities.

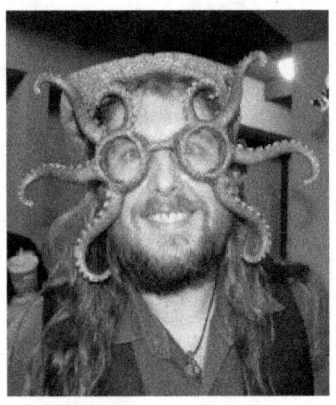

Photo by Dee Astell

Just in case you care, his favourite movie is Peter Jackson's debut, *Bad Taste,* his favourite actor is Warren William and he thinks Carl Theodor Dreyer's *The Passion of Joan of Arc* is the greatest movie ever made. He's always happy to talk your ears off about the joys of odd films, whether precodes, fifties B-movies or Asian horror flicks.

He's usually easy to find at film festivals, conventions and events because he's likely to be the only one in a kilt. He's friendly and doesn't bite unless asked.

About Apocalypse Later

Initially, Hal C. F. Astell wrote film reviews for his own reference because he could never remember who the one good actor was in otherwise forgettable entries in long crime series from the forties. After a year, they became long enough to warrant a dedicated blog.

As he was reviewing his way through every movie in the IMDb Top 250 for a project tentatively titled Apocalypse Later, that name promptly stuck. Originally it was just a joke with a punchline of reviewing *Apocalypse Now* last, but hey, there are worse names.

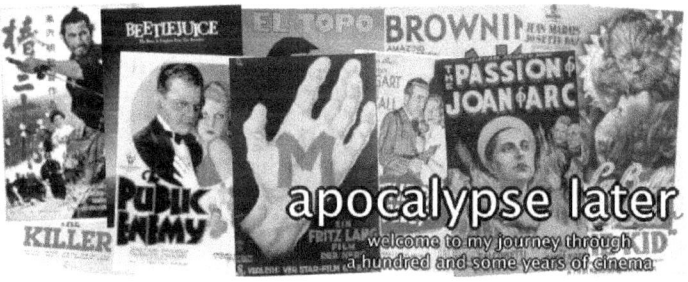

Over time, it became something of an anomaly, a movie review site full of reviews of movies most reviewers don't review. There are reviews of silent films, classic films, foreign films, indie films, short films, microbudget films, obscure films, genre films, festival films... pretty much everything except modern mainstream films. It's also one of the rare sites reviewing new microbudget horror movies that doesn't kill your eyes with white text on a black background.

Think of it this way. If you want to read about *Frankenweenie*, the $39m Tim Burton animated feature from 2012, you can go to Roger Ebert's website or any one of a thousand others. If you want to read about the other *Frankenweenie*, the black and white short film that Burton made for Disney in 1984, you'll find that Apocalypse Later is one of a few that'll help you out. And if you want go back to the odd movies that Burton made before that with a bunch of colleagues at Disney who all needed to blow off steam, then there might just be somewhere other than Apocalypse Later but I wouldn't count on it. If there are any, they'll probably be good reads too.

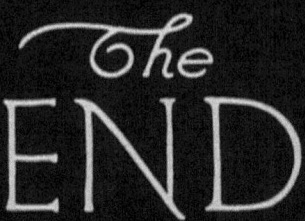

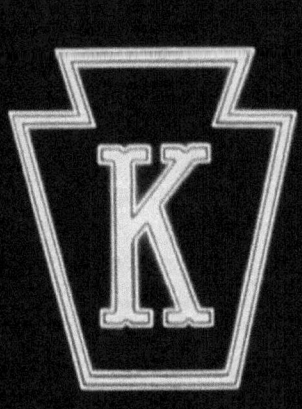

www.ingramcontent.com/pod-product-compliance
Lightning Source LLC
Chambersburg PA
CBHW060823170526
45158CB00001B/62